Lucy Page

To Mother —

WE REMEMBER GROWING
up in the "gardens"

Love
SARAH & CHIPS

Mary Rose —   4/17/2011

To Mother —

WE REMEMBER Growing
up in the "garden"

Love

SARAH & CHRIS

THE ARCHITECTURE OF
GROSVENOR ATTERBURY

Robert Weeks de Forest house

Wawapek Farm, Cold Spring Harbor, New York, 1898–1900

LEFT *Entrance court*

TOP *North facade*

ABOVE *Carriage drive-through and kitchen wing*

Congregational Church

Seal Harbor, Maine, 1901–2

Edward Cushman Bodman house

Felsmere, Seal Harbor, Maine, 1901–2

ABOVE *Congregational Church: Entrance facade*

ABOVE *Bodman house: Entrance facade*
RIGHT *Bodman house: West facade*

City Hall Restoration

New York, New York, 1907–25

ABOVE LEFT *Rotunda and skylight*

LEFT *Fireplace in Governor's Room*

ABOVE *Cupola*

FACING PAGE *Governor's Room*

Forest Hills Gardens

Queens, New York, 1909–22

LEFT *Group III on Slocum Crescent, 1911*

TOP *Entrance detail of the Lytle Hunter house on Greenway Terrace, 1922*

ABOVE *Group XII at Greenway North and Markwood Road, 1912*

Church-in-the-Gardens

Forest Hills Gardens, 1915

FACING PAGE *Greenway North facade*

RIGHT *Interior*

BELOW RIGHT *Detail of the chancel screen*

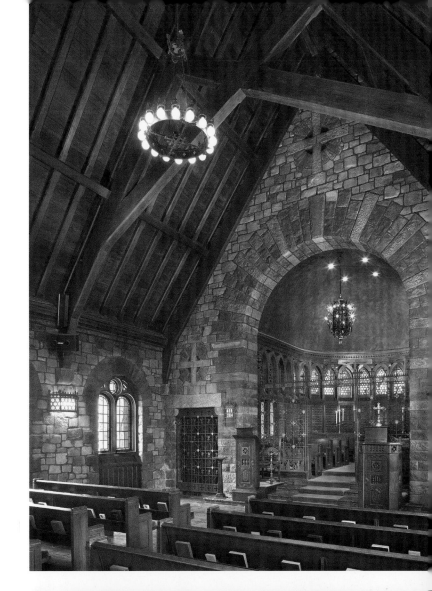

Parrish Art Museum

Southampton, New York, 1897–1913

ABOVE   *Entrance loggia*

ABOVE RIGHT   *Window detail*

FACING PAGE   *Job's Lane entrance*

FOLLOWING PAGES

LEFT   *Sculpture garden with the 1913 addition to the left and the 1897 building to the rear*

TOP RIGHT   *Side gate on entrance court*

BOTTOM RIGHT   *Gate detail on Job's Lane*

Ernesto G. and Edith S. Fabbri house

New York, New York, 1913–17

TOP *Entrance facade*

ABOVE *Stair hall*

RIGHT *Library*

Arthur Curtiss James estate

Surprise Valley Farm, Newport, Rhode Island, 1914

ABOVE *Stairs to icehouse*

RIGHT *View to the north with carpenter's shop, cow barn, and bridge*

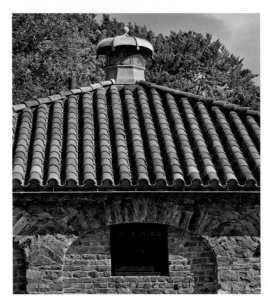

TOP TO BOTTOM

Roof detail

Detail of carpenter's shop

Stone, brick, and tile detail of the maternity building

RIGHT *Cow barn and maternity building*

Mrs. William Horace Schmidlapp house

Ca Sole, East Walnut Hills, Ohio, 1925–27

TOP *Detail of entrance facade*

ABOVE *Stair hall*

RIGHT *Garden facade*

Barns for John D. Rockefeller Jr.

Pocantico Hills, New York, 1930–33

(now the Stone Barns Center for Food and Agriculture)

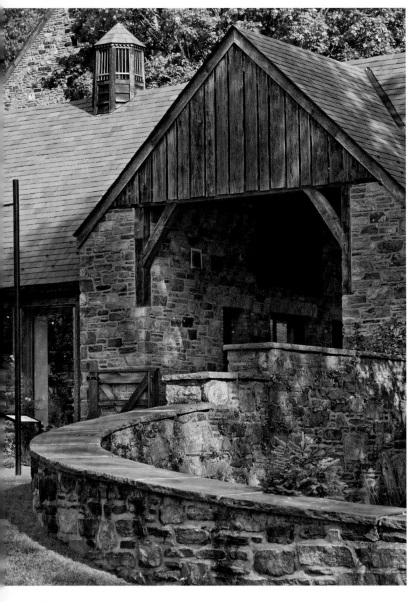

ABOVE *Entrance into farm group*

RIGHT *View to the southwest*

ABOVE *Hay barn*

FACING PAGE *Detail of silos*

Gate Lodge, Brown Mountain, Acadia National Park

Northeast Harbor, Maine, 1930–32

Gate Lodge, Jordan Pond, Acadia National Park

Seal Harbor, Maine, 1930–32

ABOVE LEFT *Brown Mountain: Carriage road entrance*

LEFT *Brown Mountain: Detail of gate lodge*

ABOVE *Brown Mountain: Detail of brick and stonework*

FACING PAGE *Jordan Pond: West facade*

Yale Medical Library and Harvey Cushing Memorial Rotunda, Yale University

New Haven, Connecticut, 1939–41

LEFT *Harvey Cushing Memorial Rotunda*

ABOVE *Wrought-iron detail of balustrade in the Medical Historical Library*

FOLLOWING PAGE *Medical Historical Library*

THE ARCHITECTURE

of

GROSVENOR ATTERBURY

PETER PENNOYER AND ANNE WALKER

NEW PHOTOGRAPHS BY JONATHAN WALLEN

FOREWORD BY ROBERT A. M. STERN

W. W. NORTON & COMPANY

New York • London

HALF-TITLE PAGE *An Atterbury-designed streetlamp in Forest Hills Gardens, Queens, New York*

For information about permission to reproduce
selections from this book, write to Permissions,
W. W. Norton & Company, Inc.,
500 Fifth Avenue, New York, NY 10110

For information about special discounts for bulk
purchases, please contact W. W. Norton Special Sales at
specialsales@wwnorton.com or 800-233-4830.

Composition and book design by Abigail Sturges
Manufacturing by Friesens
Production Manager: Leeann Graham

Library of Congress Cataloging-in-Publication Data

Pennoyer, Peter.
  The architecture of Grosvenor Atterbury / Peter Pennoyer and
Anne Walker ; foreword by Robert A.M. Stern ; new photographs
by Jonathan Wallen. — 1st ed.
      p. cm.
  Includes bibliographical references and index.
  ISBN 978-0-393-73222-1 (hardcover)
  1. Atterbury, Grosvenor, 1869-1956—Criticism and interpretation.
  2. Architecture—United States--History—19th century.
  3. Architecture—United States--History—20th century.
  4. City planning—United States—History—20th century.
I. Walker, Anne. II. Wallen, Jonathan. III. Title.

NA737.A86P46 2009
720.92—dc22

                                                    2008055941

ISBN 13: 978-0-393-73222-1

W. W. Norton & Company, Inc.,
500 Fifth Avenue, New York, N.Y. 10110
www.wwnorton.com

W. W. Norton & Company Ltd.,
Castle House, 75/76 Wells St., London W1T 3QT

0 9 8 7 6 5 4 3 2 1

CONTENTS

FOREWORD

At last, a comprehensive history of twentieth-century architecture begins to unfold as a new generation of architectural historians, many of them also practicing architects, write about the work of important traditional architects whose contributions have hitherto been either ignored or derided by historians blinkered by Modernism's presumed sense of inevitability. At first, the new generation of historians picked up the most luscious low-hanging fruit from the tree—exceptional talents such as Charles F. McKim, Stanford White, James Gamble Rogers, C. F. A. Voysey, Sir Edwin Lutyens—and such accessible typologies as country houses, private gardens, and skyscrapers. Now, happily, less well known talents and less glamorous typologies are getting the attention they deserve.

Peter Pennoyer, a practicing architect, and Anne Walker, an architectural historian, have been tireless and imaginative in their scholarly pursuit of overlooked talents. They began with *The Architecture of Delano & Aldrich* in 2003, which treated a partnership of architects who, despite having long been dismissed as "society architects," revealed themselves to be thorough professionals with a surprisingly varied approach. Then, in 2006, Pennoyer and Walker tackled the partnership of Whitney Warren and Charles Wetmore, superb stylists and practical businessmen whose

range of accomplishments extended from country and town houses for the well-to-do to skyscraping office buildings and chains of luxury hotels that were the most modern in their day and that established standards still in effect in our own time.

Now, with *The Architecture of Grosvenor Atterbury*, Pennoyer and Walker have gone into virtually uncharted territory, carefully researching and beautifully presenting the work of an architect whose name is all but lost to the discourse but whose accomplishments, so long ignored, promise to place him in the prominent position he deserves.

"Grosvenor Atterbury?" one may ask. "Never heard of him." But, as Pennoyer and Walker make clear, Atterbury deserves to be known and respected as a talented designer, as a scholarly preservationist, and as a pioneer of advanced building technology. Most especially, it is the last of these achievements that seems to me to be the basis for Atterbury's claim to long-overdue recognition.

Among the more pervasive, persistent, and pernicious myths about twentieth-century traditional architecture is its supposed social insensitivity and technological backwardness. The generally accepted wisdom, largely unchallenged, has been that the best traditional architects were uninterested in the reform movements affecting housing and industrial working conditions as well as in new ways of building, while architects who devoted themselves to these issues were one and the same as those who shed traditional composition and historical form. Exceptions are allowed in a few cases, most notably that of Auguste Perret (1874–1954) of France, who in the first half of the twentieth century consistently explored the possibilities of reinforced-concrete construction while keeping to Classical composition and form. But Perret, who was part of a family of builders, was easily pigeonholed as a *constructeur* rather than an architect, thereby getting around the fact that, despite the Classicism of his approach, he, and not his archrival Le Corbusier (1887–1965), was the great technologist of European architecture. Le Corbusier is hailed for his celebration of technology, despite the fact that his work was typically symbolic in its approach rather than literal, and despite the fact that many of his most notable buildings exploited traditional materials for their most powerful effects, beginning with his de Mandrot villa of 1930–31, which so notably gave pause to Henry-Russell Hitchcock and Philip Johnson in their 1932 book *The International Style: Architecture Since 1922*.

Grosvenor Atterbury (1869–1956) helps give the lie to the Modernist argument about technology. Atterbury, an accomplished formalist capable of working in many styles and a brilliant technologist, combined theory and practice to develop patented components and whole systems of prefabrication using reinforced concrete. He demonstrated his ideas in a number of projects, the best known being Forest Hills Gardens, Queens, New York, a highly significant community planning project designed in association with the Olmsted Brothers.

Pennoyer and Walker's book takes one more significant step toward setting the record straight about what really happened in twentieth-century architecture—helping to settle scores, as it were. But it is not written as polemic. It is history, wonderfully researched and clearly organized. As such it is a pleasure to read, and this writer begs for more in the same vein.

ROBERT A. M. STERN
June 2008

CHAPTER 1

INTRODUCTION

One of the most influential architects, town planners, and inventors of the first half of the twentieth century, Grosvenor Atterbury (1869– 1956) embodied the progressive spirit that began to permeate the American psyche after the Civil War. As an optimist, Atterbury believed in the power of change and improvement; as a member of the conscience-driven WASP elite, he felt an obligation to help the less fortunate; as an architect, he was inspired by the romantic and sculptural forms of European and English buildings; and as an inventor, he pursued the promise of new technology to introduce beauty—in the form of well-designed, low-cost, prefabricated concrete construction— into the lives of the working classes. Atterbury's extraordinary career, which spanned six decades, affected the course of American architecture, planning, and construction.

In 1895, when Atterbury set up his own practice in a small office on Fifth Avenue and 19th Street, he launched himself into a profession that stood in its infancy in America. As the financial center of the country, New York City presented a field of endless opportunity for a young architect. The closing decades of the nineteenth century had produced an unprecedented number of rich men. Due to the Industrial Revolution, the city—and the nation—experienced exponential growth and a boom in building. Beaux-

Arts–trained architects like Atterbury found their rarified knowledge much in demand as the emergent country strove to express its cultural and social arrival. During what has been described as the age of metropolitanism, a wealth of European-inspired monuments, museums, and grand houses came to redefine the cityscape.[1] As the offshoot of the 1893 World's Columbian Exposition in Chicago, many of the same group of architects—considered part of the cultured elite—applied their command of classicism to the problem of civic design, transforming city centers into grand, ordered, urban environments indicative of the country's emergence as a world economic and cultural power. The son of a successful corporation lawyer, Atterbury personally enjoyed the fruits of the flourishing economy and benefited as an architect with a series of commissions for rambling summer cottages, country estates, and city mansions from a host of affluent financiers, lawyers, and manufacturers.

However, not only was New York a symbol of the country's progress but also it was a microcosm of the problems and issues that plagued the period's unfettered expansion and growth. As immigrants poured into the country between 1880 and World War One to fuel America's industrial engines, the gap between the wealthy and the working classes widened substantially. Many of the vibrant neigh-

Portrait of Grosvenor Atterbury.
Courtesy of the Maine Historic
Preservation Commission

borhoods in which the working poor lived swelled and deteriorated into overcrowded slums. With his book *How the Other Half Lives* (1890) and a stream of related articles, reporter and photographer Jacob Riis (1849–1914) revealed the shocking and deplorable conditions of these districts. Harvard professor James Ford, author of the seminal two-volume *Slums and Housing* (1936), later described them as areas "in which housing [was] so deteriorated, so substandard or so unwholesome as to be a menace to the health, safety, morality or welfare of the occupants."[2] Riis's illuminating photographic essays galvanized reformers to concentrate on the alarming underside of the era's gilded excess.

As described by Richard Plunz, author of *A History of Housing in New York City,* the history of housing is encapsulated by New York because the repercussions of its problems were most severely felt. Consequently, the city was the first to embrace housing philanthropy and reform legislature. At a time when the government did not allocate money to housing—indeed, before the income tax—the reform movement relied on funding from the rich. While pro-business and well assured of a world where their class would rule in perpetuity, many of the wealthiest families (for the most part white Anglo-Saxon Protestant) saw reform work as a moral obligation of their position. As an example, the Charity Organization Society, headed by lawyer and philanthropist Robert Weeks de Forest (1848–1931)—the "philanthropic equivalent of the Standard Oil Trust"—was a Protestant-based group administered by patrician New Yorkers well removed from the problems and plights it sought to alleviate.[3] However, as much as the wealthy were detached from the issues at hand, it was this type of gentile benevolence that eventually spurred the government to assume a larger role in reforming housing standards, eventually leading to federal building projects.

In 1898, the Charity Organization Society established a Tenement House Committee on which Atterbury served alongside de Forest, Riis, and leading reformers Lawrence Veiller (1872–1959); Felix Adler (1851–1933), founder of the Society for Ethical Culture; Andrew Carnegie (1835–1919); and Dr. Elgin R. L. Gould (1860–1915), president of the City and Suburban Homes Company. Their initiative led to the Tenement House Act of 1901, a bill that outlawed "old-law"—or dumbbell—tenements (which had a narrow section in the middle through the depth of the block) and mandated that all tenements must have running water, toilets, and windows in each room. Atterbury stood out, along with Ernest Flagg (1857–1947), I. N. Phelps Stokes (1867–1944), and Henry Atterbury Smith

(1872–1954), as one of the few architects to explore design techniques to maximize light and ventilation for multi-family dwellings constructed within the confines of the city grid. Indicative of the movement's momentum and progress, Atterbury started out by designing "model" tenements and communities funded by private foundations; by the end of his career, he was contributing to the designs of government-sponsored housing schemes. As a planner, problem solver, and technician, Atterbury earnestly applied his talents to finding solutions that could shape the potential for change—an effort that no doubt arose out of his genuine chagrin at the conditions caused by Manhattan's overpopulation and congestion. "In building the city," he contended, "we are forgetting the humans that must dwell in it, and in striving for monumental beauty we are forgetting the beauty of life."[4]

Atterbury feared that the lofty goals of the prevailing City Beautiful movement were misguided and unconnected to the neighborhoods he and his colleagues sought to improve. He complained that "the movement to make our towns and cities healthy, practical, convenient and pleasant to live in has suffered . . . from the idea that wide boulevards, monuments and civic centers constituted the main objects of city planning. Nothing . . . could be further from the truth."[5] However, as exemplified by the era's reform-minded architects, the artistic sensibilities that drove the ideals of the City Beautiful movement also permeated the realm of scientific planning. With a sharp analytical mind, Atterbury looked at the expense of land, the cost of infrastructure, the structure of assessments, and property taxes. As an inventor of one of the first precast concrete-panel systems, he proved the viability of prefabrication, now a standard construction technique. But the grace and craftsmanship with which he combined the technical with the artistic set Atterbury apart from other practitioners. Believing that an idiom inevitably grew out of its site and conditions, he placed an emphasis on composition and materials, evolving a picturesque, practical, and derivative approach that frequently defied stylistic labels. Out of all his contemporaries, he successfully brought architectural form and language into a true partnership with planning and science, indelibly infusing style with more abstract goals.

Most concerned with creating livable and practical buildings from modern materials and methods, Atterbury eschewed the rising tide of modernism during the 1930s and 1940s. Because he was so entrenched in perfecting his concrete building system, he did not fixate on the movement's pervasive influence, and his late projects reflected a

THIS is now APT BUILDING Will is buying into

PROPOSED HISTORIC DISTRICT EXTENSION

- ▬ To return to the extension map ▬ -

RUSSELL SAGE FOUNDATION
(now Sage House)
122-130 East 22nd Street
Architect: *Grosvenor Atterbury*
1912-15; extension at 122 East 22nd Street, 1929-31

The Russell Sage Foundation was founded in 1907 by Margaret O. Sage as a memorial to her husband, the prominent politician and Wall Street financier who had died in 1906. The foundation was established with an initial endowment of $10,000,000 and the goal of promoting the improvement of social and living conditions for the poor. The Russell Sage Foundation was active in the development of social work and urban planning as professions, published many books and articles about social welfare and sponsored and supported many progressive activities. The foundation is also known for Forest Hills Gardens, a model housing project conceived in 1908. The architect for Forest Hills Gardens was also commissioned to design the foundation's headquarters.

Following the organization of the foundation, office accommodation was sought in the United Charities Building on East 22nd Street and Park Avenue South, but since this building was fully occupied, space was rented in several buildings in the surrounding area. In 1912, Mrs. Sage and her leading adviser, Robert de Forest, chose to build a headquarters building that would be a physical memorial to Russell Sage. The site at the corner of Lexington Avenue and East 22nd Street was purchased, and Grosvenor Atterbury was commissioned to design the new nine-story building (a 10th-floor penthouse was added in the early 1920s).

Since the new headquarters building was planned as a memorial, more money was spent on the design and

GRAMERCY PARK
EAST:

37
38

GRAMERCY PARK
NORTH:

40
44
45
60

LEXINGTON AVENUE:

1
Gramercy Park Hotel
Park Gramercy

PARK AVENUE SOUTH:

Church Missions House
New York Society for the
Prevention of Cruelty to
Children

EAST 22ND STREET:

United Charities Building
Manhattan Trade School
for Girls
Gramercy Arms
Sage House
Family Court Building
Children's Court
145
Gustavus Adolphus
Swedish Lutheran Church

construction than would have been appropriate if it had simply been built to house the offices of the charitable group. The street elevations are clad in a particularly beautiful rough-cut red sandstone, known as Kingwood stone, thought to have been used only once before in New York (at the synod house at the Cathedral of St. John the Divine). For the Russell Sage Foundation, Atterbury adapted the form of a Florentine Renaissance palazzo to the needs of a modern office building. The street elevations display the tripartite horizontal massing and rhythmic arrangement of openings that is typical of Florentine palazzi.

A particularly interesting feature of the building is the use of carved panels symbolic of the ideals and goals of the foundation. Located on the second floor, these panels, each in the form of a shield, represent health, work, play, housing, religion, education, civics, and justice. Above the former main entrance, on 22nd Street, is a rectangular panel representing the specialized work of the organization - study, service, and counsel. This use of ornamentation to communicate symbolically the purpose of a building was popular among the Beaux-Arts-trained architects such as Atterbury, and is evident on many late-19th- and early-20th-century public and institutional buildings in New York City. These panels are early examples of the architectural sculpture of René Chambellan, a sculptor better known for his later installations at Rockefeller Center and the Chanin building.

The foundation's new building not only housed the offices of the Russell Sage Foundation, but also contained offices of other social-service organization, including the American Association of social Workers and the Family Welfare association of America. The charitable organizations housed in this building received their space at no charge. The two top floors of the building housed the Social Work Library, one of the finest libraries of its type. In 1929, the foundation decided to expand the building by erecting a wing on East 22nd Street that was to be a profitable venture with space rented to social-service organizations. Atterbury designed a wing that would complement his original building by a five-story hyphen. The construction of a low building on the midblock site was required by a covenant attached to the deed by the site's prior owner, the Gramercy Park Hotel, who wished to preserve the light entering the hotel rooms that faced north. The New York School of Social Work became the primary tenant of the addition.

In 1949, the Russell Sage Foundation moved from this building and it was sold to the Archdiocese of New York, which used the structure to house the offices of Catholic Charities. in 1975, the

Parish House
Lexington
Miss E.L. Breese Carriage House
Gramercy Court
158

THIRD AVENUE

EAST 19TH STREET:

105
109
111 & 113
115 & 117
IRT Company Substation
112-114
116
118
120
122

IRVING PLACE:

65 & 71
67-69
81

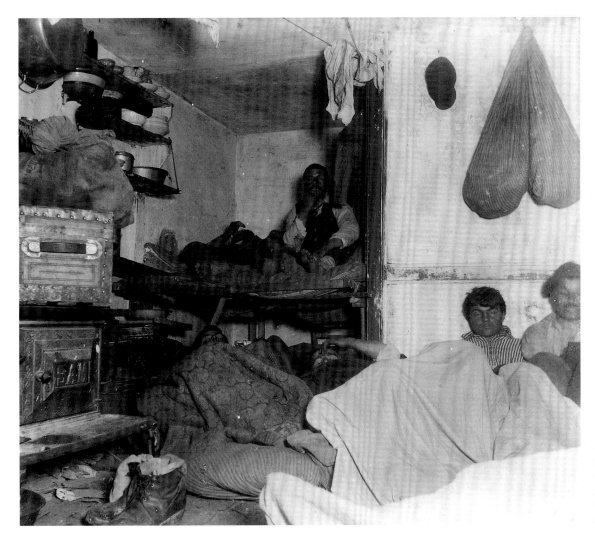

Five Cents a Spot, c. 1890. Museum of the City of New York, Jacob A. Riis Collection, #90.13.4.158

sparer and more abstract reading of classical precedent. Like many of his Beaux-Arts–trained peers, he stressed the "thorough study of classic fundamentals of beauty" which enabled the "older architects to produce buildings that [reflected] the contemporary point of view without violence to principles that have stood the test of ages."[6]

Atterbury embodied the picture of a gentleman architect. Like his father and grandfather before him, he graduated from Yale College, after which he attended the School of Mines at Columbia University; apprenticed in the offices of McKim, Mead & White; and studied in Paris under the French architect Paul Blondel (1841–1897). However, he recognized that his profession held a deep responsibility to "further widen and expand the fields in which . . . architects may serve," and he funneled his idealism and altruism into opening the field of architecture beyond merely that of gentlemen's work.[7] As a champion of the American Institute of Architects' first form of the contractual arrangement defining the field's framework, Atterbury helped craft the basis of the three-party relationship among client, architect, and builder. His work not only emphasized the status of the architect but also created protocols and paths of authority that raised architecture to a higher plane. The many professional organizations and committees with which he was associated slowly unlocked the world of potential commissions to those beyond the circle of well-connected men who had met at school, belonged to the same clubs, and summered together. Atterbury's myriad pursuits as an architect, inventor, preservationist, planner, and author produced an erudite and sophisticated synthesis of science and art. Unlike many of his contemporaries, he moved agilely between worlds, providing tasteful, appropriate, and artistic design to the moneyed set into which he was born and to the working classes, about whom he felt most passionate. The threads that form Atterbury's greatest projects expressed an understanding of materials and vernacular and iconic architecture as well as revealed his enduring quest for an engineered solution.

CHAPTER 2

GROSVENOR ATTERBURY AND HIS OFFICE

Of English and French Huguenot descent, Grosvenor Atterbury could trace his heritage back to the fourteenth century.[1] He was born on July 7, 1869, in Detroit, Michigan, where his father, Charles Larned Atterbury (1842–1914), was forging his career as a successful corporation lawyer.[2] The son of Yale graduate and lawyer Reverend John Guest Atterbury (1811–1887), Charles Atterbury was one of seven children, born in the prospering commercial center of New Albany, Indiana, across the Ohio River from Louisville, Kentucky—the city where Rev. John Atterbury had assumed one of his first posts after deciding that the ministry better suited his spiritual convictions and character than the law. At Yale, Charles Atterbury stood out academically and socially. A Townsend speaker and inductee of the exclusive secret society Scroll and Key, he also won the distinction as the Class of 1864's "wooden-spoon" man—an honor based on wit, speaking talents, and popularity, especially with women. After leaving New Haven, Charles Atterbury moved to Detroit, where he remained until 1874 when he decamped for New York to form the law practice of Betts, Atterbury & Betts with his college classmate Frederick H. Betts (1843–1905).[3]

As described in a chronicle of the family, "[Charles] Atterbury was a man of unusual ability in his own field,

and by his legal acumen, balanced judgment and human sympathy commanded the respect and admiration of all with whom he was associated. . . . In the social realm, his influence spread about him good cheer and a spirit of kindliness and geniality, the qualities that led to his selection as the most popular man in his class at Yale." At the same time, "in spite of having to make his own way and the continuous hard work he gave to his profession, he developed a fine aesthetic sense and became a lover of the fine arts. He was one of the original members of the Grolier Club, organized by bibliophiles to advance the art of printing in this country, and with McKim, Mead & White, the architects; Warner, the sculptor; Ryder, the painter; and Daniel Cottier, the art dealer, formed a small group known as the Jereboam Club, whose meetings were given over to discussions of art of all kinds at a time when this country was emerging from an era of bad taste."[4]

In 1868, Rev. John Atterbury married his son to Katharine Mitchell Dow (1844–1921) in New York at the Madison Square Church. The daughter of Marcus French Dow and Caroline Mitchell Dow of New York and Detroit, Mrs. Atterbury excelled as an organist and was known as a "beautiful character" and a woman of "great taste and judgement."[5] As the couple's only child, Grosvenor—or "Grove" as he was called—had a close relationship with his

Adele McGinnis Herter, Grosvenor Atterbury, c. 1915,
pastel on canvas, 60 x 30 inches. National Academy Museum,
New York (565-P)

parents, whom he described as "two rare spirits," and lived much of his adult life with them in both New York and the Shinnecock Hills, an oceanfront resort near Southampton on the east end of Long Island of which Charles Atterbury was an original summer resident.

During their early years in Manhattan, the Atterburys lived in a house at 7 East 33rd Street, before moving uptown to the newly stylish Upper East Side residential district and eventually settling at 131 East 70th Street, a brownstone that Grosvenor lovingly remodeled in the 1910s. During the 1890s, Charles Atterbury, one of the founding members of the Shinnecock Hills Golf Club, purchased eighty acres in the Hills, known as Sugar Loaf Acres, and built a rustic shingle-style summer house overlooking the bay. As a boy, the handsome and sporty Grosvenor enjoyed summers in Southampton, tennis at the Meadow Club, and leisurely wagon rides through the area's rural landscape as well as occasional trips to Europe and jaunts to the Adirondacks and Florida for fishing. In New York, he attended John Silas White's Berkeley School, then one of the country's top preparatory schools, before entering Yale in the fall of 1887.[6] Youthful and petite, Atterbury quickly earned the nickname "boy-face."[7] His childlike appearance notwithstanding, he made his mark academically; not only was he considered the brightest in his class but also like his father he was a Townsend speaker. He was selected as an editor of the *Yale Record* and the *Yale Literary Magazine*—

Grosvenor Atterbury, 1891. Yale University, Harvey Cushing/ John Hay Whitney Medical Library

the highest literary honor of the academic course—and elected to Phi Beta Kappa, the academic honor society.[8] While Atterbury received awards in political science and delivered his thesis on the French Protestants of the sixteenth century at graduation, he was also recognized by his classmates for his artistic skill. He took art classes with artist Professor John F. Weir (1841–1926), the first director of Yale's School of Fine Arts. He was known to sketch scenes around campus and won awards for his cartoons. Also among the most popular men, Atterbury joined clubs and fraternities, including Psi Upsilon, Chi Delta Theta, and the literary Elizabethan Club, as well as Scroll and Key. Throughout his later life, Atterbury maintained his college friendships and ties, particularly among the group that had made up his year's class of Scroll and Key. Several of these friends—John S. Barnes, Starling W. Childs, Charles P. Cooley, and Harvey W. Cushing—would become clients.

In New Haven, Atterbury made vague plans to form an architectural practice after graduation with his closest friend Harvey Cushing (1869–1939). However, when the two young men toured New York Hospital with the Atterburys' family doctor, Cushing opted for a career in medicine and went on to become one of the twentieth century's greatest

Grosvenor Atterbury in a wagon crossing the Shinnecock Hills. Courtesy of the Southampton Historical Museum

neurosurgeons and the Sterling Professor of Neurology at Yale.[9] Atterbury chose to attend Columbia University's architecture program in 1892 as a special student, at the same time apprenticing in the offices of McKim, Mead & White. While Yale had offered no formal training in architecture, Columbia's curriculum was far from inspirational, focusing more on the practical than the artistic. William Adams Delano (1874–1960), who attended the program four years later, related that Columbia "offered little to an enthusiastic approach to architecture. . . . Columbia in those days was like going back to Kindergarten."[10] Although Atterbury was enrolled in the school, he did not stay long enough to receive his degree. During the summers, from 1890 to 1893, he studied plein-air painting under William Merritt Chase (1849–1916) at the Shinnecock Summer School of Art near his family's home. Travels abroad in Spain, Cairo, and Tangiers stimulated the budding architect's sensibilities. Upon hearing of a memorial addition to Scroll and Key's New Haven headquarters designed by Richard Morris Hunt (1827–1895) in the Moorish style, Atterbury wrote Cushing in 1892 from Cairo that "ever since then I have been looking for ideas and suggestions in these Moorish mosques and palaces. Almost all of the oldest and most beautiful are built in two colors of marble like the Hall and more than once suggested it in detail."[11]

In 1894, Atterbury left for Paris to study in the atelier of Paul Blondel, which had been founded in 1881. He shared a large apartment and studio with artist friends Albert (1871–1950) and Adele Herter (1869–1946) and enjoyed the creative freedom of the city. As he reported to Cushing, "Already I feel the difference in being in an atmosphere entirely free from work and business—and perhaps it is the sudden change [that has created] very noticeable stimulus in my own work."[12] It is unclear, however, if Atterbury was officially registered at the Ecole des Beaux-Arts, the preeminent course of study for an aspiring American architect, or if he worked solely in Blondel's studio for the year.[13] As described by Ernest Flagg, who had joined Blondel's atelier in 1889, "one may enter the atelier without having been admitted to the school but he can never become an ancien without having been admitted."[14] In addition, the process for admission into the Ecole was long and arduous, and many Americans spent years in Paris preparing for and passing its rigorous entrance exams. Nonetheless, Atterbury not only experienced the energized and motivating atmosphere of the atelier—the heart of the Beaux-Arts system—but also gained the prestige associated with having studied abroad.

Stowe Phelps.
Courtesy of Stowe C. Phelps

Perhaps Atterbury chose Blondel as his *patron* for the same reasons as Flagg. As opposed to the official ateliers run by the Ecole des Beaux-Arts, independent studios such as Blondel's were considered "more chic . . . and the student [received] more attention from the *patron*, as there [were] generally fewer pupils." In 1889, Flagg opted for Blondel because there "were no Americans. Monsieur Blondel [was] a man with [a] brilliant record and [was] in the prime of life, he had won every prize in the school, including the Grand Prix de Rome [and] besides his large practice he was architect of the Government." Additionally, he "had the deserved reputation of taking more pains with his pupils than any other *patron* in Paris. His own work was stamped with that character, mainly refinement and elegant originality which one sees in the works of [Louis] Duc, whose friend and ardent admirer he was."[15] Blondel had studied under Honoré Daumet (1826–1911) at the same time as Charles McKim (1847–1909), in whose office Atterbury had apprenticed. Among Blondel's most celebrated commissions was the neo-Grec–inspired Furtado-Heine (1884), a medical clinic in Paris, which featured stratified walls of brick and limestone—a technique that would later appear

John Almy Tompkins 2nd.
Courtesy of the Division of Rare and Manuscript
Collections, Cornell University Library

in Atterbury's work. Prior to Flagg's association with Blondel, few Americans had chosen to study in his atelier; however, during the ensuing decade, many followed Flagg's example. While Atterbury was in Paris, he overlapped with fellow Americans Benjamin Wistar Morris (1870–1944) and James Gamble Rogers (1867–1947).

A Beaux-Arts education instilled a specific way of problem solving founded in formal composition. The importance of the *parti*—or practical and artistic solution—as an organizational principle was impressed upon Atterbury as well as techniques to incorporate evolving modern technology with more traditional building materials. Through competition and *esquisses*, students were forced to commit to a *parti* as the basis of their plan, which, in turn, gave rise to sections, massing, and elevations. As an admirer of Louis Duc (1802–1879), Blondel espoused a more rational approach toward composition and ornament, moving away from the idealized French neoclassicism practiced by Charles Garnier (1825–1898), architect of the Paris Opéra. He supported forging a dialogue between structure and decoration and giving expression to architecture through symbolic detail and carved motifs. As a legacy of his Beaux-

Arts education, Atterbury would later tell his colleague William Adams Delano that the "first principle of good planning [was] simple and obvious circulation."[16] While "interpretative powers [were] properly trained," he also felt that the Beaux-Arts system was deficient to some degree because it was "formed largely on historical traditions, and not organized simply and solely to meet in the most effective way the demands of modern conditions of teaching and practice."[17]

Upon returning from Paris in 1895, Atterbury set up an office in New York at 111 Fifth Avenue and pursued house commissions for friends and for his father's colleagues, including Arthur B. Claflin, Albert and Adele Herter, Robert W. de Forest, and Frederick H. Betts.[18] By 1900, Atterbury was joined by Stowe Phelps and John Almy Tompkins 2nd, who worked with him until their respective retirements in 1927 and 1937. Phelps (1869–1952) had been a class ahead of Atterbury at Yale, and the two men had worked together as editors of the *Yale Record*; both belonged to Scroll and Key. The son of dry-goods merchant Charles Phelps (1844–1890) and Helen Minerva Stowe Phelps (1843–1919), he was raised in Brooklyn on Prospect Street and attended the Brooklyn Polytechnic School before matriculating at Yale.[19] After college, while studying to be a chemist at the School of Chemistry in Mulhausen, Alsace, Phelps discovered a talent for drafting. With no architectural training, he entered Atterbury's practice and quickly rose from draftsman to specifications engineer, a position he held until his retirement in 1927, when he moved to Lausanne, Switzerland, and Santa Barbara, California.

According to his son, Stowe C. Phelps, Phelps was modest and self-effacing. Handsome and convivial, he had been a popular fixture in New York's social scene during his bachelor days, having led more cotillions than any other man of "The Four Hundred." In 1907, he married artist Edith Catlin (1874–1961) at the Catlins' family house, Fairholme, in Morristown, New Jersey, and had three children. They settled in a townhouse at 161 East 74th Street in 1910, part of a block of houses that Phelps helped develop.[20] Phelps's sociability easily won over clients. As a later firm employee described, while Phelps was the general specifications head, "his main job however was to get the wealthy clients."[21]

Atterbury met John Almy Tompkins 2nd (1871–1941), the firm's standout talent, at Columbia. Of old Staten Island stock, Tompkins was born in Baltimore to Charles H. Tompkins (b. 1832) and Jane Carr Tompkins (b. 1834) of Rhode Island and, shortly thereafter, moved back to Staten

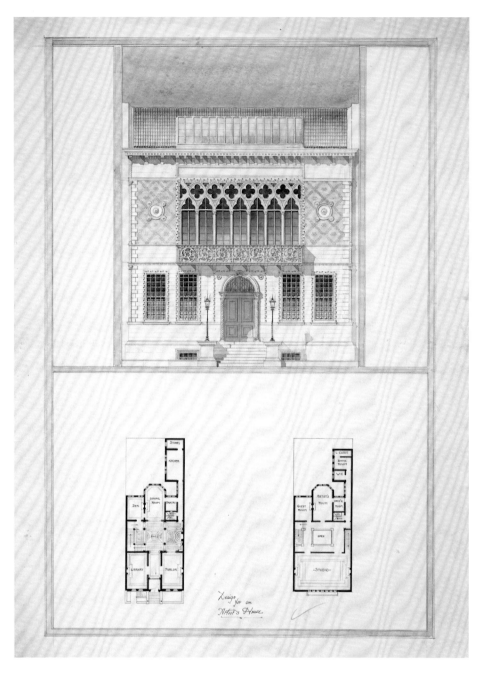

John Almy Tompkins 2nd, design for an artist's house, c. 1894. Avery Architectural and Fine Arts Library, Columbia University in the City of New York

Island with his family. At St. Paul's School in Concord, New Hampshire, which he attended between 1883 and 1889, Tompkins excelled at sports, particularly tennis as well as ice hockey, crew, and bicycling. After graduation, he attended Columbia College and studied in the School of Mines' architectural program alongside Benjamin Wistar Morris, Kenneth M. Murchison (1872–1938), and John Russell Pope (1874–1937). At Columbia, Tompkins assisted his professor, William R. Ware (1832–1915), on a treatise detailing the Casa del Aurora in Rome while he worked to develop his skills as a designer and renderer. Unlike Atterbury, who stayed only briefly as a special student, Tompkins immersed himself in college life, joining the sketch club, the class football team, the board of *The Columbian*, and Alpha Delta Psi, the college's oldest fraternity, before receiving his joint degree in political science and architecture in 1894.

After practicing independently for several years, Tompkins joined Atterbury in 1897. As chief designer, Tompkins was "gifted, patient and prolific. He took the rough sketches Atterbury made from client discussion and turned them into many possible schemes leading to solutions OK'ed by [Atterbury] and the clients."[22] According to Tompkins, he "had complete authority and supervision over design and rendering," and most of the firm's striking project renderings were executed in his hand.[23] While each of the associates was responsible for his own work, all of the projects in the office, as a 1909 article in *The New York Architect* described, had "a distinct personality and uniformity of type." A lifelong bachelor, Tompkins lived much of his adult life with his sister Eliza Tompkins in New York and shared the English-style studio he designed at 41 Deepdene Road in Forest Hills Gardens with his friend, writer and editor Samuel Chapin.

In addition to Tompkins and Phelps, the modest-sized office consisted of several capable draftsmen, two project captains, apprentices, a specifications assistant, and a secretary. By 1920, it had relocated to two three-story houses that Atterbury had combined at 139 East 53rd Street. Over its forty-year operation, Atterbury's office produced more than 1,300 projects, big and small, and attracted the talents of such architects as Roger H. Bullard (1884–1935), Elisabeth Coit (1897–1987), Henry Higby Gutterson (1884–1954), Julian Peabody (1881–1935), Albert E. Wilson (1879–1955), Edward T. Parker (1878–1930), Charles C. May (1882–1937), Philip E. Langworthy (1896–1967), W. Leslie Walker (1877–1937), William Wilson (1880–1965), W. F. Anderson (1975–1948), and Raymond C. Celli (1906–1959).[24] Elisabeth Coit, who worked as a draftsman and designer between the years of 1919 and 1929, went on to form her own practice and became the principal project planner for the New York City Housing Authority (1948–62). She credited her experience in Atterbury's office as an important stage of her career. Coit recalled that "Mr. Att's method was to visit each new client, come back with penciled small scale notes and sketches on 5 by 7 pale orange pads and hand them to Mr. Tompkins, who would produce ⅛ inch sketches of several possible layouts that might suit the owner and perhaps thumbnail sketches of the building. No fancy models or rendering that I can remember. . . . Full-size charcoal details on tracing paper were hung against a wall and Mr. Tompkins . . . [and] one or two of the staff would study it carefully and tack little changes. . . . The team worked well and hard" and "relied on design study."[25]

As head of the office, Atterbury could be both reasonable and particular. At five feet six inches, he was a small, dapper man with brown hair, clear blue eyes, and a full mustache. Often found with a corn-cob pipe in hand, he was indefatigable, almost imperious, in getting across his points and opinions. Always analyzing each problem in great detail, he verged on loquaciousness and long-windedness. As he expressed to Cushing, "my tendency is prolixity."[26] However, beyond his artist's eye, his keen intelligence included a mastery of science and numbers. He excelled at drawing and painting and relished such activities as antique collecting—a hobby born out of his college days in Connecticut. In the Shinnecock Hills and on East 70th Street, his creative instinct took on its own personality, infusing his houses with a distinct character. But, in addition to his gifts as an architect, he could easily approach problems from the standpoint of an inventor and quantitative thinker. Throughout his career, he became increasingly intrigued with the scientific aspects of building materials and filed more than fifteen patents for methods of economic concrete construction. A 1931 submission detailed

Seth Low house, Broad Brook Farm, Bedford Hills, New York.
Pencil sketch. Collection of The New-York Historical Society

LEFT *Joseph Pennell's illustration of Le Puy-en-Velay and Saint Michel d'Aiguilhe.* Elizabeth Robins Pennell and Joseph Pennell, **French Cathedrals** (New York: The Century Co., 1909): 101

OPPOSITE *Grosvenor Atterbury immortalizing Le Puy-en-Velay from the north, August 30, 1900.* Yale University, Harvey Cushing/John Hay Whitney Medical Library

a camera with safety devices to prevent double exposures; as an architect and an inventor, Atterbury's mind was constantly in motion.

In 1923, at the age of fifty-three, Atterbury married the beautiful Dorothy Axtelle Johnstone (1899–1986), thirty years his junior, in a veil of secrecy. According to one newspaper account, the union "surprised society," which had viewed Atterbury as a "lifelong bachelor." As the story has been told, Atterbury stepped in as Miss Johnstone's guardian after her father, Homer Clifton Johnstone of Short Hills, New Jersey, suffered from a debilitating carriage accident. Most likely, Astelle, as she was known, recognized that Atterbury would lift her from dire circumstances and that their union would create financial security for her and her family. Over time, this marriage of convenience grew into a partnership of mutual respect and friendship.[27] While Atter-

bury had been popular with the ladies in his bachelor days and, like Phelps, was a popular cotillion leader, he had been spurned by the real object of his affection: Dorothy Whitney (1887–1968), the daughter of William C. Whitney. In the period leading up to the heiress's 1911 marriage to Willard D. Straight (1880–1918), Atterbury pursued her relentlessly, frequently sending her illustrated letters and poetry. According to W. A. Swanberg, Dorothy Whitney's biographer, "she avoided Atterbury as much as possible despite his prestige in the field: he was too insistent, sixteen years older than she, and a half-inch shorter, too dapper, and she had not the slightest intention of marrying him."[28] After she turned down his wedding proposal, he could not bear to be in her company.

Upon Tompkins's retirement in 1937, Atterbury's involvement in Forest Hills Gardens wound down and the

architect, then age sixty-eight, completed few projects on his own. Instead, he focused all of his energies toward further developing a panelized concrete system to save on construction costs. The childless couple moved permanently to Southampton in the late 1940s after a stroke left the architect's left side paralyzed. With advice from friend and colleague Frederick Law Olmsted Jr. (1870–1957), the Atterburys subdivided their beloved property in the Hills and began selling off house lots to support their livelihood. Financially drained from the Depression and years of doctors' and legal bills, Atterbury's wealth had substantially dwindled by the end of his lifetime. After his death in October 1956, Astelle lived off of the mortgages of her various neighbors.[29] Sadly, the strong proprietary feeling toward Sugar Loaf Acres that she shared with her husband extended to Atterbury's memory. When she cleaned out the

Little Sugar Loaf House—the renovated outbuilding in which they later lived—she sent all of Atterbury's plans and oil paintings to the dump so that they would not and could not be underappreciated by strangers.[30]

As did most architects of their time, Atterbury, Tompkins, and Phelps traveled abroad extensively. Tompkins listed "travelling" on his résumé, and Phelps had just returned from a trip around the world in 1894 and 1895 before he entered Atterbury's practice. Harvey Cushing, a talented artist and medical delineator, recorded one of Atterbury's sketching trips in his illustrated travel diary, later published as the charming *A Visit to Le Puy-en-Velay*. In the late summer of 1900, Cushing, having just completed his surgical residency at Johns Hopkins, joined Atterbury in a tour of the rural Auvergne district in southern France. Inspired by the writing of Mrs. Schuyler Van

Rensselaer (1851–1934) and the illustrations of Joseph Pennell (1857–1926), Atterbury convinced his friend to accompany him to the region before traveling on to Venice with his parents.[31] Equipped with sketchbooks, paint boxes, and Kodaks, the two men took in the picturesque sites of Le Puy-en-Velay. "Grove," as Cushing noted, "[became] oblivious to the world in a sketch." On August 28, they "climbed to the top of the pinnacle of rock in the afternoon—the strange sentinel rock which is capped by the old, old Eglise de Saint Michel d'Aiguilhe—and fairly gloated over the view of the countryside which toward the east especially in the light of the late afternoon was enchanting—distant purple hills, a leaden sky broken by patches of beautiful blue—a foreground of many shaded greens with the well-groomed gardens at our feet; the red tiled roofs splashed here and there in the color scheme."[32] The medieval stone church, built into a peaked volcanic formation in 962, was reached by carved-out steps that wound up the hovering rock. The architecture of Saint Michel d'Aiguilhe must have made an impression on Atterbury. Elements of its design— the coursed stone walls, asymmetry, red tile roof, turrets, walled enclosures with arched openings, and bending facades that wrapped the form of the land—later found their way into the architect's work.

Like most men in his circle, Atterbury belonged to many clubs. In New York, he joined the University Club, of which his father had served on the building committee when McKim, Mead & White's grand clubhouse was constructed, and the Century Association, the city's oldest and most prestigious arts-related club.[33] An enthusiastic tennis player, he was also a member of the Meadow Club in Southampton, which stood at the top of the colony's social strata.[34] However, while Atterbury moved easily within high society, he seemed to prefer the informal company of artists, architects, and literary types. He wrote frequently on the subject of architecture—particularly on aesthetics and low-cost construction—and considered himself an amateur author. He also formed the Digressionists with James Monroe Hewlett (1868–1941) to assemble exhibits that would perpetuate the nonarchitectural productions of architects, and he joined the Dutch Treat Club, where he fraternized with various people involved in the arts over a "dutch" lunch. In addition, he supported the convergence of the fine arts as a member of the American Fine Arts Federation and as an academician of the National Academy of Design, an honor he received in 1918. Carrying on the Atterburys' strong Episcopalian tradition, he served as

director of St. Bartholomew's Clinic, a clinic connected with the church located on Park Avenue.

Atterbury dedicated most of his free time to the advancement of his profession and, in particular, the development of low-cost and sound methods for construction. As chairman of the American Institute of Architects' standing committee on contracts and specifications (1906–11), he played a pivotal role in producing the first edition of standard documents governing the relations between owner, architect, and builder—an important early contribution to the professionalization of his field.[35] As he later related to Professor Weir, Atterbury had wished "that [he] could find something about [architecture] when [he] was thinking of taking up the profession" during his last year at college.[36] To make up for what his education may have lacked, he lectured at Columbia and as a Trowbridge lecturer at Yale on such topics as "The Administration of the Office" to describe the workings of an architect's office to interested students. When Columbia's School of Architecture was in the process of reorganizing after Dean William R. Ware's retirement in 1903, Atterbury sat on a visiting committee with twelve other architects, including John M. Carrère (1858–1911), Charles F. McKim, George B. Post (1837–1913), and Lloyd Warren (1868–1922), to offer advice on strengthening the curriculum and to create a vital link between the school and professional practice. In his suggestions, Atterbury underlined the importance that an architect should consider "his problems in their essentials, and [place] these essentials in the order of their relative importance, before allowing himself to be influenced by minor conditions and details."[37]

In 1919, Atterbury served as a member of the American Expeditionary Forces' educational commission. At the close of World War One, General Pershing instated a comprehensive educational system to ensure that the returning American troops were prepared to assume an active and intelligent role in the country's progress. As part of the initiative, Pershing established a university in Beaune, France, near Dijon, enabling soldiers, many of whose educations had been interrupted by the war, to receive instruction while awaiting transport home. Atterbury supervised the rapid conversion of a large hospital complex into the equivalent of an American college capable of accommodating 15,000 students, and he taught planning and construction in the A. E. F.'s School of Architecture with Jacques Carlu (1890–1976), Victor Laloux (1850–1937), Archibald M. Brown (1881–1956), Aymar Embury II (1880–1966), and John Galen Howard (1864–1931). During the short period in which the university was in operation, some 1,300 men received instruction.[38]

Like most Beaux-Arts–trained architects and many of his associates, Atterbury supported the perpetuation of the traditional educational system as a member of the Society of Beaux-Arts Architects—an association created in 1894 by Thomas Hastings (1860–1929), Whitney Warren (1864–1943), and Ernest Flagg, among others, to carry on the traditions and teachings of their shared Parisian experience for the benefit of future students unable to study in France.[39] Atterbury served as president of the Architectural League of New York (1915–17), frequently exhibiting his firm's work in the organization's annual exhibition, and as president of the New York chapter of the American Institute of Architects.[40] In 1953, he earned its Medal of Honor for his achievements as architect and inventor—his "special and felicitous gifts of intellectual curiosity combined with practical invention."[41]

In retrospect, Atterbury maintained that he would have laid "much greater emphasis on the value of wide culture and knowledge of all the arts and mediums in which beauty can and is expressed since [he was] one of those who [held] to the old-fashioned belief that the two handmaidens of Architecture are use and beauty."[42] However, throughout his career, from the country estates to the small workingmen's cottages, he continually strove to incorporate beauty into his work and encouraged others to do so as well. He frequently collaborated with landscape designers and planners, most notably Frederick Law Olmsted Jr. and John Nolen (1869–1937), and artists such as Albert Herter, Gertrude Vanderbilt Whitney (1875–1942), A. Stirling Calder (1870–1945), and René Chambellan (1893–1955). Whether through artistic collaboration or through his materials, he always attempted to add an artistic dimension to his work. But for all his accomplishments as the designer of private houses for the rich, Atterbury's greatest accomplishments lay in low-cost housing and in developing rational, innovative methods of construction. As he expressed, "The matter of the housing of the people is one of fundamental importance if you wish to create and foster an esthetic sense that can grow and blossom and produce works of art."[43] To instill a sense of beauty into the lives of the working class, he advocated, first and foremost, improving their living situations to eradicate "dark rooms in slums of the most hideous character."

To help effect housing reform, Atterbury associated himself with many of the committees and organizations that stood at the forefront of the movement. He was gravely concerned about the problems that plagued New York, such as congestion and slums, but considered them to be only a microcosm of the far-spreading effects of bad design, misguided planning, and inefficient government. While such organizations served as a platform for Atterbury's ideas, it was through his own work that he made his greatest contribution. He adamantly believed that the solution to the housing problem was scientifically based. As a town planner, he advocated a collective approach and cost-saving design methods, such as the semi-detached house—a technique he used in Forest Hills Gardens and in Indian Hill, Massachusetts. According to Atterbury, less-expensive housing was a logical outgrowth of reduced construction costs—a change, he argued, that only a drastic overhaul of the building profession could accomplish. Convinced that the prefabrication and standardization of structural elements was the key to the solution, Atterbury developed and continued to perfect the Atterbury system of hollow, prefabricated concrete panels, cast in steel molds offsite, which made it possible to build a cheaper, damp-proof, and fireproof house in just a matter of days. While he relished the creative freedom and the large budgets of his grander projects, Atterbury jumped at the challenge of producing well-designed, smaller, and less-expensive homes that incorporated a comparable level of detail and artistry. He enjoyed a long and prolific career and produced many extraordinary projects, but he was quick to recognize that, as a man of talent, taste, and intellect, he held a greater responsibility to shape the landscape and, in turn, uplift the people around him with his gifts.

CHAPTER 3

ESTABLISHING A PRACTICE
1895–1917

Upon his return from Paris in 1895, Atterbury embarked on a series of country houses, summer cottages, and city homes for various well-heeled clients. In developing his design approach, the twenty-five-year-old architect transformed the lessons of the Beaux-Arts into a particular—almost unique—brand of architecture that was at once picturesque and practical. As later noted by firm associate Elisabeth Coit, Atterbury's "deep feeling for architecture as an art was shown in his mansions . . . large residential mansions and expensive decorative Beaux-Arts buildings were his delight."[1] A reflection of his Parisian training, compositional rigor underpinned the artistic quality of Atterbury's work. In most of his designs, small and large, he created a sense of place in which sequences of controlled spaces—interiors, porches, courts, gardens, and stairs—unfurled in a natural, albeit intended, progression. While accomplished at using the Colonial Revival style, especially for city houses and institutional buildings, Atterbury's real talent lay in emphasizing the qualities of his materials to create romantic designs that referenced medieval ecclesiastical buildings of Europe and England and their antecedents.

Ernesto and Edith Fabbri house, 7 East 95th Street, New York, New York. View from library into second-floor hall, 2007. Jonathan Wallen

While making his mark as a designer of country and city houses, Atterbury had the good fortune to acquire several clients who would play key roles in helping the young architect realize his talents in the public arena: Robert de Forest and Henry Phipps. His relationship with de Forest, in particular, led to several important commissions that changed and redirected the nature of his practice, including the restoration of New York's City Hall and later Forest Hills Gardens and the American Wing at the Metropolitan Museum of Art. At the same time, Henry Phipps (1839–1930), whom Atterbury most likely met through de Forest, funded the architect's research on low-cost construction and presented him with the opportunity to design his first model tenement, thereby marking Atterbury's foray into the realm of low-cost housing and socially responsible design. In the twenty-year period during which Atterbury established a flourishing general practice, he and his associates convincingly displayed the versatility of classical vocabulary, exploring an assortment of styles in buildings ranging from site-specific summer cottages to the architecturally correct restoration of City Hall.

South Road, Sugarloaf in Distance, Shinnecock Hills, L. I.

South Road, Sugar Loaf in the distance, Shinnecock Hills, New York. Eric Woodward Collection

COUNTRY HOUSES, CLUBS, AND CHAPELS

Atterbury's thriving country-house practice grew up out of the estates and cottages he designed in Southampton and the Shinnecock Hills for a group of close-knit friends and acquaintances who formed the architect's world on the East End. In the 1870s, Charles Atterbury—along with other members of patrician New York such as William and Nettie Hoyt, Samuel Parrish, and Atterbury's business partner Frederick Betts and his wife Mary—had discovered the charm of Southampton, then an informal village with pristine beaches. Initially, Charles Atterbury purchased property near Lake Agawam, the town's freshwater pond, where the summer colony originally clustered. When the Long Island Railroad was extended to the East End in the early 1870s, more fashionable New Yorkers were drawn to the area, and its sleepy atmosphere began to slowly change. In the late 1880s and 1890s, the establishment of the Meadow Club, Shinnecock Hills Golf Club, and Southampton Club created the social infrastructure of Southampton's well-maintained order—an organism bred on dignified formality and tradition. The village's cultural life, created by William Merritt Chase's Shinnecock Summer School of Art (1891) and Samuel L. Parrish's Art Museum of Southampton (see pages 135–7; designed by Atterbury in 1898), made the area an artistic center.

However, wealth was not incidental. Indeed, as one chronicler noted, "summer residents [devoted] their fortunes to purchasing comfort rather than social distinction."[2] The robust economy and prevailing tastes spawned a number of larger and more luxurious architect-designed estates to replace the modest cottages and refurbished farmhouses that defined the architectural landscape of the East End. While the summer colony was composed largely of affluent professionals, such as doctors, lawyers, and bankers, rather than the titans and robber barons who frequented Newport, Southampton's reputation as the "Newport of Long Island" had been launched by 1897. As the *Southampton Press* noted, "Southampton is not far behind Newport. The elegance of its equipages, luxury in its cottages and the display of its entertainments compare favorably with the older city."[3] Although the architectural expression of the colony had taken a more opulent turn, it was always more relaxed than the more socially rigorous resort and never aspired to the same level of pretension embodied by Bellevue Avenue's grand palazzos and châteaus.

Well entrenched in Southampton society, Grosvenor Atterbury shared a common background and similar ideas of leisure as his clients who, like him, played tennis at the Meadow Club and golf at Shinnecock—described as "probably the most perfect . . . course in this country" by the *New York Times*. In 1887, Atterbury's father, a founding member of the club, had invested in the Shinnecock Hills as part of a syndicate that wished to build homes in the wild, undeveloped hills that were up for purchase by the Long Island Improvement Company, a real estate venture headed by the president of the Long Island Railroad, Austin Corbin.[4] Consisting of three thousand acres, the land stretched west from the village to Canoe Place Creek

Sugarloaf in the Distance, Shinnecock Hills, L. I.

Sugar Loaf in the distance,
Shinnecock Hills, New York.
Eric Woodward Collection

between the Peconic and Shinnecock Bays. Sugar Loaf, Charles Atterbury's cottage built after the suggestions of family friend Stanford White (1853–1906), was located high on a bluff looking south over the water. This house and its evocative natural setting captured Grosvenor Atterbury's imagination.

Cast in the East End's golden light, the rugged beauty of the site's dunes and outcroppings, treeless rolling hills, and tangles of briers, brush, and scrub created a picturesque backdrop for the Atterburys' home. What began as a one-story shingle-style cottage gradually spread—with Atterbury's additions—into a gracefully rambling structure of weathered pine and cedar, rough overburned brick (known as lammie), and native stone that grew up as a natural extension of the hills.[5] The movement of the facades created by undulating rooflines, jutting dormers, towers, and the arched stone carriage gateway suggested the unbridled process of organic growth, or accretion over time. Between a hexagonal bedroom tower and the Norman kitchen tower, whose treatment White had suggested, stretched a 60-foot-long living room. Its low-hung timbered ceiling, exposed lammie-brick walls detailed with peeled logs, diamond-paned English casement windows, and two large rustic fireplaces created an informal space ideal for summer living.

The organic quality of the Atterburys' homestead and its splendid sun-drenched landscape greatly informed the architect's work. Sugar Loaf's informal design inspired him not only to hold dear the possibilities of native mate-

rials but also to develop a heightened sensitivity for setting. As described by architectural critic C. Matlack Price, the foundation of Atterbury's work lay in "a study of the climate, the general nature of the country and the special nature of the site, the natural planting of the trees and the local traditions and the local materials."[6] "The true answer to a problem," Atterbury expounded, "must be derived logically from its own premises and conditions." He placed great emphasis on the importance of building materials, "the palette with which the architect paints."[7] However, Atterbury recognized that a design's success was also the measure of something less tangible: a house must truly be appreciated and "possessed" by its occupants—in this case, his parents, "two rare spirits." "Although I had a good deal to do with its design," Atterbury later related, "its greatest charm didn't come from anything architectural. It came as an expression of that greatest of all arts—the Art of Living."[8] This notion would shape Atterbury's plans. Rather than include unnecessary rooms or replicate spaces for the sake of rounding out a scheme, he tried to ensure that each of his interiors was useful and livable. Many of his rooms—or what read as rooms—revealed themselves as porches, loggias, and indoor-outdoor spaces. "Of course," he divulged to one house client, "I think that rooms only justify themselves when they are livable, and how much they are lived in depends both on how well they are designed and how attractively furnished and also how well the inhabitants know how to live themselves."[9]

ABOVE *Charles L. Atterbury house, Sugar Loaf, Shinnecock Hills, New York.* Courtesy of the Southampton Historical Museum

RIGHT *Sugar Loaf. Kitchen tower and carriage drive-through.* J. W. Gilles. *Arts and Decoration* 24 (March 1926): 35

OPPOSITE
TOP *Sugar Loaf.* Samuel H. Gottscho. *The Architect* 9 (January 1928): 475

BOTTOM *Sugar Loaf. Stone fireplace, living room.* Gottscho-Schleisner Collection. Library of Congress

Surprisingly, Atterbury's first known commission was not in New York or on Long Island but in the Adirondacks, an area to which the young architect also had ties. Several of Southampton's pioneer settlers, including Charles Atterbury, Frederick H. Betts, and Alfred M. Hoyt, as well as Robert de Forest, had banded together in 1877 to form the Adirondack Club (later the Tahawus Club), the first large private fish-and-game club of its kind. Located on land formerly controlled by the McIntyre Iron Company, the club leased some 75,000 acres and the rustic buildings once occupied by miners. De Forest's friend, William West Durant (1850–1934), created the Adirondacks' first great camps and enlisted Atterbury's assistance in designing his third lodge, Camp Uncas, on Mohegan Lake (1894–95). The son of railroad tycoon Thomas C. Durant (1820–1885), William Durant developed his father's extensive Adirondacks land holdings into self-sufficient bastions of rustic luxury that catered to the ruling class's penchant for comfort and privacy. Both Atterbury and de Forest had visited Durant's first great camp, Camp Pine Knot, on Raquette Lake, built over a period of twenty years.[10] For Camp Uncas—located seven miles southeast of Raquette Lake, Atterbury executed a series of drawings of various interior features, including a fireplace and furniture. Buried deep in the woodlands, the compound, which was purchased by J. Pierpont Morgan (1837–1913), consisted of casual log structures and a low-lying stylistically eclectic manor house.[11] Inside, the space was decorated with peeled logs articulating the building's structural framework and anchored by a monumental fieldstone fireplace. The eclectic rustic quality of Camp Uncas's architecture would permeate and shape the young architect's work, particularly in the Shinnecock Hills.[12]

In 1891, soon after Charles Atterbury purchased land in the Hills, William Merritt Chase's art school opened at Shinnecock, drawing a mix of affluent female students and talented young American artists such as Rockwell Kent, Howard Chandler Christy, Joseph Stella, and Gifford Beal. Having been introduced to the plein-air method of painting abroad, Mrs. William S. Hoyt, a prominent summer resident, convinced several of her wealthy friends to sponsor an art school on the East End. As large property owners in the area, Atterbury's father and Samuel Parrish (1849–1932)—one of Atterbury's early clients, later known as the "first citizen of Southampton"—donated land for Chase's studio. Parrish also commissioned a number of cottages on the surrounding lots to create what

came to be known as the Art Village located between Sugar Loaf Acres and Southampton village. Atterbury, who attended Chase's school for three summers, was responsible for at least one house within the charming enclave of informal shingle-style cottages; it was later moved to Sugar Loaf in 1908. In 1894, Atterbury purchased several lots and two years later incorporated the Art Village Improvement Association with Parrish, Zella Milhau, John R. Weeks, Sarah R. Lee, and James P. Lee to acquire and lease real estate. However, the attribution of most of the houses is unclear; their style was characteristic of Atterbury's hand, but several other architects who worked there—including Katherine C. Budd (1860–1951) and McKim, Mead & White—may have executed some of the houses.[13]

Atterbury was also responsible for a handful of the eighteen summer houses that had transformed the Hills by 1906.[14] Around the turn of the twentieth century, he executed cottages for lawyer and former assistant secretary to the Navy James Russell Soley (1850–1911) and his wife Mary Woolsey Howland Soley (1853–1935) and for Alfred H. Swayne (1870–1937), a son of Union army general-turned-corporation lawyer General Wager Swayne and later the chairman of General Motors.[15] Working within a similarly rustic and informal vein as Sugar Loaf, Atterbury produced a pair of modest shingled homes with porches, dormers, varying window patterns, and low sweeping roofs. Shaped primarily by their symbiotic relationship with the land, these houses did not fall into any defined stylistic category. Atterbury, so familiar with the exposed planes and windswept grass of the area's undulating hills, convincingly fused his houses with their sites to evolve a distinctive approach in which the massing and the muted shades of shingle and brick blended with the dull colors and flatness of the setting. Atterbury's cottage for lawyer Lucien Oudin (1854–1929) and his wife Jessie (1860–1924), east of Southampton village in Water Mill and overlooking Mecox Bay and the dunes beyond, displayed a similar composition.[16] The architect sought to downplay the presence of the house and accompanying stable on the barren waterside site by keeping them close to the ground. Like the Soley and Swayne houses, he achieved this with a long low roof suggestive of the land's sloping contours. To relieve the intensity of the house's lines, he incorporated dormers; to add play to the facades, he incorporated a variety of window types and sizes. Experimenting with the artistic quality of his materials, he juxtaposed the textured brick of the porch

ABOVE *Camp Uncas for William West Durant, Mohegan Lake, Adirondacks, New York. Living room, manor house.* Courtesy of The Adirondack Museum, P9516, ca. 1900

LEFT *Atterbury's sketch of a fireplace at Camp Uncas.* Courtesy of The Adirondack Museum, 1981.26.51, dated 1893

TOP *James Russell Soley house, Shinnecock Hills,*
New York. American Architect 94 (August 26, 1908)

BOTTOM *Alfred H. Swayne house, Algoma,*
Shinnecock Hills, New York. American Architect 94
(August 26, 1908)

TOP *Lucien Oudin house, Water Mill, New York.*
American Architect 94 (September 2, 1908)

BOTTOM *Oudin house. Dining room.*
American Homes and Gardens (April 1908): 148

columns with smooth surfaces of shingle. Despite the modest size of the house, Atterbury's interiors conveyed a sense of roominess. Shaded porches and open-air rooms, carved into the building mass, extended off all of the major living spaces and opened up the house to the outdoors. Like Camp Uncas, the rooms were simply finished and included several rustically textured fireplaces of brick or stone. The studs was exposed inside, creating screen-like panels that framed planed boards—the backside of the outer wall sheathing.

While Atterbury's first major house commission for textile magnate Arthur Brigham Claflin (1858–1939) and his wife Minnietta Anderson Claflin (1863–1945) was larger and more formal than his weathered shingled cottages, it expressed comparable design features.[17] Located on an exposed elevated 60-acre site overlooking Shinnecock Bay, the estate, completed in 1898, encompassed a twenty-five-room home, a carriage house, and an eighteenth-century windmill that had been moved to the property by its former owner, Mrs. William S. Hoyt, in the early 1890s. On the exterior, the house's balanced asymmetrical composition, bloated size, and sandy-colored stucco walls conveyed a certain formality. However, its open plan flowed easily from the wide 37-foot-long living hall into the den, living room, dining room, and stair alcove. A number of large shaded verandas providing ample indoor-outdoor space—articu-

lated by flat arched openings on the facade—penetrated into the building mass. Because the major rooms undulated in and out of the plan, corner exposures were created, ventilation was improved, and panoramic vistas were enhanced. And while ostensibly the house was large, Atterbury dedicated much of the first-floor area to the porch and outdoor space and did not fill the plan with unnecessary rooms.

Although Atterbury clearly designed the house with its context and vistas in mind—setting it into the slope of the site below the existing windmill—its large bulky mass, light-colored facades, and tall hipped roofs did not connect to the landscape successfully. However, the cottage that Atterbury designed nearby in 1906 for industrialist Thomas Gerard Condon (1894–1930) and his wife Emily Beach Condon sprawled convincingly across a sweeping lawn, attaining the low-lying, cumulative effect that the architect preferred.[18] The property also encompassed a laundry, servants' quarters, and a tower whose oblong silhouette, jerkin-headed roof, and thin vertical openings would inform future compositions, including the towers of the Church-in-the-Gardens and the inn at Forest Hills Gardens.

Due to the relative flatness of the village's terrain, the designs of Atterbury's early houses near Lake Agawam were not based as much upon the possibilities of land-

Arthur Brigham Claflin house, Shinnecock Hills, New York.
South facade. American Architect 94 (August 26, 1908)

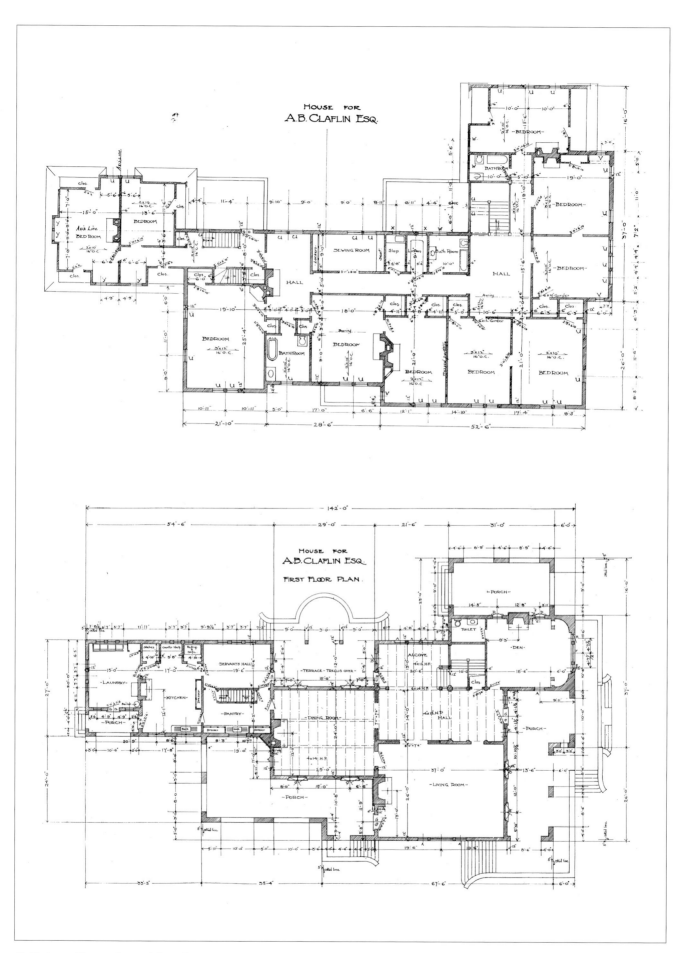

Claflin house. First- and second-floor plans.
American Architect 94 (August 26, 1908)

LEFT *Thomas Gerard Condon house, Shinnecock Hills, New York.* Eric Woodward Collection

MIDDLE *Dr. Albert Herman Ely house, Elyria, Southampton, New York.* Courtesy of the Division of Rare and Manuscript Collections, Cornell University Library

BOTTOM *Dr. Albert Herman Ely house, Fort Hill, Shinnecock Hills, New York.* Courtesy of the Division of Rare and Manuscript Collections, Cornell University Library

TOP *Henry Graff Trevor house, Southampton,
New York. Entrance façade. The Brickbuilder* 22
(November 1913): 175

BOTTOM *Trevor house. First- and second-floor plans.
The Brickbuilder* 22 (November 1913): 176

scape. Nonetheless, they displayed a similar artistic layering of textures, materials, and architectural features. For Dr. Albert Herman Ely (1860–1934) and Maud Merchant Ely's (1868–1942) house, Elyria, on Ox Pasture Road (c. 1900), Atterbury reshuffled elements such as porches, loggias, asymmetrically placed gables, eyebrow dormers, an expansive roof, and diamond-paned windows into a long rectangular envelope perforated by a flat-arched carriage drive. Atterbury interestingly juxtaposed stucco and curved concrete window-box details with the more textured quality of the shingles on the upper floors and the tile of the roof. This combination of materials was further pronounced in Dr. and Mrs. Ely's later house, Fort Hill, near the Condons' property in the Shinnecock Hills, designed by the architect in 1918, which featured a distinctively rounded tile roof constructed to simulate thatch.[19] At Vyne Croft (c. 1900) on the west shore of

Lake Agawam, belonging to banker Robert Waller (1850–1915) and his wife Emily Stewart Waller (1851–1941), Atterbury shifted to the Colonial Revival style—a mode he rarely used for country houses. However, in its design he threw off the formal geometry and rigor associated with the style by introducing asymmetrical bays and randomly placed windows, dormers, eyebrows, and bull's-eyes. Departing from his customary use of stucco, cement, or brick for the facades, Atterbury sheathed this house in wood with large pilaster details and oversized bracketed eaves—similar to that of the Oudin house—to attain the semblance of a dentilated cornice.[20] His underdeveloped interpretation of the Colonial Revival at the nearby gentlemen's Southampton Club (1899) resulted in a more straightforward expression: a large rectangular gambrel-roofed building distinguished by a central portico and Ionic columns.

ABOVE *Frank Bestow Wiborg house, The Dunes,*
East Hampton, New York. Courtesy of the East
Hampton Library, Long Island Collection

OPPOSITE

TOP *Albert and Adele Herter house, Près Choisis,*
East Hampton, New York. South facade.
Architecture 40 (September 1919): pl. 135

BOTTOM *Près Choisis. South facade and*
boathouse. Architecture 40 (September 1919): pl. 136

Atterbury and his associates continued to experiment with color, texture, plan, and intersecting roof and wall planes in his design for sportsman Henry Graff Trevor (1865–1937) and Margaret Schieffelin Trevor (b. 1870). Trevor, a founder of the Shinnecock Hills Golf Club, commissioned Atterbury to design his Southampton estate in 1910.[21] Atterbury animated the facades of Trevor's sprawling L-shaped house with multihued lammie laid in a variety of bonds and patterns. In addition to his almost aggressive use of brick, Atterbury's heavy, low-slung roof, punctuated with chimneys, eyebrow dormers, and octagonal stair tower, dominated the design. The house contained large entertaining rooms, a 40-foot-long hall, ample porch space, and a servants' wing; however, unlike the Claflin house, the plan was more compartmentalized and less fluid.

During the mid-1890s, when the Long Island Railroad extended out to East Hampton, an entire stretch of farmland was opened up for the type of high-flying development that had begun to transform Southampton a decade earlier. Previously, the rail line had run to Bridgehampton before veering north to Sag Harbor, once a bustling whaling port. The village of East Hampton, located five miles east, existed as a sleepy backwater of farmers and fishermen. In 1878, the Tile Club, a group of enterprising artists—Winslow Homer, Julian Alden Weir, Edwin Austin Abbey, and Robert Swain Gifford among them—discovered its charm on a jaunt out east. A record of the visit, published by *Scribner's Monthly*, drew attention to the area's scenic beauty. Perhaps, in part, East Hampton came to be more closely associated with an artistic and bohemian lifestyle—with such artist residents as Thomas

Moran, Childe Hassam, and Albert and Adele Herter among the ranks. As noted by Mrs. John King Van Rensselaer in the 1920s, the village was "based on a community of intellectual tastes rather than feverish craving for display and excitement."[22]

In East Hampton, Atterbury continued to shape and define his distinctive vernacular and to focus more on the design possibilities of cement and stucco—materials with which he would become increasingly preoccupied. Atterbury received his first commission in East Hampton in 1895 from Frank Bestow Wiborg (1855–1930) and Adeline Sherman Wiborg (1859–1917).[23] As Wiborg's printing-ink manufacturing firm Ault & Wiborg flourished, the Cincinnati-based client decided to lay down roots on the East Coast—an easy jumping-off point for Europe where Wiborg was developing his company's presence. Wiborg purchased 600 acres between Hook Pond—one of the village's saltwater lakes—and the ocean, and Atterbury transformed a diminutive gambrel-roofed farmhouse on the windblown dunes into a sprawling thirty-room estate, The Dunes, with a 70-foot-long living room. Given the nature of the project, The Dunes acquired the graceful rambling cumulative quality toward which the architect aspired. Additional houses for Albert and Adele Herter, Clarence and Jeanne Rice, Mrs. Benjamin Richards, and William and Annie Woodin manifested the prevailing themes of the architect's work. With some of the area's best views, the Herter, Rice, and Woodin properties provided an inspirational canvas for Atterbury's idiosyncratic hand. As noted by *Architecture*, he did "not stop at designing the mass of the building to work into the contours of the ground; he harmonized his color scheme . . . and [worked] out a sub-

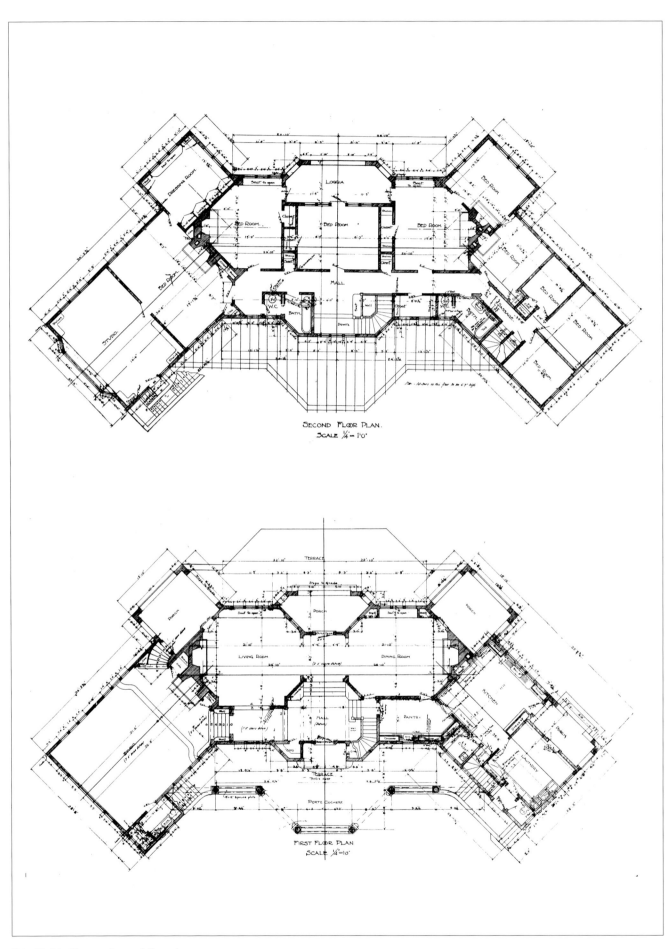

SECOND FLOOR PLAN.
SCALE ¼" = 1'0"

FIRST FLOOR PLAN
SCALE ¼" = 1'0"

Près Choisis. First- and second-floor plans.
Architecture 40 (September 1919): pls. 137, 138

Près Choisis. Studio. Architecture 40 (September 1919): pl. 139

tle harmony of reds, browns and buffs suited primarily to the autumn landscape or the burnt-up foliage of the sea coast." As a result, Atterbury's houses lost "all the rawness of a new building."[24]

Set into a low promontory on Georgica Pond, the Herters' house, Près Choisis (later The Creeks), completed in 1899, lay at the head of the lake's longest axis and looked southwest out to the ocean.[25] Parisian-trained portrait and mural painter Albert Herter and his artist wife Adele occupied a central place among East Hampton's cultured elite. Albert Herter was a scion of an artistic family; his father and uncle had founded the prominent interior design and furnishings firm Herter Brothers. Adele McGinnis Herter's father had been a successful banker. The Herters' inherited wealth allowed the couple to pursue careers in the arts and to establish a summer residence—complete with two studios—rich in color and character. As a wedding gift, Mary Herter gave her son and daughter-in-law 75 acres of land between two estuaries. After lengthy discussions with the Herters about the house's orientation, Atterbury produced a salmon-colored stucco house with blue trim, a roof of mottled copper tile, diamond-paned windows, terraces,

and porches. Italian in spirit, the design's success rested within its dialogue with the waterfront setting and surrounding gardens. When approached from the creek side, a set of steps flanked by cement retaining walls led up from the dock and below-grade boathouse to the garden terraces and porch entrance.

Within the house's ostensibly symmetrical butterfly-shaped footprint—the architect's earliest exercise using this plan—Atterbury nimbly maximized the site's potential for light and views. Due to the relative thinness of the building mass, all of the major rooms looked south over the water, and the artist studios, located in the eastern wing, received the benefit of morning light. Taking their cues from the site's contours, the first-floor interiors featured an interesting layering of levels; a pair of octagonal rooms for living and dining was accessed by a short set of steps while another flight of stairs led down to the 34-foot-long studio to the east. Within the interstice created by the diagonally projecting wings, Atterbury carved out a semi-enclosed space, forming a layer between the house and the landscape. He continued to explore the possibilities of the butterfly plan in many of his future commissions, including a renovation of an 1886 house for stove manufacturer

Près Choisis. Garden and north facade. Long Island History Collection.
Nassau County Department of Parks, Recreation & Museums

Grange Sard Jr. (1843–1924) and his wife Catherine in Southampton—a design that also incorporated piazzas, rounded spaces, and a multicolored red tile roof.[26]

The Herters effortlessly encapsulated the essence of Atterbury's idea of "the Art of Living." As artists, they lived freely and fully, effusing their house and its gardens with personality and atmosphere. Grace Wickham Curran, writing for the *American Magazine of Art*, described the couple as "intensely artistic, with tastes, sympathies and aspirations so harmonious that wherever they are they create an environment of beauty, not only of material

things but of heart and spirit as well."[27] At Près Choisis, color played an important role in linking the interiors to the outdoors, carrying visitors from a formal radiating garden of oranges, pinks, and reds under a vine-covered cement porte cochere built into the curve of the pink stucco facade and into a red lacquered stair hall. On the creek side, cooler blues and whites permeated the plantings and Persian tiles set into the retaining walls, tying the scheme to the color of the water and sky as well as to the hues of the overlooking living and dining rooms. The color of the rooms was amplified by rich decorations, ele-

Près Choisis. Dining room. Long Island History Collection.
Nassau County Department of Parks, Recreation & Museums

gant tapestries from the Herter Looms—the successor to the Herter Brothers—and paintings and murals by the artists-in-residence.

On the eastern plain, the former commonly held pastureland extending east of East Hampton village, Dr. Clarence C. Rice (1855–1935), a throat specialist with many famous patients (including the tenor Enrico Caruso and the decorator Elsie de Wolfe), and his wife, pottery maker Jeanne Durant Rice, commissioned a stucco and shingled house with a red tile roof in 1899.[28] Atterbury's idiosyncratic and irregularly placed towers, dormers, porches, windows, and outside stairs produced a somewhat ungainly effect but, as noted by *Architecture*, were well suited to the sandy stretch of coastline: "This house is at its best in the autumn when the creamy gray of the stucco, the dull red roof, the dark brown of the shingles and half timber work are only differentiated from the browns, purples and scarlets of the marsh grass, sumac and heather."[29] Like the Claflins' cottage, completed one year earlier, the interior floor area of the entrance level was not as commodious as the exterior of the house suggested; loggias subsumed into the building mass rounded

TOP *Dr. Clarence C. Rice house, East Hampton,*
New York. Entrance facade. F. B. Johnston and
M. E. Hewitt. *Architecture* (October 1911): pl. 98

BOTTOM *Rice house. Exterior veranda.*
American Architect 94 (August 26, 1908)

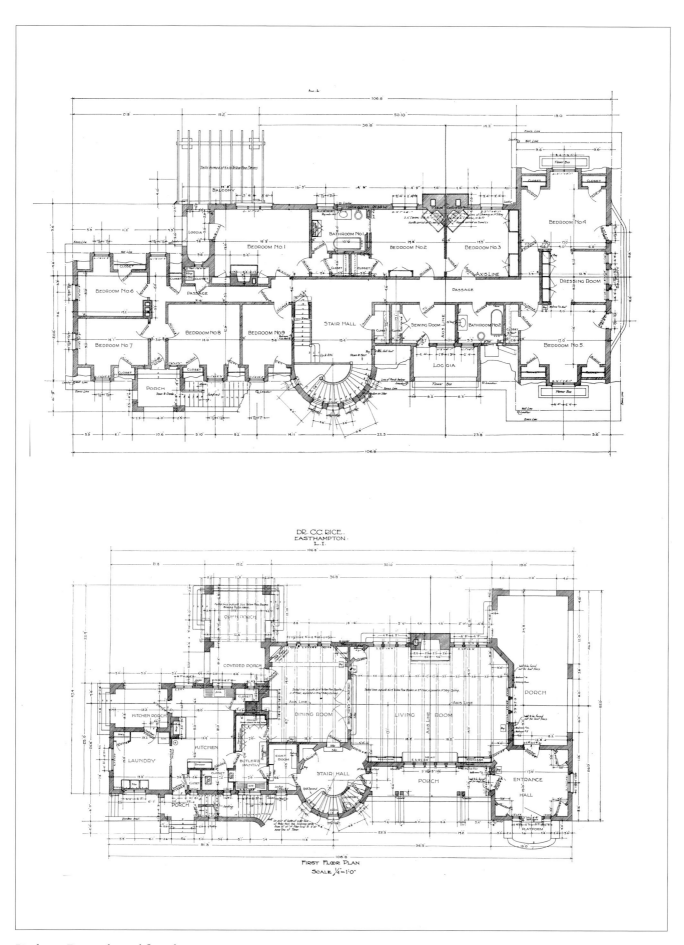

Rice house. First- and second-floor plans.
American Architect 94 (August 26, 1908)

COTTAGE AND GARDEN
FOR VILLAGE PLOT FOR
MRS AND MISS RICHARDS
·AT EAST HAMPTON L·I·
GROSVENOR ATTERBURY ARCHITECT
DRAWN BY ANNE GRANT

TOP *Mrs. Benjamin Richards house, East Hampton,
New York. Cottage and garden scheme.* House &
Garden *3 (April 1903): 214*

BOTTOM *William Hartman Woodin house, Dune House,
East Hampton, New York.* Gottscho-Schleisner. Courtesy
of the East Hampton Library, Long Island Collection

out the size of the exterior, making it seem larger than it actually was. By contrast, Atterbury's stucco cottage for Mrs. Benjamin Richards and her daughter on Dunemere Lane in East Hampton, completed in 1900, exemplified the type of compact, well-planned house that would come to define the architect's developments in Forest Hills Gardens and Indian Hill.[30] Unlike the Rice house, it was "small without and large within." While outside sheathing and ceiling beams formed the simple finishes of the interiors, the planned walled garden (never carried out) created a vital link between the house and the surrounding landscape.

In 1916, Atterbury completed a large beachfront house in East Hampton on Lily Pond Lane for Annie Jessup (1866–1941) and William Hartman Woodin (1868–1934), later the president of the American Car and Foundry Company (the corporation that would fund the architect's prefabrication research) and secretary of the Treasury under Franklin D. Roosevelt.[31] While Atterbury oriented the stair hall and service areas of Dune House, as it was known, to the north, his main living spaces projected toward the water. Octagonal rooms on either side of the house spread toward two octagonal garden pavilions which, in turn, reached out to the dunes. Unlike the Rice house, here Atterbury designed with a cleaner hand, giving the house a more-streamlined, less-organic expression. In 1925, Atterbury applied his interest in semidetached housing to an estate commission by adding a charming two-family gardeners' cottage to the property.

With his cluster of houses on the East End, Atterbury gradually began to build up his practice, and the commission for Bayberry Point, a unique and widely publicized project on the South Shore, only bolstered the architect's burgeoning career. Around 1896, Henry Osborne Havemeyer (1847–1907), founder of the American Sugar Refining Company, and his brother-in-law, Samuel Twyford Peters (1854–1921), purchased 125 acres on the Great South Bay near West Islip and commissioned Atterbury to design a summer colony of inexpensive and stylish concrete cottages as part of a real estate venture. For Havemeyer—a man of strong opinions—the fledgling architect was a curious and unlikely choice, especially since Havemeyer had previously worked with Charles C. Haight (1841–1917) on the design of his Manhattan mansion at 1 East 66th Street in 1891 and Robert S. Peabody (1845–1917) and John G. Stearns (1843–1917) on his Greenwich country house, Hilltop, in 1890. Havemeyer and his wife, Louisine (1855–1929), admired the work of Louis Comfort Tiffany (1848–1933), designer of their city home's interiors. Tiffany, a great friend and neighbor of Robert and Emily de Forest's in Cold Spring Harbor, likely collaborated with Atterbury at the couple's recommendation. Influenced by the architecture of northern Africa, Tiffany made suggestions to the young architect who had also recently traveled there; Atterbury may have acquiesced to realize Tiffany's ideas in order to further his name. While it is unclear for which aspects of the overall scheme each was responsible, the design undoubtedly influenced the tenor of Atterbury's future work.[32]

Bayberry Point faced on to the Great South Bay, in West Islip, 55 miles closer to Manhattan than Southampton. Atterbury's 1897 plan, as revealed in the promotional brochure, *Moorish Houses*, featured ten stark stucco cottages on a barren windswept plain bisected by a 100-foot-wide man-made canal on the western portion of

Henry Osborne Havemeyer houses, Bayberry Point, Islip, New York. Rendering from Moorish Houses, *1897.* Courtesy of William Havemeyer

Havemeyer's property. Advertised as "creations of the fancy," the modern Venice, which it was also called, was described as an "advanced social experiment" of collective living. However, with Havemeyer as a resident, the *New York Times* proclaimed that Bayberry Point's modest cottages and acreage were bound to become a "Tuxedo of the Seaside." The marshy land on the point was raised four feet with sand dredged from the western canal as well as another canal dug to the east, and then divided into modest one-and-a-half-acre lots, each with 200 feet of water frontage. In the enclave, "membership [was to] be very select and all elements . . . congenial." For the ten houses

ABOVE *Bayberry Point. House C from canal.* Courtesy of William Havemeyer

RIGHT *Bayberry Point. First- and second-floor plans of house C.* Courtesy of William Havemeyer

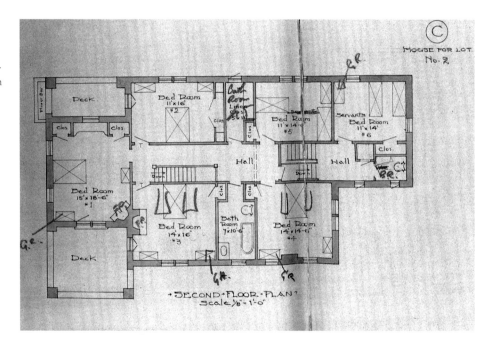

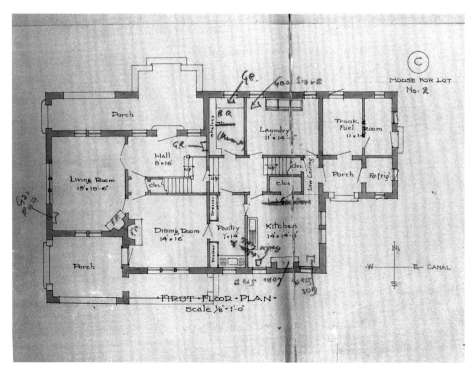

comprising the artistic ensemble, Atterbury developed four well-organized compact plans and oriented them differently to create variety. Shockingly stark in their architectural expression, especially when compared to similar summer colonies of the period, the low-lying flat-roofed stucco cottages were well suited to their seaside location with an abundance of porches, piazzas, trellises, and outdoor stairs. Red and green Spanish tile detail relieved the expanses of rough sandy-colored concrete. Although strikingly different from any of Atterbury's other commissions, Bayberry Point still displayed the architect's ability to forge a dialogue between the cottages' broad massing and light

ABOVE *Bayberry Point. Side view of house D.* Courtesy of William Havemeyer

RIGHT *Bayberry Point. First- and second-floor plans of house D.* Courtesy of William Havemeyer

SECOND FLOOR PLAN—"D"—HOUSE.

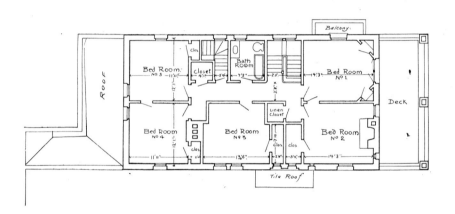

FIRST FLOOR PLAN—"D"—HOUSE.

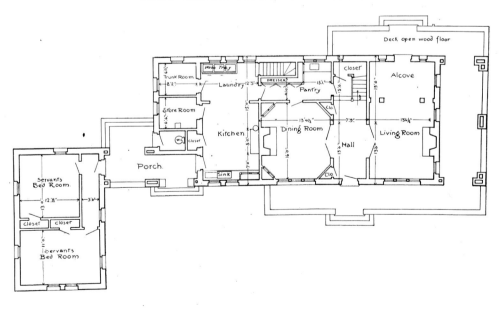

stucco walls and the landscape's flat contours and sandy terrain. While smaller in scope than his planning commissions to come, it presented Atterbury with the opportunity to contemplate relationships between dwellings and to generate picturesque variety through modest means and materials and limited plan templates.

However, perhaps Havemeyer's vision for Bayberry Point was too progressive. He moved into the southwest-ern-most cottage for the summer season of 1901 but, finding it difficult to sell the other homes, finally rented them out to family and friends.[33] While the community failed as a business venture, it represented an important first step in what would become a central quest of Atterbury's career. As an early housing advocate for the working poor, Atterbury would increasingly apply concrete, which offered superior construction standards to the

TOP *Bayberry Point. Courtyard and bridge.*
American Architect 96 (September 8, 1909): 98

BOTTOM *Bayberry Point. House D. American Architect*
96 (September 8, 1909): 98

ubiquitous wood-frame house, to a range of projects. To the extent that the use of concrete was completely atypical of single-family house construction in the United States, Atterbury was embarking on an experimental path; his goals were both pragmatic and aesthetic. Other early experiments in concrete, such as the California houses of Irving J. Gill (1870–1936), were similarly motivated by the prospect of sounder construction. But unlike Gill, who stove for a highly planar expression shorn of any ornament, Atterbury realized the full potential of the material's plasticity. Gill crafted a tilt-up slab method to fuse the flat plane of his wall into a modern style, whereas Atterbury strove for fuller sculptural possibilities with rounded corners, arched windows, brackets, exterior stairs, and rooftop verandas that imbued the development with an essential Moorish character. In this early project, Atterbury demonstrated his uncanny ability to master the formal rules of a style of architecture; concrete and its manipulation were used as a method for better housing instead of as a means to formulate a modern design.

While Bayberry Point brought Atterbury recognition in the architectural press, Wawapek Farm in Cold Spring Harbor, on the north shore of Long Island, thirty miles east of Manhattan, begun in 1898, would be his most fruitful commission. Robert de Forest, a member of the Adirondack Club and a business colleague of Charles Atterbury, would become Atterbury's most staunch patron, not only aligning the young architect with the right people but also bringing him unprecedented opportunities that tested—and expanded—the limits of his expertise. As one of his most successful and charming summer houses, Atterbury's work at Wawapek Farm clearly impressed de Forest and his wife, Emily Johnston de Forest (1851–1942), daughter of the Metropolitan Museum of Art's first president, John Taylor Johnston. While de Forest practiced law, he was better known for his contributions to the world of philanthropy. Sitting on innumerable boards and presiding over countless charitable organizations, he was, as the *New York Times* noted, "to the world of public-spiritness what J. Pierpont Morgan [was] to the realm of finance."[34] Descended from a Huguenot family whose roots in Manhattan stretched

Bayberry Point. Boathouses and bridge.
American Architect 96 (September 8, 1909): 101

Robert Weeks de Forest house, Wawapek Farm, Cold Spring Harbor, New York. North facade. Spinzia Collection. Hofstra University. Long Island Studies Department

back over two centuries, de Forest's father, Henry Grant de Forest, had also been an attorney; his maternal grandfather, Robert D. Weeks, had been president of the New York Stock Exchange. With connections and ties to all of patrician New York, de Forest was well inclined to recommend his architect for residential commissions and projects associated with his various charities.[35]

While the de Forests had frequented Cold Spring Harbor since the 1870s, they decided to build a new house on a hillside overlooking Cold Spring Harbor on a portion of the land originally owned by de Forest's parents. Emily de Forest challenged Atterbury by requesting a Long Island house with the aspect of an Adirondack lodge; the de Forests were devoted to preserving the Adirondacks, particularly the Upper Ausable Lake region. Atterbury—well versed in the rustic architecture of that region—did not exactly meet his clients' expectations, designing a charming shingled house with a heavy stone base composed of granite imported from Vermont. Rather than the

more indefinable regional style he had developed on the East End, Atterbury worked in a vein more closely related with the Colonial Revival style, embellishing the entry facade with a two-story screen of Ionic columns and a Palladian window. Deftly incorporating his angled scheme into the curve of the hillside, Atterbury gave rise to a masterful composition of picturesquely arranged porches, piazzas, towers, and shifting rooflines. While an arched carriage drive-through emptied into an enclosed entrance court contained by the house on one side and the rising land on the other, all of the rooms in the house were oriented to the south and the west to take advantage of the stunning views of the harbor.

In the center block of the house, Atterbury located a rustic living room with a large brick and stone fireplace and red tile floors. Two wings angled off of the broad central hall; to the north Atterbury placed a brightly lit paneled dining room and kitchen wing and, to the south, a large parlor with a bow window and a rounded stair hall

with small windows that stepped up the curve of the wall. Tiffany, the couple's close friend and neighbor, decorated the parlor in a Pompeian style with a "Turkish" corner, glass shades, tiles, and a large window depicting an underwater scene of shells and pebbles collected from the family's property in Montauk. Throughout, no opportunity for detail was lost: side doors were inlaid with patterned leaded-glass panels, and floors and ceiling boards were joined with decorative butterfly joints. Exotic items from the family's travels, Emily de Forest's collections of American antiques and Pennsylvania German pottery, and paintings by de Forest's brother, Lockwood de Forest (1850–1932), furthered the artistic and atmospheric splendor of the interior spaces.[36]

One year later, Dr. Walter Belknap James (1858–1927) and his wife Helen Jennings James (1860–1946) commissioned a large stucco house, Eagle's Beak, near the de Forests in Cold Spring Harbor. Also with ties to the Adirondacks, James later invited the architect to visit his

camp on Upper St. Regis Lake in 1906.[37] At Eagle's Beak, Atterbury joined the stark—almost abstract—stucco quality of Bayberry Point with a butterfly plan to produce a bulky fortress-like edifice. The outcome of Atterbury's amalgam of architectural elements, including oversized mannerist dentil-like features and the huge expanse of roof, was ungainly and unresolved. However, its application to the smaller carriage house and squash-court cottage on the 75-acre property was more effective and properly scaled. In 1910, Atterbury also designed a large brick house for Mutual Life Insurance Company President Charles A. Peabody Jr. (1849–1931) and his wife Charlotte on 68 acres nearby. It is possible that the commission came through Peabody's son Julian (1881–1935),

an architect who worked briefly in Atterbury's office. Again Atterbury experimented with variations in plan and materials by combining his signature butterfly plan with brick and half-timbering on the exterior. While the house's footprint was symmetrical, Atterbury's irregular placement of doors, dormers, and timbered service stair tower created a dynamic balance.[38]

While many of Atterbury's North Shore commissions were centered in Cold Spring Harbor, he did venture into some of the other exclusive hamlets sprinkled along the Gold Coast. In 1906, Atterbury designed a large sprawling house for James Byrne (1857–1942) and his wife Helen McGregor Byrne (1869–1945) on a 353-acre property in Locust Valley.[39] A successful corporation lawyer,

TOP *Planting Fields. Kitchen wing and outdoor stair.*
Architectural Catalog (April 1918)

BOTTOM *Planting Fields. Courtyard and garden. The*
Brickbuilder 17 (January 1908): pl. 10

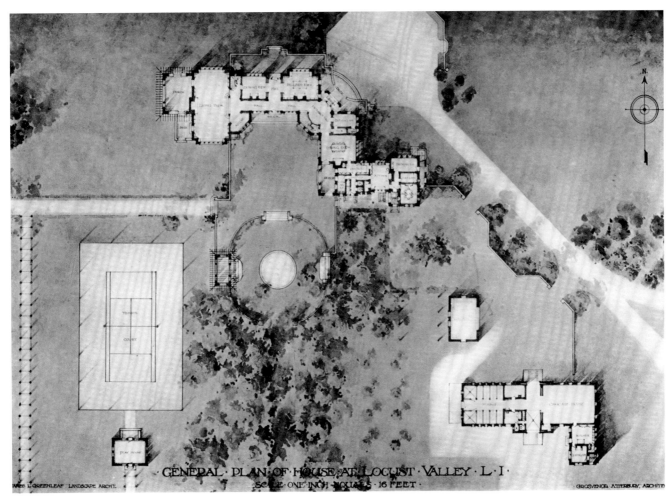

Planting Fields. Plan. The Brickbuilder 17 (January 1908): pl. 14

James later became the first Catholic member of the Harvard Corporation, the university's seven-man governing body, and also helped establish the Rice Institute in Houston, Texas. Mrs. Byrne, an avid collector and traveler, decorated the interiors of the house in a style reflective of the period's prevailing tastes.

Perhaps Atterbury's most picturesque essay in irregular massing, unexpected windows, outdoor stairs, lammie brick, and rough half-timber detail, the Byrne estate, Planting Fields, gave the appearance of growth over a period of time. With low-lying wings extending in a variety of directions, Atterbury's well-guided, ostensibly rambling composition blended well with the property's flat topography and gave limitless possibility for addition. The varied—almost accidental—quality of its architecture prompted architect Aymar Embury II to note that Planting Fields was "so wonderfully charming in every way that no single viewpoint serves to bring out all of its delightful features."[40] A monumental stair-hall tower anchored the plan; due to the thinness of the wings, most

of the rooms received light from several sources. From the front hall, a long chestnut-paneled hall bathed in light culminated in a 50-foot-long living room with a large lammie-brick fireplace set on axis. As Embury pointed out, "The great strength in modern design lies in precisely such adjustment of old motives to suit modern conditions and their combination with new motives."[41] At Planting Fields, Atterbury demonstrated the versatility of his idiom, striking a finite balance between picturesque form and livability. The grounds of Planting Fields, which included a diminutive playhouse, pergola, and carriage house, were enclosed by textured lammie-brick walls and distinguished by the landscape design of James L. Greenleaf (1857–1933).

Around 1900, Atterbury completed Oakdene for Walter George Oakman Sr. (1844–1922), chairman of the Guaranty Trust Company, in nearby Roslyn. Carried out in the Colonial Revival style that the architect had employed for Robert Waller's contemporaneously built house, Vyne Croft, in Southampton, the 70-acre property commanded

Walter George Oakman Sr. house, Oakdene, Roslyn, New York. Courtesy of John F. Santos

Oakdene. Stable. Courtesy of John F. Santos

views of Hempstead Harbor and included a shingled house, distinguished by a two-story Doric portico, gardens, cottages, and a charmingly idiosyncratic towered stable block. Mrs. Oakman (1856–1931), née Eliza Conkling—the daughter of politician Roscoe Conkling—was an enthusiastic collector, and the eclectically decorated interiors reflected her myriad interests, which ranged from Spanish history to religious imagery. The library featured carved columns taken from a Spanish cathedral, while the living room and hall were decorated with relics, architectural fragments, and religious imagery, creating an environment that *Town & Country* described as "ideal . . . in which to study history and art; and [in which] the balance [was] so nicely maintained that comfort [waited] at every turn."[42]

By the early 1900s, Atterbury and his associates were able to expand their practice beyond Long Island to more distant summer resorts and fashionable retreats frequented by New York's elite circles, including Mount Desert Island, Maine, notable for its natural rugged beauty and remote location. In

Bar Harbor and the more tranquil Seal Harbor, two of Mount Desert's important summer villages, Atterbury realized a collection of informal shingled retreats that evoked the atmosphere of an Adirondack lodge. Atterbury's chapel for the Seal Harbor Congregational Church (1901–2) at the intersection of the roads leading to the anchorage and Northeast Harbor, perfectly reflected its Maine environment with a high foundation, entrance, and walls of native gray stone. In 1901, Atterbury submitted a design to the building committee, composed of summer residents Edward Cushman Bodman (1840–1917) and Albert Herter.[43] Completed in August 1902, the charming shingle and stone chapel featured an arched stone entrance and a deeply hooded gable peak, which, according to *The Craftsman*, gave the "vivid impression of the protecting character of the edifice, for both roof and hoods have a hovering look as if gathering the little building under its widespreading wings. . . . The whole effect is that of kindliness and sheltering strength as well as of great solidity and permanence."[44]

Congregational Church   Seal Harbor, Maine

TOP *Congregational Church, Seal Harbor, Maine.*
Courtesy of the Maine Historic Preservation Commission

BOTTOM *Dr. Christian Archibald Herter house, Miradero, Seal Harbor, Maine.* Courtesy of the Maine Historic Preservation Commission

TOP *Edward Cushman Bodman house, Felsmere,
Seal Harbor, Maine.* Courtesy of the Maine Historic
Preservation Commission

BOTTOM *Ernesto and Edith Fabbri house, Buonriposo,
Bar Harbor, Maine.* Courtesy of the Maine Historic
Preservation Commission

Misquamicut Golf Club, Watch Hill, Rhode Island, c. 1916. Watch Hill Then and Now, Watch Hill Preservation Society, Roberta Burkhart, Michael Beddard, and Ardith Schneider

Atterbury's first Maine cottage, Miradero (1901), for Dr. Christian Archibald Herter (1865–1910) and his family, was located on Ox Hill in Seal Harbor. In all likelihood, this commission also came through Albert Herter, the pathologist's brother and the architect's friend. The Herters purchased an inaccessible rocky site and commissioned Beatrix Jones (later Farrand), a niece of Edith Wharton, to lay out a road and situate the house. Jones (1872–1959), who summered nearby at Reef Point in Bar Harbor, bolstered her developing career as one of the era's most prominent landscape designers with commissions from Mount Desert's affluent summer contingent. Atterbury's charming design was built in record time. Foundations were laid in February 1901, and his rectangular block—differentiated by groups of diamond-paned windows, overhangs, eaves, and wood details—was completed in time for the summer season. Inside, the articulation of the structural framework gave the rooms a simple decorative appeal.

Although Jones completed a contour plan for Felsmere, Edward Cushman Bodman and Ida Berdan Bodman's (1855–1937) nearby Ox Hill property, in 1900, Atterbury's cottage, guest cottage, and stable were not ready until the summer of 1902.[45] With its sturdy fieldstone base, the main house rose dramatically from a rocky ledge and possessed dramatic views of the Gulf of Maine in the distance. Atterbury enlivened the long thin mass with two round turrets enclosing various porches and piazzas.

Ernesto and Edith Fabbri's cottage, Buonriposo, on Eden Street two miles from Bar Harbor, was completed in 1904. Ernesto Fabbri (1874–1943), a linguist and world traveler, had inherited substantial wealth from his uncle, a J. P. Morgan partner, and had married Edith Shepard (1872–1954), a great-granddaughter of Commodore

Cornelius Vanderbilt. In massing and plan, the Fabbris' large stucco and shingled house, described as "one of the most beautiful as well as nicely furnished in town," closely resembled Albert and Adele Herter's cottage in East Hampton, which also revolved around a butterfly plan and encompassed a number of porches.[46]

At Watch Hill, Rhode Island, another fashionable seaside resort, Atterbury and his associate John A. Tompkins garnered a number of commissions that sprang up on a thin wedge of land between Little Narragansett Bay and Block Island Sound. The locale drew summer residents primarily from Philadelphia, Pittsburgh, and Cincinnati, as well as points north. The New England coastline, with stretches of light sand beaches and coves, rolling knolls, and wooded upland acreage, created a geographically diverse backdrop for Atterbury's finely attuned regional style. In 1900, he designed a clubhouse for the Misquamicut Golf Club on Ocean View Highway.[47] Founded in 1895, the club owned a nine-hole golf course and an old corn crib-cum-clubhouse. The club's new home, completed in 1901, reflected the architect's characteristic touch. The combination of simple massing with picturesque features—broad jerkin-headed dormers, curved porches, massive hipped roof, and rough fieldstone base—created an appropriately informal clubhouse well suited to the seaside location. In 1916, Atterbury and Tompkins would return to Misquamicut to expand the structure. A new L-shaped wing, stone porch, porte cochere, and two-story shingle and fieldstone octagonal tower considerably enlarged the size of the building and enhanced the exterior as an expression of growth over time. Atterbury's involvement in the clubhouse brought in additional commissions from Watch Hill's summer residency. Sowanniu, a broad rambling cottage with jerkin-headed gables for Alanson Trask Enos

Mrs. William R. Thompson house, Sunset Hill,
Watch Hill, Rhode Island. Watch Hill Then and
Now, Watch Hill Preservation Society, Roberta Burkhart,
Michael Beddard, and Ardith Schneider

(1856–1931) and his wife Jennie Taylor Enos (d. 1946), and The Folly, for Mrs. George Hoadley and her friend Mrs. Scarborough, were completed around the turn of the twentieth century, followed by Chenowith, a charming bungalow for Mrs. G. H. Stanton in 1913. Again the architect demonstrated his prowess at designing picturesque, yet practical, cottages of local materials well rooted in the landscape.[48]

In 1913, Mrs. William R. Thompson (1856–1944) of New York, née Mary Thaw—the daughter of Pennsylvania Railroad magnate William Thaw—commissioned Sunset Hill, Atterbury's most interesting project in Watch Hill. Perched on the crest of a rocky windswept hillside, the house possessed magnificent views of the Long Island Sound from every direction. As at the Woodin house, Atterbury integrated two squat octagonal towers into his butterfly plan to take advantage of the site's dramatic vistas and shelter the garden from salty breezes. Particularly interesting was the architect's unusual entrance sequence that incorporated a cloister-like barrel-vaulted arcade carried out in Portland cement. Hugging the inner curve of the house, the arcade overlooked a lush walled garden with shuttered arched openings detailed with quaint cutout silhouettes. An octagonal gazebo and lovely terraced lawns executed by the New York firm of florists and garden designers Wadley & Smythe stepped down the sloping site. In his scheme, Atterbury paid careful attention to

color and detail; his gray-green shingled roof, soft gray native stone facades, burned cypress woodwork, concrete sills, and copings brushed with aggregate and peacock-blue trim blended well with the seaside environment. Leader heads were wrought with figures of crabs and seahorses. The interiors of the house appropriately reflected the relaxed quality of the summer colony: a double stair opened into the large central living room; all trim and woodwork were kept simple; and the octagonal sun parlor featured exposed stonework.[49]

Associate Stowe Phelps's friendship with Arthur Curtiss James (1867–1941) brought about one of Atterbury's most unique and spectacular projects: Surprise Valley Farm in Newport.[50] Considered "one of the fifty-nine men who ruled America," James was also one of the country's wealthiest citizens. In addition to inheriting the Phelps, Dodge & Company mining empire from his father, he controlled the largest amount of railroad shares held by any individual owner. His vast 125-acre property Beacon Hill—which included a Georgian "cottage" (1910) designed by John Mead Howells (1868–1959) and I. N. Phelps Stokes, Vedimar (1910), a Spanish style stucco guest house, and Zee Rust, an artist's studio, both designed by Atterbury and Phelps—was among Newport's most significant. While described as understated and unobtrusive, James, a commodore of the New York Yacht Club, and his wife Harriet Parsons James (1867–1941) lived large. James also owned a massive 100-foot-wide townhouse at 39 East 69th Street and a magnificent 218-foot full-rigged bark in which he sailed the world.[51]

In 1914, when James decided to move his father's prized herd of Guernsey cattle from New Jersey to Newport, he commissioned Atterbury to design a farm to house them. Atterbury ingeniously fused the architecture with the landscape to produce, as one critic described them, the "most unusual group of farm buildings in America."[52] As part of the project's first step, Atterbury blasted out the site's rocky outcroppings to create an open bowl-shaped basin—or "Surprise Valley"—for the buildings, using the property's warm gray and buff colored granite to clad his charmingly diminutive and picturesque farm structures. For inspiration, Atterbury looked to the Italian region of Switzerland—an area whose architecture James admired; Atterbury's miniature village could perhaps have appeared more convincing high in the Italian Alps than at the exclusive summer resort one mile from the ocean. However, through careful site planning, the self-contained group hugged the

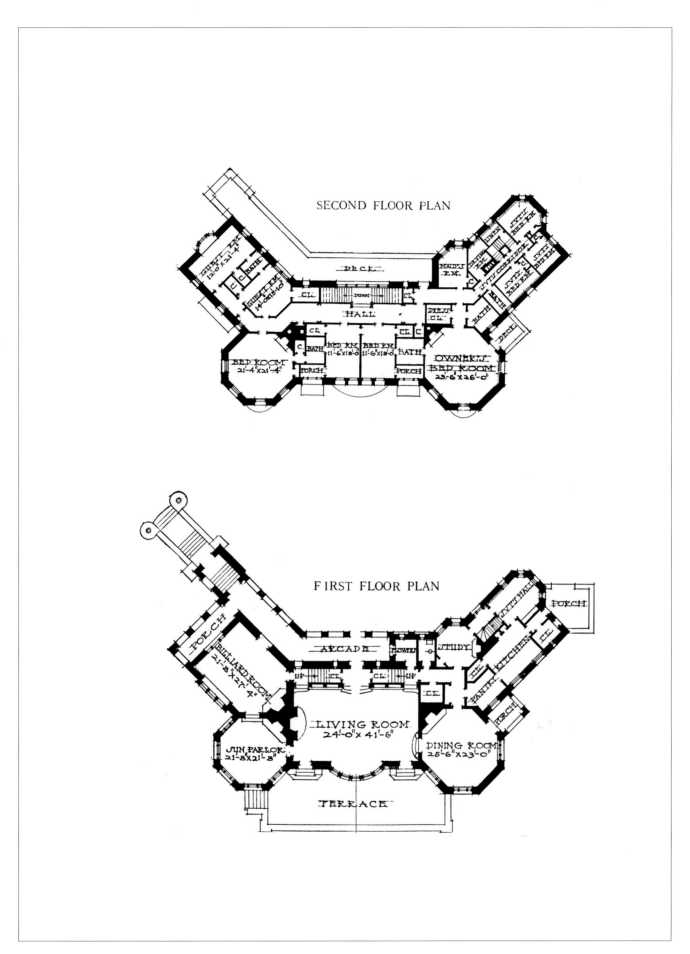

SECOND FLOOR PLAN

FIRST FLOOR PLAN

Sunset Hill. First- and second-floor plans.
The House Beautiful 46 (August 1919): 70

*Sunset Hill. View
of enclosed garden.*
The House Beautiful 46
(August 1919): 69

sloping contours of the site to create an extraordinary sense of place.

The architect's multitiered scheme incorporated curving roads and walls that echoed the sweeping arc carved out of the ledges. His arching windows and openings, which juxtaposed the buildings' vertical lines, produced a picturesque balance. As the pivot of the design, Atterbury's great arch marked the entrance into the center of the group formed by the dairy, maternity building, bull pen, farmers' cottages, and subterranean icehouse built into the hill. At the same time, the arch supported a bridge connecting the cow barn to the delightfully rustic carpenter's shop with a turret modeled after a fourteenth-century watchtower. A series of smaller arches supported a curved ramp that funneled down into the center green;

the low-slung piggery, poultry house, and slaughterhouse were located to the west. For the interiors, Atterbury continued in the Italian vein, combining open fireplaces and murals with advanced farm technology.

As always, Atterbury relied on texture and color to articulate his design. He meticulously oversaw the stonework, making sure the ashlar was laid properly with wide flush joints to achieve the effect he sought. The granite facades, paired with luminous pink and yellowish brick detail, weathered timber, and vibrant claret, purple, and green clay Ludovici roof tile, produced an appearance of rugged agelessness. However, Atterbury's diminutive scale and the brightly colored bas relief by Boston artist Joseph Lindon Smith (1863–1950) comically conveying the purpose of each building lightened the spirit of

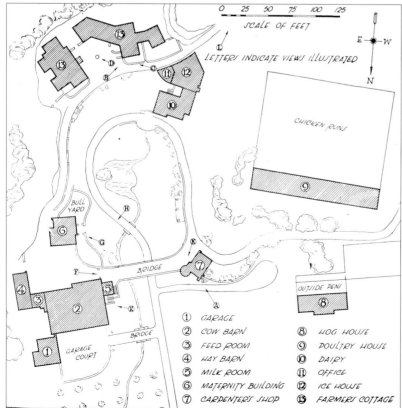

ABOVE *Arthur Curtiss James estate, Surprise Valley Farm, Newport, Rhode Island. View to south.* Frances Benjamin Johnston. Courtesy of the SVF Foundation

LEFT *Surprise Valley Farm. Site plan.* Architectural Forum 34 (February 1921): 57

OPPOSITE

TOP *Surprise Valley Farm. Cow barn and maternity building.* Frances Benjamin Johnston. Courtesy of the SVF Foundation

BOTTOM *Surprise Valley Farm. Cottages and milk toast.* Frances Benjamin Johnston. Courtesy of the SVF Foundation

LEFT *Surprise Valley Farm. Carpenter's shop.* Frances Benjamin Johnston. Courtesy of the SVF Foundation

BELOW *Surprise Valley Farm. Slaughterhouse, 2007.* Jonathan Wallen

OPPOSITE
TOP *Surprise Valley Farm. Entrance gate, 2007.* Jonathan Wallen

BOTTOM *Surprise Valley Farm. Piggery, 2007.* Jonathan Wallen.

the place. Critic Augusta Owen Patterson observed that "if [Surprise Valley Farm] were built for the owner to live in, rather than as an expression of a play mood, it would be judged by very different and much harsher standards. . . . It has a certain element of undeniable theatrical effectiveness which is as exhilarating as any masquerade."[53]

Atterbury also realized a number of large residential commissions in New York's suburban communities. For former New York mayor Seth Low (1850–1916) and his wife Annie Curtis Low (1847–1929), the architect designed a stone and shingle house and dairy farm group on their 200-acre Bedford Hills property, Broad Brook Farm, in 1904.[54] During his long and productive career, Low had figured largely in the city's civic life. Starting out, he had headed his father's business, A. A. Low and Brothers, a firm owning China clipper ships trading in tea, silks, and porcelain. From 1882 to 1885, Low served as the Republican mayor of Brooklyn, his birthplace, and later, from 1890 to 1901, as president of Columbia University. During his tenure at Columbia, he oversaw the development of the institution's Morningside Heights campus and financed the great library that formed the heart of McKim, Mead & White's master plan for the university. In 1901, Low was elected mayor of New York, a

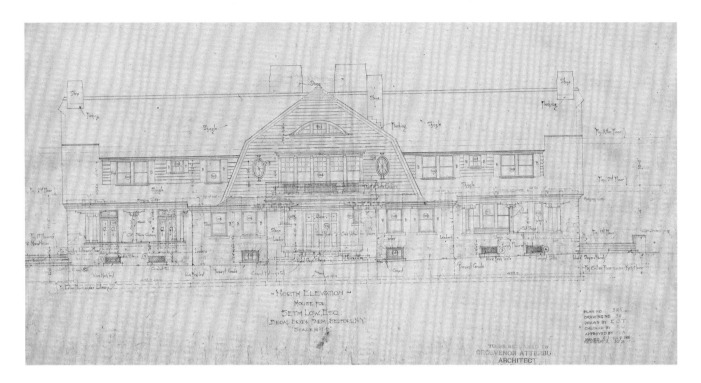

ABOVE *Seth Low house, Broad Brook Farm, Bedford Hills, New York. North elevation.* Collection of The New-York Historical Society

LEFT *Broad Brook Farm. North facade.* Bedford Historical Society, Bedford, New York

position he held until 1903. As an activist, Low identified with affairs and issues with which other civic-minded reformers, particular Robert de Forest, strongly associated. Likely it was the de Forest connection that brought Atterbury the Low commission.

At Broad Brook Farm, Atterbury collaborated with Frederick Law Olmsted Jr., who laid out the gardens, and Downing Vaux (1856–1926), the son of Calvert Vaux (1824–1895), who created an extensive planting plan of chestnut groves, peach and apple orchards, and raspberry fields. With his design of the Lows' house, Atterbury displayed the sculptural potential of a shingled frame structure. The graceful swoop of its large projecting central

gambrel embraced the form of the building down to the gently curved lip where the rounded fieldstone base anchored it to the land. The taut skin of the shingled surfaces hovered over the rough stone, which created an abundance of shadows at the porches, loggia, and porte cochere, while the almost whimsical arrangement of windows—a broad expanse at the center flanked by ovals and topped by an eyebrow—marked the entrance. In Atterbury's hands, the various details pulled at the facades, giving rise to a playful anthropomorphic composition. Atterbury's charming dairy farm group transformed the same elements—gambrels, shingles, jerkin-headed gable ends, and rough fieldstone—into a rustic relative of the house. The angled forms of the wagon sheds, hay lofts, carriage rooms, cow stalls, and dairies, arranged around a center court, stood as a counterpoint to the pure cylinders of the silos. By expressing the group's primary facade with a thicker, taller, and denser wall, Atterbury successfully gave the illusion of age and accretion, as if his building incorporated an earlier structure.

In 1907, Atterbury also completed Savin Hill in Lewis- boro, New York, for Rev. Dr. William Stephen Rainsford (1850–1933) and his wife E. Alma Green Rainsford (1855–1923).[55] The 570-acre property, which stretched into Ridgefield, Connecticut, was a gift from J. P. Morgan, an elder of St. George's Episcopal Church on Stuyvesant Square, over which the tall outspoken Dublin-born Rainsford had presided as rector for twenty years.[56] With help from his wealthy parishioners—Seth Low, Robert Fulton

LEFT *Broad Brook Farm. Dairy farm group.* Bedford Historical Society, Bedford, New York

BELOW *Broad Brook Farm. North and south elevations of the farm group.* Collection of The New-York Historical Society

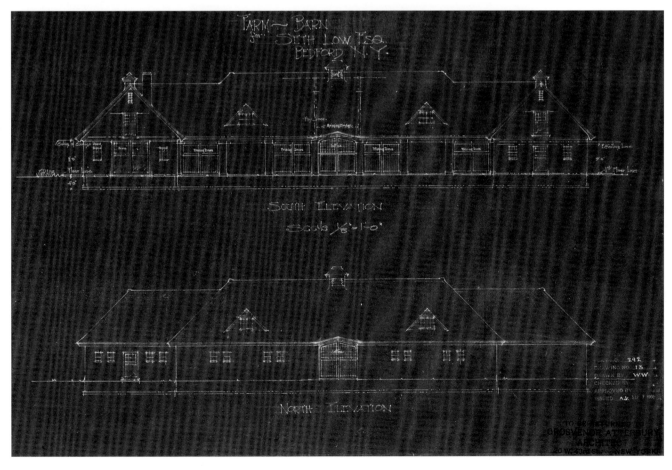

Rev. Dr. William Stephen Rainsford house, Savin Hill, Lewisboro, New York, and Ridgefield, Connecticut. Living-room terrace. Architectural Catalog (April 1918)

Cutting, and Frederick Betts among them, Rainsford had turned St. George's into the city's first great institutional church by establishing schools, clubs, and camps under its auspices. Although Atterbury was concurrently working on the Low farm, the architect likely knew the rector, a founding member of the Shinnecock Hills Golf Club, from Southampton. After his retirement in 1906, Rainsford moved permanently to Savin Hill. As noted by *Architectural Review*, Atterbury's design was a particularly successful "example of the logical development of a design from the conditions" of the site. The architect's nimble composition of robust local fieldstone, lammie, and half-timbering created the impression that the large blocky building was born out of the high ridge on which it was located. The relationship Atterbury forged between the house and the topography of the site was deepened by a series of alluring terraced gardens carved into the hill-

side with southwesterly views of the Hudson River Valley. His rustically elegant wood-paneled interiors created a warm and appropriate environment in which Rainsford, a big-game hunter, could display his trophies, skins, and arms collected during years of exotic travel. Under Atterbury's direction, the hand-hewn woodwork in the main hall, which extended from the deeply recessed front vestibule to the garden terrace to the west, was textured with a pattern of marks from a broad axe, which added decorative appeal.

In the Somerset Hills of New Jersey, Atterbury rearranged architectural elements, materials, and plans to create several visually dynamic designs. Investment banker George Dillwyn Cross (1869–1936) and his wife Leonie de Bary Cross (1873–1928) commissioned Baricross, a fieldstone manor on Bernardsville Mountain, for which Atterbury employed his signature butterfly plan, in 1905.

ABOVE *George Dillwyn Cross house,*
Baricross, Bernardsville, New Jersey.
Courtesy of John Dessarzin

RIGHT *George Rudolf Mosle house,*
Hillandale, Peapack, New Jersey.
Courtesy of W. Barry Thomson

While Atterbury frequently incorporated fieldstone into his facades, the Crosses' home was one of the architect's few commissions carried out completely in rough stone. At Hillandale (1906), George Rudolf Mosle (1865–1941) and Katherine Kunhardt Mosle's estate in Peapack, New Jersey, the architect designed a large lammie-brick house, articulating the lintels, arched openings, sills, and quoins with robust pieces of multihued fieldstone.[57] Atterbury's associate, W. Leslie Walker, who lived in suburban New Jersey, pulled in a number of commissions in Montclair.[58] In addition to the elegant stucco and shingle Unity Chapel (1905), Atterbury and Walker designed several half-timbered dwellings in the area as well as Edgewood Terrace, a large brick Colonial Revival house on Upper Mountain Road for Edwin A. Bradley (1839–1925), owner of a large building material manufacturing company, and Marianna Gulick Bradley (1846–1919).[59]

Throughout his career, Atterbury maintained a strong relationship with Yale, nurturing his college ties and Scroll and Key associations with an almost religious ardor. Not surprisingly, the architect was frequently called back to New Haven to provide professional service, not only for the university but also for private clients. On Prospect

TOP *Edwin A. Bradley house, Edgewood Terrace, Montclair, New Jersey. The Brickbuilder* 18 (August 1909): pl. 104

BOTTOM *New Haven Country Club, Hamden, Connecticut. Entrance façade. American Architect* 94 (September 2, 1908)

Hill, he completed several smaller Tudor- and Colonial-style houses in the elegant residential neighborhood populated by New Haven's most prominent residents.[60] Three miles north of the city in Hamden, Atterbury designed the New Haven Country Club, a picturesque clubhouse with a red tile roof completed in 1908. The club, founded in 1898 by Yale professor Theodore S. Woolsey (1852–1929), quickly became a mainstay of New Haven society with a strong Yale presence among its membership. On a strip of farmland near Lake Whitney, Atterbury transformed the club's preexisting building into a dynamic composition of shifting roof planes, irregular volumes, rough stone, and half-timbering.[61]

CITY HOUSES

As he was busily building his country-house practice, Atterbury enjoyed a series of commissions in Manhattan for townhouses, many of which were concentrated within the fashionable Upper East Side residential district. Architectural taste was constantly in a state of flux, and by the turn of the twentieth century, trendsetting society had started to gravitate away from the elaborate archaeology exemplified by Richard Morris Hunt and C. P. H. Gilbert (1860–1952), preferring freer interpretations of Italian Renaissance and so-called Modern French styles and especially the restrained Georgian idiom, mastered by the erudite hand of Delano & Aldrich. Shedding the influences of geography, Atterbury's work in New York seemed to reflect C. Matlack Price's observation that "the city house [was] far less affected by local conditions, being usually at its best when it most closely follows convention."[62] In the fifteen years leading up to World War One, architects like Atterbury were kept busy transforming the midblock stretches of nondescript brownstones between Fifth and Lexington Avenues into sections of restrained brick townhouses with minimal decoration.[63] In 1901 and 1902 alone, more than 200 dwellings were constructed—or more typically reconstructed—on the Upper East Side, from the 50s to the 90s.[64] Despite the general taste for conventional Georgian, Atterbury was able to give his houses some individuality, incorporating artistic detail such as wrought ironwork and leaded glass. With commissions for alterations and additions to houses originally designed in the 1880s, Atterbury expanded his client base to include Gertrude Vanderbilt Whitney and railroad magnate Edward Harriman (1848–1909).[65]

Frederick H. Betts house, 22 East 65th Street, New York, New York, c. 1940. Municipal Archives, Department of Records and Information Services, City of New York

In 1897, Frederick Henry Betts and his wife Mary Holbrook Betts (b. 1847) commissioned Atterbury to design a five-story house at 22 East 65th Street on the southwest corner of Madison Avenue. Atterbury's father and Betts had been classmates at Yale—as had Atterbury and Betts's son—and law partners, as well as pioneering members of both the Southampton summer colony and the Adirondack Club.[66] Atterbury executed a Georgian-inspired brick mansion, which included an entire floor dedicated to Betts's daughter's family, with restrained facades accented by robustly articulated stone lintels, band courses, and quoins. The architect's interest in color permeated the design; to express the exterior of the house Atterbury chose a light pink, almost mauve, brick.[67]

Atterbury also designed large limestone houses for Mrs. George Trowbridge at 25 West 54th Street in 1900; philanthropist and steel magnate Henry Phipps at 6 East 87th Street in 1902 (see pages 119–20); and Atterbury's

ABOVE *Mrs. George Trowbridge house, 25 West 54th Street, New York, New York (far right).* Milstein Division of United States History, Local History & Genealogy, The New York Public Library, Astor, Lenox and Tilden Foundations

RIGHT *John Sanford Barnes Jr. house, 10 East 79th Street, New York, New York.* Museum of the City of New York, Byron Collection, #93.1.1.4383

Yale classmate, paper broker John Sanford Barnes Jr. (1870–1942), at 10 East 79th Street in 1901. Compared to the flat restraint of the Phipps design, Atterbury's schemes for the Trowbridges and the Barneses acquired a sculptural—almost malleable—quality, reflecting modern French taste. Both houses featured robust rustication combined with smooth expanses of stone, rounded bays, and a variety of segmental-arched and rectangular window openings. The formal facades of the Barnes house belied the intimate and warm interiors, which were detailed with beamed ceilings, butterfly-jointed floors, elaborately carved woodwork, and leaded glass.[68]

However, for the most part, Atterbury opted to work in brick, producing a collection of spare, reserved townhouses with interesting plan features. He used a more finished,

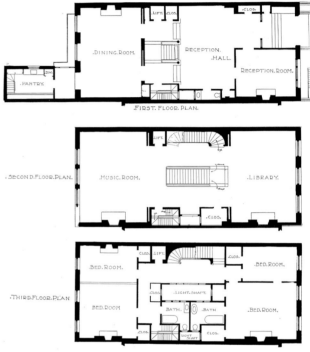

LEFT *Sarah Jewett Robbins house, 33 East 74th Street, New York, New York.* The Brickbuilder 17 (September 1908): 200

ABOVE *Robbins house. First-, second-, and third-floor plans.* The Brickbuilder 17 (September 1908): 200

refined brick rather than the lammie that he preferred for his country houses. In 1901, he designed a 35-foot-wide brick and limestone house at 33 East 74th Street for banker Julian Wainwright Robbins (1857–1934) and his wife Sarah Jewett Robbins, granddaughter of Hugh Judge Jewett, former president of the Erie Railroad.[69] As *Architectural Record* noted, Atterbury treated the facade "as a flat surface with no very telling projections" and incorporated wrought ironwork and leaded glass to create a "very pretty picture."[70] He differentiated the limestone entrance level with

wide segmental-arched openings and demarcated the *piano nobile*—occupied by the music room and library—with three great round-arch windows. The spacing of the windows combined with the expanse of Flemish-bond brick gave the facade a flat appearance, especially in contrast with its brownstone neighbors. The emphasis on light, which infused Atterbury's country-house designs, manifested itself differently within the confines of a city lot. Rather than positioning the main stair off to one side, as was commonly practiced, Atterbury placed it at the center of the plan

.THIRD.FLOOR.

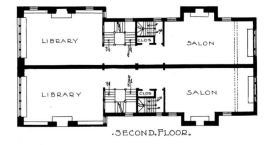

.SECOND.FLOOR.

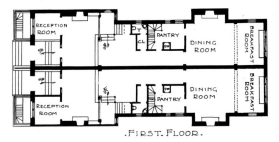

.FIRST.FLOOR.

RIGHT *105–7 East 73rd Street, New York, New York.* Museum of the City of New York, Wurts Collection, #110398

ABOVE *105–7 East 73rd Street. First-, second-, and third-floor plans.* The Brickbuilder 17 (September 1908): 189

bathed by a light well above the main run between the first and second floors.

At 105–7 East 73rd Street (1903), Atterbury experimented with the idea of attached houses. For the pair of speculative dwellings commissioned by the Residence Realty Company, he designed two identical homes with mirrored plans for a fifty-foot-wide lot.[71] With a common tile roof and a cornice of oversized brackets, they read as one structure. Atterbury maximized the amount of light entering the houses by incorporating broad rows of multi-paned double-hung windows and allowing for windows through the depth of the lot. The second and third floor windows read as one unit separated by molded panels. Atterbury's redesign of two existing row houses at 119–21 East 62nd Street for his cousin, Dr. Lewis Atterbury Conner (1867–1950), a leading authority on heart disease, and his wife Emma Harris Conner (d. 1921), was more restrained.[72] In 1910, he combined two narrow Greek Revival dwellings into an austere Federal-style American basement house with brick laid in Flemish bond.

Dr. Lewis Atterbury Conner house, 119–21 East 62nd Street, New York, New York. Milstein Division of United States History, Local History & Genealogy, The New York Public Library, Astor, Lenox and Tilden Foundations

Atterbury's brick Georgian townhouse for Edwin Cornell Jameson (1864–1945) and Mary Gardner Jameson (d. 1974) at 9 East 69th Street was more ambitious.[73] One of the country's leading insurance men, Jameson commissioned his six-story 28-foot-wide dwelling in 1915. Atterbury's dignified scheme featured a marble base, Ionic columns marking the front entry, and band courses, keystones, and balconies on the upper floors. Inside, Atterbury included a charming elliptical dining room with murals inset over the doors and a living room with three huge arching French doors overlooking 69th Street. An ample rectangular stair, which rose from the first-floor reception space up to the sixth story, conveyed the sheer size of the house. On the *piano nobile*, it opened directly into a parlor—or music room—with a leaded-glass lay light. Perhaps one of the most interesting aspects of the house was Atterbury's way of drawing light and air into the upper floors. As he had at the Robbinses' house, he

Edwin Cornell Jameson house, 9 East 69th Street, New York, New York. Museum of the City of New York, Wurts Collection, #117536

extended a light shaft through the core of the building above the second-story lay light. With the ability to put windows on all four sides of the well, Atterbury placed windows in unexpected places.

The 1871 brownstone Atterbury redesigned for his parents in 1909 at 131 East 70th Street on the northwest corner of Lexington Avenue was one of the architect's most interesting city schemes.[74] During the 1900s and 1910s, as the streets leading off Park Avenue became

increasingly desirable, the rows of high-stooped brownstone houses were transformed into historically inspired American basement houses by a host of Beaux-Arts–trained practitioners. These extensive renovations involved removing stoops, relocating front doors to street level, and pushing front facades forward to the lot line. Instead of altering the house past recognition, as was common, Atterbury emphasized the renovation's cumulative quality. On Lexington Avenue, he retained elements

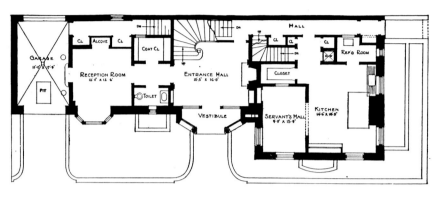

ABOVE *Charles Larned Atterbury house,*
131 East 70th Street, New York, New York.
The House Beautiful 39 (May 1916): 169

RIGHT *Atterbury house. First- and second-*
floor plans. Samuel H. Gottscho.
The Architect 6 (September 1929)

BELOW *Atterbury house. Living room.*
Samuel H. Gottscho. The Architect 6
(September 1929): pl. 131

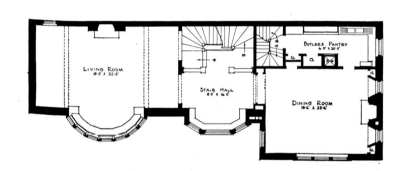

of the Italianate brownstone but reoriented its main entrance to the longer eighty-foot facade on 70th Street. He then enhanced what had originally been an unadorned side facade with irregularly placed bays, casements, and a two-story elliptical oriel window—an effect that gave the impression of accumulation over time. His garage, which was conveniently connected to the house through an intimate reception room with leaded-glass windows and gold-toned walls, was an unusual feature for the period.[75] In 1911, Atterbury moved into the house with his parents; he eventually inherited it after the death of his father in 1914 and his mother in 1923.

The elegant English interiors that showcased Atterbury's well-honed taste and artistic creativity were by no means narrowly focused in their inspiration. From the warm oak-paneled entrance hall, a curved stair spiraled up to the *piano nobile* and the bedrooms and library on the third floor. According to Janet Howison Marsh, writing for *Arts and Decoration*, its balustrade, pierced with Gothic-inspired cusps, was "sufficiently spectacular" and defined the "character of the entire interior treatment."[76] Within the second-floor living space, Atterbury's taste for dark paneling, beamed ceilings, and leaded glass abounded. Broad elliptical arches divided the space into a stair hall, an oak-paneled Gothic living room to the west, and a dining room overlooking Lexington Avenue. However, while Atterbury used dark colors and materials, the rooms were not gloomy; as *The House Beautiful* noted in 1916, "gloominess would be the last word to apply to Mr. Atterbury's house. Mr. Atterbury has progressed beyond the state of mind of a puristic practitioner. . . . Happy is the man who has reached the point when he dare do anything whether by rule or against it."[77] In the living room, light spilled through a seven-sided leaded oriel window that had once belonged to Louis Comfort Tiffany.[78] The bronze-faced fireplace, treated with a Gothic design of English ivy and Scotch berries, was set off by dark wood elements: the Stuart paneling, the carved linen-fold panels at the cornice line, the thistle and rose details, and the structural ceiling beams highlighted with brown, gold, and red. In the paneled dining room, Atterbury added color with a broad frieze of blue-green Spanish leather above the spring line of the arched entry. Atterbury's collection of English, Italian, and French Provincial furnishings, paintings, and bas reliefs enhanced the artistic quality of the interior spaces.

In 1913, Atterbury began planning a large Italian Renaissance–style house at 7 East 95th Street for Ernesto

Atterbury house. Stair. *The House Beautiful* 39 (May 1916): 170

and Edith Shepard Fabbri.[79] In 1896, as a wedding gift, Edith's mother commissioned her nephew—and Edith's cousin—Augustus Shepard and his partner Abner Haydel to design an exuberant modern French mansion for the couple at 11 East 62nd Street. In 1903, the Fabbris decided to build another house in Bar Harbor, Maine, and asked Atterbury to draw up plans for their summer retreat Buonriposo; Atterbury's scheme was completed in 1904 (see pages 90–91).

By 1913, after living and traveling extensively abroad, the Fabbris' preferences had swung from the elaborate French styles predominating popular taste at the turn of the twentieth century to the more refined, almost monastic, flavor of Italian Renaissance architecture. Atterbury's initial plan for their new house included brick Gothic facades, a loggia at the fifth floor, and a Venetian room with a fountain. As plans progressed, the Fabbris struck an agreement with their westerly neighbors, the Goodhue

Ernesto and Edith Fabbri house, 7 East 95th Street,
New York, New York, 2007. Jonathan Wallen

TOP *Fabbri house. Library. Architecture and Building* 49 (April 1917): pl. 17

BOTTOM *Fabbri house. Drawing room. Architecture and Building* 49 (April 1917): pl. 18

Livingstons, to leave a front portion of each of their lots open to maximize air and light. While the Livingstons' plans never went forward, the L-shaped footprint of the Fabbris' 34-room house—62 feet at its widest point—reflected that arrangement.[80]

After hearing of her brother-in-law's success as a designer, Edith asked Ernesto's older brother Egisto (1866–1933), an amateur artist and architect living abroad, to become involved in her house project. The Fabbris had accumulated an impressive array of Italian Renaissance and Baroque furniture and architectural fragments that Edith wished to incorporate into the interiors. Egisto, as he described, executed "drawings for the library, dining room, halls and stairs. Edith wanted them to be simple and architectural, otherwise I couldn't have done them. I haven't the least experience as a decorator." He also "could not help being more interested in the facade and having an idea, [he] made a drawing which so pleased [Edith] that she declared she would have carried it out or not build the house."[81] While Atterbury was the

Fabbri house. View from library into second-floor hall, 2007. Jonathan Wallen

Fabbris' architect of record, the extent to which his design was carried out is unclear. Nonetheless, his cooperation with Egisto Fabbri resulted in strikingly taut soft redbrick facades punctuated by limestone-framed window and band courses. As he had at his own home, Atterbury made accommodations for the automobile. Among the front courtyard plantings, he located a turntable for parked vehicles. Nailcrete—the nailable concrete Atterbury had developed at Forest Hills Gardens—was utilized in the construction of the building's floors.[82]

Due to its spare design, a quiet serenity permeated the interiors decorated by Righter & Kolb. One critic noted that as he passed "from one room to another in this well equipped house, [he was] met with architecture of delightful proportions and simplicity of line, as well as decoration of exceptional merit."[83] The entrance hall, monumental stair, and second-floor gallery, inspired by Filippo Brunelleschi's old sacristy at San Lorenzo, featured a series of arches highlighted with dark trim cleverly molded out of concrete—another Atterbury touch. The sunlight that streamed through the large French windows along the western wall overlooking the courtyard enlivened the spare white walls and red tile floors of the various spaces. On the entrance floor, the Italian motif continued in the white vaulted dining room to the rear of the house and in the reception room with an antique ceiling from Edith's collection.

However, it was the expansive library on the *piano nobile* from which the entire scheme for the house sprung. Stretching almost the full width of the house, the library was constructed from wood paneling (c. 1400s) removed from the ducal palace in Urbino, Italy, and shipped to this country during World War One. In the soaring 25-foot-high vaulted space, the paneling—replete with a secret passageway, balustraded upper gallery, and bookshelves—was masterfully reconstructed. While a monumental mantel, also from the palace, carved with male figures adorned the western end of the room, the decorative quality of the room emerged mainly from the thousands of multicolored book spines and vibrant coat of arms—attributed to Raphael—juxtaposed against the dark woodwork and white walls. A coffered ceiling and a mantel from Edith's collection added heightened interest to the drawing room on 95th Street. The house, completed in 1917, was Atterbury's last major residential commission on the Upper East Side. As it was the eve of the United States's involvement in World War One, the Fabbris opted for a subdued two-night musical affair in the library to open their new home to friends.

Henry Phipps house, 6 East 87th Street, New York, New York. Wurts. *Architecture* 9 (January 1904): pl. 4

PHIPPS COMMISSIONS

In 1902, Atterbury had the good fortune to take on Henry Phipps as a client. For the steel magnate, the architect designed a house off of Fifth Avenue, a collection of speculative office buildings, model tenements, a psychiatric clinic, and a tuberculosis treatment center. Phipps's goals as a philanthropist aligned with Atterbury's developing architectural interests. Under Phipps's tutelage, Atterbury began to broaden his field of expertise beyond the residential commissions for society's upper crust that formed the core of his early practice with the opportunity to apply the lessons of the Beaux-Arts to more socially relevant assignments.

The son of an English bootmaker, Henry Phipps (1839–1930) was born in Philadelphia and raised in

Allegheny City (now part of Pittsburgh) where he played a substantial and profitable role in establishing the Carnegie Steel Company with his lifelong friend and neighbor, Andrew Carnegie. While less visible than his strong-willed partner, the quiet and retiring Phipps's sharp business skills and ability to control costs were integral to the company's extraordinary success as a low-cost steel manufacturer. Auspiciously established in the 1860s when a preindustrialized United States teetered on the brink of change, their venture responded to and abetted the country's rapid expansion and transformation. After Phipps retired as president of the corporation in 1888, he focused his energies and wealth on charitable causes, funding several conservatories, parks, reading rooms, playgrounds, and baths in his native city. In 1901, when Phipps sold his interests in Carnegie Steel to J. P. Morgan to form U.S. Steel, he became one of the country's richest men, enabling him to expand the scope of his philanthropy. Phipps was attracted to the field of public health—in particular to the fight against tuberculosis and mental disorder. The distinguished dean of Johns Hopkins medical faculty, Dr. William Welch (1850–1934), described Phipps as a "man whose heart [was] overflowing with kindness and with a desire to benefit his fellowmen" and stated that he had "never known one more imbued with this spirit of humanity and more eager to find ways of relieving human suffering."[84]

While Carnegie had moved to New York by 1870, Phipps only decided to put down roots in Manhattan in 1901 after traveling extensively abroad with his family. At that time, he commissioned Atterbury to design a five-story, 38-foot-wide townhouse at 6 East 87th Street, four blocks south of his erstwhile partner's Fifth Avenue home at 2 East 91st Street. Instead of working in the more austere Georgian mode that had defined most of his city projects to date, the architect produced a grander Italian Renaissance–inspired edifice with a rooftop pergola and a thirteen-foot-wide side garden. Completed in 1904, Atterbury's palazzo featured smooth limestone facades with carved detail isolated to the entrance level, *piano nobile*, and cornice. As noted by *The New York Architect*, its principal interest lay "in the quiet and orderly arrangement of its facade, its reasonableness of scale, and its careful selection and placing of its ornament."[85] Wrought-iron entrance doors, grilles, fanlight, and fence railings as well as bifurcated windows embellished with tracery at the attic story added an artistic note to the otherwise subdued and well-proportioned design. Although Phipps resided at

6 East 87th Street only briefly, the eclectically detailed Italian and Georgian interiors included all of the requisite rooms required of a captain of industry, including a basement bowling alley outfitted with paneled lockers.[86]

Also in 1901, Atterbury executed drawings for an even larger home for Phipps and his wife Anne Childs Shaffer Phipps (1870–1934) intended for a site across the street stretching from 87th to 88th Street along Fifth Avenue. Displayed at the Architectural League of New York's annual exhibition in 1902, the plans revealed a great four-story Italian Renaissance mansion nestled among gardens and trees. Atterbury's scheme, however, never came to fruition; rather, the commission was given to the firm of S. Breck Parkman Trowbridge (1862–1925) and Goodhue Livingston (1867–1951) who, working in collaboration with London architect George A. Crawley (1864–1926), produced an imposing white marble mansion, replete with a porte cochere, terrace, and orangerie.[87] It appears that Phipps intended 6 East 87th Street to be his intermediary home; after he relocated to the newer, more luxurious residence in 1905, Phipps's eldest son, John (Jay) Shaffer Phipps (1874–1958), and subsequently his daughter, Mrs. Bradley Martin Jr., occupied the Atterbury-designed house. Sportsman-financier Jay Phipps and wife Margarita Grace Phipps (1876–1957) later consulted with Atterbury in 1904 on his country estate, Westbury House, in Old Westbury, Long Island. While Phipps had commissioned George Crawley to design the house, Crawley lacked the practical knowledge and experience to carry out the scheme. Acting as architect of record, Atterbury provided detailed plans and specifications; however, this arrangement was fraught with dissonance because the opinionated architect continually changed Crawley's drawings without approval to reflect his own ideas.[88] A tenuous agreement was struck after Phipps intervened to put Atterbury in charge of all technical issues and Crawley the aesthetics.

Over the course of the ensuing years, Atterbury went on to design a number of speculative office buildings and lofts for the Phipps family in Pittsburgh and New York City. By 1904, Henry Phipps had consolidated his considerable Pittsburgh real estate holdings into the Phipps Pennsylvania Land Trust as a gift to his three sons. Between the years 1904 and 1908, the trust commissioned Atterbury to design four buildings along the Allegheny River waterfront adjacent to the city's Sixth Street Bridge. The thirteen-story Italian Renaissance–inspired Bessemer Building (1904–5) was

Proposal for the Henry Phipps house, Fifth Avenue, New York. Yearbook of the Architectural League of New York 17 (1902); Avery Architectural and Fine Arts Library, Columbia University in the City of New York

the first completed. As Atterbury's first attempt at tall office design, it departed from the typical base-shaft-capital composition followed by most architects by articulating the building's riverfront facade as three bold vertical sections, distinguished by quoins and capped by bracketed wide-eaved pavilions and red tile.[89] Despite the architect's effort to "open up a vista of [design] possibilities," *The New York Architect* was vaguely critical of the outcome, writing, "The top of the Bessemer Building [was] an effort toward a new order of things as a crowning feature of a high building . . . it may point the way to a reasonable solution, and again it may not."[90] In tribute to Sir Henry Bessemer, inventor of

the revolutionary steel-making process so integral to Carnegie Steel's success, Atterbury incorporated details of steel strapwork on the facades and riveted brackets inside the lobby and elevator hall.

The Bessemer Building formed an impressive pair with the adjacent Fulton Building to the east finished the next year.[91] While Atterbury treated the Fulton Building's massing and cornice line similarly, he articulated its courtyard, punched into the central section of the facade, with a colossal seven-story arch. The giant steel form, which supported the top two floors of the building, gave the somewhat bland brick facades a certain structural

ABOVE *Fulton, Bessemer, and Manufacturer's Buildings, Pittsburgh, Pennsylvania. View from Federal Street Bridge looking east.* Pittsburgh History & Landmarks Foundation

LEFT *Bessemer Building, 100 Sixth Street, Pittsburgh, Pennsylvania.* Carnegie Library of Pittsburgh

OPPOSITE *Fulton Building, 107 Sixth Street, Pittsburgh, Pennsylvania.* Carnegie Library of Pittsburgh

integrity and opened up what otherwise would have been interior rooms to the river. An ornate three-story white-marble lobby modeled after the open-aired courtyards of Italian Renaissance palazzos occupied the building's granite base. Featuring a monumental double stair, upper-tier colonnade with paired columns, and massive copper skylight, the imposing space was perhaps Atterbury's most elaborate and seemingly uncharacteristic interior. In comparison to the Fulton and Bessemer pair, Atterbury's treatment of the Manufacturer's Building (or Phipps Building) in Pittsburgh (1906–7) and the U.S. Cigar Building at 44 East 18th Street (1906–7) in New York was more conventional. For each, the architect attempted to distinguish the top of the structure with

U.S. Cigar Building, 47 West 17th Street and 44 East 18th Street, New York, New York. Museum of the City of New York, Wurts Collection, #120710

arching rooflines embellished with brickwork patterns, arched windows, and bull's-eyes.[92]

The design of Phipps's four-story natatorium (1907–8), located to the rear of the Manufacturer's Building, was more remarkable.[93] Also intended as a commercial venture, the city's first great bathhouse and swimming pool encompassed a magnificent barrel-vaulted space with arched skylights, orb-shaped pendant lights, and upper-level gallery. As *The New York Architect* aptly noted, it was "an interesting example of vaulted tile construction in which the color of materials employed evidently [played] an important part."[94] In its design, Atterbury's growing intrigue with color and texture vividly emerged. By combining smooth terra-cotta ribbing, marble walls, brick banding, and glazed green Guastavino tile, he gave rise to a grand, architecturally rich space.

As the flip side to his speculative ventures, Phipps gravitated toward more socially relevant projects, retaining Atterbury as his architect, beginning with the first Phipps model tenement in New York at 321–37 East 31st Street in 1905.[95] Inspired by Lawrence Flick (1856–1938), a Philadelphia-based doctor dedicated to finding a cure for tuberculosis, Phipps had established the Institute of Study, Treatment and Prevention of Tuberculosis in his birth city of Philadelphia in 1903 and later founded the Phipps Tuberculosis Dispensary at Baltimore's Johns Hopkins Hospital in 1905. Considered the plague of the late nineteenth and early twentieth centuries, tuberculosis—or consumption—ran rampant in city slums where cramped quarters and unhealthy living conditions abetted the spread of bacteria and germs. As described by the *New York World*, Phipps's "entrance into the field of tenement-house reform [was] . . . a logical extension" of his fight to eliminate the disease. "It was natural," the article added, "that Mr. Phipps should now direct his fight against tuberculosis to its strongest ally, the breathless and crowded tenement."[96]

In late 1904, Phipps set out to build affordable and sanitary fireproof tenements and pledged one million dollars to the cause. By early 1905, he had assembled some of the city's most noted housing reformers, including Robert de Forest; Dr. Elgin R. L. Gould, president of City and Suburban Homes Company; Alfred Tredway White (1846–1921), Brooklyn tenement builder; and I. Straus (1845–1912), businessman, housing reformer, and owner of the R. H. Macy & Company department store, to form his executive board.[97] Gould suggested organizing the tenements after expatriate George Peabody's trust for

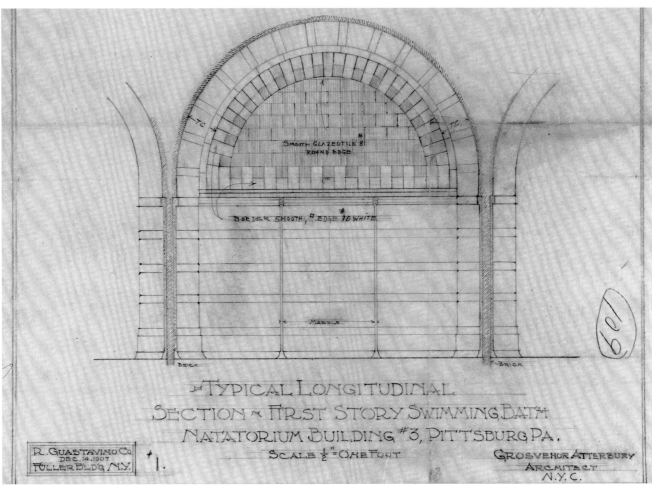

TOP *Phipps Natatorium, 540 Duquesne Way,*
Pittsburgh, Pennsylvania. The Brickbuilder 18 (March
1909): pl. 30

BOTTOM *Phipps Natatorium. Typical longitudinal*
section. Guastavino Collection, Avery Architectural and Fine
Arts Library, Columbia University in the City of New York

workers' housing in London. As a limited dividend company, it would not rent the apartments below market rate, and a projected four percent earning would be applied toward future buildings.[98]

As chairman of the executive committee, de Forest was fundamental in guiding the development process, at once obtaining the state charter that the organization's innovative corporate structure required. Although de Forest had initially recommended a limited competition to select an architect for Phipps's first project on East 31st Street, the board eventually decided that Atterbury, who had served as both de Forest and Phipps's personal architect, was well suited to the task. As recorded in the board's meeting minutes, they chose "Mr. Atterbury [who had] already been extensively employed by Mr. Phipps and [had] his confidence." In addition, many of the members knew "Mr.

Bath-tub in Airshaft, c. 1890. Museum of the City of New York, Jacob A. Riis Collection, #90.13.2.31

Atterbury personally [and were] aware of the position which he [had] already attained among the younger architects and [had] confidence in his ability and zeal." Because he did not have special experience in city tenements, Atterbury suggested that he work with an expert, whose fees would be taken out of his commission. In accepting the architect's proposal, the committee agreed that Dr. Gould, "a gentleman eminently qualified to act as this expert," would serve as Atterbury's advisor.[99]

In designing the East 31st Street apartments, Atterbury aspired to improve upon recent "admirable efforts to solve the tenement problem" and sought to "frankly benefit by their lessons and contribute toward the general advance by carrying the problem one step further."[100] In advance of the Tenement House Act of 1901, architects had begun exploring alternatives to the dumbbell tenement. Although the plan of a dumbbell allowed for windows in the middle of the building, it did not offer much relief to the oppressive density, and as neighborhoods developed, a series of narrow airless courtyards were entombed in the middle of each block. Regardless of the new law, corrupt officials and confusing jurisdictions prevented thorough enforcement, and many new buildings were approved for construction even though their plans created densities greater than allowed by code. With his influential courtyard plan of 1894, Ernest Flagg revealed the efficiency of combining 25-foot-wide lots into a larger footprint with one central courtyard opening off of the street. By redistributing floor area, he was able to increase the amount of air and light entering the building. The 1901 tenement law, which outlawed dumbbells, rendered development on lots less than 40 by 100 feet ineffective, and Flagg's prototype was readily adopted.

After a "careful and systematic analysis and comparison of the best plans previously executed," Atterbury produced three six-story tenements with 142 suites of two to five rooms on a 180-by-100-foot lot. The three buildings enclosed two large courtyards open to the street, which Atterbury innovatively furnished with fountains, benches, and a central loggia to provide safe and attractive social areas. Supporting his claim that construction and decoration "should doubtless be synonymous and result in a building that will produce a decorative effect through ornamental construction, without constructed ornament," the architect deftly translated the building's structural features into decorative elements.[101] The heroic four-story archways—similar to that of the Fulton Building—that delineated the entrance courts became the key

LEFT *Phipps Model Tenement, 321–337 East 31st Street, New York, New York.* The Brickbuilder 16 (September 1907): pl. 129

BELOW *Phipps Model Tenement. Interior courtyard.* Picture Collection, The Branch Libraries, The New York Public Library, Astor, Lenox and Tilden Foundations

notes of the 180-foot-wide street facade, breaking it into three well-proportioned sections. Brickwork, terra-cotta trim, varied window patterns, and wide sills for plants contributed to create a semblance of home that Atterbury felt other more "barrack-like" tenements lacked.

In contemplating his goals as a tenement designer, Atterbury at first satisfied the tenement and buildings laws before turning his attention toward producing an economical plan. Although his rooms were small, their arrangement was well ahead of the typical tenement with carefully interspersed hallways and vestibules separating the various living spaces and no rooms connecting

through one another—a common practice in old-law tenements. Due to the absence of closed interior courts, most of the rooms were well ventilated, and large double-hung windows in the living rooms flanked by casements amplified light and air. Atterbury's modern fireproof construction—brick exterior walls, steel columns and beams, reinforced-concrete floors, and plaster block partitions—and modern amenities such as steam heat, showers, gas ranges, private bathrooms, incineration systems, electric conduits, and sanitary laundries raised the standards for safety, hygiene, and convenience. At the same time, his rooftop gardens—with shrubs, vines, pergolas, pavilions,

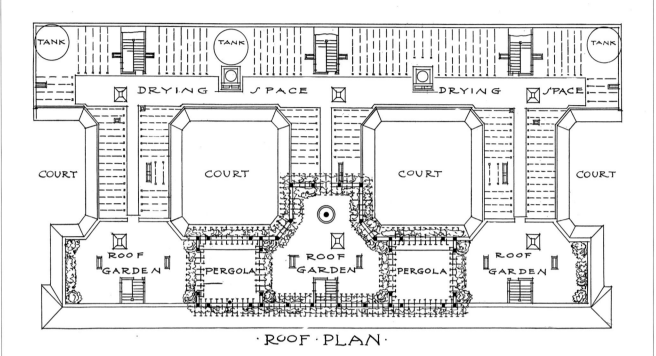

· ROOF · PLAN ·

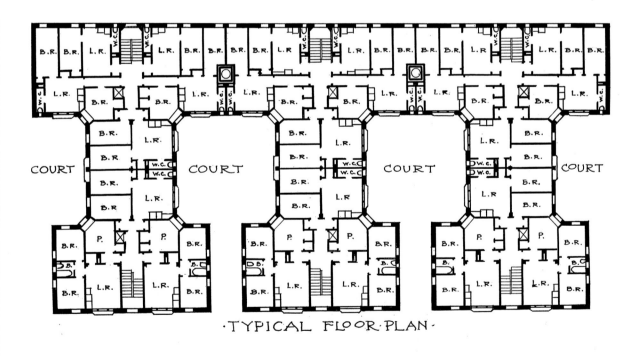

· TYPICAL · FLOOR · PLAN ·

Phipps Model Tenement. Roof plan and typical floor plan.
The Brickbuilder 16 (September 1907): pl. 133

Phipps Model Tenement. Roof terrace. The
Brickbuilder 16 (September 1907): pl. 130

and drying yards—and a basement kindergarten signifi-cantly enhanced the inhabitants' quality of life. Atterbury's attractive and artistic interiors with mosaic floors, marble staircases, oak woodwork, and tinted walls were well lit, clean, and well maintained. However, the architect derided "the despised galvanized iron cornice and metal tile," which he deemed out of place in the "otherwise sub-stantially and honestly constructed building."[102]

Atterbury was concerned that the improved tenements available at prevailing rates would be inaccessible to the lower classes of wage earners, writing in 1906 that "the danger of such a policy is that the buildings may draw down instead of up."[103] True to the architect's prediction, the apartments, which opened in 1907, attracted middle-class professional men and women. Limited dividend companies like Phipps's enterprise were often criticized for catering more to skilled laborers than to the less-priv-ileged, needier slum inhabitants. In order to protect their investments, the companies often built in advance of their tenants' conscious needs, inadvertently raising their stan-dards of living. On the other hand, they succeeded in dif-fusing the problem by displacing the less fortunate out of the lowest grade of housing.[104]

Atterbury did not contribute to the subsequent 1906 and 1912 tenements that Phipps funded in the San Juan Hill slum of the West 60s. In 1909, when the board was contemplating sites for its third venture, he was briefly called upon to develop a feasibility study for a lot pur-chased in the Crown Heights section of Brooklyn with-out Phipps's consent. After Atterbury and an advisory group consisting of Ernest Flagg, Henry D. Whitfield, and I. N. Phelps Stokes determined that either one- or two-family houses would be necessary for the venture to be at all profitable, the board abandoned the project for the West 60s.[105] The architect may have played a role in plan-ning apartments on the north side of Pittsburgh in 1908. Located in the once-vibrant immigrant neighborhood in which Phipps had been raised, the tenements—known as the Allegheny Apartments—have also been attributed to London-born architect Alfred C. Bossom (1881–1965),

Phipps Psychiatric Clinic, Johns Hopkins Hospital, Baltimore, Maryland. The Alan Mason Chesney Medical Archives of the Johns Hopkins Medical Institutions

who worked with George A. Crawley on Jay Phipps's country house in Old Westbury.[106]

Henry Phipps's generous gift of $1,500,000 to Johns Hopkins University to establish a psychiatric clinic formed the basis of Atterbury's next commission.[107] The university and hospital, established in the 1870s at the bequest of banker and philanthropist Johns Hopkins (1795–1873), stood at the forefront of American medicine as one of the country's first teaching facilities.[108] Upon visiting the tuberculosis dispensary he had endowed at the hospital in 1905, Phipps expressed a desire to the medical school's dean, Dr. William Welch, to fund future projects. At that time, Welch gave Phipps a copy of Clifford Beers's *A Mind that Found Itself*. The startling autobiographical account, which revealed the inhumane practices within mental institutions, spurred Phipps to turn his attention and wealth toward the field of psychiatry.

After the announcement of the gift in 1908, the officials of Johns Hopkins Hospital in East Baltimore recruited the well-regarded Swiss psychobiologist Dr. Adolf Meyer

(1866–1950) to serve as the clinic's director. Meyer worked closely with Atterbury to design a modern facility capable of accommodating clinical, educational, and research divisions. In June 1908, the two men embarked on a two-month tour to study the organization and construction of Europe's leading psychiatric institutions, particularly those in Vienna and Munich and, upon returning, worked closely with the various specialists and scientists scheduled to occupy the space to complete plans in 1909. Describing the scheme as being "in a class by itself in this country," the *New York Times* noted that it was not "a reproduction of any clinic in the world but [was] designed to embrace the most desirable features of all."[109] Construction of the landmark facility started in the summer of 1910; as construction progressed, Atterbury continued to consult with Meyer on every detail of the building from light switches to curtain rods to window grilles.[110]

Inspired by an epitaph from the entrance of Berlin's Virchow Hospital—"In treating the patient, do not forget the man"—Atterbury sought to re-create the comforting

Phipps Psychiatric Clinic. Quiet ward. The Alan Mason Chesney
Medical Archives of the Johns Hopkins Medical Institutions

familiarity of a house within the state-of-the-art clinic. "After many weeks spent visiting institutions throughout Europe," he described, "the impression made by the ward of a recently completed hospital in London still stands out vividly in my memory. The room was rather low ceiled, and made no architectural pretense. But the sunlight came through prettily dressed windows and fell on stands of flowering plants, while the reflection of a brisk open fire danced on a dark polished floor. And lying in brass knobbed beds, crisp and fresh against warmly tinted walls, the patients themselves provided a finishing touch of cheerfulness by wearing bed jackets of hunting pink." At Johns Hopkins, Atterbury strove to construct interiors capable of projecting a similar warmth or, in his words, were "cheerful but not exciting; varied but without disturbing contrast; roomy but without the large scale that stamps it as an institution. In a word, a building expressing that familiar quality of the individual home to a degree sufficient not only to rob the individual of its tendency to arouse the feeling of strangeness but also to produce if

possible a more soothing and agreeable reaction in the patient than is his ordinary lot in life."[111]

Contrasting with the clinic's dark redbrick, rather institutional, five-story edifice, designed to blend with the older Queen Anne buildings by the Boston firm of Edward Clark Cabot (1818–1901) and Francis Ward Chandler (1844–1926) on Johns Hopkins Hospital's campus, the interiors were imbued with a "homelike feeling," furnished with fireplaces, calming colors, a pipe organ, and architectural finishes more apt to appear in a house than in a hospital ward. When possible, Atterbury hid restraints and bars and refrained from using cold sterile materials such as tile, marble, and mosaic, except when necessary for hygienic purposes. By locating laboratories and offices in the northern portion of the U-shaped building, he maximized light in the wards in the southern wings. His charming south-facing cloistered courtyard with fountains and bay trees provided an attractive outdoor space to uplift patients. Despite the quality of the building's craftsmanship, the administration found Atterbury's comfortable—if not luxurious—accommodations excessive, criticizing the architect's exam rooms as too large and his use of brass and copper as expensive to maintain.[112] Nonetheless, Meyer allotted half of the clinic's resources to serving the poor. Dedicated in 1913, the Phipps Psychiatric Clinic became renowned in the medical community as the first psychiatric facility to be associated with an academic institution.

While he was working in Baltimore, Atterbury was also entrenched in the design for the Henry Phipps Institute for the Study, Treatment and Prevention of Tuberculosis in Phipps's birthplace of Philadelphia. During the late nineteenth and early twentieth centuries, the repercussions of the debilitating, often fatal disease were severely felt in the city. Dr. Lawrence Flick, an ambitious and enthusiastic physician who sought to combat the devastating plight, inspired the philanthropist to focus on fighting its effects.

In 1902, Phipps and Flick, himself a victim of pulmonary tuberculosis, established the Philadelphia clinic "devoted exclusively to the work of exterminating tuberculosis." The two men visited Europe to study various foreign examples after which Flick returned to set up an institute in two remodeled townhouses on Lombard Street. With aspirations of "[setting] the world aflame with a burning zeal to stamp out tuberculosis," Flick, with Phipps's support, began thinking about building a more permanent home for his work after the institute had run successfully for a year.[113] An exhaustive seven-year search produced an appropriate site nearby on Lombard and Seventh Streets, thick in the midst of the city's most congested slums, where its services were most needed. As the first scientific institution specifically dedicated to eliminating the disease, Atterbury's designs for the new building combined a sanatorium, hospital for advanced cases, dispensary for in-

Phipps Institute for the Treatment of Tuberculosis, Seventh and Lombard Streets, Philadelphia, Pennsylvania. The Brickbuilder 23 (September 1914): 129

Phipps Institute for the Treatment of Tuberculosis.
Entrance detail. The Brickbuilder 23 (September 1914): 130

patients, laboratories, libraries, and social study division under one roof. After Flick's retirement as director in 1909, the University of Pennsylvania took over the institute; ground was broken the following year.

Reflecting the prevailing progressive ideals of the period, Flick described the institute as a place "consecrated to the uplift of man" in what was "perhaps the most degraded spot physically, sanitarily and morally" in Philadelphia.[114] Situated among more downtrodden surroundings, Atterbury's five-story Georgian edifice, completed in 1913, made a strong impression.[115] While the architect used limestone lintels, sills, and keystones to complement the redbrick facades, the scheme's decorative qualities emerged more through Atterbury's massing and fenestration patterns. To the west, he presented a closed entrance facade, embellished with a well-proportioned front door with leaded transoms and side lights and an inventive interpretation of a Palladian window on the second floor. He cleverly opened up the building's primary symmetrical facade to the south and hinged its composition around a central round stair tower accentuated with iron balconies. Within the U-shape of the building's first three floors, he inserted a little garden and located exam rooms and nurse, servant, and student quarters. Patients were sequestered on the upper stories, where they could enjoy the restorative qualities bestowed by Atterbury's inclusion of ample indoor-outdoor spaces. Pleasant terraces decorated with pergolas and shrubs incorporated into the building's third-floor setback and an expansive arcaded porch connected directly to the wards. The fourth- and fifth-story pavilion encompassed open-air wards and a bright, cheerful solarium with large arched windows as well as dining rooms and exam rooms.

Like the Phipps Psychiatric Clinic at Johns Hopkins, the institute was incorporated into the medical school, this time at the University of Pennsylvania, providing a venue in which students could receive training in disease treatment and prevention.

Phipps's contributions to the area of public health would advance the field significantly, encourage several health movements, and lead to his appointment to the Committee of One Hundred, the organization that sought support from politicians and various public health, medicine, and social welfare representatives in order to establish a National Department of Health. Atterbury's association with such promising and visible projects as the Phipps commissions gave the architect a strong foothold into the world of social reform and would influence the direction of his practice in the ensuing decades. With the awareness that was born out of this involvement, Atterbury strove more resolutely to make his work meaningful and relevant to society at large.

Photographer unknown, (n.d.) interior before 1912 looking toward the north hall; (at right) the Spinario and the Hermes; (center) the Caesar Augustus of Prima Porta; (center left) busts of Dante and Homer; on each side of the hall, copies of Roman imperial busts; also visible are paintings from Parrish's collection and reproductions of sections from the Parthenon frieze. Collection of The Parrish Art Museum Archives

Photographer unknown, (n.d.) exterior main entrance as it appeared shortly after the 1913 addition. Courtesy of The Parrish Art Museum Archives

MUSEUMS, RESTORATIONS, AND SCHOOLS

At the same time that he was helping to shape the Southampton summer colony's residential character, Atterbury also designed for Samuel Longstreth Parrish in 1897 the Art Museum of Southampton, which he described as "one of the earliest country museums"; he later executed two additions in 1902 and 1913.[116] Having recently retired from his career as a corporate lawyer at the age of forty-eight, Parrish devoted his time and interest to such pursuits as politics, golf, and art collecting.[117] As one of the earliest and most prominent summer residents, he was active in the village life of Southampton and was among the group of men who founded the Shinnecock Hills Golf Club. Also passionate about Greek, Roman, and Italian art, "the thought came to [Parrish] suddenly while traveling from Ravenna to Florence . . . to transplant to a small, once Puritan village on the east-

ern end of Long Island a delicate exotic in the form of an artistic collection that would express at least something of the spirit of the Italian Renaissance."[118] Like other philanthropists of the Progressive era, Parrish felt a certain responsibility to share the ideals of civilization, beauty, and culture for the betterment of mankind.

Atterbury's Parrish Art Museum fittingly fused the stately proportions of an Italian Renaissance palazzo with the informal quality of a summer house in an unassuming shingled building festooned with climbing vines. While Parrish admired the work of William Merritt Chase, Southampton's artist-in-residence, he focused primarily on plaster and marble copies of Greek, Roman, and Italian masterpieces to fill the space. At the turn of the twentieth century, in the United States and abroad, casts and copies of antiquity's great works were considered attractive and worthy as a means of education and a source of beauty. By 1898, Parrish's eclectic collection of simulacra, which included plaster sections of the Parthenon frieze, a hand-

135

colored facsimile of the Bayeux tapestry, and various life-sized sculpture, was displayed in a large rectangular room with orangey-brown burlap-covered walls, dark wood-work, brick piers, flat skylight, and an organ, added in 1903, at the western end. Accessible by path from the village's main street, the museum was open during the season and sat amid an arboretum laid out by Boston landscape designer Warren H. Manning (1860–1938), a disciple of Frederick Law Olmsted Sr.

While Atterbury's northern brick exhibition hall of 1902 doubled Parrish's display space, his 1913 addition transformed the modest wood structure into a sophisticated brick interpretation of an Italian villa.[119] The architect joined three enfilade galleries to the south of the original building and reoriented its main entrance onto Job's Lane. Brick walls capped with intricate ironwork gently curved up to a paved forecourt, where a charmingly diminutive three-bay loggia, designed in the spirit of Brunelleschi, embraced the public. As firm associate

Charles C. May, writing for *Architectural Record*, accurately noted, "In plan, in exterior treatment and in detail the building is simplicity itself. It relies for its effect not upon picturesqueness of form or feature but upon the grouping of large masses, bold contrasts of shadow and texture of expansive wall surfaces."[120] As displayed by his house designs, Atterbury held the virtues of irregular overburned brick—a rough by-product often discarded by architects and builders—in high regard. While the massing and forms that the architect employed for Parrish's museum were appealingly straightforward, the warm and richly textured veneer of reds, browns, and blacks, paired with black mortar, added a level of energy and vivacity to the facades. Atterbury's flanking side gates, notably featuring ornamental concrete panels and details brushed with colored aggregate, framed vistas into the museum's gardens; the varied hues of the walls, exquisite ironwork, and panels and plaques incorporated into the facades—an attribute inspired by Brunelleschi's Foundling Hospital in

York Hall, Yale University, New Haven, Connecticut.
Gottscho-Schleisner Collection. Library of Congress

York Hall. Rendering of window detail. American Architect (June 12, 1897)

Florence—gave rise to a tasteful and colorful vision amplified in contrast to the greenery of the country setting.

Inside, Parrish commingled the work of different eras and countries with originals and replicas to create a pleasing and balanced display based on aesthetics rather than on a set chronology. The Latin cross plan created by the combined old and new galleries produced, according to May, "a grateful sense of freedom from supervision or necessity of viewing the collection in prescribed sequence."[121] As a backdrop for the art, Atterbury's interior architecture and deep-toned blue burlap-covered walls were appropriately quiet and neutral. Diffused light from the glazed doors and elliptical barrel-vaulted sky-light cast a mellow glow, creating an enchanting and intimate museum experience.

While cultivated Americans took their cues from Europe in defining tastes and culture, they also began to take a larger interest in their own heritage—a reflection of the sweeping Colonial Revival movement. During the early years of the twentieth century, the preservation of the country's historical sites became increasingly important and timely. In 1905, Atterbury embarked on his first major project in architectural conservation: the restoration of Connecticut Hall at Yale, or South Middle College as it was then known, the sole survivor of the college's original redbrick row of buildings overlooking New

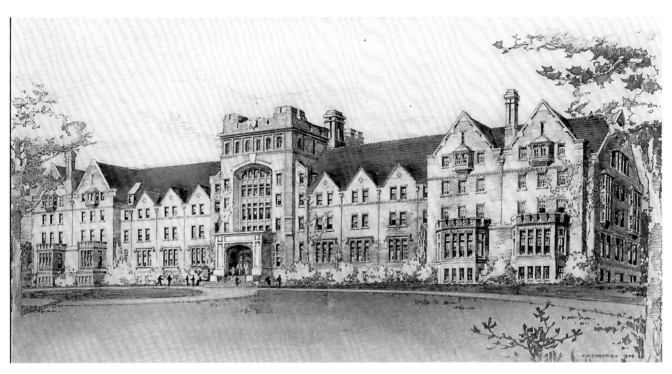

Haven's green. By that time, Atterbury had already designed York Hall (1897) on Yale's campus, a large four-story brick dormitory for the Chi Psi fraternity inspired by Venetian palazzos, such as the Palazzo Contarini Fasan. While the building was anomalous in Atterbury's body of work, it demonstrated his virtuosity when approaching a project that required a specific formal language. As a graduate of Yale, he had absorbed the power and charm of the campus's architecture and was familiar with buildings, such as Scroll and Key's Moorish temple, that clothed their inner secrets in a variety of potent architectural styles. Atterbury's associate, Tompkins, may have influenced the scheme, having designed an artist's house (c. 1894) at Columbia in creditable Venetian form. Most intriguing, though, given Atterbury's interest in bringing natural light into the center of his urban buildings, was his use of a delicate three-bay terra-cotta loggia on Wall Street to screen a broad expanse of glazing in the stair hall. Its imaginative Gothic ornament was reinterpreted in an elaborate terra-cotta balcony that served effectively as a cornice for the building.[122]

Atterbury's restoration of Connecticut Hall presented the architect with an entirely different problem. When it was first completed in 1753, it was described as the "best building in the colony." The college's president, Thomas Clap, modeled the distinguished three-story brick Geor-gian dormitory after Harvard's Massachusetts Hall and brought in builders Francis Letort and Thomas Bills from Philadelphia and New York to construct the 100 by 40 foot structure, detailed with fine brownstone trim, ornamental keystones, and subtle courses of brick. Designed to house the college's 150 students, the dormitory featured a gambrel roof and dormers, hand-hewn woodwork, oak floors, and suites of rooms. During the 1790s, artist John Trumbull (1756–1843), in collaboration with Connecticut politician and developer James Hillhouse, conceived the college's first master plan, incorporating Connecticut Hall into what came to be known as Old Brick Row—a row of long rectangular dormitories with taller assembly buildings and chapels interspersed. In 1796, Trumbull added a fourth floor to Connecticut Hall and replaced its gambrel with a gabled roof to blend more readily with its Adam-style neighbors.[123] As the first planned college campus in the United States, Old Brick Row was highly influential in informing the shape of campuses throughout the country.

While Trumbull's plan served Yale for over a century, new buildings rendered the well-worn Old Brick Row obsolete at the turn of the twentieth century, leading to its demolition in 1900. A group of alumni, however, headed by Professor Henry Farnam, came forward to save "South Middle"—the oldest building on the Yale campus and in

Shaw Field House. Pawling School, 1926. Courtesy of the
Trinity-Pawling School

New Haven—as a memorial to the college's history. They
commissioned Atterbury to restore it in 1905. To faith-
fully return the hall to its 1750s form, the architect spent
considerable time researching its original details, and at a
cost of $16,354, he reestablished its gambrel roof and
dormers and modernized the building. At a time when
preservation was only emerging, Atterbury's restoration
of Connecticut Hall—which reclaimed its original name
after the renovation—was an important early contribution to the development of the field.[124]

With his work at Yale, Atterbury acquired some expertise in the realm of collegiate architecture. Four years later,
he and his associate Stowe Phelps began work on the
Pawling School, a preparatory school near Millbrook,
New York.[125] Dr. Frederick L. Gamage (1860–1947) had
founded the school in 1907 after defecting from the St.
Paul's School in Garden City, Long Island, with a loyal following of teachers and former students. George B. Cluett
(1832–1912), a wealthy manufacturer of collars and cuffs
from Troy, New York, funded Pawling's new school building, known as the Alfonzo Rockwell Cluett Foundation,
in memory of his son, a graduate of St. Paul's in Garden
City.[126] It is likely that Atterbury received this commission through George D. Cross, president of Pawling's
Alumni Association, for whom Atterbury had recently
designed a house in Bernardsville, New Jersey. In 1909,
Atterbury and Phelps laid out the campus and designed a
four-story battlemented Gothic edifice that stretched 314
feet across a gentle rise on the school's 150-acre farmland
property in Pawling. Completed in 1910, the imposing

redbrick structure accented with white marble trim and a
crenulated central section stood as a rare example of
Atterbury's collegiate Gothic style.[127] Development of the
campus unfolded gradually according to the architects'
plan with construction of a gym (1911), field house
(1913), headmaster's house (1924), chapel (1926), and
science building (1936). Atterbury's later development
plan (1923) for St. Paul's School in Concord, New Hampshire—Tompkins's alma mater—in collaboration with
Frederick Law Olmsted Jr. did not result in any commissions.[128]

Atterbury was able to apply his experience preserving
Connecticut Hall to future commissions. His relationship
with Robert de Forest led to his involvement in restoring
City Hall, one of New York's great architectural treasures,
designed by the Scottish-born architect John McComb Jr.
(1763–1853) and his short-term partner, Joseph François
Mangin (1794–1818), in the early 1800s.[129] Their proposal, which took first place out of the twenty-six submitted in a competition, blended aspects of Italian
Renaissance, French neoclassicism, and Georgian architecture. A disciple of the English designer Sir William
Chambers (1723–1796), McComb carried the pair's 1802
entry to completion.[130] However, in the 1890s, the future
of the building lay in the balance as various administra-
tions and architects advocated its destruction. The Municipal Building Commission held a competition for a new
City Hall, with Richard Morris Hunt, Napolean Le Brun
(1821–1901), and William Robert Ware acting as jury;
however, the state legislature passed a law forbidding con-

ABOVE *Restoration of New York's City Hall, New York, New York. Governor's Room.* New York State Archives. Education Dept. Division of Visual Instruction

LEFT *City Hall. West room. American Architect* 96 (July 7, 1909)

struction on the site, and plans for other projects, including the Hall of Records (1899–1911) and the Municipal Building (1907–14), accommodated the overflow from City Hall.[131] During his twenty-five-year tenure as president of the Municipal Art Commission, de Forest safeguarded the architectural integrity of the century-old building, overseeing several restorations and renovations to maintain and improve its historic fabric.

In 1907, Atterbury was engaged to restore the Governor's Room—a suite of three enfilade spaces occupying the central southern portion of the building's second floor. Throughout the nineteenth century—a time when city and state governments worked more closely together—the rooms had been designated for the governor's use when he was in residence. However, since the building's completion in 1811, the interiors had undergone a series of alterations and repairs that had disfigured McComb's artistry. The most recent renovation, executed by Bernstein & Bernstein in 1905, had been carried out in the then-popular French mode with red walls, parquet floors, new ceiling and cornice moldings, imported French Savonnerie rugs, and elaborate gilt-and-crystal chandeliers. It was the subject of criticism, and city officials soon began contemplating yet another overhaul to scale back the extravagant gesture. In 1907, McKim, Mead & White prepared a new scheme with a domed ceiling and white walls hung with silk velour; however, the city soon abandoned the plans, which were deemed expensive and unnecessary in the wake of Bernstein & Bernstein's extensive three-year renovation. Later that year, Margaret Olivia Slocum Sage (1828–1918), founder of the recently established Russell Sage Foundation, spread her benevolence to the Governor's Room, announcing her interest in the "complete and satisfactory restoration of the Governor's Room . . . as one of the most important historical rooms in the city." Under the condition that the new scheme "should present as nearly as possible the appearance it originally had," Mrs. Sage pledged $25,000 toward its improvement and named the Municipal Art Commission, headed by her trusted advisor and personal lawyer, de Forest, its steward.[132] As the decade unfolded, Atterbury's livelihood as an architect became increasingly linked to de Forest and Mrs. Sage. Soon after the architect began his redesign of the Governor's Room, de Forest and the Russell Sage Foundation started funding Atterbury's research on concrete construction and contemplating plans for Forest Hills Gardens.

Since McComb's architecture had been unduly ravaged by time, Atterbury was confronted with what was as good as a blank slate; the only original elements existing in the Governor's Room were the window trim, shutters, sashes, and trim around the suite's three main entrances. The commission's challenge rested in the architect's ability to interpret what the rooms had once looked like to accurately capture the spirit of the early 1800s. Careful and thorough in his research to reconstruct them, Atterbury first delved through McComb's original drawings for the building in the collections of the New-York Historical Society. With many aspects of the design unclear or undocumented, the architect turned to books, details found in other parts of City Hall, and other late eighteenth-century buildings, particularly in and around

City Hall. Detail in the Governor's Room.
© 2009. City of New York. All Rights Reserved. Jonathan Wallen

City Hall. Mayor's office. New York State Archives.
Education Dept. Division of Visual Instruction

Philadelphia, to fill in the blanks. He also referred to McComb's annotated copy of Chambers's *Treatise on the Decorative Part of Civil Architecture* (1791), drawings owned by the McComb family, and pattern books such as William Pain's *The Practical House Carpenter* (1797), loaned by R. T. Haines Halsey, a member of the art commission who was later instrumental in creating the Metropolitan Museum of Art's American Wing. As restoration architect, Atterbury's groundwork for designing the new scheme was perhaps more important than the scheme itself. His meticulous preparation and the considerable time he spent reconstructing details provided the foundation for a just and appropriate interpretation of McComb's ideas.

The restored rooms opened on May 28, 1909, to critical success. *The Daily Tribune* pronounced them "perhaps the finest in a public building in the country" and noted "the details of the ceiling, cornices, mantels, and woodwork [as] the greatest beauty of the room."[133] By opening two previously blind windows in the center room—a decision predicated on McComb's drawings—Atterbury created a wall of light to the south that amplified the room's soaring ceilings and attenuated proportions. Using the five round-arch windows as a basis for the interior architecture, the architect composed the north wall paneling and compartmentalized plaster ceiling moldings to follow a similar five-bay configuration, as opposed to the previous tripartite arrangement. Atterbury relied on *The Practical House Carpenter* and plates from such books as *Old Colonial Architectural Details in and around Philadelphia* (c. 1890) and *Colonial Architecture in South Carolina and Georgia* to construct lighter and simpler ornament. At the same time, he incorporated symbols and patriotic iconography to convey a sense of purpose and personality. Over the two sets of doors adjoining the east and west rooms, he inserted seals of the state, nation, province, and New Amsterdam and allegorical symbols of library, justice, war, and peace.[134] The pair of mantels in the center room were

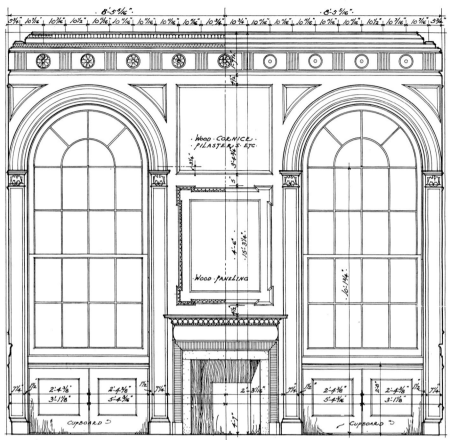

* WEST * ELEVATION ~ MAYOR'S * PRIVATE * OFFICE *
* ⅜ * INCH * SCALE *

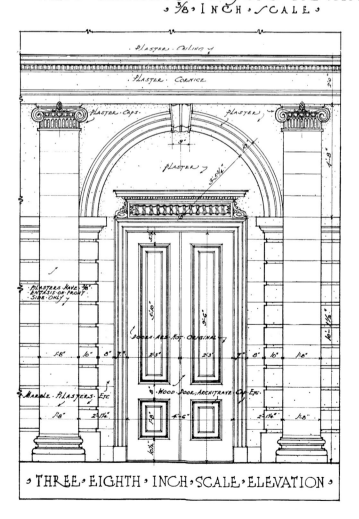

* THREE * EIGHTH * INCH * SCALE * ELEVATION *

detailed with exquisitely carved seals and vignettes, including one of a figure of fame blowing a trumpet—an image taken from a pitcher once owned by George Washington.

The extent of the city's pride in the restoration's authenticity was reflected clearly in John Quincy Adams Jr.'s *The Governor's Room in the City Hall*, published by the art commission upon the room's opening. The twenty-five-page booklet included a brief history of the space and a catalogue of Atterbury's details and their respective sources. Also responsible for the decoration, the architect introduced a more restrained palette, using shades of white for the walls, hardwood for the floors, and green upholstery and curtains. His chandeliers, based on McComb's sketches, and benches were classic and clean with less carving and more refined profiles. Combined with antique pieces, including George Washington's desk and library table, John Adams's desk, high-backed sofas and armchairs from Federal Hall, and John Trumbull's collection of portraits of noteworthy politicians, the completed picture conveyed a sense of dignity, gravity, and a restrained grandeur. The city celebrated the museum

City Hall. Rotunda and dome. New York State
Archives. Education Dept. Division of Visual Instruction

145

City Hall. Restoration of the cupola.
Architectural Catalog (April 1918)

quality of the historically significant space. As Atterbury's associate Charles C. May noted, "The Governor's Room has exercised an immeasurable influence. . . . Let no one question the value of [this] municipal museum."[135]

Until the mid-1930s, Atterbury was periodically called upon to redecorate and repair the Governor's Room.[136] The success of the restoration also led to additional commissions throughout the building, both inside and out. From 1910 to 1916, the architect restored, modernized, and fireproofed many of the interiors, returning the rooms to something closer to McComb's original conception. In addition to rehabilitating and redecorating the Board of Estimate Chamber and the Committee Room for the Board of Aldermen on the second floor and the

mayor and council wings on the first floor, he also reworked the circulation in the hallways and added Georgian screens, transoms, and fanlights.[137] On the third floor, he created offices for the art commission in an apartment suite once occupied by City Hall's superintendent and family. As a guiding principle, the architect and the art commission held the building's original woodwork as sacred and did as much as possible to preserve McComb's delicate profiles and moldings, which had been obscured by layers of paint and plaster over the years. Combining the old with the new, Atterbury supported areas of the building where water damage and haphazard renovations had caused structural damage with steel members and beams. City Hall's splendid central rotunda with its ten fluted Corinthian columns also received the attention of Atterbury's hand. With a $25,000 grant from Mrs. Sage, he reinforced the soaring coffered dome with a protective coating of cement and reestablished the integrity of McComb's details. By repainting the dome in shades of white—removing offending gilt from the rosettes—and enlarging the skylight, Atterbury created a bright ethereal space. His light fixtures and sculptor John LeMaire's (1767–1852) exquisitely carved marble band around the circumference of the rotunda, revealed from beneath layers of grime, added to the beauty and impressiveness of the building's pivotal moment.

With the exception of the cupola, the exterior of City Hall stood untouched from the time of its completion in 1811. When McComb was designing the building, he produced several versions for the crowning element, and since the scheme that was carried out had been so heavily altered through time, the form of McComb's original motif was unknown. In 1830, the city decided to incorporate a clock into the cupola, inserting an eight-foot section under the dome to receive the four dials. Although McComb attempted to tie in the added height with inverted consoles, the overall effect was awkward and unwieldy. This cupola fell victim to a fire in 1858 during a celebration of the first Atlantic telegraph cable when it was customary to set off fireworks from the roof of City Hall. A stray rocket hit the tower, instantly reducing it to rubble. While the predicament presented an opportunity for a better design, the new cupola, when rebuilt, "retained all the faults of the altered cupola of 1830." According to John Walker Harrington, writing for *The American Architect*, "The clock was in the same place, the drum went back in the same unsightly fashion and those signs manual of a degenerated architecture, the inverted consoles, were retained, although the urns which stood near them were omitted."[138]

In May 1917, another conflagration—this time started by men working on the roof—claimed the cupola again. Atterbury, who was setting up a temporary exhibit in City Hall park, saw the smoke and ran to the office of the mayor's secretary, shouting, "The City Hall is on fire; send in an alarm."[139] Although help arrived shortly thereafter, the cupola was destroyed down to the stone supports. Since Atterbury had so aptly demonstrated his sensitivity to the building's historic fabric, he was called upon to reestablish its crowning feature. Like his work in the Governor's Room, Atterbury's design for the new cupola could best be described as "an interpretation rather than a restoration." In his quest to "combine the maximum of architectural beauty and the strictest harmony with the main structure," he carefully studied McComb's drawings and various schemes to determine his "finest conception." However, McComb's multiple designs left the question of the cupola's final form open. In addition, Atterbury decided the clock had become so familiar to New Yorkers that it was "entitled to be considered as an essential part" and therefore "highly desirable . . . to incorporate . . . but only if it can be done without violence to the architectural design.[140]

Completed in 1919, the new cupola followed the lines of McComb's designs and conformed beautifully to the building's established architecture. By incorporating the four round glass dials into the upper rounded section of the windows, the clock became an integral aspect of the design rather than a clumsy afterthought. Although some city officials objected to the reduced size and position of the new clock faces, Atterbury fastidiously measured its sight lines and maintained that it would be visible from all points, "excepting only a small area immediately in the rear of City Hall in front of the old Court House—a practically negligible area."[141] As noted by Harrington, Atterbury's solution was "especially interesting" since "it [represented] a problem worked out with modern materials and complicated by vast changes in environment." While the cupola was shorter than its predecessors, Atterbury's skillful play of proportions rendered it "well poised and strong" against a backdrop of "looming skyscrapers."[142] Atterbury expertly articulated its architecture in wood, combined with a core of steel and concrete, creating a modern monument that seamlessly fused with McComb's edifice.

· PRESENT · CUPOLA ·
AS BUILT AFTER THE FIRE OF 1858

· PROPOSED · CUPOLA ·
DESIGNED AFTER ORIGINAL STUDIES BY McCOMB

City Hall. Cupola as built after the fire of 1858 and Atterbury's proposal. American Architect 112 (September 12, 1917): 179

CHAPTER 4

THE RUSSELL SAGE FOUNDATION AND FOREST HILLS GARDENS

1909–1940

On September 8, 1910, the Pennsylvania Railroad opened its long-anticipated tunnel under the East River, connecting midtown Manhattan to the Long Island Railroad and opening New York's business districts to areas of Queens and Long Island that had been previously isolated and remote. At the same time, the Russell Sage Foundation publicly announced its intention to develop a new suburban community in Queens called Forest Hills Gardens. Margaret Olivia Slocum Sage had established the foundation, among the first in the country, in 1907 after her husband Russell Sage (1816–1906), one of the era's foremost figures on Wall Street, left her his fortune of $65 million.[1] With advice from her lawyer, Robert de Forest, Mrs. Sage allocated $10 million—an amount described as "the largest single gift to philanthropy in the history of the world"—toward the foundation's endowment with the goal of ameliorating the social and living conditions of the working poor in the United States. At Forest Hills Gardens, one of the organization's first ventures, the foundation set forth to demonstrate how a well-planned, tastefully designed, and economically accessible community could dramatically improve the living conditions of those of modest means and, in turn, present an influential model to guide future developments of its kind.

In addition to receiving nationwide press and interest,

Forest Hills Gardens brought considerable renown to Atterbury, who in 1909 had been asked to collaborate on the project with Frederick Law Olmsted Jr. For both men, Forest Hills Gardens was a golden opportunity to experiment with new ideas about town planning, open space, housing types, and building construction. Taking inspiration from the garden cities of England and Germany, Atterbury and Olmsted designed an architecturally distinct suburb shaped around a well-defined landscape plan and using innovative materials and methods of building. Although the concept of the garden city had been gaining momentum in England and Germany for a generation and especially since 1898, its principles were still relatively unexplored in the United States. Atterbury and Olmsted had thoroughly studied European designs and building techniques.[2] Together, they interpreted the ideals of the movement to create a unique and enchanting community that remains one of the most important early examples of city planning and design in this country.

In her role as the foundation's president, Mrs. Sage appointed de Forest as vice president. Well qualified to guide the organization, de Forest was a partner in his family's firm, de Forest Brothers, director of myriad railroad and insurance enterprises, and extraordinarily dedicated to philanthropic and civic pursuits. Hailed as the "captain of

building was sold again, and it was subsequently converted into apartments.

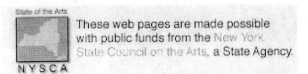

These web pages are made possible with public funds from the New York State Council on the Arts, a State Agency.

To EXIT and return to Preserve & Protect

last revised 31 August 1998

nL

Group VI and view of the Forest Hills Inn from Greenway Terrace, Forest Hills Gardens, Queens. The Sage Foundation Homes Company, *Forest Hills Gardens* (December 1913)

philanthropy," by 1909 he divided his time between the Charity Organization Society (COS), of which he had been president since 1888; the Metropolitan Museum of Art; the Municipal Art Commission; the American Red Cross; Presbyterian Hospital; the Welfare Council of New York; and the National Association for the Study and Prevention of Tuberculosis, which he had founded, among others.

Especially interested in housing as an agent for social reform, de Forest was responsible for helping draft the new tenement law of 1901 as chairman of the New York State Tenement House Commission, a position to which his friend Governor Theodore Roosevelt appointed him in 1900; he went on to serve as the first commissioner of the New York City Tenement House Department in 1902–3. In addition to de Forest, Mrs. Sage filled her board with a series of like-minded, public-spirited citizens, including Cleveland H. Dodge, Robert C. Ogden, Helen M. Gould, Mrs. William Rice, Louisa Lee Schuyler, and Daniel Coit Gilman.[3] Board member John M. Glenn (1858–1950), a leader in Baltimore's philanthropic world, was named manager of the foundation. Atterbury had sat on the COS's tenement house committee in 1898 with de Forest and, in 1907, had joined seventy other researchers in putting together the Pittsburgh Survey, a pioneering study funded by the Russell Sage Foundation to relieve living and working conditions of the people in a typical American city. The six-volume survey, issued between 1909 and 1914, was the organization's first and most influential research and publishing effort.

Once incorporated, the foundation moved quickly to create Forest Hills Gardens, in 1909 purchasing from the Cord Meyer Development Company 142 acres nine miles from the railroad's new station at 34th Street; two miles from Jamaica, Queens; and adjacent to the 536-acre Forest Park. Cord Meyer (1854–1910), chairman of the Democratic state committee, had inherited his father's sugar-refining fortune and had acquired 600 acres in the Hopedale section in Queens three years earlier to create a 6,000-house subdivision called Forest Hills. Since the Brooklyn and Williamsburg Bridges were the only connections between Queens and Manhattan, much of Queens's farmland had remained untouched up until that time. However, with the opening of the Queensboro Bridge in 1909 and the Pennsylvania Railroad's tunnels under the East River a year later, Queens's open pastures became ripe for development. To build Forest Hills Gardens, the Russell Sage Foundation established the Sage Foundation Homes Company, a separate entity headed by de Forest to improve the undulating plot of land purchased from Meyer.[4]

While de Forest was not personally acquainted with Olmsted, he was well aware of Olmsted's pioneering work within the field of landscape design. Olmsted's father, Frederick Law Olmsted Sr. (1822–1903), had advised on the landscape plan of the Montauk Association in 1892, of which de Forest and his father, Henry G. de Forest, were members; the de Forest house was one of eight cottages within the elite summer enclave designed by McKim, Mead & White. A leader of the emerging city-planning movement, Olmsted Jr. had established the first professional landscape architecture program at his alma mater Harvard in 1900. He had also been a member of the Senate Park Commission of 1901 with Daniel Burnham (1846–1912), Charles McKim, and Augustus Saint-Gaudens (1848–1907), which, under Michigan senator James McMillan (1838–1902), had been responsible for preparing a plan for the core of Washington, DC, after Pierre Charles L'Enfant's historic scheme. With his partners, Olmsted continued his father's eponymous firm after his death in 1903, evolving the elder's emphasis on picturesque landscapes as an antidote to the urban realm in order to embrace the city as a living organism in need of shaping. Olmsted's specific planning expertise was in high demand, and by 1909 he had prepared city plans for Detroit, Utica, Boulder, Pittsburgh, New Haven, Rochester, and Newport. He had also contributed to the suburban plan for Roland Park, outside of Baltimore.[5] In 1906, he began designing a number of de Forest family projects in Cold Spring Harbor.[6]

In December 1908, de Forest wrote to Olmsted, laying out his ideas about Forest Hills Gardens and gauging Olmsted's interest in the project. De Forest's timing was propitious since Olmsted, at that time, was traveling in Berlin to study urban development in Germany and was planning to visit England's garden cities. Olmsted responded at once, writing, "Nothing should interest me more than such a problem as you have on hand. . . . I cannot think of any landscape man in America who knows any more, if as much." While he was happy to cut his trip short, Olmsted was anxious to "get a better knowledge of what the Germans are doing in the systematic control of urban development for the greater well-being of the people" and hoped to see Hamburg, Frankfurt, and Darmstadt as well as manufacturing cities in France and the garden cities of England because "the celebrated Garden City is still largely on paper, but I want to look at it, as far as it has got, and also Port Sunlight, and one or two other 'model villages' again, with new eyes."[7] De Forest offered to hold the project until Olmsted's return and confirmed that "the English garden cities, though in embryo, are well worth seeing and suggestive.

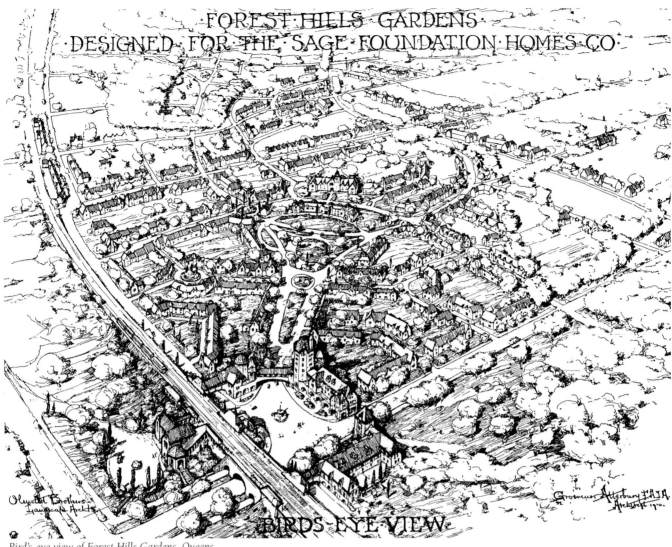

·FOREST·HILLS·GARDENS·
DESIGNED·FOR·THE·SAGE·FOUNDATION·HOMES·CO·

BIRDS·EYE·VIEW·

Bird's-eye view of Forest Hills Gardens, Queens,
New York. Arts and Decoration 1 (January 1911): 120

You can readily see Hampstead and Letchworth. We have here fairly complete data respecting them."[8]

From the outset, de Forest had a clear notion of what he wished to achieve at Forest Hills and strongly believed "there [was] money in taste." Mrs. Sage and her associates were "profoundly impressed with the need of better and more attractive housing facilities in the suburbs for persons of modest means, who could pay from $25 a month upwards in the purchase of a home. They have thought that homes could be supplied like those in the garden cities of England, with some greenery and flowers around them, with accessible playgrounds and recreation facilities, and at no appreciably greater cost than is now paid for the same roof room in bare streets without any such adjacency."[9] To Olmsted, de Forest wrote that the foundation was not striving "merely to give houses but to lay out these tracts in some way different from the abhorrent rectangular city

block, and to make our garden city somewhat attractive by the treatment and planting of our streets, the possibility of little gardens, and possibly some public places." Above all, he wanted to "set an example to the growing suburban districts of New York and other cities of how the thing can be done tastefully and at the same time with due regard for profit."[10] While de Forest revealed to Olmsted that "the more I see of abroad, the less I think we have to learn there, for our conditions are so different," the burgeoning Garden City movement in England provided Forest Hills Gardens's creators with a wealth of inspiration and a template for interpretation.[11]

Ebenezer Howard (1850–1928), an English court stenographer with limited formal education, had initiated the Garden City movement in 1898 with his publication *Tomorrow: A Peaceful Path to Real Reform*.[12] To relieve the squalid conditions within city slums, Howard envisioned

151

relocating the working class to a band of self-sufficient, collectively owned garden cities that embodied the best of both town and country living. These conjectural cities would have the liveliness of a metropolis—with restaurants, shops, and street life—set within an attractive rural landscape. Limited in size and density by a continuous agricultural greenbelt, they incorporated parks and private gardens and were to be connected to one another by a transit system. With his theoretical schemes, Howard intended to spur social and economic change rather than to promote a specific image or form.

In 1904, Howard organized a private corporation with several wealthy colleagues to explore his vision by developing the self-contained industrial community of Letchworth, located in Hertfordshire thirty-four miles north of London. Olmsted visited Letchworth, designed by the Buxton-based architectural team of Richard Barry Parker (1867–1947) and Raymond Unwin (1863–1940), in the spring of 1909, soon after corresponding with de Forest about Forest Hills Gardens. Unwin, a trained engineer, had joined his brother-in-law Parker in practice in 1896; the partners went on to become leaders in town planning and design, and in 1909 Unwin authored the influential book *Town Planning in Practice: An Introduction to the Art and Design of Cities and Suburbs*.[13] Advocating the connection between aesthetics and moral and mental health, Parker & Unwin demonstrated that working-class housing could successfully embrace style and design. The firm's 1,200-acre town, executed in an Arts & Crafts style reminiscent of Charles F. A. Voysey (1857–1941) and M. H. Baillie-Scott (1865–1945), incorporated a sophisticated balance of planning, circulation, landscape design, and architecture. Olmsted noted with

Leys Avenue, Letchworth, Hertfordshire, England. Scribner's *Magazine 52 (July 1912): 5*

Workmen's cottages, Letchworth. Scribner's Magazine *52 (July 1912): 7*

pleasure the "narrow roadways within highway limits of ample width" and how the designers kept "pretty clearly in view the fundamental requirement of economical efficiency while attaining much individual interest and charm." However, "coming to Letchworth directly from a study of town planning in Germany, where the value of a picturesque irregularity based upon Medieval examples is being enthusiastically urged," he did feel "some sense of regret at the apparent predominance . . . of straight and parallel-sided roads with entirely formal rows of trees, too suggestive of the shortcomings in this regard of nearly all American town planning."[14] Letchworth's tree-lined streets, cottages, and cheap rents rapidly attracted occupants, and the city's population grew from 400 to 7,000 in seven years.[15]

As he had mentioned to Olmsted, de Forest had also gathered information on Hampstead Garden Suburb (1905–8), a residential community located half an hour from central London by train. The brainchild of cosmetic heiress and social worker Henrietta Barnet (1851–1936), the suburb arose as an effort to counteract the unsavory development going up around the city.[16] In 1906, Barnet organized a group of like-minded citizens to purchase 243 acres near Hampstead Heath with the goal of providing a beautiful place where "thousands of people of all classes of

TOP *Asmuns Place, Hampstead Garden Suburb, London, England. Scribner's Magazine* 52 (July 1912): 9

BOTTOM *Hampstead Garden Suburb. Architectural Record* 44 (August 1918): 144

RIGHT *Hellerau, Dresden, Germany.* Architectural Record 35 (February 1914): 157

BELOW *Margarethenhöhe, Essen, Germany.* Scribner's Magazine 52 (July 1912): 19

society, of all sorts of opinions, and all standards of income, [could] live in helpful neighbourliness."[17] The newly formed Hampstead Garden Suburb Trust commissioned Parker & Unwin to design the layout and many of the suburb's early cottages and brought Edwin Lutyens (1869–1944) on to execute the principal buildings on the central square. To benefit the community, Barnet and her architects limited the number of houses per acre; incorporated gardens, closes, parks, and cul-de-sacs into the design; and thoroughly examined the relationship of cottages to one another. Inspired by German models, Parker & Unwin's houses, both detached and semi-detached, were simply constructed structures with half-timber details and handcrafted slate roofs grouped to produce interest and variety.

Garden cities derived from Howard's writings also materialized throughout Germany. Industrial communities, such as the Krupp Foundation's Margarethenhöhe (1906) in Essen, designed by Georg Metzendorf (1874–1934) for steel workers, and Hellerau (1909), north of Dresden, designed by Richard Riemerschmid (1868–1957) as an initiative of the Deutsche Werkstatten, also showed a happy balance of planning and architecture and the effect of "picturesque streetviews and charming vistas" that captured the charm of "older German towns."[18] Like Olmsted, Unwin held the virtues of German architecture in high esteem. In designing Hampstead, he "[learned] from the German School both a greater respect for the opportunities afforded by the undulations and other characteristics of the site and a greater appreciation of the possibilities which town planning affords for the creation of beautiful architectural groups of buildings."[19]

Hampstead was a residential suburb where its residents relied on the neighboring city for their livelihoods, whereas Letchworth was an essentially self-contained city in which factories employed many of its inhabitants. Both Letchworth and Hampstead Garden Suburb were collectively owned cooperative efforts of a group of like-minded people seeking to reform the current living conditions. While these goals defined the garden city in Europe, when transplanted to America, the garden city shed both its association with collective control and its goal of ameliorating housing for the laboring class and the poor.[20] A pragmatist by nature, de Forest noted that "[in this country] methods of land tenure are very different, social habits are very different, and to run counter to ordinary methods of land tenure and social habits, even under the stimulus of continental or English success, would be a very doubtful experiment."[21] Since the foundation and the architects believed that their development would only influence builders if it were based on market-driven principles, they had to adjust their goals as the project proceeded.

Rising land costs in Queens, due to its increased accessibility, precluded the Russell Sage Foundation from appealing to the day laborer, as was initially intended. Atterbury offered an apology, explaining that "many people will doubtless be disappointed to find that the first housing demonstration . . . will not reach the so-called laboring man, or even the lower paid mechanic, which is impossible in this instance by reason of the cost and location of the land."[22] As an alternative, the foundation promised to focus on housing the working class in the future—a pledge that never materialized. The fact that Forest Hills Gardens was a business investment—not a charity—was an important factor in its development. In its various promotional brochures, de Forest attempted to dispel the popular conception that the foundation was strictly philanthropic by reiterating that Forest Hills Gardens would be "conducted on strictly business principles for a fair profit" and that "whomever deals with it, whether as tenant or purchaser, will be expected to pay fair value for everything received."[23] Atterbury bridled at the term "model," used throughout the press to describe the project, writing in 1911 that it was "unfortunate that the somewhat misleading word 'model' must be applied to such an eminently practical scheme as this development of the Russell Sage Foundation, for the further reason that there is a kind of subtle odium which attaches to 'model' things of almost any kind, even when they are neither charitable nor philanthropic—a slightly sanctimonious atmosphere that is debilitating rather than stimulative of success."[24]

The first gathering of the Sage Foundation Realty Development Committee on April 29, 1909, marked the beginning of a series of meetings at which Forest Hills Gardens's character, layout, architecture, pricing, and advertising were discussed and determined. Atterbury and Olmsted met in the offices of William E. Harmon (1862–1928), a suburban real estate expert brought on to the project by de Forest to advise on the business end of the enterprise. Having successfully developed suburbs throughout the country by allowing purchasers to buy property with low down payments and installments, Harmon—partner of Wood, Harmon & Co.—had a firm command of how to market and price suburban properties.[25] Throughout the ensuing months, the group met frequently, toured suburban properties suggested by Harmon, and traveled to Baltimore by private railroad car to look over Roland Park, a residential community (1890–1920), parts of which were designed by Olmsted around similar planning and design ideas. Edward H. Bouton (1858–1941), the manager of Roland Park whom Olmsted knew well from his involvement in the project, was appointed general manager of the Sage Foundation Homes Company.[26]

In a fast-paced sequence of meetings in the spring and summer of 1909, Harmon, Olmsted, and Atterbury successfully convinced de Forest to purchase additional property south of the railroad station.[27] Records show that Olmsted and Atterbury worked closely together, discussing the development's architectural treatment over dinner at the Century Association and meeting at the architect's house at 23 East 62nd Street to sketch out plans and reserve locations for a school, playgrounds, club, casino, offices, public hall, church, and library.[28] Together and independently, they carefully analyzed the layout of the streets, the virtues of various house types, and the relationship of each to open space while the development committee continued to weigh the requirements and capacities of single-family block houses and semi-detached residences to create the best and most-affordable housing balance.

In his desire to design "something rather strikingly different in kind as well as in quality," Olmsted proposed to Atterbury the idea of contrasting their plan with the "geometrical character of the rectangular street system." He suggested a "smooth-flowing curvilinear system" but admitted he leaned more toward adopting an "accidental plan which has generally resulted from unpremeditated city growth, combining straight streets with subtle deflections, bends and variations in width."[29] Opposed to Olmsted's "accidental" plan, which he felt lacked educational value, Atterbury was more inclined to do "something distinctly reasonable and straightforward" with "detail treatment and architectural effects for the variety and picturesqueness" and recommended evolving a solution "from the fundamental conditions of the problem." As a combination of both formal and curvilinear systems, Atterbury proposed "a geometric beginning at the point of arrival, a slightly less, but still distinctly practical and reasonable layout of the next zone adjoining, in which I take it the 'civic center' or 'mall' so called would be, and a frankly curvilinear treatment in the remoter sections where we are placing detached houses only and where such treatment would be largely suggested by the present irregular topography." This approach, he reasoned, enabled the use of "such features as you find in some of the foreign model towns, in the shape of circles,

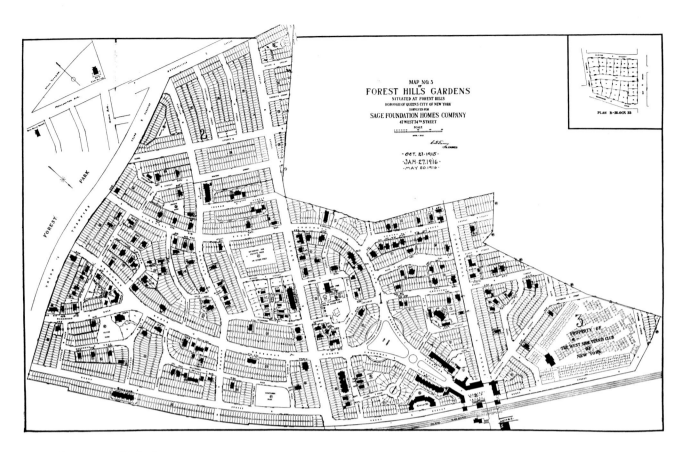

Progress plan. Forest Hills Gardens. Architecture 34 (August 1916): 164

terraces, and groups of houses in that part of the development, intermediate between the formal vestibule so to speak and the absolutely informal domestic section devoted to detached houses only."[30]

After much collaboration, Atterbury and Olmsted produced a sequential plan that moved from the more formal Station Square, the primary focal point and business hub, to the less-ordered outer reaches of the development. As the principal link to the city, the railroad station, to be jointly paid for by the Russell Sage Foundation, the Cord Meyer Development Company, and the Long Island Railroad, was integral to bringing people in and out of the community.[31] Atterbury and Olmsted's plan transferred "the principal architectural points of interest from the position adjoining the station and Continental Avenue diagonally into the Sage development, minimizing the plaza at the station, so as to represent more nearly the function of a vestibule."[32] Following this concept, the designers developed the square as a single composition enclosed by the station, a nine-story inn, and a series of three- and four-story apartments with Atterbury working through several schemes to balance the size of the square's buildings with the scale of the plaza.[33] With the station set up alongside the elevated tracks, Atterbury in essence cre-

ated a bank—or hill—to define the northern edge of the square. Three of the Gardens's major thoroughfares—Continental Avenue, Greenway North, and Greenway South—fanned out from the relative intimacy of the enclosed space to the far boundaries of the neighborhood. Initially, Olmsted proposed a "distinctly unsymmetrical scheme for the green, recognizing the predominant importance of Greenway North." However, since Atterbury felt that a deliberate plan seemed "forced," they adopted a symmetrical plan for the green, the residential heart of the community.[34]

While the Sage Foundation Homes Company intended to sell a large proportion of the land undeveloped, it planned ten initial housing groups, as the first phase of the operation, to set an architectural standard for the community. In an attempt to temper house prices, Atterbury and his associate Tompkins designed the houses to correspond to lot values, locating multi-family groups on the more expensive property closer to the station and the larger single-family dwellings nearer to Forest Park. As part of the first phase, the development committee tentatively decided to build two hundred forty-seven homes in the form of attached and semi-detached houses on the central section of the property. Seventy-four units of four

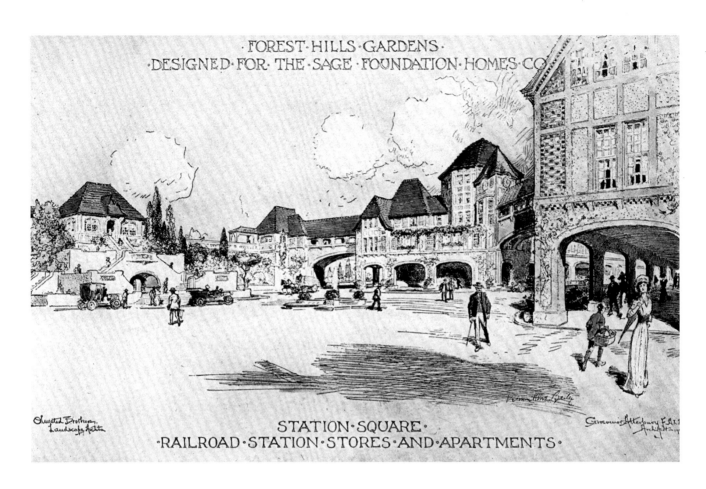

TOP *Station Square. View to the east.* Courtesy of the Frances Loeb Library, Harvard Graduate School of Design

BOTTOM *Station Square. View to the southeast.* *Arts and Decoration* 1 (January 1911): 118

to five rooms would be offered at $3,000, one hundred fourteen units of six to eight rooms at $4,000, and fifty-nine units of nine to eleven rooms at $8,000.[35] Later, Atterbury remarked that purchasers might be surprised "when it is realized that the larger number of the houses . . . are contiguous or block houses, and on plots often-times smaller than our usual city ones."[36]

Olmsted's landscape plan complemented Atterbury's attached houses and smaller lots. In laying out the Gardens, Olmsted used organizing principles that, according to the designer, were "coming to be more and more clearly recognized as part of the rapidly advancing expert knowledge of the subject."[37] Areas for common use and enjoyment, including the one-and-a-half-acre green directly southeast of Station Square and two small parks (Olivia and Hawthorne Parks), were integral to Olmsted's plan. In an ingenious innovation, he shortened lot depths on certain blocks to create private interior parks intended for shared use by the surrounding houses, which could be reabsorbed into the plan as additional house lots if they proved to be

unpopular.[38] To emphasize the Gardens's park-like setting, Olmsted maintained "direct, ample and convenient" through streets and designed the secondary streets as quiet residential retreats with a "cozy domestic character."[39] Prior to the foundation's purchase of the property, Cord Meyer had laid out the location of Ascan and Continental Avenues, two eighty-foot-wide thoroughfares fixed by the railroad bridges. Olmsted added two seventy-foot-wide, gently curved avenues (Greenway North and Greenway South) that radiated from Station Square toward Forest Park and set the width of the smaller inroads at forty feet to discourage traffic. He planted American elms on the main thoroughfares and specified a variety of trees on the local streets that would flower or bear fruit during different seasons to ensure color throughout the year.

Once Atterbury and Olmsted had formalized their plans, the committee estimated that properties in Forest Hills Gardens would be ready to sell in 1911. As the streets were graded, sewers laid, and temporary buildings erected, Atterbury continued to develop and refine plans for Sta-

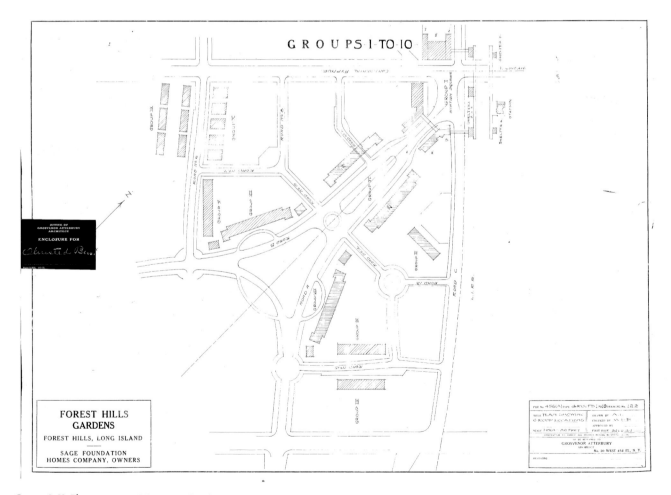

Groups I–X. Plan. Courtesy of the National Park Service, Frederick Law Olmsted National Historic Site

tion Square and his various housing groups. Construction was well under way by the early spring of 1911: the railroad station was nearing completion; the first levels of Station Square were taking shape; and the foundations of Group III, the first housing group consisting of ten two-story, seventeen-foot-wide houses, were laid. In June 1911, Forest Hills Gardens officially opened for sale. To create a "homogeneous and congenial community," the Homes Company required references and thoroughly investigated the character and standing of each applicant.[40] Overall, early buyers consisted of middle-class professionals. Of the 155 purchasers recorded in the foundation's Characterization List of Purchasers from February 1912, the majority were architects (11), clerks (17), educators (22), lawyers (8), and managers (19).[41] One month after opening, 172 lots had sold, and by September 1911, 153 buyers had purchased 364 lots.[42]

To spur lot sales, the Homes Company offered the first one hundred purchasers free architectural designs, specifications, grading, and planting plans.[43] Buyers were subject to a series of restrictions regarding setbacks and side yards, height and building width, and minimum house costs—a control intended to maintain the architectural integrity of the community—as well as an annual maintenance fee for lighting and park and garden upkeep. Atterbury, as supervising architect, approved all plans and alterations for houses designed by the Homes Company or the various designers brought in by the new landowners. In 1911, the development committee established an architectural department to prepare specifications and consult with customers, which operated under the general manager's direction. Bouton, well occupied by his duties in Roland Park, resigned as manager in 1911, and John M. Demarest (1877–1935), a real estate executive from New Orleans, assumed the position.

As construction progressed throughout 1911, Atterbury's architectural groupings began to emerge from the scaffolding. By incorporating arching covered bridges over the intersecting thoroughfares, Atterbury expressed the nine-story inn and various three-to-four-story apartments surrounding Station Square as one cohesive visual unit. He furthered this effect by using materials rich in color and texture and accentuating the continuous rhythm of the roofline—a bold sequence of turrets, domes, jerkin-headed gables, dormer windows, and naïve chimney caps.[44] Crowned with an octagonal dome and flèche, his tower rose commandingly above the square and stood as the apex of the group. Architectural critic Samuel Howe noted that

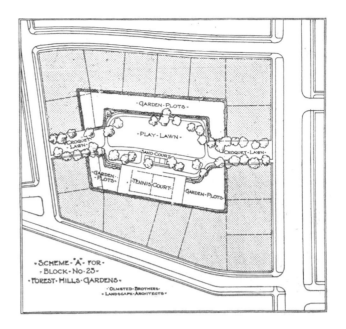

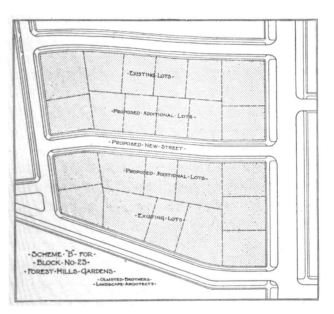

TOP *Scheme for interior park. Scribner's Magazine* 52 (July 1912): 30

ABOVE *Scheme without interior park. Scribner's Magazine* 52 (July 1912): 31

the square's soaring tower and cloister-like arcades and passageways gave the impression of a "medieval cathedral city." The stairs and terraces of the elevated stucco railroad station, located to the north, spilled down into the brick-paved plaza, "giving something of the terraced garden effect of the northern section of Italy."[45]

As the Gardens's commercial section, Station Square housed a variety of stores, offices, and restaurants at street level. The Forest Hills Inn functioned as the community's social hub with tennis, squash, billiards, and an enclosed tea garden attractively organized around a fountain, pergo-

Station Square and the Forest Hills Inn. Courtesy of the Frances Loeb Library, Harvard Graduate School of Design

las, and flowerbeds. Occupying the upper floors of all the buildings on the square, it provided 230 rooms, arranged in suites from one to four rooms, included nonhousekeeping apartments for men and women, and connected directly to the railroad platforms. Advertised as a "modern fireproof apartment hotel open all year," it featured steel skeleton construction combined with hollow terra-cotta blocks reinforced with rods and concrete.[46]

Atterbury's innovative use of color and materials deepened the artistic appeal of the architecture and set the tone for other buildings throughout the development. A master of color and texture, the architect primarily used lammie

and red and brown shingle tile, laid at random, to blend with the wall surfaces. He resourcefully used cast concrete to represent details, such as half-timbering, grilles, chimneys, and corbelling, and applied pebbles, mica, quartz, and broken tile treated with muriatio acid to draw out the different shades—a technique he developed in 1909 with Charles E. Pellow, a chemistry professor at Columbia University. Louis Graves, writer for *Building Progress*, was particularly "impressed with the thoroughness with which things [were] done" at Forest Hills. He noted that "on one corner of the property is a sort of factory and test house, where building materials are made and tested before they are put into use. For example, the architects may decide upon a reddish stucco for a certain group of houses. Then follow a series of experiments to determine just what proportion of chipped tile ought to be used, how big the chips should be to give the most satisfying effect, and to what extent the mixture ought to be treated with acid to bring out the rich coloring."[47] Atterbury carefully designed the development's ornamental iron lamps and street signs, delicately wrought in the shape of commuters rushing for

Group VI and view of the Forest Hills Inn from Greenway Terrace. The Sage Foundation Homes Company, *Forest Hills Gardens* (December 1913)

Balcony showing use of precast decorative brushed concrete.
Concrete-Cement Age 6 (January 1915): 6

trains, birds, animals, trees, and the Russell Sage Foundation logo, after bracket-form lampposts Olmsted had admired in Germany and Switzerland.

With his housing groups, Atterbury struck a fine balance between variety and economy. "Good collective planning," he maintained, would secure a certain measure of economy. When buildings were "intelligently planned as one group, the average width of the lot might be reduced twenty percent and the conditions be really better for each individual house."[48] Group III, located on Slocum Crescent, was the first group to be completed. Consisting of ten seventeen-foot-wide single-family dwellings of six to eight rooms, each house contained a parlor, dining room, kitchen, bath, and four bedrooms. To break the monotony of the row-house strip, Atterbury articulated the primary facade of the block as three distinct sections with varying roof and entry-level patterns. He grouped the three houses on either end together with gable fronts, Palladian windows, and arched porches while differentiating the four interior dwellings with jerkin-headed dormer windows at the third floor and shared front-door overhangs. Like the Station Square buildings, Atterbury used a similar combination of lammie brick, brushed concrete stucco, and red roof tiling.

On either side of the village green, Atterbury designed nine larger, more-impressive twenty-six-foot-wide row houses (Group VI-A and B), each consisting of ten to twelve rooms. An extension of Station Square, the pair of crescent-shaped house groups on Greenway Terrace, at the mouth of Greenway North and Greenway South, displayed a similar picturesque quality and attention to detail. Also composed of precast hollow sections filled with concrete in situ, the buildings' brick walls were complemented by precast concrete window jambs, lintels, sills, cornices, gable trimmings, and half-timbering. Atterbury enlivened the facades of the row houses by creating shifts in the planes of the street wall with trellised balconies, turrets, and protruding end houses. In addition, he anchored the facade of Group VI-A with a four-story gable and two turrets that marked an arched driveway tunneling through the block. Aside from the two-family house located over the central driveway, each residence was accessed through an arching gate and a private garden enclosed with stone walls.

According to firm associate W. F. Anderson, interiors were designed as "simple yet attractive and practical" spaces with hardwood floors in all the principal rooms and white wood in the bedrooms.[49] However, Clarence True, an architect briefly employed by the Homes Company, thought the

LANTERN·AT·FOREST·HILLS·GARDENS
· GROSVENOR · ATTERBURY · ARCHITECT ·

LANTERN·AT·FOREST·HILLS·GARDEN
· GROSVENOR · ATTERBURY · ARCHITECT ·

Lanterns. Architecture 34 (August 1916): pl. 125

Group III, Slocum Crescent. The Brickbuilder 21
(December 1912): pl. 158

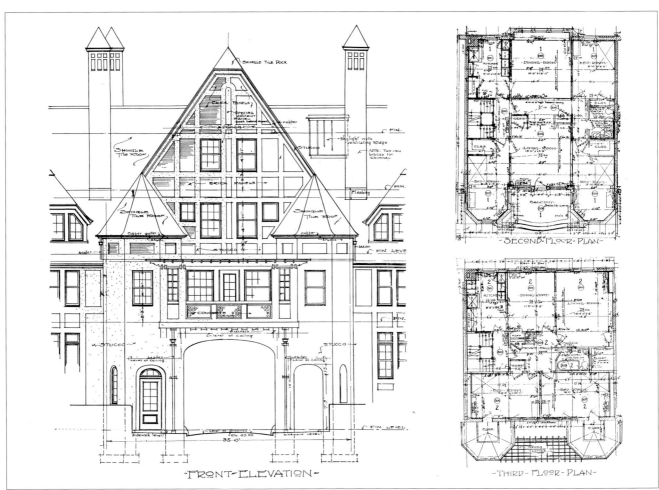

TOP *Group VI, Greenway Terrace. Architecture 34*
(August 1916): pl. 120

BOTTOM *Group VI. Elevation and plans. Architecture*
34 (August 1916): pl. 121

164

architect's sparing touch verged on substandard. In remarking that the expense of the project would impede its success, he observed that the interiors of Group VI were "cramped and plain even to cheapness and inconveniently arranged" while its "whole cost [was] being put in a very handsome and expensive exterior."[50]

Toward the end of 1910, the development committee temporarily abandoned additional row-house plans and moved forward with groups of detached and semi-detached homes at less central locations. The members also decided to invite outside architects, such as Aymar Embury II, Wilson Eyre (1858–1944), Lewis Colt Albro (1876–1924), Harrie T. Lindeberg (1880–1959), and J. T. Tubby (1875–1958), to design some of the groups to create an "agreeable variety . . . from differing methods of treatment" which would "avoid a noticeable distinction between houses built by the company and houses erected by others."[51] Located on Beechknoll Road, Atterbury's first group (Group XI, 1912) was composed of two detached (seven rooms) and two semi-detached (six rooms) brick and shingle houses, all of which faced inward onto a common garden. The individual homes, each situated on a fifty-foot-wide lot, presented their gable ends to the street, while the semi-detached dwellings, located between the two outer houses, were recessed with their long ends outward; kitchens opened to the rear and drying yards were concealed from the street. Aymar Embury II noted the "[importance of] the relations which exist between the four."[52] By organizing the houses in such a manner, Atterbury maximized light, air, and appearance on the midblock lots and improved the outlook of each house.

As firm employee Charles C. May remarked, "The plan of Forest Hills provides in most cases that the vision be satisfied—either the vista has a group or important buildings at its extremity; a turn of the roadway lends decision and interest to the perspective; or the buildings are arranged to form a confining frame for a view of open country beyond."[53] Atterbury's housing group at the juncture of Greenway North and Markwood Road (Group XII, 1912) effectively closed the long view up Greenway North. A culminating moment in the street picture, the large crescent-shaped building, composed of two ten-room homes, curved inward to follow the irregular lot line and presented a symmetrical, multilayered facade to the street. To the rear, Atterbury designed two detached seven-room homes parallel to the central block and four garages set on axis.

Group XI, Beechknoll Road. The Sage Foundation Homes Company, *Forest Hills Gardens* (December 1913)

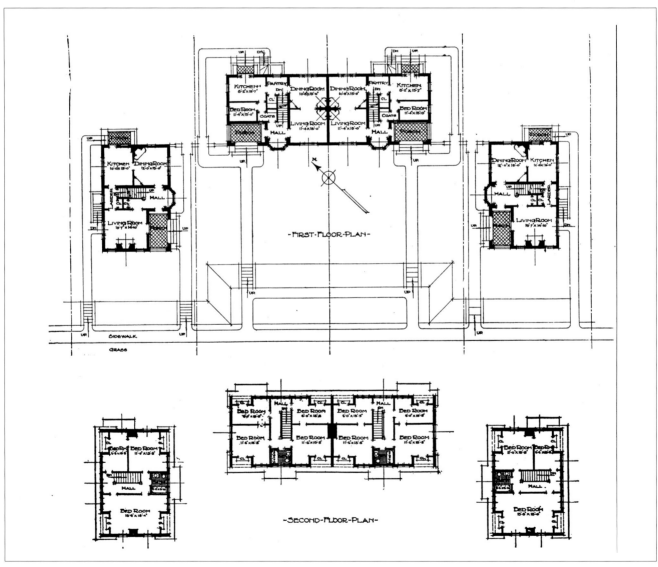

TOP *Group X.* The Sage Foundation Homes Company, *Forest Hills Gardens* (December 1913)

BOTTOM *Group XI. First- and second-floor plans.* The Sage Foundation Homes Company, *Forest Hills Gardens* (December 1913)

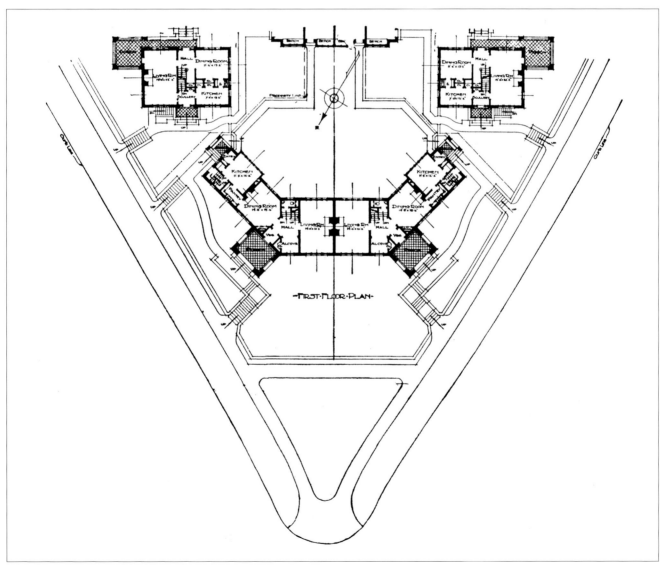

TOP *Group XII, Greenway North and Markwood
Road. Architecture* 34 (August 1916): 170

BOTTOM *Group XII. Plan. Architecture* 34 (August 1916): 170

T. Commerford Martin house, Greenway North. The Sage Foundation
Homes Company, *Forest Hills Gardens* (December 1913)

Despite Atterbury's innovative planning approach, one critic noted that the complexity of the roofing angles and the awkward relationship of the detached houses to the side street detracted from the group's overall effectiveness.[54]

The detached houses in the Gardens designed by Atterbury and other approved architects—such as William Lawrence Bottomley (1883–1951), Aymar Embury II, Robert Farrington, Eugene Schoen (1880–1957), Alfred Fellheimer (1875–1959), Julian L. Peabody, Albert E. Wilson, and Archibald M. Brown—created an exceptional depth of character and variety. In addition to his row-house blocks and groups of detached and semi-detached

residences, Atterbury designed well over fifty freestanding homes, for both the Homes Company and individual clients, which displayed the range of the architect's palette and "[suggested] the homes of rich men . . . because their proportions [had] been carefully thought out, their detail studied lovingly, and their color planned by artists who [understood] and [respected] color."[55] Among Atterbury's first houses were those originally purchased by Thomas H. Todd, founder and publisher of the *Long Island City Daily Star*; electrical engineer T. Commerford Martin; and cotton broker Robert M. Harriss, all located along Greenway North.

Atterbury evoked the Elizabethan style in his scheme for the Martin house, a center-hall design, deepening the color and texture of its facades with shades of buff-colored brick veneer laid in Flemish bond.[56] For the seven-room Todd house, Atterbury paired lammie brick, laid in headers, with brushed concrete stucco panels, producing a design that responded to the site's hilly contours. While locating the dining room and kitchen on the first floor, he improved the living room and adjoining porch's outlook by placing them on the second story with an exterior stone stair for access.[57] With its steeply pitched roof, dormers, and jerkin-headed gables, the eight-room Tudor-style Harriss residence displayed Atterbury's ability to create interesting facades from a relatively simple plan by varying the layers and planes of the roof and street wall.[58] Always encompassing a number of porches and piazzas, Atter-

Thomas H. Todd house, Greenway North. The Sage Foundation
Homes Company, *Forest Hills Gardens* (December 1913)

bury's house designs integrated ample indoor-outdoor space to bring in sunlight and air and increase the living area. Olmsted, who worked with Atterbury on the site plans for the Gardens's earlier homes, incorporated terraces, creepers, wisteria, lush and fragrant flowerbeds, and trees into the landscape to create colorful gardens and yards.[59]

While the size and style of his work ranged from modest brick cottages to elaborate Tudor manses, Atterbury and his associates always took care to set each design apart. At the smaller end of the spectrum was Mary E. Taylor's charming tapestry-brick Colonial-style cottage on Puritan Avenue, while H. H. Buckley's English-style residence on Markwood Road stood as one of the largest and most architecturally distinct houses in the community.[60]

Robert M. Harriss house, Greenway North. The Sage Foundation Homes Company, *Forest Hills Gardens* (December 1913)

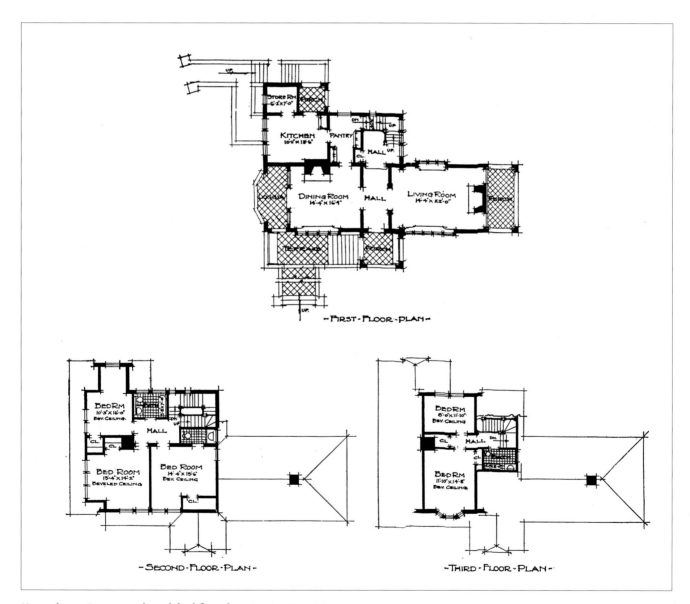

Harriss house. First-, second-, and third-floor plans. The Sage Foundation Homes Company, *Forest Hills Gardens* (December 1913)

TOP *Mary E. Taylor house, Shorthill Road.*
Architectural Catalog (April 1918)

BOTTOM *H. H. Buckley house, Markwood*
Road, 2007. Jonathan Wallen

John Almy Tompkins 2nd house, Deepdene Road.
Country Life in America 43 (December 1922): 72

Tompkins house. Studio. Country Life in America 43
(December 1922): 73

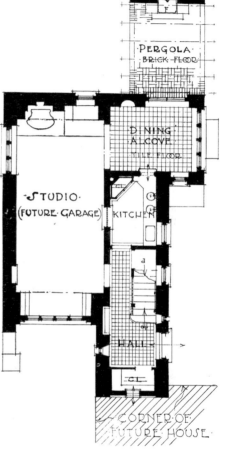

Tompkins house. First-floor plan. Country Life in
America 43 (December 1922): 73

Like Atterbury's designs for large private estates, the Buckley house featured a heavy stone base, half-timber details, lammie-brick panels, and a stair tower. Atterbury's associate John A. Tompkins was also a Gardens resident; his English-style cottage on Deepdene Road, which he shared with editor and writer Samuel A. Chapin, was among the Gardens's most enchanting homes. Designed to convert to a garage once an adjacent house was constructed (never built), the native stone and brick-trimmed cottage enclosed a large studio with soft gray cement and stone walls, brick fireplace, wrought-iron grilles, two upstairs bedrooms, and a dining alcove with leaded-glass casement windows that opened onto a pergola and yard planted by Olmsted.[61]

Over the ensuing years, Atterbury and Tompkins designed several of the community's landmark buildings, including the West Side Tennis Club and the Church-in-the-Gardens. In 1913, the West Side Tennis Club purchased ten acres from the Homes Company between Burns and Dartmouth Streets so as to relocate from its cramped location on Amsterdam Avenue and 117th Street. Recognizing the benefits of luring the club to Forest Hills, the development committee offered to negotiate its land purchase with the Cord Meyer Company and to provide its

TOP *West Side Tennis Club, Tennis Place. Entrance facade. Architectural Forum* 28 (June 1918): pl. 72

BOTTOM *The Church-in-the-Gardens, Ascan Avenue. Architecture* 34 (August 1916): pl. 122

West Side Tennis Club. Courtside facade.
Architectural Forum 28 (June 1918): pl. 73

services free to develop the site, up to a certain limit. Not only would its location west of Continental Avenue create an appropriate boundary to the community, but also the committee felt that its prestige would undoubtedly draw purchasers and spur additional house sales.[62]

Eager for their club to assume a prominent position in American tennis, club members commissioned Atterbury to design "one of the finest [clubhouses] in the country . . . equipped with every modern convenience" and Olmsted to consult on the layout of the club's grounds and positioning of its fifty courts.[63] Built exclusively for tennis, Atterbury's three-story Tudor-style stucco building was completed in 1914. To the street, he presented an austere symmetrical facade divided by a large central chimney while designating the porches, piazzas, and upper viewing deck to the courtside. The building's thin rectangular footprint allowed all of the major rooms, including the central assembly room, café, bar, and second-floor locker room, to enjoy views of tennis and the stadium.

In a gesture of religious spirit, Mrs. Sage generously donated $50,000 to build the Church-in-the-Gardens as a gift to the community. After the parish purchased land on the corner of Ascan Avenue and Greenway North, Atterbury and Tompkins designed a charming Norman-style church building, completed in 1915, steeped with the "old-world character" embodied by village churches in Europe.[64] The architects' creative massing and use of materials gave rise to a unique and stunning design that, as Tompkins described, "was planned as a simple, unostentatious little country church" that was "not built in any particular style."[65] Using native stone for the walls with antiqued half-timber cypress details in the chancel and above the entrance porch, they gave the building an ageless quality rich in texture and color. Atterbury's striking square tower, capped by truncated gables and a wrought-iron flèche, echoed the silhouette of the inn on Station Square. Inside the church's main auditorium, capable of holding 250 parishioners, the architects accentuated the integrity of the room's architectural features. By choosing simple pews and plain tile floors for the interior, they drew attention to the muscular stone walls and the pattern of the exposed trusses and roof timbers. The beauty of the details—such as the amber glass in the windows; the chancel's leaded-glass rondels; the wrought-iron light fixtures; and the gold chancel screen in the shape of biblical figures, flowers, symbols, and quotations with accents of color—was highlighted against the rustic simplicity of the space.

For the block located at the head of the green (known as block twelve), Atterbury and Olmsted envisioned a monumental feature to close the vista from Station Square.

Despite the various schemes produced over the years for houses, community centers, movie theaters, and apartment buildings, the elliptically shaped site sat empty throughout Atterbury's tenure as supervising architect. In 1920, Atterbury executed several designs, including one for an apartment house with an asymmetrical tower that would "extend the architectural interest which now centers in the station square more nearly into the heart of the development."[66] Olmsted, however, was concerned that the tower would be "somewhat restless and over-full of effort at the picturesque" and felt that the landscaping of the green would need to be reworked for the scheme to succeed.[67] Over the next twenty years, as block twelve became the focus of a prolonged lawsuit over the question of whether an apartment house could be erected on the site, Atterbury proposed a number of different schemes, including a group of single-family homes for a community group (1923), a picturesque three-tower apartment complex for 39 fami-

RIGHT *View of the undeveloped block twelve from the tower of the inn.* The Sage Foundation Homes Company, *Forest Hills Gardens* (December 1913)

BELOW *Scheme for block twelve, 1925.* Courtesy of the Division of Rare and Manuscript Collections, Cornell University Library

SKETCH for DEVELOPMENT OF BLOCK 12

Two concrete-panel houses at Sewaren, New Jersey.
Standardized Housing Corporation, *The Manufacture of*
Standardized Houses (1918): 23

lies (1924), and later, both a six- and a nine-story building (1938).[68] In 1933, the Court of Appeals ruled that an apartment house could be constructed but, much to Atterbury's consternation, none of his plans were adapted. The Gardens Corporation moved forward with Steward Wagner (1887–1958) and Alfred Fellheimer's six-story, 96-family apartment house, The Leslie, completed in 1944.[69]

Atterbury experimented with cost-effective materials and techniques—such as brushed precast concrete elements—to build low-cost quality construction because, as he revealed, he could "find no real reason why the garden suburb [would] enable us to raise the standard of living without raising the cost of living, except insofar as we can accomplish saving of waste by an increase of efficiency either in design, development, or construction."[70] Atterbury had been investigating building materials under the auspices of the Russell Sage Foundation since 1908 with the goal of establishing an economic fireproof construction system for workingmen's homes that was architecturally flexible and based on the best available materials, technol-

ogy, and aesthetics. With help from his office staff, after three years of work in the laboratory and in the field, Atterbury successfully developed a prefabricated concrete-panel system capable of erecting the shell of a small house in five working days with minimal labor. He went on build a diminutive shack on 64th Street and two small two-story workingmen's cottages located on lots that the Sage Foundation had acquired rent-free from the Sewaren Improvement Company in New Jersey, an enterprise owned by de Forest's wife's family.[71]

Atterbury's system involved standardized hollow concrete slabs, cast from steel molds in a factory, which were then transported to the site and placed on the building with a power crane. Damp-proof, fireproof, and maintenance-free, a typical eight-foot-high and nine-inch-thick wall section weighed one-and-a-half tons and consisted of two one-and-a-half-inch concrete membranes with a six-inch air space in between. Significantly reducing labor and expense, Atterbury's process could produce a precast concrete-panel dwelling for $2,020 as opposed to a terra-cotta

Group II. Construction. Standardized Housing Corporation,
The Manufacture of Standardized Houses (1918): 25

block house ($2,536) or a brick house with concrete floors ($2,566) of the same size, overhead notwithstanding.[72]

Atterbury applied his research at Sewaren to the construction of Group II, a crescent-shaped row of ten thirteen-foot and four twenty-four-foot single-family homes located on Burns Street. In early 1910, the development committee endorsed Atterbury's pioneering construction techniques, for which there was "at present no exact precedent," and approved a concrete-panel factory on Burns Street, located close to the site.[73] Also providing a testing ground for terra-cotta, concrete blocks, cement, roofing materials, and finishes, the factory consisted of a large casting shed, storage yards, and an electric crane. From the casting shed, partially hardened sections of molded cement were lifted onto cars and moved into the storage yard on movable industrial rails for drying. They were then finished with aggregate on the exterior-facing side and grout on the interior side. Once cured, they were transported on the tracks to the building site, picked off the car by an electric crane, and set into place. Atterbury's system enabled workers to complete the shell of one thirteen-foot-wide house, made up of 140 panels, in nine days, after which plumb-

ing, heating, and plaster were installed. Nailable concrete, or Nailcrete, also developed by Atterbury in connection with the Russell Sage Foundation, was used as the nailing base for wood flooring and roof coating as well as the mortar for laying up partitions and furring blocks.[74] However, due to its high overhead, Atterbury's pioneering work at Forest Hills was more economically suited for larger groups of houses and was regarded more as "a contribution to the science of building with precast units than a successful investment."[75]

When completed in 1913, Group II compared favorably to the other housing blocks in the development. Frederick Squires, writing for *Concrete-Cement Age*, enthusiastically noted that "the group holds its own in color, texture and design in spite of the fact that it is composed of 'standard' sections made out of ordinary sand, gravel and cement, and that the manufacture of the floor and wall sections of the entire group of houses was accomplished with only six steel molds."[76] With Group II, Atterbury effectively demonstrated the architectural flexibility of his system. By inserting four twenty-four-foot-wide composite houses with octagonal parlors between spans of thirteen-foot-wide stan-

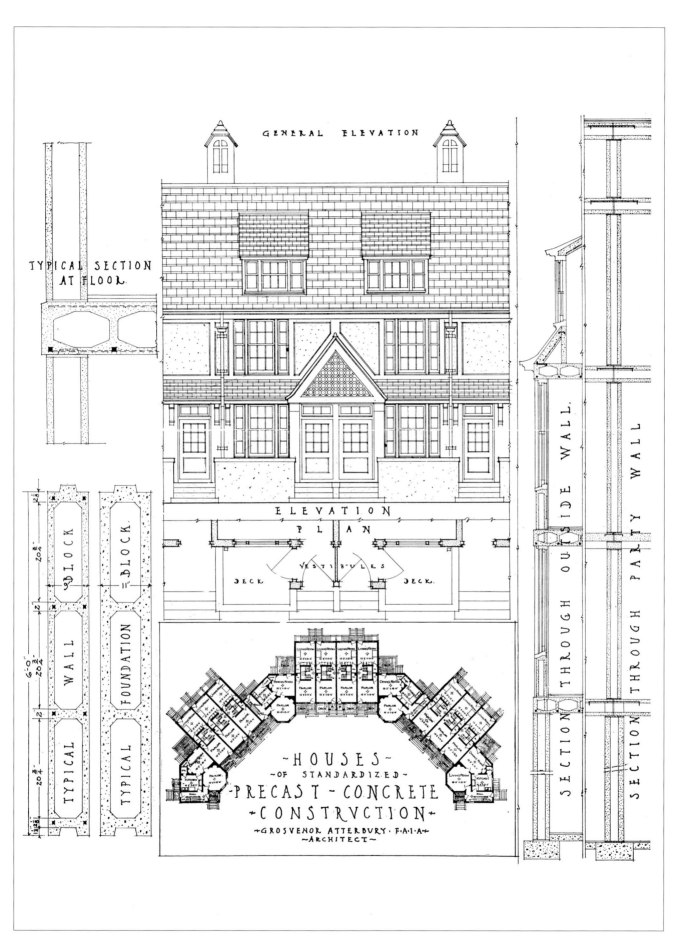

GENERAL ELEVATION

TYPICAL SECTION AT FLOOR.

ELEVATION

PLAN

VESTIBULES

DECK   DECK.

TYPICAL WALL BLOCK

TYPICAL FOUNDATION BLOCK.

SECTION THROUGH OUTSIDE WALL.

SECTION THROUGH PARTY WALL

~HOUSES~
~OF STANDARDIZED~
~PRECAST~CONCRETE
~CONSTRVCTION~
~GROSVENOR ATTERBVRY·F·A·I·A·
~ARCHITECT~

*Group II. Houses of standardized precast
concrete construction. Architecture and Building 46*
(February 1914): 82

ABOVE *Group II, Burns Street. Architecture* 34 (August 1916): pl. 124

RIGHT *Group II. Concrete detail.* Standardized Housing Corporation, *The Manufacture of Standardized Houses* (1918): 28

Group II. Interior. Standardized Housing Corporation, *The Manufacture of Standardized Houses* (1918): 27

dardized houses, he broke up any monotony in the design; his roofline, punctuated with chimneys, turrets, decorative panels, dormers, and overhangs, and the aggregate-enhanced brushed facades gave the group the same picturesque quality that characterized the architect's other buildings in the development. In all, Atterbury applied his prefabricated techniques to approximately forty houses at Forest Hills, including two rows of houses (Group 48 and 49) in 1918 and 1919 as well as a group of semi-detached homes (Group 56) in 1920.

Building continued at an even pace throughout the 1910s. By 1913, ten groups of houses had been completed, four were underway, and thirteen were in abeyance. Land buyers had built forty-four homes and the Homes Company six.[77] Two years later, one hundred ninety-two residences were up, and Atterbury's Group XXXIII at Middlemay Place and Bow Street—which consisted of two detached and two semi-detached fieldstone houses—was

in the midst of construction.[78] However, as new houses went up, a disparity in quality began to emerge between Atterbury's work and that of less-qualified designers. In his role as supervising architect, Atterbury had "for some time been worrying over the difficulties . . . in maintaining the degree of quality and distinction, in the small house, that is necessary if the place as a whole is to maintain the standard we have set." To counteract the "gradual spread of the commonplace suburban character," he suggested interspersing group houses at important points throughout the property, pointing out that "the group plan—no matter how small the unit it contains—at once makes good proportions and simpler lines possible."[79] Olmsted recommended establishing an official list of architects to discourage purchasers from hiring incompetent designers and proposed delaying house approval until after grading plans had been submitted to force buyers to focus on the landscape—an element they tended to ignore.[80]

Group XXXIII, Middlemay Place.
Architecture 34 (August 1916): pl. 123

By 1922, the foundation "was of the opinion that its chief purposes in organizing and developing Forest Hills Gardens had been accomplished" and sold its Homes Company stock to a syndicate headed by vice president and general manager John Demarest.[81] Though, by that point, more than four hundred houses had been built, Atterbury regretted the foundation's withdrawal from the project since he felt the development had not passed its "danger point."[82] When the transfer of ownership occurred, Atterbury was not immediately retained as supervisor, and for several months the community was without architectural guidance. As the architect became more and more concerned about the situation, several houses went up and, while he continued to offer his services, no decision about his position was made. In a plea to the community council, he wrote, "I trust you realize that both Mr. Olmsted and I have the interest of Forest Hills Gardens so much at heart that we would go a

long way in our efforts to maintain the standards which have not only involved our own time and effort during the past ten years but have likewise meant a very real contribution and in certain cases some sacrifice undoubtedly by the property owners themselves."[83] Subsequently, Atterbury was officially named supervising architect of the Gardens Corporation, a body organized to maintain the living and aesthetic conditions of Forest Hills Gardens.

Although the syndicate upheld the covenants established by the Homes Company and continued to administer design restrictions, over time Atterbury found his responsibilities growing increasingly tedious.[84] The majority of the designs submitted by lot owners needed to be substantially modified to meet standards, and as a result, the architect's workload doubled. Conveying his frustration in a letter to the president of the Gardens Corporation, Lawrence Abbott, he complained that "the very fact that it is known that plans are coming to [my] office for criticism doubtless influences some people to be less careful as to whom they employ in the first instance as their architect or builder."[85] By 1936, Atterbury was more removed from the project, and his associates carried out much of the work; however, at that point, they were not as fully vested since the quality of design had further deteriorated and too much work was expected for little remuneration.[86] The Gardens Corporation noted that "where [Atterbury's office] used to comb the plans with a fine toothed comb making all too many corrections, they now hardly mark the plans at all and hold them until our builders are frantic, then shove them through and stamp them as approved with such cursory attention that I never feel sure they have even been looked at. For $40.00 per house I think we may naturally expect more than this. We are forced to infer that the Atterbury interest in Forest Hills Gardens has waned and we have seriously considered doing away with the service all together."[87] In 1940, Atterbury renounced his role as supervising architect and Steward Wagner took over the position as a volunteer.

While the press criticized Forest Hills Gardens's narrow reach, its creators were clear from the beginning that they never intended its housing to appeal to the city's poor, as England's garden cities, such as Letchworth, had. They did, however, expect their experiment, as a business proposition, to generate a small return and weighed its success as an educational example against its economic viability. As expressed by John Glenn, "failure to make the project a reasonable commercial success would mean that the educational policy of the foundation would miscarry."[88] Atterbury similarly expounded upon the subject, writing that "the so-called model town must succeed on a commercial basis. It must do even better in this respect than the ordinary commercial or speculative development. Its educational, architectural and sociological possibilities, therefore, in the last analysis depend on its economic success."[89] However, at the time of the foundation's sale in 1922, the foundation's books revealed bleak numbers, showing a loss of over $350,000.[90] Despite the failure of the project as a business venture, de Forest held faith in the foundation's investment and firmly stressed that "from every other point of view—planning, restrictions, maintenance charge, basis of sale, investigation of prospective purchasers—it has been to me entirely successful and has accomplished what the Sage Foundation intended."[91]

Although aesthetically Forest Hills Gardens was a triumph, the influential example its creators strove to set was not as sweeping as they might have hoped. Due to the price of land, Forest Hills quickly grew into an upper-middle-class enclave instead of a development for persons of "modest means," and as a result, designers of upscale suburbs rather than of low-income housing were more apt to absorb its design and planning lessons. For example, in Shaker Heights (1912), an upper-class suburb outside of Cleveland, O. P. and M. J. Sweringen similarly focused on creating a unified design, establishing stringent architectural standards and regulations to maintain its integrity. While Atterbury's carefully planned housing groups, semi-detached homes, and economic methods of construction worked well in Forest Hills, they did not become widespread models for development since the single-family detached house was, and continues to be, the American ideal, and Atterbury's prefabricated system was better suited for larger building endeavors.

During World War One, a tremendous number of new towns were proposed, and many of them rapidly built, under the auspices of the U.S. Housing Corporation (a new division of the Labor Department established in 1918) and the U.S. Shipping Board's Emergency Fleet Corporation, to accommodate itinerant workers involved in war-related industries and shipbuilding.[92] Yorkship Village (1918) outside Camden, New Jersey, which provided much-needed housing for the New York Shipbuilding Corporation's employees, exemplified the type of well-planned wartime industrial community that the Forest Hills Gardens model inspired. Designed by Electus D. Litchfield (1872–1952), it contained 1,700 Federal-style row houses, detached, and semi-detached houses, in varying sizes and Colonial detail, set on winding tree-lined streets.[93] In addition to light and airy dwellings with up-to-date appliances, Litchfield's layout included a public square and ample outdoor recreational space. At Atlantic Heights in Portsmouth, New Hampshire (1918), the Boston firm of Walter Harrington Kilham (1868–1948) and James Cleveland Hopkins (1873–1938) incorporated fifty-five four-room semi-detached houses modeled after Atterbury's roomier version at Forest Hills Gardens.[94] The construction of well-designed developments proliferated during the war years; however, the few industrial communities built after its end faltered in quality.

Gardens resident Clarence Arthur Perry (1872– 1944), a planning theorist and the Russell Sage Foundation's associate director of recreation, was perhaps the most influential figure in popularizing Forest Hills Gardens's community appeal. Basing his "neighborhood unit" concept on his own

*Russell Sage Foundation Building, 122–30 East
22nd Street, New York, New York.* Museum of the
City of New York, Wurts Collection, #120662

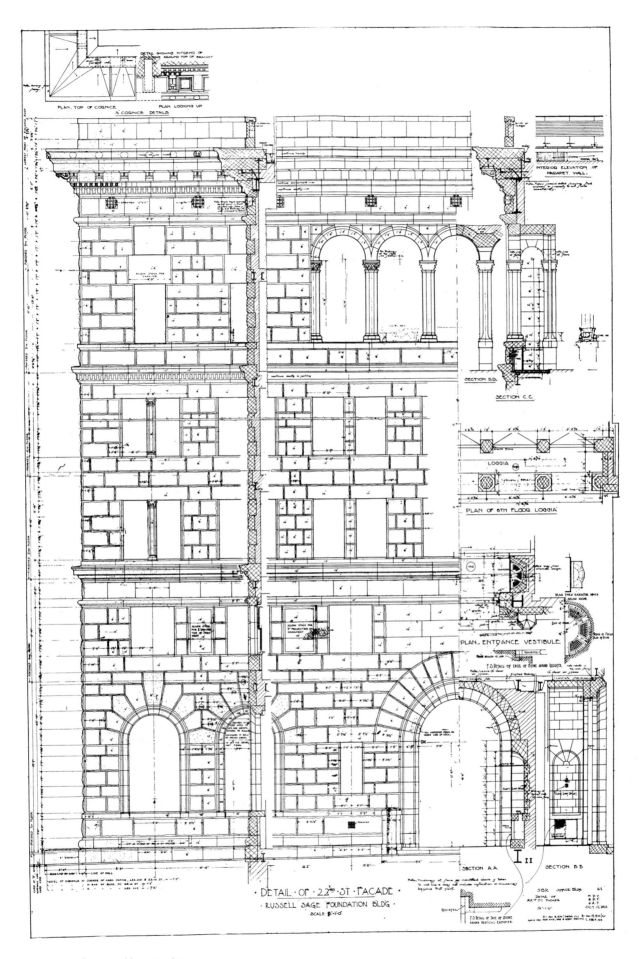

Sage Foundation Building. 22nd Street entrance.
American Architect 108 (October 20, 1915)

TOP *Sage Foundation Building. Detail of 22nd Street entrance. American Architect* 108 (October 20, 1915)

BOTTOM *Sage Foundation Building. Sculptural details by John Donnolly and Eliseo V. Ricci. American Architect* 108 (October 20, 1915)

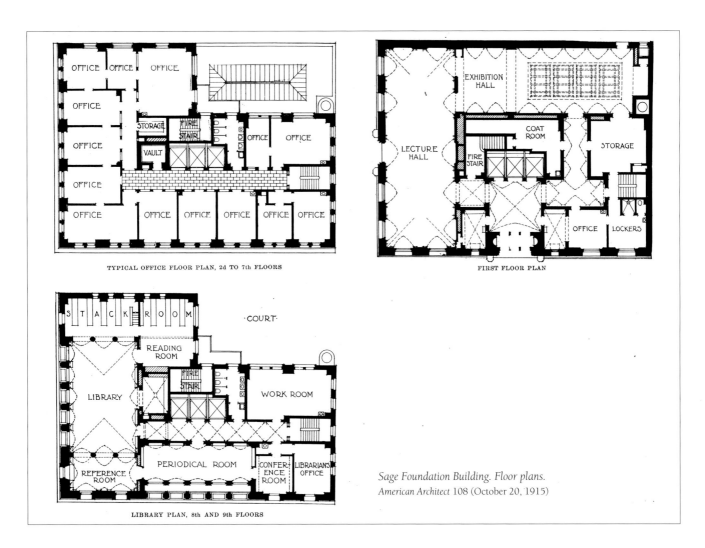

TYPICAL OFFICE FLOOR PLAN, 2d TO 7th FLOORS

FIRST FLOOR PLAN

LIBRARY PLAN, 8th AND 9th FLOORS

Sage Foundation Building. Floor plans.
American Architect 108 (October 20, 1915)

living experiences there, Perry stressed the importance of physical, educational, social, and recreational facilities in shaping a neighborhood. His theories came to be widely exercised by city planners and adopted by such architects as Clarence Stein (1882–1975) and Henry Wright (1878–1936) in the design of Sunnyside Gardens, Queens (1924–28), and Radburn, New Jersey (1929).

While in the throes of the development of Forest Hills Gardens, the Russell Sage Foundation embarked on another building project at the southwest corner of Lexington Avenue and 22nd Street in 1912 which, at Mrs. Sage's urging, would simultaneously serve as a headquarters for the organization and a memorial to her husband. As a result, "more thought was given to beauty of design, materials, and construction, and more money was spent to obtain it, than otherwise would have been deemed suitable."[95] Already engaged by the foundation, Atterbury was the logical choice for architect. De Forest selected an appropriate site adjacent to the Princeton Club—Stanford White's former home—and across the street from the United Charities Building, where the organization located its offices.[96]

Atterbury looked to the palaces of sixteenth-century Florence as inspiration to express the stature and significance of the foundation. His monumental nine-story palazzo, carried out in a warm buff-colored Kingwood sandstone—a material used only elsewhere in the Synod Hall of the Cathedral of St. John the Divine—gave the impression of weight and importance.[97] The heavily textured quality of the facades, produced by the rock-faced ashlar, set off the delicate ironwork and leaded-glass detail surrounding the main entrance on 22nd Street and created a sturdy base to the building's massive cornice decorated with copper rosettes, putti, and owls' heads. In his praise of the design, Rudolf Hempel, of *The American Architect*, observed, "Mr. Atterbury gives fine evidence of his originality as a designer, coupled with a sense of restraint and good taste. It is traditional without being academic, and original without being unscholarly."[98]

On the ninth floor, Atterbury incorporated six granite panels communicating the foundation's purpose, carved by noted sculptors John Donnolly and Eliseo V. Ricci. In 1922, the architect began working on a second set of reliefs to be carved into granite blocks above the ground

floor's arching windows. They consisted of a series of crests—René Paul Chambellan's first known commission in New York—conveying the foundation's various goals and ethics: religion, education, civics, justice, health, work, play, and housing.[99] To represent housing, Atterbury chose honeycombs, which, according to the architect's research, were "the most perfect examples of housing

to be found anywhere—well built, ventilated and protected by the whole community."[100] The iconography of Atterbury's triptych above the main entrance reinforced the foundation's educational focus and its goal to improve social and living conditions in America.

To accommodate the foundation's employees, visiting scholars, and researchers, Atterbury designed a succession of architecturally rich interiors. The stone ashlar in the intimate vaulted entrance and elevator hall off the 22nd Street entrance gave the space an ageless quality. The heaviness of the walls offset the intricate metalwork of the doors, grilles, and chandeliers. Along Lexington Avenue, Atterbury located a 200-person lecture hall, carried out in a neutral green, that connected to a top-lit exhibition hall to the west. Far removed from the street noise, Atterbury's bright and airy library occupied the eighth and ninth floors. A double-height, northerly oriented loggia opened off a large barrel-vaulted periodical room decorated with red Welsh floor tiles, Colima oak details, and Kingwood stone columns and pilasters with symbolic capitals representing the foundation's activities. Stretching nearly the full width of the building to the east was the main reading room. Its five double-height arched windows echoed the form of the room's vaulted ceiling, which was supported by Tennessee marble columns and corbels. Decorated by Tiffany Studios, the lofty gray-blue room with blue and gold accents on the walls and ceilings created a striking study space. Offices and workrooms were located on the intermediary floors.

As the foundation's scope expanded, Atterbury added a tenth-story penthouse (1922–23) to provide space for a drafting room for the Committee on Regional Planning. In 1930, he designed a fifteen-story annex on 22nd Street to harmonize with the original structure in style and material. A four-story hyphen connected the addition, occupied by the New York School of Social Work, to the main building. By that time, its main cornice had been stripped at the side at the insistence of a neighboring landowner. Stressing that "the sawed off cornice and unsightly finish of the corner [was] a very serious detriment," Atterbury convinced the foundation to restore the original design despite John Glenn's claim that using the organization's funds for "what seems . . . a minor and unnecessary adornment" was irresponsible.[101]

Between the years 1909 and 1913, Atterbury's involvement with the Russell Sage Foundation was all-encompassing. Thoroughly occupied with the design and management of Forest Hills Gardens, Atterbury's firm had little time for other commissions and designed only a handful of houses in Manhattan and Long Island during that period for private clients. As architectural supervisor of Forest Hills Gardens, he remained associated with the foundation throughout his career, and his personal connection with de Forest would continue to bring Atterbury important commissions, including the American Wing of the Metropolitan Museum of Art.

CHAPTER FIVE

SPECIALIST IN TOWN PLANNING AND AFFORDABLE HOUSING

1909–1925

With much of the Gardens's initial design work complete by 1912, Atterbury was to some degree freed up to take on new commissions. While he continued to design the estates and city houses that had defined his early practice, albeit with less frequency, his focus shifted to affordable housing and town planning. By 1919, his firm's letterhead listed "industrial housing and community planning" as a specialty.

Atterbury had already contributed considerably to the energy of the housing-reform movement as New York City's population exploded in the 1900s. In addition to his involvement in the COS's Tenement House Committee, he joined the Committee on Congestion of Population's executive board in 1907, headed by activist Benjamin C. Marsh. The group was concerned with reducing congestion in the areas around developing transportation hubs through decentralization to create decent living conditions for the poor. In 1908, it organized the so-called Congestion Show at the American Museum of Natural History. The exhibit's maps and charts exposed New York's overcrowdedness and proposed a number of planning solutions to the problem. In contrast to the aesthetic basis of the pervasive City Beautiful movement, the show presented a more scientific and socially conscientious approach to city

First Methodist Episcopal Church, Kingsport, Tennessee. Courtesy of the Archives of the City of Kingsport

planning.[1] The committee was also responsible for sponsoring the first national conference on city planning in 1909; this event eventually led to the establishment of the first national city-planning organization.

With strong opinions, Atterbury was not reticent in his criticism or hesitant to suggest alternatives to housing deficiencies. At one conference held by the COS in 1910, he condemned the city's existing regulatory structure by remarking that the builder of model tenements was "up against an impossible problem": the city's taxation system. Because property taxes, Atterbury argued, were based on assessed value rather than on property returns, model tenements were subject to the same, if not more, taxes as a tall revenue-producing building. Although Atterbury abhorred skyscrapers, he grudgingly suggested that "if the people must stay in the city, skyscrapers for the poor are the only remedy"—a recommendation that was widely opposed, particularly by John M. Murphy, commissioner of the Tenement House Department.[2]

As a charter member of the National Housing Association, Atterbury worked with de Forest, the organization's president; secretary Lawrence Veiller; and John M. Glenn, the director of the Russell Sage Foundation—among others—to improve the country's housing

conditions before they became as dire as New York's slums. The association, founded in 1910, studied the problem nationwide and encouraged the formation of local associations devoted to improved housing. Its annual conference created an ideal venue for Atterbury to share his ideas on housing and economic construction with like-minded colleagues. In 1912, he spoke on the subject of "Garden Cities" in Philadelphia, and in 1916 on "How to Get Low Cost Houses: the Real Housing Problem and the Arts of Construction Illustrated from Research Work Done under the Auspices of the Russell Sage Foundation" in Providence.[3]

In 1912, Atterbury brought the benefits of scientific planning before a wide public in his article, "Model Towns in America," published in *Scribner's Magazine* as part of an issue on the "New Suburb." Described as "a series of articles by high authorities on the planning and building of the ideal town," the magazine included pieces by reformer Frederic C. Howe (1867–1940) on England's garden cities and by California architect Elmer Grey (1872–1963) on Pacific Coast suburbs. Writing from his experience at Forest Hills Gardens, Atterbury championed scientific planning and collective development as the basis for building "model towns." Since bad city planning—"street plan, lotting, restrictions, and city ordinances"—often created unhygienic houses and tenements, he underlined the importance of "collective purchase, design, development, and control"—the most "distinctive feature of a model town"—for better living conditions.[4]

During World War One, Atterbury espoused the idea of collective planning to solve the housing crisis for laborers working in wartime industries as chairman of the National Housing Association's Committee on Wartime Housing. In 1917, the committee—which also included Lawrence Veiller and the prominent urban planner John Nolen from Cambridge, Massachusetts—urged President Woodrow Wilson to establish a federal housing administration to preside over wartime housing.[5] Whether, as Veiller recalled, their "letters or other factors led the President to act," he was unsure, but "at any rate, [the committee's] suggestions crystallized" into a "definitive war housing programme" with Otto Eidlitz, one of New York's leading builders, as the secretary of labor.[6] Atterbury later sat on the New York chapter of the AIA's committee on civic design and development.[7]

As he continued to design model tenements in Manhattan, Atterbury also embarked on several industrial communities outside the city, capitalizing on his work at Forest Hills Gardens. These communities included Indian Hill,

in Worcester, Massachusetts, for the Norton Company (1915–16); Erwin, Tennessee, for the Holston Corporation (1915–16); and Mocanaqua, Pennsylvania, for the West End Coal Company (1918–25). He also contributed schemes for workers' housing in Kingsport, Tennessee (1917), and Mariemont, Ohio (1925), two developments laid out by John Nolen. A graduate of Harvard's School of Landscape Architecture, Nolen had, by 1915, designed parks in Charlotte, North Carolina; Savannah, Georgia; and Madison, Wisconsin; he also produced plans for San Diego, California; Roanoke, Virginia; Reading, Pennsylvania; and Myers Park, an affluent suburb of Charlotte, North Carolina. In the case of Forest Hills (later renamed Woodbourne), a planned community fifteen minutes outside of Boston, Atterbury's contributions as well as those of his colleague Frederick Law Olmsted Jr. were never realized.[8] Additionally, Atterbury sat on the advisory board of Roland Park and was a consultant for industrial developments in Dundalk, Maryland, for Bethlehem Steel and in Passaic, New Jersey, for woolens manufacturer Forstmann & Huffman.[9]

TENEMENTS

Model tenements such as the Phipps Model Tenements (1905–7) were efforts by the philanthropically and socially minded that offered Atterbury the opportunity to improve upon previously accepted prototypes for tenement design, such as Ernest Flagg's internal courtyard scheme. In 1912, Atterbury designed a five-story model tenement at 425–27 West 44th Street in the heart of Hell's Kitchen for Mrs. Catherine C. D. Rogers (d. 1958), the wife of prominent New York lawyer John S. Rogers (1877–1935).[10] Well constructed and equipped with modern amenities, Atterbury's work far surpassed the minimum standard acceptable for tenements. However, model tenements were not looked upon as realistic solutions to the housing problem. For example, Lawrence Veiller argued that, by 1910, only twenty-five model groups capable of housing 3,588 families had been erected in Manhattan, whereas speculative builders, who tended to skimp on code regulations, had built 27,100 tenements for 253,510 families.[11] Atterbury was aware of the stigma attached to the word "model," finding it more debilitating than "stimulative of success."

In the design of 425–27 West 44th Street, Atterbury experimented with the layout to maximize light and to generate a community atmosphere among its inhabitants.

Rogers Model Tenement, 425–27 West 44th Street,
New York, New York. Courtesy of the Division of Rare
and Manuscript Collections, Cornell University Library

Adapting Flagg's courtyard plan, developed in 1894, but taking it one step further, he enlivened the austere, balanced street facade with a variety of brick patterns and white painted-iron balconies at the windows.[12] The building consisted of two fifty-foot-wide sections, each twenty-nine feet deep, connected by a two-story hyphen through an oversized courtyard, built fifty percent larger than what the law required. On the second floor of the connection, Atterbury incorporated an assembly room with large skylights, bookshelves, and built-in seats for the building's tenants to congregate in, while his rooftop playgrounds and laundry yards provided additional communal space. Each of the building's twenty well-arranged apartments—consisting of two bedrooms, living room, kitchen, and bath—received ample light from the street and courtyard and, in compliance with the Tenement House Act of 1901, had a window in every room. In addition to its hardwood floors, marble hallways, and stairs, Atterbury's fireproof steel and concrete building had electric lighting; included many modern conveniences, such as gas ranges; and, as an economic by-product, had hot water created from the heat generated by the building's basement incinerating system.

Rogers Model Tenement. Entrance facade.
The Brickbuilder 24 (May 1914): pl. 64

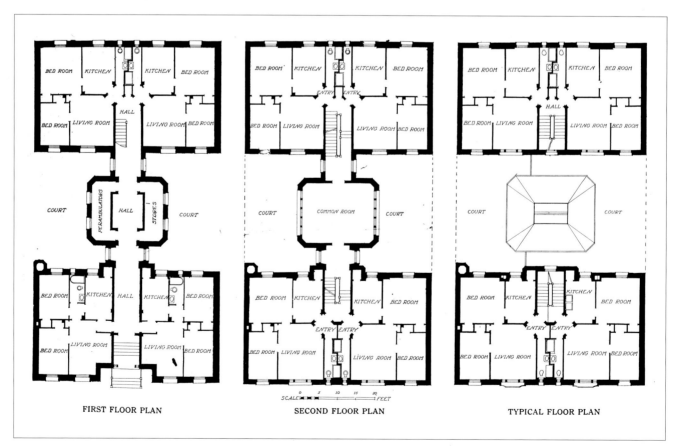

Rogers Model Tenement. First-, second-, and typical floor plan. The Brickbuilder 24 (May 1914): pl 65

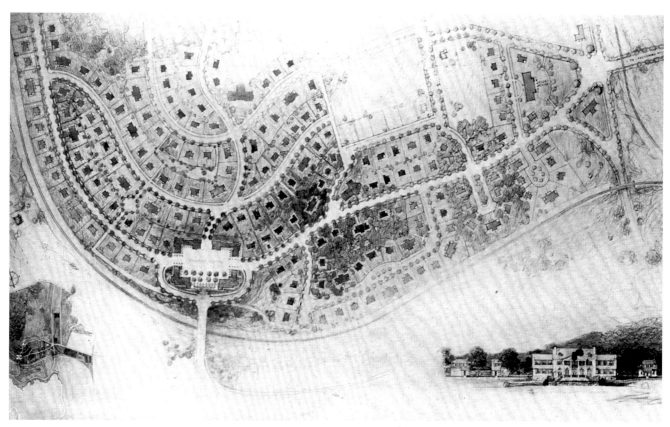

Indian Hill, Worcester, Massachusetts. Site plan.
Architectural Record 41 (January 1917): 22

TOWN PLANNING AND AFFORDABLE HOUSING

Atterbury's reputation as a tenement house designer and his highly publicized success at Forest Hills Gardens brought the architect new commissions to plan complete industrial-housing villages. His first venture, Indian Hill, in Worcester, Massachusetts, built between the years 1915 and 1916 for the rapidly expanding Norton Company, was deemed "one of the noteworthy industrial communities in the country."[13] Founded in 1885 by Milton P. Higgins, Norton was a leading manufacturer of abrasives and machinery. In 1913, it purchased a 116-acre site just west of its factories under its real estate subsidiary, the Indian Hill Company, and embarked on an ambitious housing program for its 3,700 employees. At that time, the company was threatened by strikes, and Worcester—an industrial city—was experiencing a labor shortage due to a decline in immigration and competition from other companies. By giving its workmen and their families the opportunity to own homes, Norton hoped to attract new employees, boost company spirit, and increase efficiency.

Hiring Atterbury based on his work at Forest Hills Gardens—"without question, the finest similar development in this country"—the Norton Company was confident that its housing campaign was "under the most expert direction available in the United States." In early 1915, after a year of working with the company's engineering department, Atterbury presented his design to Norton's workers and officials, who found the architect's scheme "unusual and interesting."[14] With plans, elevations, and models, Atterbury communicated the benefits of planning and, through photographs, contrasted well-designed communities to industrial neighborhoods where American families lived in "squalor and filth."[15]

In arriving at his scheme, Atterbury concentrated on a thirty-acre area on the hillside overlooking Indian Lake next to the plant. Deferring to the site's natural features and topography, he planned the community's formal center on level ground at the mouth of the development to the south. A bridge spanning a deep cut created by the Boston and Maine Railroad, which looped around the base of the hill and separated the settlement from Norton's factories, formed Indian Hill's main entrance. Just north, the center—designed as an enclosed square with shops—opened

Indian Hill. Indian Hill Road. Architectural Record 41 (January 1917): 25

slightly steeper smaller roads to connect them. Where the grade was too steep for roadways, he interspersed footpaths and easy crosscuts, breaking up longer blocks and providing direct access to the center. As a self-sufficient community, Indian Hill's plan included locations for such facilities as a dining hall, located on the settlement's eastern fringe next to the factory's entrance; the Satucket Inn, a large Colonial-style boarding house with club-like features for bachelors; a boarding house for women in the company's office force; a school; and a chapel.

As he had done at Forest Hills Gardens, Atterbury allocated a generous amount of land toward playgrounds and communal outdoor spaces. In addition to lakefront amenities, he planned a recreation center along the hill's eastern base as well as an amphitheater, bathing pools created by diverted natural springs, cul-de-sacs, and private interior parks for some of the blocks—an innovation he and Olmsted had introduced at Forest Hills Gardens. All of the two hundred lots Atterbury laid out in his scheme enjoyed southern views of the lake and the city in the dis-

to the south with terraces commanding views of the lake. To create the best possible street grading for the sloping land, Atterbury stretched sweeping curved thoroughfares east to west across the hillside and added a number of

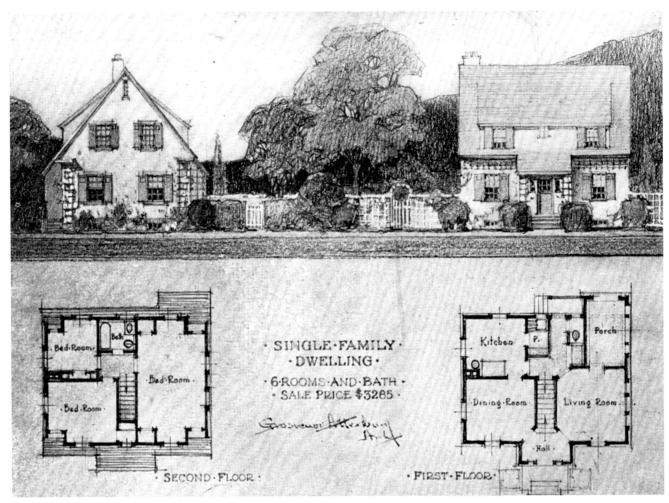

Indian Hill. Six-room house. Architectural Record 41 (January 1917): 26

Indian Hill. Six-room house. Architectural Record 41
(January 1917): 28

Indian Hill. Living room. Architectural Record 41
(January 1917): 31

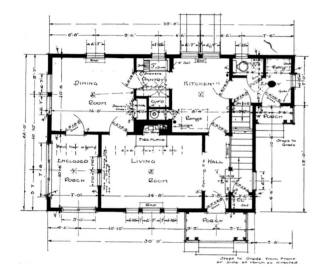

Indian Hill. First-floor plan of a seven-room house.
Architectural Record 41 (January 1917): 30

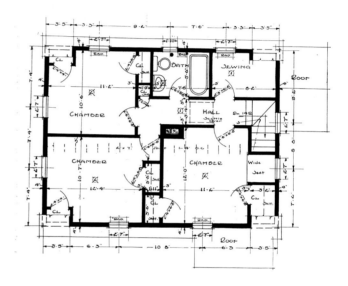

Indian Hill. Second-floor plan of a seven-room house.
Architectural Record 41 (January 1917): 30

tance. Infrastructure that was unusual at the time included storm-water drainage, water mains, sewers, and electricity.

In keeping with New England's architectural tradition, Atterbury adapted Colonial models for his house designs, creating a glorified picture of an American village. As the movement to Americanize a primarily immigrant workforce swept through the country, particularly with the onset of World War One, the heavy Germanic overtones of Forest Hills Gardens were considered less appropriate for the type of patriotic message American companies, such as Norton, wished to emphasize. Rather, industrial villages such as Whitinsville, fifteen miles south of Worcester, presented a more compelling American image for Atterbury to interpret in designing Indian Hill. Atterbury admired Whitinsville's "considerable architectural harmony and charm" and neat white Colonial-style houses, which had been built gradually after the Civil War as part of a cotton machinery settlement.[16]

While Atterbury's simple, well-proportioned houses were economically built, they were well constructed by the day's standards with brass pipes, copper flashing, concrete foundations, and slate roofs. Offered in several different models, the smaller houses were configured around a center hall with a living room, dining room, kitchen, and enclosed porch downstairs and three bedrooms and bath upstairs. Atterbury differentiated his larger, more-expensive model by placing the front entrance and stair at the

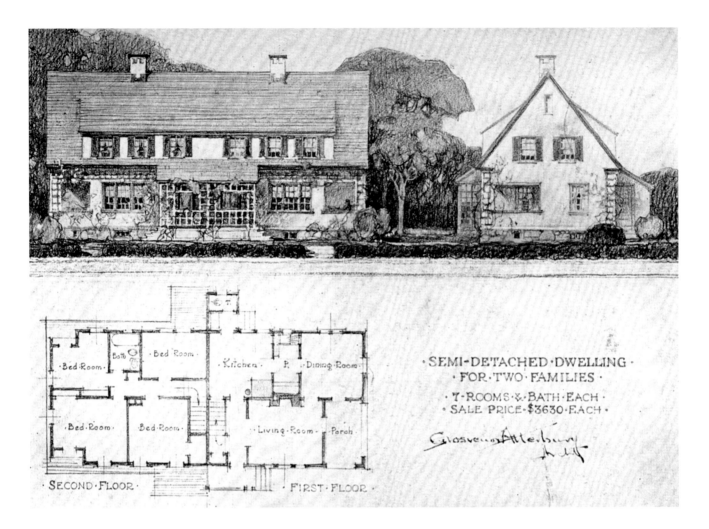

Indian Hill. Semi-detached house. Architectural Record 41
(January 1917): 2

Indian Hill. Rear elevation of a semi-detached house.
Courtesy of the Division of Rare and Manuscript Collections,
Cornell University Library

Indian Hill. Nashoba Place, 1918. Collections of the
Worcester Historical Museum, Worcester, Massachusetts

side of the house and adding a fourth bedroom to the
upper level. Having experimented with semi-detached
houses at Forest Hills Gardens, he interspersed a number
of seven-room double houses throughout the settlement.
Although Atterbury championed their economy, architectural interest, and flexibility, Norton's workers, who placed
more value on individual home ownership, did not readily
embrace the grouped homes, which had been so successful abroad and in Queens; only two were built at Indian
Hill on Nashoba Place and Weelahka Circle.

To distinguish his various housing models, Atterbury
alternated between variations of stucco, clapboard, and
shingle cladding, gambrel and pitched roofs, and brick and
fieldstone basements. He incorporated different types of
entries and porches, patterns of lattice trelliswork, and
shutter-panel details, such as silhouettes of moons, stars,
and rabbits, and he positioned the houses at different setbacks, heights, and angles, "varying [them] so positively in
their placings along the street," one writer noted, that "the

general effect [was] most picturesque."[17] To tie the individual units together, Atterbury specified white exteriors, consistently used a grayish-green roof slate, and planted the
main streets and individual lots with maples, cedars, fruit
trees, and hedges. Ornamental streetlights and signs,
retaining walls, and terraces refined the street picture, giving the impression of a more expensive development.
According to firm associate Charles C. May, Atterbury's collective planning "produced dignity and carrying power in
an aggregation of which the units, taken singly, must be too
small or too insignificant to be effective."[18]

During the summers of 1915 and 1916, Norton constructed fifty-eight homes from Atterbury's plans, selling
them to foremen and higher-paid workers— primarily
Swedish immigrants—for what the land and house had
actually cost the company. Employees were responsible for
a ten percent down payment and two mortgages, each
payable over twelve years with five percent interest. However, despite the various draws, Norton's employees were

Indian Hill. Window display, Duncan & Goodell, 1916.
Collections of the Worcester Historical Museum, Worcester,
Massachusetts

not overanxious to purchase homes in Indian Hill.[19] The company advertised the property aggressively, even commissioning a window display at the Worcester hardware store Duncan & Goodell in November 1916, and eventually handpicked qualified employees to move there.

Originally, the houses were offered for $2,800 to $3,200; however, their prices increased nineteen percent between 1915 and 1916. Despite the presentation of Norton as the embodiment of corporate altruism, critics emerged who viewed the concept of planned company towns as patronizing and venal. Ida M. Tarbell, the famous journalist who exposed the excesses of John D. Rockefeller's trusts in *The History of the Standard Oil Company*, pointed out that the houses met "the needs of only the highly paid workmen."[20] Because of the escalating cost of labor and materials due to the war, Norton curtailed building at Indian Hill in 1917. As a result, none of the community facilities Atterbury envi-

sioned were erected, and the first fifty-eight houses were confined to the eastern portion of the property. Rising labor shortages prompted the company to supplement its predominantly Swedish workforce with unskilled Italian and Polish laborers. In an attempt to integrate them into the community, Norton asked Atterbury to prepare a new plan, which included houses for foremen, office employees, and skilled workmen priced out of Indian Hill as well as rental units for unskilled laborers. Atterbury proposed a hierarchical system with residences, five-unit terraced dwellings constructed from concrete blocks, and two- and three-story rental apartment houses using his precast concrete panels.[21] However, after the project was delayed, Norton rapidly built ninety-four small houses just north of Indian Hill as an emergency measure in 1919 without Atterbury's supervision.

With his design for Indian Hill, Atterbury shattered the controversial image of industrial housing and effectively showed what could be made possible through sensitive and well-intended planning. Corporate workers' towns before Indian Hill offered mass-produced housing with a minimum of design and construction and rarely achieved any sense of civic order or aesthetic aspiration. As Tarbell observed, "Of recent undertakings, there is no doubt but that Indian Hill . . . is the most suggestive and promising. It is planned for utility, economy, and beauty. It will be the most attractive town of its kind in the United States if it is carried out as begun."[22] Although Indian Hill's plan was never brought to completion, Atterbury's design, like Forest Hills Gardens, had a resounding effect on the level of architecture and planning in industrial communities built during World War One. Prominently featured in the press, Indian Hill's compact Colonial Revival–style houses and well-laid-out grounds created a compelling vision and offered a more fundamentally American interpretation of the garden city that grew in popularity throughout the country. Among the most distinguished developments to arise during the war period was George B. Post's village of Eclipse Park (1917–18) in Beloit, Washington, for the Fairbanks Morse Company. Described by Lawrence Veiller as "one of the most artistic and attractive [developments] thus far evolved in this country," Eclipse Park included Colonial cottages, narrow curved tree-lined streets, varied lot sizes, and a town square.[23] Housing and planning specialists such as Kilham & Hopkins of Boston and the New York firm of Mann & MacNeille also embraced Colonial styles to better express the country's "national character" at Lowell (1917), a seven-acre village near the town's mills, for the Massachusetts Homestead Commission, and Perryville, Maryland (1918), a 160-house development for the Atlas Power Company on the Susquehanna River.[24]

In 1916, the Holston Corporation, the legal land entity of the Carolina, Clinchfield & Ohio Railroad (CC&O), commissioned Atterbury to plan and design a housing community at its newly established hub in Erwin, Tennessee.[25] During the last quarter of the nineteenth century, businessmen and industrialists had begun to develop railroads and coal mines in eastern Tennessee, transforming the sleepy agricultural region rich in minerals into a thriving area. With support from a New York syndicate made up of financiers Thomas Fortune Ryan, C. Ledyard Blair, and John B. Dennis, George L. Carter (1857–1936), CC&O's first president, succeeded in running his railroad through portions of the Appalachians, connecting eastern Kentucky's coal mines to the mill towns of South Carolina—an expensive and ambitious feat. Set on a level plain

equidistant from the railroad's termini at Elkhorn City, Kentucky, and Spartanburg, South Carolina, Erwin created the ideal location for train crews to switch before or after traveling through the Blue Ridge section of the route. In 1908, as Carter constructed railroad facilities, shops, and yards in the small Appalachian outpost, Erwin experienced rapid growth, its population more than tripling.

In 1911, well-connected New York lawyer Mark W. Potter (1866–1942) succeeded Carter as CC&O's president. Familiar with Atterbury's work at Forest Hills Gardens, Potter enlisted the architect in 1916 to design a community to accommodate the influx of railroad workers. Originally intending to sell unimproved lots, the Holston Corporation decided to build rental houses over which it could maintain architectural control. Like Norton and other progressive companies wishing to foster opportunity and growth, the railroad executives believed that well-designed, attractive homes would draw skilled workers to the area and entice them to stay. Atterbury visited Erwin in 1916; later that year, the Holston Corporation began to act upon the architect's drawings and plans, which laid out housing to accommodate up to 30,000–40,000 people.

As he had at Forest Hills Gardens and Indian Hill, Atterbury worked cleverly with the site's conditions and topography. On land sandwiched between the Unaka Mountains, the Nolichucky River, and the railroad tracks, Atterbury laid out a system of undulating roads connecting to Erwin's existing street grid, creating a variety of irregularly shaped lots and long sweeping boulevards that led in and out of town. So as not to compete with the breathtaking mountain backdrop and bordering parklands, he did not design a distinct or monumental entry into the settlement, as he had in Queens and Worcester. Since Holston's residential addition was located next to Erwin's existing town, a commercial area along the lines of Forest Hills's Station Square or Indian Hill's community center was unnecessary. Atterbury's streets—enhanced by circular roundabouts at the development's northern and southern extremities, cul-de-sacs, greens, plantings, and fruit trees—brought a defining variety and interest to the plan.

Atterbury's well-proportioned houses resembled the cottages he had designed at Indian Hill in both plan and detail. However, in the tradition of southern construction, they were designed with storage rooms off of the kitchens rather than cellars. The models Atterbury proposed ranged from a one-story, four-room bungalow to an eight-room house with a large porch and garage (each with a fireplace) as well as groupings of detached and semi-detached homes. With

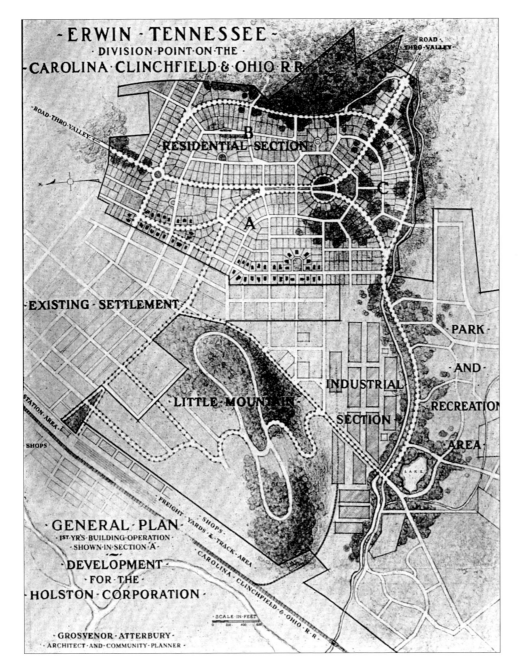

Development for the Holston Corporation, Erwin, Tennessee. General plan. Architectural Record 43 (June 1918): 549

similar layouts, each house was to be differentiated by either shingle, stucco, or a combination of the two; porches; trellises; and shutter-panel details—cutouts of cats, windmills, birds, or rabbits. For the first phase of development, the company went forward with the four-room bungalow and the five- and six-room, two-story cottages, and it decided not to build either the semi-detached houses or the larger eight-room residences.

By June 1918, the railroad had constructed forty-five of Atterbury's houses along Ohio Avenue and Unaka Way (in residential section A) at an average price of ten cents per cubic foot—a figure that reflected the cheaper southern construction costs. The homes were larger in size and only

slightly inferior in finish to the cottages at Indian Hill, where the cost to build had risen from sixteen to nineteen cents per cubic foot between 1915 and 1916. While Atterbury integrated several cul-de-sacs into his larger plan, only one—Holston Place—was completed. Surrounded by seven houses of varying type, the quiet green off of Ohio Avenue exemplified the type of defining plan features the architect incorporated for pleasing variety. In praise of Atterbury's work, Lawrence Veiller noted that "Erwin is especially significant as showing the possibilities of well-ordered, harmonious, and attractive designing in the development of what is ordinarily so sordid a thing as a railroad shop settlement, and illustrates anew the great advantage of

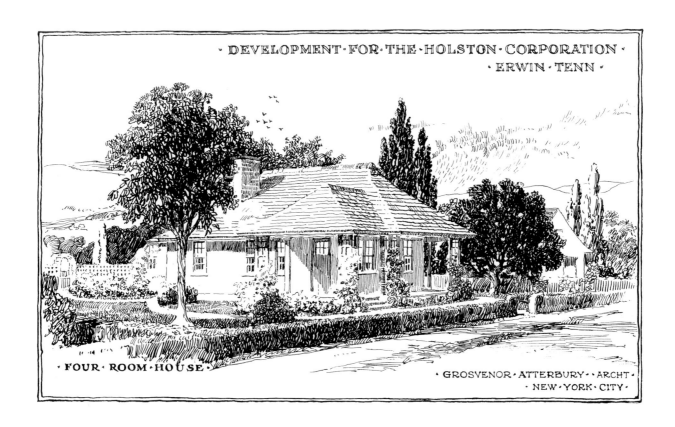

·DEVELOPMENT·FOR·THE·HOLSTON·CORPORATION·
·ERWIN·TENN·

·FOUR·ROOM·HOUSE·

·GROSVENOR·ATTERBURY·ARCHT·
·NEW·YORK·CITY·

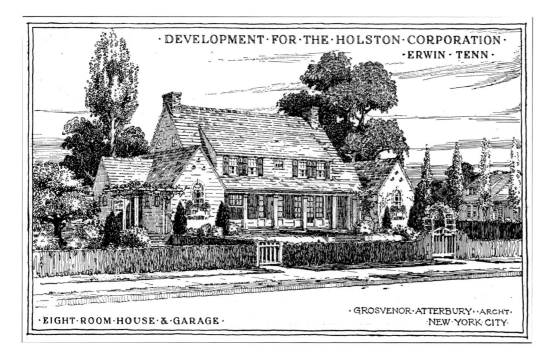

·DEVELOPMENT·FOR·THE·HOLSTON·CORPORATION·
·ERWIN·TENN·

·EIGHT·ROOM·HOUSE·&·GARAGE·

·GROSVENOR·ATTERBURY·ARCHT·
·NEW·YORK·CITY·

ABOVE *Erwin. Four-room house.* Courtesy of the Division of Rare and Manuscript Collections, Cornell University Library

ABOVE *Erwin. Eight-room house.*
Architectural Record 43 (June 1918): 548

RIGHT *Erwin. Shutter-panel designs.*
Architectural Record 43 (June 1918): 553

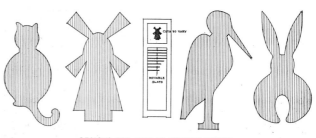

DESIGNS FOR CUTS IN SHUTTER PANELS

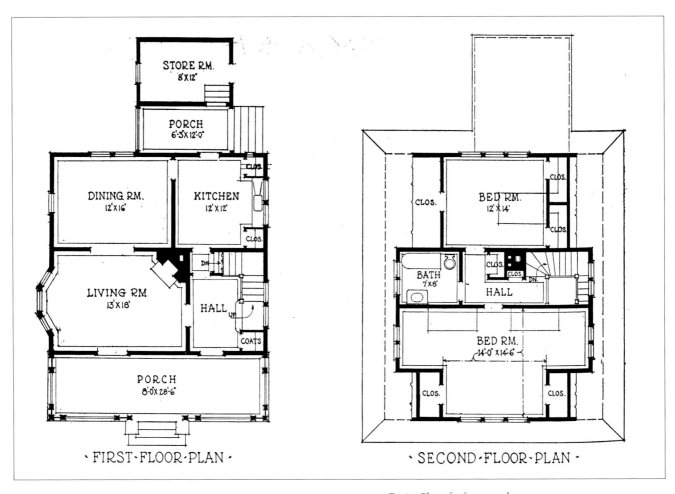

· FIRST · FLOOR · PLAN ·

· SECOND · FLOOR · PLAN ·

TOP *Erwin. Five-room house.* Courtesy of the Division of Rare
and Manuscript Collections, Cornell University Library

BOTTOM *Erwin. Plan of a five-room house.*
Architectural Record 43 (June 1918): 552

·DEVELOPMENT·FOR·THE·HOLSTON·CORPORATION·
·ERWIN·TENN.·

·SIX·ROOM·HOUSE·

GROSVENOR ATTERBURY ··ARCHT.·
·NEW·YORK·CITY·

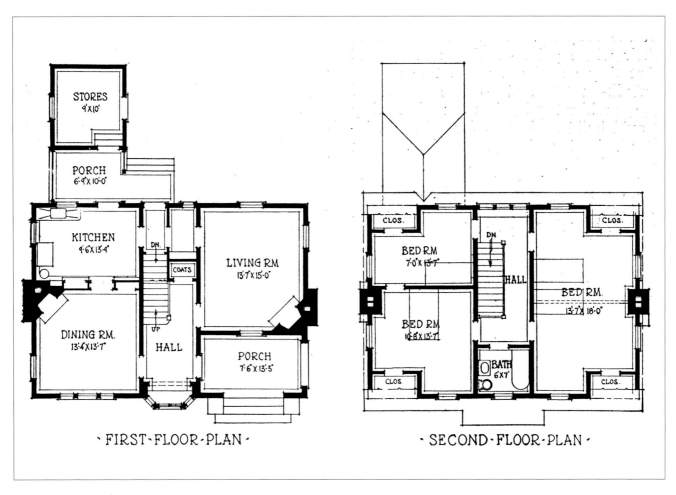

·FIRST·FLOOR·PLAN·

·SECOND·FLOOR·PLAN·

TOP *Erwin. Six-room house.* Courtesy of the Division of Rare
and Manuscript Collections, Cornell University Library

BOTTOM *Erwin. Plan of a six-room house.*
Architectural Record 43 (June 1918): 553

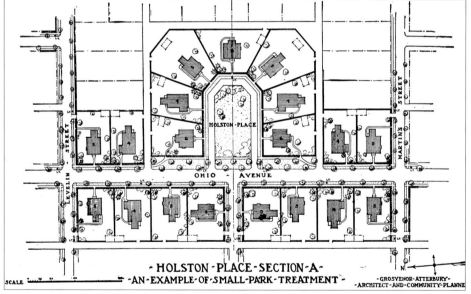

employing for the development of even the humble work-ingman's dwelling the best expert advice and direction."[26] However, as the railroad's financial condition steadily declined during the war, the Holston Corporation termi-nated its building program. In addition, Potter—the driv-ing force behind the development—resigned as president of the railroad in 1920 after President Wilson nominated him to the Interstate Commerce Commission.[27] As a result,

Erwin did not become the industrial center of 30,000 inhabitants the CC&O had predicted, and Atterbury's planned community never grew past the initially laid streets and forty-five original houses.

As Erwin was undergoing change, Kingsport, also along the CC&O's route in northeast Tennessee, was being similarly transformed. In developing the railroad, George Carter had recognized Kingsport's potential as an

RIGHT *House for the Kingsport Improvement Corporation, Kingsport, Tennessee.* Courtesy of the Division of Rare and Manuscript Collections, Cornell University Library

BELOW *Kingsport. Rendering of houses.* Courtesy of the Division of Rare and Manuscript Collections, Cornell University Library

BOTTOM *Kingsport. Plan of houses.* Courtesy of the Division of Rare and Manuscript Collections, Cornell University Library

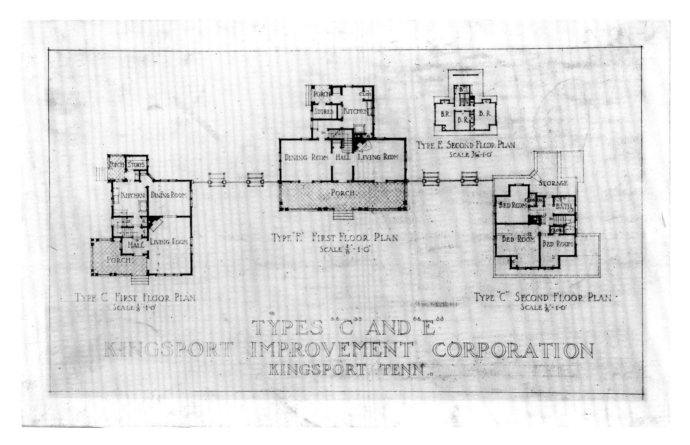

First Methodist Episcopal Church, Kingsport, Tennessee.
Courtesy of the Archives of the City of Kingsport

industrial city and bought up land in the area. A small agricultural community on the Holston River forty miles north of Erwin, Kingsport was also rich in natural resources, including water, timber, coal, and minerals. In 1914, when Carter began experiencing financial difficulties, the syndicate backing the CC&O—composed of John B. Dennis; C. Ledyard Blair; and Mark W. Potter, CC&O's president—purchased 10,000 acres in the Kingsport river valley from Carter to form Kingsport Farms, which later became the Kingsport Improvement Company. The Kingsport Improvement Company, headed by Dennis, successfully recruited industry to the area, including the chemical company Tennessee Eastman, owned by Eastman Kodak of Rochester, New York. As Kingsport's businesses thrived, the city—much more so

than Erwin—grew into the "model" industrial city its founders envisioned.

John B. Dennis, a partner at Blair & Company in New York, was the project's motivating force. In 1915, he commissioned John Nolen to prepare a scheme. A disciple of Fredrick Law Olmsted Jr., Nolen also considered comprehensive planning for cities, parks, and their peripheries an essential element of modern life to instigate a happy and healthy balance. At Kingsport, he divided the city into industrial districts, a commercial and civic center, and residential sections with parks and curvilinear roads. A central circle serving as the pivot of the plan connected the town center to the residential areas, which Nolen arranged according to housing prices. Unlike Atterbury, who preferred to serve as both architect and planner, Nolen worked only in a planning capacity. In carrying out his vision, he collaborated with New York architect Clinton Mackenzie (1871–1940)—who designed most of the city's houses and civic buildings, including its country club, community house, inn, and railroad station—along with a number of other architects, such as Atterbury, Thomas Hastings, Evarts Tracy (1868–1922), and Electus D. Litchfield.

Atterbury and his associate Philip Langworthy designed a cluster of residences set around a hilltop park in the area referred to as the White City.[28] Representing some of the city's best housing, Atterbury's white-framed Colonial Revival houses were essentially larger versions of his Erwin houses. Completed in 1919, they had large porches, fireplaces, pitched roofs, and accompanying garages, and they were located far from the industrial district. Atterbury adroitly built a number of the houses into the hillside and grouped them to improve each of their outlooks. In addition, he designed the First Methodist Episcopal Church in 1921 on Kingsport's church circle.[29] While Atterbury had designed a number of churches and chapels, including Seal

Harbor's Congregational Church and the Church-in-the-Gardens at Forest Hills, the Kingsport church was the largest as well as the only one to be designed in the Georgian style. Described in the architect's building list as "Colonial Church," the Christopher Wren–inspired brick and wood edifice featured a two-story entrance portico, supported by four attenuated columns, and a copper-capped cupola embellished with delicate swags and urns. Since the minister, Reverend E. O. Woodyard, acted as superintendent for the project and construction only progressed as funds were raised, the church was not completed until 1926.

While Atterbury's work at Kingsport illustrated his ability to design attractive, standardized homes, they were primarily intended for company managers and upper-level employees. His industrial housing, however, for the West End Coal Company in Mocanaqua, Pennsylvania, demonstrated his skill at infusing even the simplest worker's cottage with character.[30] Mocanaqua, a small coal-mining village on the banks of the Susquehanna River near the Pennsylvania Railroad line, served as the residential base

Miners' village, West End Coal Company, Mocanaqua, Pennsylvania. Courtesy of the Division of Rare and Manuscript Collections, Cornell University Library

Ten houses on Sheldon Close, Mariemont, Ohio.
Architecture 54 (September 1926): pl. 185

for West End Coal's operations in the region. The company began constructing housing in the 1880s; Atterbury's contributions formed part of a third building phase (1918–24) that transformed the town. Located close to the river on Italy Street, Atterbury's compact four-room, one-and-a-half-story cottages were carried out in a diminutive Colonial Revival style. To avoid following the monotonous layout of the existing homes, Atterbury placed his houses with consideration for their neighbors, setting some dwellings back from the street so as to open up a larger yard in front for the surrounding houses to enjoy. Embellishments that he had used at Erwin and Kingsport, such as trellises and arched latticework entrance gates framed with ivy, enhanced the houses' basic rectangular forms.

In 1925, Atterbury, along with other architects, joined John Nolen in the design of Mariemont, a garden suburb developed by Mary M. Emery ten miles east of Cincinnati on the Little Miami River.[31] Like Olivia Sage, Emery (1844–1927) opted to disperse her inherited wealth through a succession of philanthropic and constructive gestures. Her late husband Thomas J. Emery (1830–1906), a prosperous businessman, had been Cincinnati's largest real estate owner. After the untimely death of her son Sheldon, Mary Emery invited his Harvard classmate Charles J. Livingood (1866–1952) to join the family firm, Thomas Emery's Sons. Livingood acted as Emery's business advisor and later as her primary liaison at Mariemont.

In 1913, Emery and Livingood began secretly amassing the land that would eventually comprise Mariemont's 423-acre spread. Versed in the patterns of city planning abroad, Livingood commissioned John Nolen in 1920 to lay out a self-contained community based on England's garden cities. As he saw it, the development would provide housing for all economic classes and create an alternative to Cincinnati's crowded downtown district.[32] With Mariemont—named after the family's Newport estate—Emery, Livingood, and Nolen sought to establish a "national exemplar, a study field for individual builders and the projectors of town and subdivisions near great cities, not only by its plan of procedure or city planning principles, but in illustration of the advantage of modern methods in building, cost saving and the value of beauty, both in placing and designing a home."[33] Nolen's general plan accommodated a population of five thousand and included a town center, replete with public buildings and a green; a range of housing options, including apartments, group houses, and detached and semi-detached dwellings; and a street pattern characterized by axes, winding roads, cul-de-sacs, and parks. To create visual diversity, Livingood and Nolen brought twenty-six architects from Cincinnati, New York, Boston, and Philadelphia onto the project to design the town's various civic buildings and housing groups. Among this group were Louis E. Jallade, Ripley & LeBoutillier, Richard Henry Dana, Clinton Mackenzie, and Paul P. Cret.

As construction began in 1923, Nolen's garden suburb, carried out primarily in Elizabethan and Colonial Revival styles, took shape.

In 1925, Atterbury was commissioned to design a group of ten larger homes on Sheldon Close, a cul-de-sac south of the town's center.[34] Atterbury used the Elizabethan style to create a charming enclave of stucco and stone dwellings with half-timber details, steep slate roofs, porches, and private rear garages. Each composed of six to seven rooms, the houses contained multiple fireplaces and, in some cases, double-height living spaces. Since Mariemont's overall scheme encouraged semi-detached homes, Atterbury at long last had the opportunity to incorporate the more cost-effective double house into his group. He placed two semi-detached residences along either side of the close and the larger single homes to the front and rear of the cul-de-sac. With lush plantings, street lamps, and arched gates, Atterbury developed a sense of privacy and intimacy off of one of the village's busier streets.

While Atterbury relished housing commissions, they only further convinced him that "an increase of efficiency either in design, development, or construction" was the only way to raise the standard of living without raising the cost of living.[35] Since land prices and construction costs rose steadily in the 1910s and 1920s, the Indian Hill, Erwin, and Kingsport houses were only affordable to upper-level workers. At Mariemont, the low-cost apartments intended for the working class became more expensive as construction prices soared; as a result, the community developed as a middle-class suburb. This inflation only galvanized Atterbury's conviction that mass production and standardized units were the key to reducing costs and solving the housing problem. The architect continued to carry out his research through the 1910s and 1920s with support from the Russell Sage Foundation (1908–16) and, subsequently, the Standardized Housing Corporation (1916–19) and the American Car and Foundry Company (1919–21). Both the Standardized Housing Corporation and the American Car and Foundry Company sought to test the viability of Atterbury's building system commercially; however, in 1921, they concluded that sluggish production rates due to the concrete's slow curing time barred its widespread success.

Single-family house, Sheldon Close. Architecture 54
(September 1926): pl. 185

CHAPTER SIX

LATE PROJECTS

1917–1941

During the final twenty-five years of his career, Atterbury gravitated toward projects with greater social relevance and became increasingly preoccupied with concrete construction as a means to solve the housing problem. As he struggled to perfect his prefabricated building system, he continued to design the country houses and city mansions that had initially been the firm's bread and butter. While the number of residential commissions dwindled, Atterbury's estates from the 1920s represented some of the architect's most interesting work. At the same time, important institutional projects such as the American Wing at the Metropolitan Museum of Art and the Bloomingdale Hospital in White Plains kept him in the public eye. During the 1930s, when the amount of work diminished significantly, John D. Rockefeller Jr. (1874–1960) almost singlehandedly kept Atterbury's practice afloat with commissions at Pocantico Hills and Acadia National Park. The gregarious Stowe Phelps, responsible for drumming up business, left the office in 1927; and after John A. Tompkins retired in 1937, Atterbury—at the age of sixty-eight—produced little work on his own, with the exception of the Yale Medical Library and Amsterdam Houses; yet, despite his failing health, he channeled his energies into improving his building system.

Mrs. William Horace Schmidlapp house, Ca Sole, East Walnut Hills, Ohio. Arcade, 2007. Jonathan Wallen

ESTATES AND CITY HOUSES

During the 1920s, Atterbury and his associates designed mainly primary residences in such far-flung locales as Cincinnati, Ohio, and Tucson, Arizona, rather than secondary homes in suburban and resort areas. As his practice began to slow down, the various elements, styles, materials, and plans with which Atterbury had been working came together, culminating in some of the architect's most exceptional houses. Always aware of the relationship between the landscape and design, Atterbury exhibited the same sensitivity and responsiveness to the site and continued to emphasize color and materials for heightened artistic effect.

In 1917, Atterbury completed his last major house commission on Long Island: Wereholme, Harold H. Weekes (d. 1950) and Louisine Weekes's (1884–1952) estate in Islip, just east of H. O. Havemeyer's compound on Bayberry Point.[1] Havemeyer had originally purchased 125 acres between Doxsee's Cove and Champlin's Creek with his brother-in-law, Samuel T. Peters; Peters's daughter Louisine and her husband Harold Weekes built Wereholme on a portion of the property they inherited. In carrying out his design, Atterbury

ABOVE *Harold and Louisine Weekes house, Wereholme, Islip, New York. North facade.* Courtesy of Peter Tcherepnine

RIGHT *Wereholme. Roof detail.* Courtesy of Peter Tcherepnine

employed some of the new construction techniques he had developed at Forest Hills Gardens to execute his first estate built entirely of concrete blocks. While the 28-room mansion was ostensibly a stone Norman manor, Atterbury innovatively used cast concrete manufactured on the site brushed with multicolored aggregate to articulate the facades. During her travels abroad, Louisine Weekes had admired châteaus in the Loire Valley—particularly Azay-le-Rideau. Atterbury interpreted Mrs. Weekes's photographs to produce a pared-down version of the French provincial style in which no detail was lost: the shades of white and dark gray cement stucco mimicked the texture of natural stone, and the cast concrete chimneys were decoratively treated with lattice-patterned caps. Mottled green and purple roof tile, peacock-blue paint for the trim, and wrought-iron Juliet balconies con-

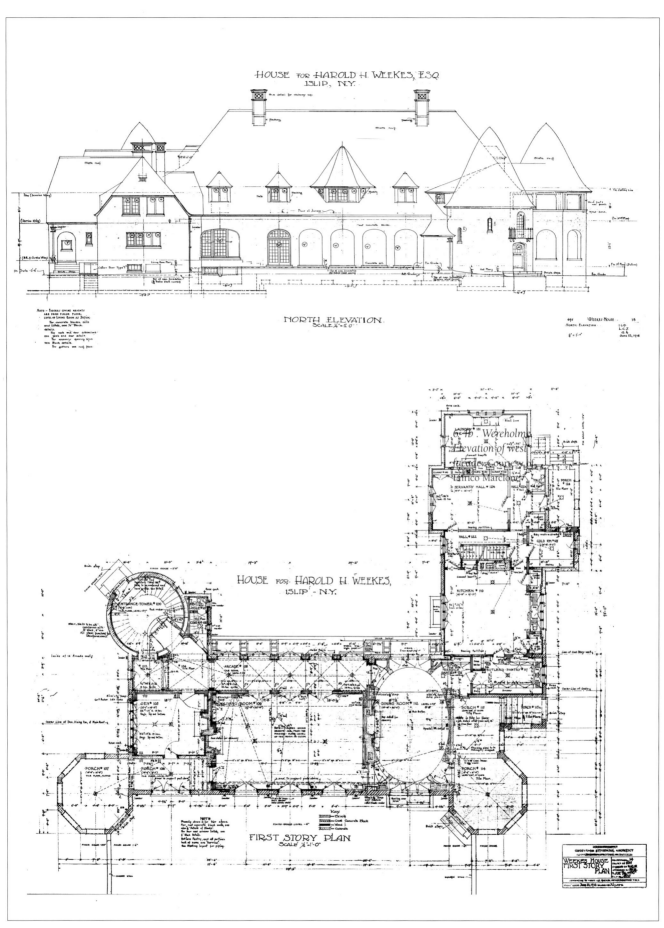

HOUSE FOR HAROLD H. WEEKES, ESQ
ISLIP, N.Y.

NORTH ELEVATION.
SCALE ¼"=1'0"

HOUSE FOR: HAROLD H. WEEKES,
ISLIP - N.Y.

FIRST STORY PLAN
SCALE ¼"=1'-0"

TOP *Wereholme. North elevation.* Courtesy
of Enrico Marclone

BOTTOM *Wereholme. Plan of first floor.*
Courtesy of Enrico Marclone

Aldus Chapin Higgins house, Worcester,
Massachusetts. View to the southeast. The Architect 5
(October 1925): pl. 9

trasted nicely with the warm gray exterior. Essentially L-shaped in plan, the house featured a series of arched openings on the first floor that expressed the main interiors. Atterbury threw off the relative symmetry of the central block by combining the front entry with the stair hall in a *tourelle* on the eastern facade and including two additional towered piazzas. Inside, Atterbury produced a spare interpretation of French provincial farmhouse architecture. His reinforced-concrete stair dressed in dark red brick and quarry tile contrasted starkly with the light sand-finished plaster walls and culminated in a rustic wood ceiling with exposed rafters radiating out from the center. The oval dining room featured walls of oak half-timbering, stucco infill, and leaded windows on either ends of the room, while the oak-paneled living room was anchored by an ornately carved mantelpiece (1684) purchased by the Weekeses in Scotland.

The Aldus Chapin Higgins house in Worcester, Massachusetts, completed in 1925, exemplified Atterbury's picturesque Tudor style in full effect.[2] Likely Higgins (1872–1948) became familiar with Atterbury's work after the architect planned the Indian Hill community outside Worcester for the Norton Company in 1915, the company of which Higgins was the president. Located four miles south of Indian Hill, Higgins's ten-acre property sat adjacent to his alma mater, Worcester Polytechnic Institute, of which he was a lifelong trustee. On the site, Atterbury created an appropriate architectural statement worthy of housing Higgins's collection of stained glass, early Flemish tapestries, and modern French paintings.

Atterbury so skillfully fit Higgins's Tudor Gothic manse into the slope of the site's gentle rise amid graceful old elms that his design reminded one visitor of "fine old manor houses, built in the days of Tudor England, which still

· Mr. Floppy Fly ·
· Mr. Daddy Long Legs ·
· The Pussy Cat ·   · Brer Rabbit ·   · The Owl ·

TOP *Higgins house. South facade.* Courtesy of the Division of Rare and Manuscript Collections, Cornell University Library

BOTTOM *Higgins house. "Nonsense" corbels.* Courtesy of the Division of Rare and Manuscript Collections, Cornell University Library

stand, unchanged, in the midst of their ancient velvety lawns."[3] As one critic aptly noted, Atterbury's careful selection of materials—warm-colored stone ashlar, brick, and rough-hewn timbers taken from old homes—and attention to detail "[contributed] immeasurably to the artistic atmosphere of the whole."[4]

The gates and the garage's Norman tower marked the entrance to the property while the sprawling main house rose to the south. The architect emphasized the expansive roofline of the house with chimneys with curved pots, decorative brickwork, and iron flèches, incorporating brick, stucco, and half-timbering carved with rich ornament in the gables. True to the house's Gothic spirit, Atterbury integrated carved stone details into the facades, including the family's coat of arms and humorous "nonsense" corbels of Daddy Long Legs; Mr. Floppy Fly; Br'er Rabbit; Mr. Squirrel; Marly, the Merovingian Duck; and Carlo, the Carlovingian Dog.

Atterbury stressed the medieval quality of his scheme, locating the front entrance in a two-story crenulated section that picturesquely projected out from the main block. A beautifully carved heavy oak door with hand-wrought ornament opened into an intimate octagonal entrance hall clad in soft red brick. Departing from his more typical butterfly plan, Atterbury arranged the rooms in an L-shape around a massive great room with stucco walls, an enormous leaded-glass window, and a clerestory level. Characteristically, the architect highlighted the structural aspects of the space, emphasizing the wood ceiling and exposed rafters as decorative features. A diminutive stair with thick stucco walls and a small window secreted down to the library to the west while a vaulted gallery, decorated with carved Gothic radiator covers, connected to the dining room and to the stone-walled sunroom to the south.

Atterbury successfully forged a dialogue between the house and the surrounding landscape by inserting gardens, terraces, and allées laid on axis with major rooms. Retaining walls constructed of the same local stone as the house gave the impression that the house was rising out of the site. Particularly charming was the rose garden with a rustic rose-covered teahouse and intricate iron gates wrought with Gothic lettering—*Un jardin tapissé d'espaliers odorans*

TOP *Higgins house. Site plan. The Architect* 5 (October 1925): pl. 2

ABOVE *Higgins house. Front entrance. The Architect* 5 (October 1925): pl. 5

ABOVE *Mrs. William Horace Schmidlapp house, Ca Sole, East Walnut Hills, Ohio. View from the northeast.* Samuel H. Gottscho. Avery Architectural and Fine Arts Library, Columbia University in the City of New York

OPPOSITE

TOP LEFT *Ca Sole. Arcade, 2007.* Jonathan Wallen

TOP RIGHT *Ca Sole. Arched opening with wrought-iron gates and bell, 2007.* Jonathan Wallen

BOTTOM *Ca Sole. Fountain and enclosed garden.* Samuel H. Gottscho. Avery Architectural and Fine Arts Library, Columbia University in the City of New York

(A garden covered with fragrant trellises)—that stretched off of the sunroom. Atterbury concealed the kitchen wing and the service yard, accessible through a half-timbered arch between the garage and the main house.

After completing the Higgins house, Atterbury and his associates embarked on several projects in Cincinnati for the daughters of Lawrence Maxwell (1853–1927), a prominent lawyer and former solicitor general under President Grover Cleveland. For Jean Maxwell Schmidlapp (b. 1884), Atterbury designed Ca Sole, a striking Italian-inspired house set high on a bluff in East Walnut Hills with panoramic views of the Little Miami River and Kentucky, in 1925. Atterbury

was acquainted with Mrs. Schmidlapp's father-in-law, Jacob G. Schmidlapp (1849–1919), a financier and well-known philanthropist with a keen interest in low-income housing. Like Atterbury, Schmidlapp was involved with the National Housing Association and had built the city's first housing development, Cincinnati Model Homes. While Atterbury was simultaneously working on Mariemont, he had previously been drawn to the Queen City to design houses for Jacob Schmidlapp and Joseph S. Neave.[5]

Ca Sole's steep hillside terrain and breathtaking views guided Atterbury's scheme. Completed in 1927, the two-story buff-colored stone residence was located in a dense

residential enclave near the Cincinnati Country Club
(1902), close to downtown.[6] On the asymmetrical entrance
facade, Atterbury emphasized the rhythmic pattern of the
windows with peacock-blue trim and pinkish-gray brick
details and accentuated the low-slung proportions of the
house and connecting outbuildings with a squat stair tower
and a gently pitched pink and gray terra-cotta roof. Set a
grade lower than the entrance to the property, the house
gently curved with the arcing driveway and appeared
closed and intimate. However, the south facade presented
the architect with the opportunity for drama. He oriented
all of the major rooms toward the river and, in collaboration with the prominent New York–based landscape architects Ferruccio Vitale (1875–1933) and Alfred Geiffert Jr.
(1890–1975), created terraced gardens that stepped down
the sloping site. Much like in his design for Mrs. William
R. Thompson's Sunset Hill in Watch Hill (1913), Atterbury
incorporated an arcade off of the main hall, living room,
and library wings that hugged the inner curve of the house
and projected out to the view. Within the concavity of the
plan, he designed a stunning hexagonally shaped walled
garden one level lower with arched openings, brick-capped
stone walls, and intricate wrought-iron gates. While the

Joseph Spencer Graydon house, Cobble Court,
Indian Hill, Ohio. Entrance facade. Courtesy of
the Division of Rare and Manuscript Collections,
Cornell University Library

architect had played with this idea before, it was particularly successful at Ca Sole.[7] In addition to protecting the exposed hillside site, Atterbury's walls, punched with wide generous arches, drew the exceptional views into the room-like space and filtered the panorama through a screen made of the same stone as the house. Its hexagonal shape encompassed a small walled garden in front of the house accessible by a small string of steps.

As he had on the exterior, Atterbury relied on the texture and color of his materials to express the interior architecture. Stretching the width of the house, the entrance hall with light red Dutch brick walls, dark wood-beamed ceilings, weathered gray timbers, and wrought-iron light fixtures opened onto a rustic arcade overlooking the gardens below. Atterbury incorporated dark wood ceilings, beams, and fixtures throughout the interiors, including the stair tower similar to that at Harold Weekes's house, Wereholme (1917), which culminated in wood sheathing and radiating rafter tails.

For Jean Schmidlapp's elder sister Marjorie (b. 1879) and her husband, lawyer Joseph Spencer Graydon (1877–1963), Atterbury reordered the elements that had made Ca Sole so special to produce Cobble Court in Indian Hill—one of the architect's most charming designs.[8] As Cincinnati's residential pockets became crowded and the desire for land swelled, the fashionable suburb of Indian Hill sprang up northeast of the city. In 1933, Atterbury executed a Norman-inspired farmhouse with a cobbled forecourt on the Graydons' gently rolling 100-acre vineyard property, skillfully arranging picturesque elements such as chimneys, dormers, and an octagonal stair tower to achieve a formal balanced design. While the two projecting wings enclosing the forecourt and axial entrance, emphasized by two large spreading elms, established a sense of symmetry, Atterbury's well-placed stair tower and library wing to the east set it slightly askew. The architect cleverly downplayed the size and impact of the house on the entrance facade by extending the steeply pitched roof just above the first story while opening the rear to a full two stories. Atterbury's combination of cool colors for the trim and roof tile—in shades of peacock-blue, warm colored stone and rose-colored brick in the gables—was particularly successful. By running single courses of the light-red Dutch brick at regular intervals through the stone portions of the facades and chimneys, he achieved a striking decorative banding based solely on

Cobble Court. South facade. Courtesy of the Division of Rare and Manuscript Collections, Cornell University Library

Cobble Court. Pilaster detail. Courtesy of the Division of Rare and Manuscript Collections, Cornell University Library

the virtues of the materials. The walls surrounding the forecourt, rear garden terrace, and lower-level pool and the stone pillars with recessed bull's-eye lights marking the entrance into the estate enjoyed a similar treatment.

Cobble Court's intricately carved wood front door—inspired by an old French farmhouse screen in Atterbury's collection—opened into a wide entrance hall with stone walls, open-beam ceiling, and slate floor. Throughout the house, Atterbury spread special flourishes to personalize the space. In the front hall, the mantel was carved with a plan of the house and the Latin inscription "*Ornamenta Domus Amici Frequentantes*" (An ornamented house is frequented by friends), while the pilasters in the vaulted corridor extending back to the double-height library were detailed with caricatures relating to vineyards and archery—subjects in which Mr. Graydon was interested. The Canterbury Room, inspired by Graydon's extensive Chaucer collection, featured quotations from major literary figures such as Chaucer, Dante, and Shakespeare carved into the stone fireplace and paneling of the upper balcony. An enormous twenty-panel stained-glass window with colorful characters and scenes from *The Canterbury Tales* lit the south side of the library for which Atterbury commis-

Cobble Court. Library. Gottcho-Schleisner Collection.
Library of Congress

·SOUTH·ELEVATION·

·SCALE·⅛ inch = 1 FT·

·T·MONDAY·4·JUNE·1928·

·HOUSE·FOR·HARRY·L·LINCH·ESQ·~·CINCINNATI·OHIO·

Harry L. Linch house, Avondale, Ohio. Rendering
of south elevation by John Almy Tompkins 2nd.
The Architect 11 (January 1929): 400

sioned his friend Albert Herter to design a drapery depicting the procession of Chaucer's pilgrims.

Just after Atterbury finished Ca Sole, he designed a smaller Italian-inspired residence for lawyer Harry L. Linch (1885–1971) in nearby Avondale. In fact, Linch had so admired elements of the Schmidlapps' home that he asked Atterbury to incorporate them in his house. Reflecting his strong opinions and considerable attention to detail, Atterbury produced no fewer than nine schemes for the Linches, presenting different variations of plan, window arrangement, orientation, and landscaping.[9] Completed in 1929, the home featured rough stone walls, light brick details, peacock-blue trim and shutters, red tile roof, and a round stair tower. The charming and intimate interiors also included design elements similar to those in Ca Sole.

Atterbury's handling of color and materials produced an even more striking effect at Stone Ashley, Miss Florence L. Pond's desert home on the outskirts of Tucson, Arizona (1934).[10] Florence Pond (1867–1955), a daughter of prominent Detroit lawyer Ashley Pond, placed Atterbury in her confidence, giving him full artistic rein over the design. As he described, "The building of Stone Ashley was a wonderful experience and the place owes whatever interest, beauty and charm . . . found in it to the extraordinary degree of trust and faith [Pond] put in an architect she had never met, until the day Astelle and I stepped off the train at Tucson."[11]

While Atterbury absorbed little of the modernist influences then beginning to permeate the profession, Stone Ashley's stripped-down rectilinear quality reflected a modernist sensibility more so than any of his other projects. In laying out his scheme for Pond's flat-roofed stone Italian Renaissance house, Atterbury gravitated toward a steep sloping site on the 320-acre estate, located in the sandy foothills of the Rincon Mountains. The decorative quality of Stone Ashley's coursed brick and stone facades and walls—similar to those of Cobble Court—emphasized the house's boxy silhouette and created an appealing backdrop to the architect's gardens and fountains. A green oasis within the desert, Atterbury's landscaping included different levels of green lawns; lush plantings; orange, olive, and eucalyptus trees; and an avenue of cypresses leading up to the entrance. In a sunken garden to the east, Atterbury located a water cooling tower—part of the circulatory system he adapted from "age-old devices" to pipe water through a series of radiators and ducts to cool the house and irrigate the site. As he recalled, "When we found that it would require the circulation of around 150 gallons a minute to give the cooling power desired for Miss Pond's house, it seemed a shame not to get some fun out of it all. And that's why our fountains were born."[12] From the east terrace, water spilled down a set of semicircular steps, through a channel to a tower embellished with shapes of flowers and suns. Atterbury's wrought-iron gates and

TOP *Miss Florence L. Pond house, Stone Ashley, Tucson, Arizona. Exterior view.* Courtesy of the Division of Rare and Manuscript Collections, Cornell University Library

BOTTOM *Stone Ashley. Plan.* Courtesy of the Division of Rare and Manuscript Collections, Cornell University Library

grilles, set within arched and square shuttered openings, and the star motifs inspired by the clear Arizona night sky, added further decorative interest to the scheme. In the design of the forecourt fountain, Atterbury incorporated a star-shaped pool from which water rose in jets from each of its five points.

Atterbury's artistic and ambitious design made a strong impression. The *New York Times* pronounced it "one of the most beautiful [houses] in the region" with "extraordinary gardens facing the mountains."[13] Atterbury's friend and client John D. Rockefeller Jr. was equally entranced by the manner in which "the house and grounds [were] tied in with their wild desert mountain surroundings." After visiting the house in 1947, Rockefeller wrote Atterbury, "To have seen this lovely house was a great treat and an inspiration, I don't wonder you enjoyed building it; you may well be proud of it. . . . Every detail I examined with interest and appreciation, the lovely iron work, the skillful handling of brick and stone, also the harmonious blending of the various materials. I liked especially the way the flanking buildings lose themselves in the plantings. The interior we thought most attractive and livable; the view from every window, as well as every room, is superb and obviously carefully planned."[14]

In designing his friend Starling W. Childs's house at the Yeamans Hall Club outside Charleston, South Carolina, Atterbury demonstrated his proficiency in the early American idiom endemic to the area). Childs (1870–1946), an investment banker from New York City, had been in Atterbury's

Stone Ashley. Garden and water cooling tower. Courtesy of the Division of Rare and Manuscript Collections, Cornell University Library

Starling W. Childs house, Yeamans Hall Club, Charleston, South Carolina. Rendering by John Almy Tompkins 2nd with architect's note: "The gentleman reclining under a blue umbrella is the Architect contemplating the fruit of his toil!—put in his own prophetic hand. The sad gentleman is the owner addressing a fond farewell after giving the house to the Architect rather than pay his bill." Courtesy of Starling Lawrence

class of Scroll and Key. He was president of Yeamans Hall, a winter colony for northerners founded in 1924 by architect James Gamble Rogers (Scroll and Key, 1889) and several of his friends and clients. The development that Rogers designed around the golf course was made up of understated white painted wood cottages with porches in keeping with the southern tradition. Inspired by the original planters' estates in the region, Atterbury produced a low rambling stucco and frame house with brick chimneys and dormers in 1928. Inside, he executed comfortable and hospitable interiors, demonstrating the notion that "rooms only justif[ied] themselves when they [were] livable."[15] Architectural critic Augusta Owen Patterson, writing for *Town & Country*, aptly noted that the rambling living room with burned cypress paneling was "a room made for people who keep their fires always lit and feel that a house was made to live in as distinct from a house designed to serve as an impersonal background."[16] Atterbury's intimate barrel-vaulted entry hall ran the length of the house; its twin stairs led to a women's dormitory on one side and a men's dormitory on the other.

Atterbury applied his characteristic blend of lammie brick and half-timbered detail to the facades of the Zimbalist residence at 225–27 East 49th Street to create his only Tudor-style house in Manhattan.[17] The Russian-born violinist and composer Efrem Zimbalist (1889–1985) was known for his "assured technique, intelligent musicianship and patrician bearing" while his wife, the handsome and charismatic Alma Gluck Zimbalist (1884–1938), had created a sensation as a soprano in the Metropolitan Opera.[18] Their 1914 marriage represented the union of two of the most respected musical figures of their time. Soon after Alma's retirement in 1925, the Zimbalists purchased a large lot in Turtle Bay on which to create their ideal home. Atterbury transformed the existing brownstones on the site into a wide four-story house with large casement windows, half-timbered details, and dormers. As a reflection of the Zimbalists' personality and artistic pursuits, he inserted an intricately carved panel over the entrance of a singing angel and a violin entwined around the five opening notes of "O', Rest in the Lord" from Mendelssohn's *Elijah*—Alma's favorite oratorio. Like his design for 105–7 East 73rd Street (1903), Atterbury incorporated two houses into one; however, this time the facade read more convincingly as one large residence with a shared center entry. At its heart lay an immense rosewood-paneled music room with twin Steinways, which overlooked an enclosed garden with Italian fountains—the location of the Zimbalists' celebrated musical soirees that attracted musicians from around the world.

Efrem Zimbalist house, 225–27 East 49th Street, New York, New York. American Architect 131 (March 5, 1927): 325

ROCKEFELLER COMMISSIONS

During the early 1930s, John D. Rockefeller Jr. (1874–1960) emerged as Atterbury's most important client. For the Rockefellers, Atterbury applied his rustic Norman style to a farm group in Pocantico Hills, New York, and to several buildings as part of the National Parks system on Mount Desert Island and Schoodic Point in Maine. While the Rockefellers could be opinionated, Rockefeller and Atterbury came out of the design process as good friends. Atterbury endearingly called his client "Doctor" since Rockefeller generously paid Atterbury's doctors' bills and sent him to Arizona to convalesce when the architect fell ill. As his health deteriorated, Rockefeller continued to help him out financially.

In 1930, Rockefeller commissioned Atterbury to design a farm group at his family's property near Kykuit on a hillside site with distant views of the Hudson River.[19] Years earlier Frederick Law Olmsted Jr.'s firm had surveyed the land to best determine the location for the farm and, having worked with Atterbury before, may have recommended the architect. Additionally, Atterbury's Surprise Valley Farm for Arthur Curtiss James in Newport had been widely published and was well known. As an effort to strengthen his family's farming operations in the area, Rockefeller requested a thoroughly modern facility with barns, ample storage space, and advanced equipment to process farm products. To achieve this, Atterbury accompanied Rockefeller and his second son, Nelson (1908–1979), to Mount Hope Farm in Williamstown, Massachusetts, in the summer of 1931 to study technological advances and new construction methods within the farming community. The 1,400-acre Mount Hope Farm was considered one of the foremost experimental farms in the country. Owned by Rockefeller's older sister, Alta Prentice (1871–1962), the

well-equipped modern facility provided a standard from which Atterbury and his clients could learn. Due to his interest in architecture, a young Nelson Rockefeller—later governor of New York (1959–73) and America's vice president (1973–77)—took the reins from his father and became involved in the design of the barns at Pocantico Hills.

By August, the architect's working drawings were well under way. As described by Atterbury, they detailed a "commonsense, straightforward and simple architectural solution to the problem, along the lines of the American farm barn." "Of course," he wrote Rockefeller, "we can elaborate this and make it more picturesque in the details" but felt "the problem [was] a practical one" and "that the interior requirements ought to be satisfied in the matter of windows before anything else." Although "the very simple treatment [he] . . . suggested [had] possibilities of working out well architecturally," he added that "much study to satisfy the problem from all points of view" would be needed.[20] To expand upon his straightforward scheme,

Barns for John D. Rockefeller Jr., Pocantico Hills, New York. Courtesy of the Division of Rare and Manuscript Collections, Cornell University Library

Atterbury evolved a multitiered Norman-style farm group consisting of a horse stable, hay barn, cow barn, silos, garages, and offices. On the exterior, he struck a fine balance of rustic sophistication by combining coursed stone—which gave the facades a banded look—with rose-colored brick and weathered half-timbering and wood. Atterbury approved of the hillside site that the Olmsted Brothers had chosen because it gave "a number of advantages, both aesthetic and practical. By a system of upper and lower levels, a much larger area of working ground space [was] available than the same sized plot of level land would allow."[21] Atterbury's steel-frame construction made large openings and spans possible. His plan featured a series of arches and storage areas on the lower level, which supported an upper-level court around which various barns and stables were arranged. The road, which ran along the lower level, swung up around to the west, ran underneath a broad opening punched through the building mass, and emptied into the central farm court. The hay barn—the tallest building in the group—formed the centerpiece of the composition, while the other low-lying structures, enhanced by dormers

and ventilation louvers, enclosed the court on the south, east, and west. The two-level arrangement enabled Atterbury to fit the farm group deftly into the hillside, allowing it to blend well with the surrounding landscape.

Atterbury elaborated upon the basic rectangular shape of the hay barn by adding a steeply pitched roof, a cupola, a series of brick-infilled stone arches above a string of large wooden carriage doors, and small leaded windows under the eaves. The flurry of correspondence between Atterbury and his clients regarding its design was indicative of the level of thought and detail that went into every aspect of the project. In many cases, Atterbury was compelled to defend his choices when asked by the Rockefellers to change elements. To save on cost, Nelson suggested omitting the "stone arches over the hay barn doors which [led] to the shed space leaving the walls plain above the door."[22] Disturbed by this request, Atterbury prompted his clients to reconsider. On a different occasion, Nelson asked Atterbury to revisit the cupola because it "was a little too tall and thin and slightly out of scale with the rest of the group." "If it were a little shorter and the pitch of the roof not quite so steep," he recommended, "it would have more of the New England farm barn atmosphere about it."[23] While it appears that Atterbury retained the barn as originally proposed, the Rockefellers did succeed in expressing their opinions and tailoring the buildings to their more subdued tastes. Atterbury was concerned about the shadows that the barn's louvered cupola would cast and suggested a different treatment. Nelson, however, "did not care for the lattice effect" Atterbury recommended and chose to stay with the more discrete louvers.[24] Nelson also asked Atterbury to tone down the "fancy bolts which appear in the stone work between the arches" because "instead of being less conspicuous than they were on the drawing they stand out so from the stone work that they attract your attention immediately."[25] Subsequently, Atterbury softened the color of the bolts to match the adjoining stone.

In the northern corner of the courtyard, Atterbury transformed the evocative vertical forms of the two silos into a pair of medieval watchtowers. Their striking silhouettes, octagonal roofs, and small windows added picturesque intrigue to the scheme. Atterbury was horrified when Nelson suggested omitting "the windows around the top of the silos and [carrying] plain stone work to the roof" and persuaded him to keep them.[26] Atterbury also succeeded in convincing the family to carry out the "inconspicuous" retaining walls behind the barns with small boulders rather than the less-expensive cement that had been specified.

After three years of work, Atterbury traveled up to Pocantico on May 3, 1933, to watch "the cows come home."[27] Despite the back and forth on various design elements, everyone was thrilled with the outcome. Though John D. Rockefeller Jr. acknowledged that the "numerous discussions from the outset regarding this detail or that" had, at times, been difficult, he concurred that "now that they are finished and occupied there is but one feeling in regard to them, and that is a feeling of complete satisfaction and delight." He expressed his gratitude to Atterbury, writing, "You and your office force have worked untiringly and patiently to meet the wishes, the whims and the vagaries of the Rockefeller family as embodied in a group of farm buildings. Never have you become exasperated or impatient, always have you been cooperative and adaptable."[28]

To alleviate the housing problem on the Pocantico Hills estate, Atterbury also designed four small and two medium-sized houses in 1930 for Rockefeller employees across from Union Church. Like the cottages he had executed for the Norton Company at Indian Hill, they were

modest one-and-a-half-story Colonial-style homes carried out in wood and shingle. Atterbury persuaded Rockefeller to build the more cost-effective semi-detached houses for his workmen if they did not object; however, since the zoning in the village only allowed single-family homes, they were never constructed. At the same time, Atterbury oversaw the redesign of several older homes that were moved to Pocantico Hills, settling questions of taste, architecture, and location.

During the period that Atterbury was working at Pocantico Hills, he became involved in additional projects on the coast of Maine—an area to which Rockefeller was also devoted—where he had enjoyed a flurry of commissions for summer cottages at the turn of the century. The thriving resort of Bar Harbor initially had drawn Rockefeller to Mount Desert Island in the 1900s as a college student. Captivated by the beauty of the island, he later purchased 150 acres and The Eyrie, a half-timbered house (1897) built by Samuel Fessenden Clarke, in the neighboring village of Seal Harbor; in 1914, John and Abby Aldrich Rockefeller (1874–1948) commissioned Duncan Candler (1873–1949) to remodel the cottage into a 100-room Tudor-style mansion. As Rockefeller was discovering the island's rugged landscape, Boston native George B. Dorr (1853–1944) and president emeritus of Harvard Charles W. Eliot (1834–1926) were busy incorporating the Hancock County Trustees of Public Reservations to preserve land in the area.[29] President Woodrow Wilson established the Sieur de Monts National Monument in 1916—a nod to the region's French heritage—after their organization gave 6,000 acres to the federal government. In 1919, this land—chiefly composed of mountain tops—became known as Lafayette National Park (1919) and later Acadia National Park (1929).

Seeing this land as "a possible nucleus for a truly magnificent park," Rockefeller began accumulating property between the public byways and the unconnected park land to provide unrestricted access.[30] With government permission, he began extending a network of carriage roads and horse trails from his land deep into the park's rolling topography, which allowed him to enjoy Mount Desert's beautiful vistas in scenic seclusion. In 1930, as he was collaborating with Frederick Law Olmsted Jr. on the construction of the carriage roads and a number of stone-faced bridges, he commissioned Atterbury to design several gate lodges on his property to prevent unauthorized automobiles from entering the trails. In due time, he would donate the lodges and the land to the National Park Service.[31]

Rockefeller barns. Silos and dormers, 2007. Jonathan Wallen

Determined to set a good example, Rockefeller first asked Atterbury to survey the architecture of the western parks and to apply his conclusions to bettering Acadia. In August and September 1929, Atterbury toured the parks at Grand Teton, Yellowstone, Yosemite, Zion, Bryce Canyon, Grand Canyon, and Mesa Verde. He took more than three hundred photographs and produced a lengthy report that "made an impression on each and every one of the officers of the Service" and was considered "a distinct contribution to . . . landscape preservation policies."[32] For the most part disappointed by the various buildings and

hotels he encountered on his trip, Atterbury underlined the importance of context in designing park architecture—a principle to which he had adhered throughout his career. "The true answer to the problem," he wrote, "must be derived from its own premises and conditions."[33] Writing in May 1930 after an expedition to Seal Harbor, Atterbury stated that he was "astonished at the great beauty and variety that [Rockefeller's] work in the parks [had] brought out and made available for everyone to rejoice in."[34] Confident in his choice of architect, Rockefeller responded, "that Acadia National Park and its possibilities have impressed you

TOP *Gates and lodge, Brown Mountain, Acadia National Park, Northeast Harbor, Maine*. Charles E. Knell. *Architecture* 71 (March 1935): 129

BOTTOM *Brown Mountain gates, 2006*. Jonathan Wallen

so strongly is gratifying and reassuring to me. I sometimes wonder whether I am over-enthusiastic about the park."[35] While the majority of Mount Desert's residents, both permanent and seasonal, applauded his efforts, some believed that Rockefeller's automobile and horse roads rendered the island's scenic beauty too accessible and destroyed its wild charm.[36]

Atterbury applied the lessons of his western exodus to the design of Rockefeller's gatehouses at Brown Mountain in Northeast Harbor and Jordan Pond in Seal Harbor. In his report, the architect had emphasized the importance of "ancient local traditions" and had suggested "developing a style from these historic precedents that will also satisfy the modern practical requirements."[37] Because Atterbury felt that Acadia "called for a somewhat more sophisticated treatment," he opted to work in the French tradition—a reference to the area's early French Colonial associations.[38] In November 1930, Atterbury completed preliminary studies. By that time, he was already in the midst of developing working drawings for a Norman-style gatehouse, teahouse, and carriage and saddle center on a thin strip of land Rockefeller owned north of Eagle Lake. However, the project was never carried out due to its controversial location next to the lake that served as Bar Harbor's water supply. Designs for a teahouse at Jordan Pond were similarly unrealized.

Brown Mountain lodge. Charles E. Knell. *Architecture* 71 (March 1935): 128

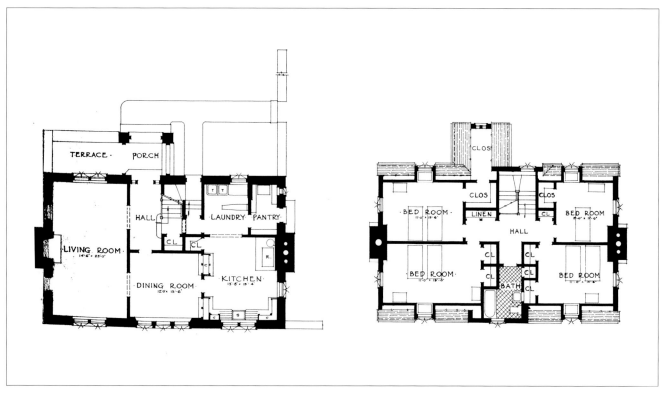

Brown Mountain lodge. First- and second-floor plans. Architecture 71 (March 1935): 129

Gates and lodge, Jordan Pond, Acadia National Park, Seal Harbor, Maine, 2006. Jonathan Wallen

234

National Park Service station headquarters building, Schoodic Point, Maine. National Park Service, Acadia National Park's William Otis Sawtelle Collections and Research Center

The gate lodges were discreetly located in wooded areas "entirely outside the picture . . . where there was no direct comparison or competition with the scenic marvels"—an attribute of which Atterbury had discovered the importance out west.[39] "Color is probably even more important than design," the architect stressed, especially "where the prime requisite architecturally is that it harmonize and fit in with its surroundings."[40] In typical fashion, Atterbury based his choice of materials on the virtues of their color. For both sets of gates and lodges, he used a seam-face granite excavated from Cadillac Mountain, weathered and treated pecky cypress, and soft colored brick from Holland mixed with James River brick from Richmond, Virginia. Like the barns at Pocantico Hills, he stratified the stone in courses to give the buildings and gates a banded appearance—a technique adapted from the Le Puys district that Atterbury had toured in 1900. Rockefeller followed Atterbury's advice to "have the brick belt course in the Brown Mountain Lodge . . . and the seam face granite in the Jordan Pond Lodge." As the architect expressed, he "personally . . . felt inclined toward the brick, which should not, of course, be a bright red, but of soft old coloring."[41] Distinguished by courses of brick, octagonal turrets, and French shingle-tile roofs, the Brown Mountain gates added a note of sophistication off of the road leading into Northeast Harbor, while the Jordan Pond gates, buried deeper in the park system, were more unassuming.

As modest-sized homes for park personnel, Atterbury's charming rustic farmhouses featured high-pitched roofs, dormers, and half-timbered detail. At both Brown Mountain and Jordan Pond, he connected the house to the gate with a stone wall that also prevented "the family life from spilling over into the front."[42] Atterbury had noted that the absence of shutters or blinds in the western parks made the buildings "unlivable," and he incorporated natural wood shutters at Jordan Pond with whimsically carved cutouts of the letter "A." His high-pitched roofs, which gave "the exterior a decided character," were, in his words, "practical, logical as well as picturesque."[43] Atterbury also had strong opinions about plantings and trees. "Without proper background and plantings," he pronounced, "no buildings . . . will ever succeed no matter how good intrinsically their design may be."[44] At Acadia, he recommended birches, evergreens, and climbing vines and suggested avoiding exotic plants, specimens, and base plantings that would alter the effect of the buildings.[45] Occasionally his opinions would clash with those of noted landscape architect and Bar Harbor summer resident Beatrix Farrand (née Jones) with whom he worked on the project. Also in Rockefeller's confidence, Farrand designed Abby Aldrich Rockefeller's gardens at The Eyrie in the 1920s, landscaped Rockefeller's carriage roads, and had collaborated with Atterbury on earlier projects in the area.

When completed in August 1932, the gate lodges were enthusiastically received. Rockefeller was delighted with the outcome, finding them "much more imposing and important than [he] dreamed [they] would be, and . . . exceedingly charming and decorative."[46] In his praise, architect W. Welles Bosworth (1869–1966) touched upon the effect that Atterbury had been striving to achieve, observing that "they [settled] into their environment with a natural picturesqueness born of what seems to me to be a very just sense of the locality."[47]

Just east of Mount Desert Island on the Schoodic Peninsula, Atterbury designed a new naval radio station in 1933.[48] Previously located near Otter Cliffs on Mount Desert—an area with good reception and radio communication with Europe—the navy's dilapidated structure had been condemned by the islanders. Rockefeller, who wished to extend his carriage roads through the land, negotiated to build the navy a new station nearby in exchange for the Mount Desert property. The navy agreed to 26 acres on Schoodic Point within a more distant precinct of Acadia National Park. Although it was just four miles from Bar Harbor by sea, the tortuous Maine coastline rendered Schoodic Point and its neighboring town of Winter Harbor more remote. Relatively isolated, Schoodic Point's rugged coast, tall red granite cliffs, rough surf, and immediate water access provided extraordinary panoramas and vistas.

Working in the rustic Norman style he had employed for the gate lodges, Atterbury designed officers' quarters, a power house and pump station, a receiving building, and a radio compass station. By August 1934, the buildings had begun to take shape. Atterbury reported to Rockefeller that his "man [had] just come back from Schoodic and . . . that the contractors [were] doing a very good piece of work and that the Navy people, at least, [were] highly pleased."[49] Atterbury's three-story apartment building, built into the slope of the land, featured two- and three-bedroom apartments for officers and also garages in the base. For the largest and most impressive of the structures, Atterbury used the same sophisticated stone and brick patterning he had at Brown Mountain and Jordan Pond but employed darker-hued materials that better reflected the location's deep coloring and open northern exposure.

Upon its completion in 1935, the Rockefellers "were charmed with the building and thought it delightful, attractive, well arranged and eminently successful." "In this instance," Rockefeller exclaimed, "you have not only built a completely satisfactory building, but have set a standard for Acadia Park architecture that will surely have its influence."[50] Over the five-year period during which Atterbury and Rockefeller collaborated, Atterbury produced some of his best and most memorable work. Both men missed the regular interaction they experienced through the design process. While Rockefeller remarked in 1935 that he "would miss the frequent contacts with [Atterbury] which [he] had for some years, [he continued] to be grateful for the many things [the architect had] done."[51]

MUSEUMS, CHURCHES, AND CLUBS

The American Wing at the Metropolitan Museum of Art, one of the most acclaimed projects with which Atterbury was involved, was perhaps his least-known commission—and intentionally so.[52] In 1919, Atterbury rejoined forces with his old friend and client, Robert de Forest, whose long and auspicious association with the esteemed art institution brought about some of the country's first and most-influential period rooms. Not only had de Forest married Emily Johnston, the daughter of the museum's first president, John Taylor Johnston (1820–1893), but also he had proposed to her on the day the museum was founded.[53] After becoming a trustee in 1889, de Forest rose through the ranks to become president of the board in 1915. His interest in American decorative arts piqued by his wife's

enthusiasm for collecting, de Forest served as the chairman of the art committee for the Hudson-Fulton exhibition in 1909, which was held in conjunction with the 300th anniversary of Hudson's discovery and the 100th anniversary of Fulton's navigation by steamboat of the Hudson River. The comprehensive exhibit illuminated the inherent quality and craftsmanship of the American decorative arts from the Fulton period, which theretofore had received little notice, and gave de Forest and his colleagues the opportunity to gauge its popularity as a museum display. H. Eugene Bolles's collection of important early American furniture, which the museum had borrowed for the event, formed the nucleus of the show. Soon after, acting upon the advice of de Forest, Mrs. Russell Sage purchased the 434-piece group from the Boston lawyer and gave it to the Metropolitan to create the core of the museum's American furniture collection.

With the idea of establishing a dedicated American wing, de Forest and his fellow trustees Henry W. Kent (1866–1948) and R. T. Haines Halsey (1865–1942), who became the chairman of the Committee on American Decorative Art in 1913, led the initiative to acquire rooms, architectural fragments, and additional pieces of furniture and decorative arts. Over the next ten years, the group, with the help of a young curator named Durr Friedly, scoured the eastern seaboard for distressed historic properties they could disassemble and bring to New York to reincorporate into the museum. Emily de Forest unearthed paneling, mantels, and cupboards from a Colonial house in Woodbury, Long Island, while her husband, as president of the Municipal Art Commission, salvaged the classical marble facade of the United States Branch Bank (1824–36) designed by Martin Euclid Thompson (1786–1877), which had served as the United States Assay Office from 1854 to 1914. The building had been located at 15 Wall Street until its dismantling in 1915. In 1922, with the collection sufficiently augmented and plans completed, the de Forests publically announced their gift of an American wing building in which the decorative arts could be framed by the environment for which they had been designed—a method adopted from European museums such as the Swiss National Museum in Zurich. According to de Forest, "American art lost its distinctive charm of simplicity" in the large galleries and "could be adequately shown only in the modest rooms for which it was made."[54] This novel technique enabled the curators to compellingly display artistic development in America from the Colonial to the early Republican periods.

American Wing, Metropolitan Museum of Art, New York, New York. Rendering. Courtesy of the Division of Rare and Manuscript Collections, Cornell University Library

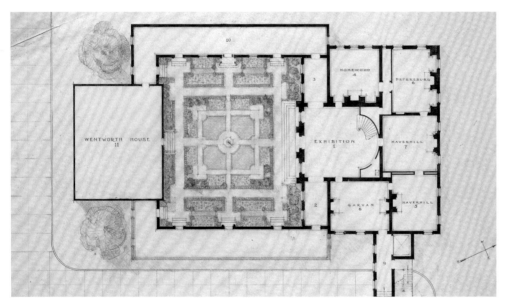

Grosvenor Atterbury, Preliminary plan for the American Wing, October 9, 1919, ink and watercolor, on paper. The Metropolitan Museum of Art Archives Image © The Metropolitan Museum of Art

From the outset, it was understood that the de Forests would provide the architect for the project.[55] As de Forest described, Atterbury "was selected as architect of the American Wing, not because he was an old personal friend (though he is), but because he combined a number of important qualifications for this particular enterprise. He had a deep sympathy with Colonial art. He had shown what he could do and what his sympathy was in the restoration of our New York City Hall and in that of Connecticut Hall in New Haven. But, besides that, he had an infinite patience, he had a most painstaking care for detail, and he had infinite tact."[56] In accepting the commission— perhaps out of loyalty to de Forest—Atterbury was faced with the difficult task of combining fifteen original rooms with various architectural elements and fragments and two reproduction rooms into a three-story rectangular building without imposing any of his own taste or style. "If you have ever tried to persuade an assemblage of twenty-five or thirty old Colonial rooms—each with his or her very definite idea of the proper ceiling height to have, the best location of windows and doors and fireplaces," pronounced Atterbury, "to live together amicably in a rectangular building of fixed dimensions, in three stories, each representing more or less accurately their chronological sequence, and, at the same time, so arranged that they can all look out through the original windows of the old Assay Office—you

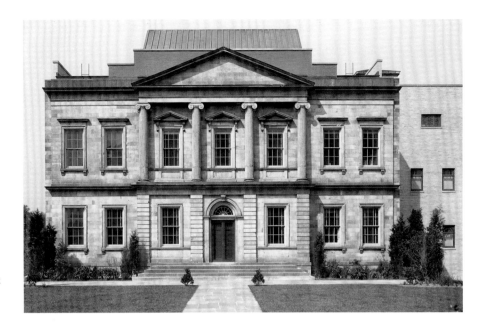

Museum views, exteriors, the American Wing, 1925. The Metropolitan Museum of Art Archives Image © The Metropolitan Museum of Art

American Wing. Room from Philadelphia. Courtesy of the Division of Rare and Manuscript Collections, Cornell University Library

will find that the most diabolical cross-word puzzle ever concocted is mere child's play in comparison."[57]

With his work cut out for him, Atterbury executed a steel, reinforced-concrete, and brick building that connected to the northwestern section of the Pierpont Morgan wing. During the 1910s, Charles Over Cornelius (1890–1937), the assistant curator of decorative arts, had devised a somewhat confused three-story scheme for the project.[58] Taking his cues from the predetermined facade, Cornelius's template, and the established chronology of the rooms, Atterbury worked out a well-organized and coherent solution that better facilitated circulation and flow. As designed in 1919, its southern facade—the

archaeologically restrained marble front of the United States Branch Bank—looked onto a picturesque Colonial garden, embellished with flagged walkways, inset mill-stones, hedges and banks of evergreens, and the center-hall Wentworth-Gardner house from Portsmouth, New Hampshire, directly opposite. However, in the aftermath of World War One, plans changed: the garden, framed to the east and west by single-story arcaded corridors, was not completed, and the Wentworth-Gardner house was never brought to New York.

Inside, the exhibition rooms on each floor were arranged around large central galleries and unfolded chronologically down from the third story. The top floor showcased the earliest Colonial rooms, two of which were full reproductions, which opened off a center hall with roof trusses and framing modeled after the Old Ship Meeting House (1681) at Hingham, Massachusetts. On the second floor, reconstructed rooms, such as a 1793 ballroom from Gadsby's Tavern near Mount Vernon, embodied the more refined spirit of the revolutionary period. The assemblage of Federal architecture and arts on the first floor featured elements designed by Charles Bulfinch (1763–1844) and Samuel McIntyre (1757–1811). Working with a host of museum authorities and curators, Atterbury had little leeway to impose his own ideas.[59] However, the often imperious architect deferred easily to the larger picture. In describing the design process, de Forest suggested that "there wasn't merely one client. . . . There were clients of both sexes. And there was a whole staff of the Museum. It was no tempting task for an architect to do nothing original himself, but to frame in a whole lot of old rooms with all their old corners and all their irregularities. And it was no small task to do this with all the changes that everybody, at one time or another, would suggest. Our friendship for Grosvenor Atterbury and our admiration for him have survived all those experiences and he is largely entitled to the credit."[60]

In November 1924, the sequence of spaces opened to the public. "In a thousand ways the Metropolitan Museum has made itself indispensable to the nation," noted architectural critic Royal Cortissoz, "but never hitherto has it rendered a service so intensely national in character. . . . The wing has an educational value beyond measurement."[61] A triumph, the American Wing spawned a succession of house museums and period rooms across the country and encouraged the Colonial Revival movement. For Atterbury, "from the point of the designer . . . [its] object . . . seems to me to be primarily that of a corrective. Our sense of beauty is like the magnetic compass. It does not always point true north. It needs to be corrected from time to time. Some day we may have a gyroscopic sense of beauty. But until that time comes, an exhibition of Colonial art . . . may furnish a very healthy corrective, if we heed its teachings."[62]

Colonial and Federal architecture provided a sound basis for Atterbury's proposals for an addition to Fraunces Tavern at 101 Broad Street and the new building for the Museum of the City of New York (1928), formerly housed at Gracie Mansion. Both projects intended to highlight the history and heritage of the city; architects entering designs into the Museum of the City of New York competition were "reminded that the building [was] to be expressive of New York of the past, which is fading, as well as of the present."

For both projects, Atterbury chose to evoke New York's old Federal Hall—the country's first example of Federal architecture. Once located on the site of the U.S. Customs House on Wall Street, the building had been constructed in the early 1700s and remodeled by Pierre Charles L'Enfant (1754–1825) in the 1780s. However, since it had been demolished in 1812, Atterbury referenced rendered images, detailing the building in 1789—the year of Washington's inauguration—and 1797 to inform his schemes. For the Sons of the Revolution in the State of New York, he proposed renovating the existing building on the site, which adjoined Fraunces Tavern to the north, as a thinner, smaller version of the landmark. His entry for the Museum of the City of New York competition, won by Joseph H. Freedlander (1870–1943), was more fantastical. To correspond to the larger lot on Fifth Avenue between 103rd and 104th Streets, he stretched the proportions of Federal Hall to form the building's center block between two Georgian end pavilions. Behind, he inserted a towering replica of Stadt Huys, New Amsterdam's City Hall, once located on Pearl Street, as an option for further expansion.[63]

In 1927, Daniel Gleason Tenney (1867–1951), a Yale classmate of Atterbury's, commissioned the architect to design and furnish a small brick chapel in memory of his parents, Charles H. and Fanny H. Tenney, in Methuen, Massachusetts. Long connected to the economic vitality of the area, Charles Tenney had invested in many of the manufacturing concerns, textile mills and public works that flourished in Methuen at the end of the nineteenth century. Having recently completed the American Wing, Atterbury referenced rooms and features at the Metropolitan Museum in carrying out his scheme. According to the *Lawrence Telegram*, "no expense was spared to make it a perfect duplicate of chapels reared by the Pilgrims."[64] Weathered materials, including lumber and slate from old dismantled homesteads in New Hampshire, combined with treated brick and stone, gave the chapel's facades a patina of age and elegance, while antique elements, such as the belfry's 1750 weather vane, added history and a certain authenticity. Like he had in the American Wing, Atterbury created an interior space evocative of Hingham's Old Ship Meeting House (1681) by encasing the steel trusses with aged wood to create the semblance of heavy beams and framing. Atterbury collaborated with artist Martha Ryther (1896–1981), a former student of Maurice Prendergast and William Zorach, who painted the reredos panels, seats, and altar chest; the chest was detailed with biblical scenes after old tiles at the Metropolitan Museum.

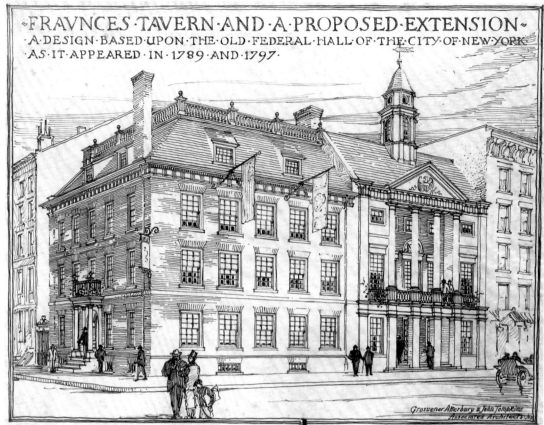

~FRAVNCES·TAVERN·AND·A·PROPOSED·EXTENSION~
·A·DESIGN·BASED·UPON·THE·OLD·FEDERAL·HALL·OF·THE·CITY·OF·NEW·YORK·
·AS·IT·APPEARED·IN·1789·AND·1797·

Grosvenor Atterbury & John Tompkins
Associated Architects. NY

"The first Congress of the United States of America was convened in Federal Hall
in the City of New York, corner of Wall and Nassau Streets, and Washington
was inaugurated in the Balcony of this Hall April 30.1789" (from a contemporary print)

*Proposal for
an addition to
Fraunces Tavern,
New York, New
York.* Courtesy of the
Division of Rare and
Manuscript
Collections, Cornell
University Library

John Tompkins Associated
Nov. 1928

A true Perspective View of the Southwesterly Prospect of the Proposed
MUSEUM of the CITY of NEW YORK
representing as the Central feature of the Facade a Fac-simile of the "FEDERAL HALL" as that Edifice was completed by Major L'En-
in 1789 with the portico where HIS EXCELLENCY GEN. GEORGE WASHINGTON took the oath as First President of this Repub-
In this building was then established by the Saint Tammanys or Colombian Order, the First Museum in the City of New York ~ In the
background is found the COURT OF NEW AMSTERDAM with the original STADT HUYS restored as it was in 1654, the
first seat of our city government the "Communalty of the Manhattans" subsequently New Amsterdam.

*Competition entry
for the Museum
of the City of New
York, New York,
New York.* Courtesy
of the Division of Rare
and Manuscript
Collections, Cornell
University Library

Remodeling of the First Presbyterian Church,
12 West 12th Street, New York, New York.
Gottscho-Schleisner Collection. Library of Congress

Aside from Kingsport's First Methodist Episcopalian Church (1921), Forest Hills Gardens's Church-in-the-Gardens (1915), and the handful of modest chapels he designed, Atterbury's ecclesiastical work existed in the form of alterations, additions, and rectories.[65] Renovations to the First Presbyterian Church on Fifth Avenue between 11th and 12th Streets arose from the architect's connections with de Forest. Its congregation represented the confluence of three established Presbyterian churches in Manhattan: Old First, University Place, and Madison Square. Due to shifting financial and geographical conditions, the churches merged in 1918. De Forest, formerly a prominent Madison Square parishioner, called upon Atterbury to add a chancel to Joseph C. Wells's Gothic edifice (1840s) on Fifth Avenue, which had been modeled after the Church of St.

Savior in Bath. The arched envelope of Atterbury's chancel created an appealing backdrop for his intricately carved choir screen, newly positioned reredos panels by Taber Sears (1870–1950), and blue-glass rose window designed by Louis Comfort Tiffany. At the behest of Mrs. Robert de Forest and Mrs. Arthur Curtiss James, Atterbury returned to the First Presbyterian in 1937 to design the Alexander Chapel in memory of the combined church's first pastor, Dr. George Alexander. Located in the church's south wing, it featured stained-glass windows and Atterbury's beautiful ironwork wrought in the shape of the Scottish symbols: thistle, heather, and ivy.[66]

While Atterbury's 1926 proposal for the Union Club's new clubhouse was never built, it was among his most creative schemes. In the 1920s, the members of New York's oldest men's club began to weigh the benefits of remodeling their Georgian clubhouse on Fifth Avenue and 51st Street, designed by Cass Gilbert (1859–1934) and John DuFais (1855–1935) in 1902, or moving farther uptown. Recognizing that the inevitable tide of development north might eventually reduce the value of their real estate, the membership began exploring different options to maximize its worth. In 1926, the club invited Gilbert, Delano & Aldrich, and Atterbury to prepare schemes for a series of theoretical sites. Gilbert investigated the feasibility of adding on to the 51st Street building while Delano & Aldrich, the firm responsible for the Knickerbocker Club (1913–15), the Colony Club (1914–16), and The Brook (1924–25), examined the possibilities of a corner lot. Atterbury's location—an eighty-foot-wide side street plot running through the block—provided the grounds for a clever and extravagant solution. His proposal featured a dignified south-facing four-story building to house the main lounge and the large vaulted library with a ten-story edifice—replete with dining rooms, assembly rooms, bedrooms, kitchens, squash courts, pools, and Turkish baths—rising to the rear. At the center of the plan, Atterbury placed a delightful open-air Italian courtyard with glass walls that could be removed in the summer. Arcades with side windows, made possible by the assumption that the Union Club would also own the flanking lots, connected the main lounge to the rear assembly rooms.[67] Because the club wisely sold the 51st Street building at the height of the market, it was able to acquire a large lot on the northeast corner of 69th Street and Park Avenue and to use the equity to build a new home debt-free. However, since the membership went forward with Delano & Aldrich's corner scheme, Atterbury's masterful and intriguing design was never realized.

Study for the Union Club, street to street with interior court, New York, New York. Main entrance facade. Delano & Aldrich Collection, Avery Architectural and Fine Arts Library, Columbia University in the City of New York

Union Club. Central court with removable glass enclosure. Delano & Aldrich Collection, Avery Architectural and Fine Arts Library, Columbia University in the City of New York

HOSPITALS, ORPHANAGES, AND MEDICAL BUILDINGS

During a time when attractive and comfortable hospital wards were rare, Atterbury's humanistic approach toward design was refreshing and well embraced. At the Phipps Psychiatric Clinic at John Hopkins University (1908–13) and the Henry Phipps Institute (1908–13) in Philadelphia, the architect had manifested his commitment to ameliorating the patient's experience. As he had expressed at the Phipps Psychiatric Clinic's dedication ceremonies, Atterbury based his design principle around an epitaph taken from the entrance of Berlin's Virchow Hospital: "In treating the patient, do not forget the man."[68] In place of nondescript tiles and white walls, he strove to construct more uplifting and nurturing environments; however, because of their locations and programs, the exteriors of both Phipps commissions gave off an institutional air associated with large singular structures. In the 1920s and 1930s at the Bloomingdale Hospital in White Plains, New York, and the Children's Village in Hartford, Connecticut, Atterbury designed smaller buildings incorporated into pastoral settings to generate the soothing restorative quality he sought.

Formally established in 1821, the original Bloomingdale Hospital or Asylum—the psychiatric division of New York Hospital—was located far from the city's southern nucleus on the then-remote Morningside Heights site of what would in the 1890s become Columbia University. To treat its patients, the asylum encouraged mental and physical

Bloomingdale Hospital, White Plains, New York. Reception room, Sturgis Hall, Women's Occupational Therapy Building. The Architect 5 (January 1926): pl. 84

rehabilitation through recreational activities and constructive hobbies within an invigorating rural setting. However, as the city's growth encroached upon the northern oasis, the hospital was forced to seek out a new location with more property. In the 1890s, it moved to a large strip of farmland in White Plains; hospital officials commissioned James Lord Brown (1859–1901) and Frederick Law Olmsted Sr.'s firm to design and landscape a new campus. Bloomingdale's superintendent, Dr. Charles Nichols, examined recent institutional developments in Europe and suggested "villas or cottages" in addition to the main hospital buildings "with small parks and tree and shrubbery plantings . . . for the use of quiet patients . . . in as nearly a homelike way as mental invalids can live." Though aware of the "cottage system," the building committee was not inclined to "recommend a very extensive outlay of villas in view of the present commitments and the large appropriations already made."[69] Rather, before his death in 1901, Brown executed seven large Colonial Revival buildings embellished with subtle classical, Gothic, and Dutch flourishes and well settled within Olmsted's park-like setting of rolling lawns, curving walkways, trees, and plantings. With its emphasis on design, the Bloomingdale facility created an exceptional model of aesthetic hospital architecture.

As an architect, Atterbury was the ideal candidate to continue Bloomingdale's development along sympathetic lines.[70] From his extensive travels and research abroad when working on the Phipps Psychiatric Clinic, he was well versed in the criteria required to put "back into the definition of hospital the full meaning of 'hospitality,' somewhat forgotten perhaps in the stress of scientific progress."[71] Over a period of ten years, Atterbury added thirteen buildings to the Blooomingdale hospital cluster, which were connected to the original structures by underground tunnels. In the Olmsted-designed portion of the property, he executed occupational treatment buildings and convalescent cottages, as Dr. Nichols had envisioned, for the patients as well as quarters for doctors, nurses, and staff on additional farm property the hospital had acquired in the early 1900s. Having collaborated with Olmsted Jr. on Forest Hills Gardens, Atterbury had a strong knowledge of the firm's work and seamlessly integrated his buildings into the landscape.

To produce buildings "expressing that familiar quality of the individual home" and "a more soothing and agreeable reaction in the patient," Atterbury designed his rehabilitation spaces to be warm and home-like.[72] Sturgis Hall, the Women's Occupational Therapy Building (1921–22), was carried out in Atterbury's variation of the Tudor Revival

style and featured a charming groin-vaulted three-bay entrance arcade reminiscent of the Parrish Art Museum with delicate wrought-iron fixtures. In the lobby, the architect relied on the materials for architectural effect: tapestry brick walls, wooden beams and rafters, slate floor, and a large stone fireplace. As a whimsical and personal flourish, Atterbury incorporated stained-glass figures of women participating in the occupational arts into the leaded windows and transoms. Atterbury's attention to detail also suffused his designs for the men's and women's gymnasiums. In the Rogers Gymnasium (1922–24), he created club-like accommodations for the male patients with a billiards room, golf room, squash court, and a large wood-paneled space with a fireplace, large curtained windows, chandeliers, and comfortable chairs. The half-timbered Taylor Building or women's gymnasium (1924–25) featured a

basement bowling alley and a large exercise room with a beamed ceiling and built-in benches. Ostensibly private homes, his two Tudor Revival cottages (1930–31)—Bard House and Bruce House—for convalescent women no longer in need of intensive study were built after the hospital received a large bequest from the estate of Payne Whitney (1876–1927), the chief benefactor of New York Hospital's York Avenue building and a leading proponent of psychiatry.

To the east of Brown's original structures, Atterbury designed an enclave of houses and dwellings for employees and physicians. As the most impressive, his large Flemish-bond brick Georgian staff building (1921–25), with sleeping quarters and communal rooms, was embellished by a double-height portico and delicate Colonial Revival details. An arcade supported by attenuated wood piers connected

Children's Village, Hartford, Connecticut. Samuel H. Gottscho. Avery Architectural and Fine Arts Library, Columbia University in the City of New York

the building's central block to two side houses, each containing three apartments. For the six cottages located to the north of the staff house (1922–23; 1930–31), Atterbury followed the same formulas he had for Rockefeller's worker housing at Pocantico Hills to produce modest shingle and brick Colonial Revival houses with steep roofs and dormer windows.

At the Children's Village in Hartford, Connecticut—an offshoot of the Hartford Orphan Asylum—Atterbury continued to emphasize the nurturing quality of small cottage units.[73] Incorporated in 1833, the Hartford Orphan Asylum was a progressive institution that instated foster care and encouraged public-school education before they were widespread notions. The agency had been housed in an imposing Victorian edifice since 1878, but in 1911 it had a small girls' cottage built on its grounds to house children in smaller, more intimate groups. Because the cottage was such a success, the orphanage decided to plan a new home on Albany Avenue around the concept. Most likely this commission came though Atterbury's Scroll and Key compatriot Charles Parsons Cooley (1868–1954), a prominent Hartford financier. As a supporter of the Hartford Orphan Asylum's mission, Cooley sat on the organization's advisory committee while his wife served as its president for several years. Atterbury went on to design a granite and brick Colonial Revival house on Prospect Avenue with a two-story cast-iron porch for the Cooleys in 1929.[74]

The diminutive group of cottages for boys, girls, babies, and staff that Atterbury designed in 1925 was arranged

around a quadrangle—or village green—with an administration building at one end and a convalescent home at the other. Executed in Atterbury's distinctive hybrid of Colonial and Tudor Revival styles, the cottages were a charming and accessible assemblage of brick and shingle houses with steeply pitched roofs and dormer windows. In much the same fashion that the architect embellished his house designs, he incorporated leaded fanlights and transoms as well as shutters whimsically carved with cutout shapes of stars, trees, and topiaries. With its enclosed campus-like setting, the homey, residential quality of the village created a community in which children could grow and thrive, where their lives were "normal and healthy and made full of those things that interest all children." As described in the Hartford Orphan Asylum's 100th anniversary booklet, "There [was] nothing whatever institutional, either in spirit or in physical aspect, in the group of attractive small houses. . . . Here [was] found a place where dependent children [could] be cared for, physically and mentally, until they [could] be returned to their own homes, or sent to foster homes where they [would] be equally well loved and cared for."[75]

In 1928, Atterbury embarked on a nine-story scheme for the Gotham Hospital in Manhattan on a site between 107th and 108th Streets and Central Park West.[76] The experimental hospital was the first facility in the country designed around the concept of group nursing—an arrangement intended to lower charges for middle-class New Yorkers unable to afford proper health care, whereby, as described by Atterbury, "one nurse [would be] able to serve two or more patients, according to their condition, thus reducing the cost proportionately. And the most important architectural feature . . . [would] be the group nursing units, which will carry out the above system on a scale hitherto unknown in the hospital field."[77] Women doctors, who then did not have as many options to practice and teach medicine, would primarily run the facility. Public-spirited citizens and doctors, including the architect's uncle General W. W. Atterbury (1866–1935), president of the Pennsylvania Railroad, and his cousin Dr. Lewis A. Conner, were involved in the effort to raise funds for the hospital's building and its endowment. Although final plans for Atterbury's initiative were approved by Gotham's board in 1930, the building was never constructed.

Atterbury found more success at Yale, where his work formed an integral part of the university's medical-school development in the 1920s under the leadership of Johns Hopkins–trained pathologist Milton C. Winternitz (1885–

1959). During his tenure as dean, Winternitz carried the school from near extinction to elite status by establishing a full-time medical system with a new faculty, departments, expanding buildings, and educational facilities in cooperation with the New Haven Hospital. The Sterling Hall of Medicine, the first of many projected buildings for the campus, opened in 1925. Designed by Philadelphian Charles Z. Klauder (1872–1938), a specialist in collegiate architecture and planning, the building consolidated formerly scattered departments, library, amphitheater, administration offices, and laboratories into a spare Georgian-inspired edifice with an attractive concave entrance facade. Considering medicine a social science, Winternitz enthusiastically endorsed the growth of social medicine at Yale. With support from the university's president, psychologist James R. Angell (1869– 1949), and dean of the Law School, Robert M. Hutchins (1899–1977), Winternitz pushed forward plans for an Institute of Human Relations in order to bring together fields of interdisciplinary research. It would, as described by the dean, "serve as a dynamo and assembling plant for those university organizations concerned from the viewpoint of research, teaching or treatment with problems of human well-being."[78] At a time when social science as an academic discipline was only emerging, the institute was considered a controversial and progressive initiative. By then, Atterbury had firmly established a reputation for hospital design and demonstrated his affinity for projects with a larger social import. The institute's mission easily aligned with what the architect sought to accomplish as a designer.

In 1929, with gifts from the Rockefeller Foundation and the Laura Spelman Rockefeller Memorial, the university commissioned an addition to the Sterling Hall of Medicine for a child development clinic; adult psychobiology units; psychology, social science, and mental hygiene divisions; and a newly founded department of psychiatry.[79] Atterbury transformed Klauder's restrained brick and limestone curved facade into a monumental limestone entrance embellished by a double-height portico and dome; he executed the remainder of the pressed-brick wing in a restrained Georgian style to blend with the preexisting school buildings. Inside, the architect executed modern facilities and laboratories worthy of a leading institution. From the north, a double-height portico with modified Corinthian columns on the now-discontinued Davenport

Sterling Hall of Medicine, Yale University, New Haven, Connecticut. Entrance. Courtesy of the Division of Rare and Manuscript Collections, Cornell University Library

Institute of Human Relations and Dr. Gesell's
Children's Psychiatric Ward. North entrance. Samuel H.
Gottscho. Avery Architectural and Fine Arts Library,
Columbia University in the City of New York

Avenue led to the psychology and sociology departments, well equipped with shops, soundproof rooms, projecting rooms, and, according to the *University News Statement*, the "most modern equipment available for the measurement of stimuli and the reactions of the human brain." The mental hygiene and psychiatry section featured forty private rooms, small wards, gymnasiums, and a series of spaces for hydrotherapy and occupational therapy. Atterbury located Dr. Arnold Gesell's child development clinic in the eastern end of the wing and, as he had at the Children's Village, designed the space to resemble a private residence to foster feelings of familiarity and comfort among the young patients. An authority on infant behavioral patterns, Gesell (1880–1961) gained renown as the first doctor to use photography and observation mirrors to collect data on children; his clinic included nurseries, observation rooms, wading pools, examining rooms, playrooms, and photography laboratories.

Five years after the completion of the Institute of Human Relations in 1931, Atterbury began working on what would become one of his most meaningful projects: the Yale Medical Library.[80] While the idea of a library had been in the pipeline for some time, it came to fruition after Atterbury's close friend and Yale classmate Harvey Cushing presented his extensive collection of rare books and medical texts to his alma mater with the condition that the university would build a library for them. Although much of Cushing's career as a pioneering neurosurgeon had played out elsewhere—primarily at Johns Hopkins and Harvard's Peter Bent Brigham Hospital—he returned to Yale in 1933 as the Sterling Professor of Neurology. The multifaceted Cushing—also a Pulitzer Prize–winning biographer—convinced his colleagues John Fulton (1899–1960), Yale's professor of physiology, and Swiss tuberculosis specialist Arnold C. Klebs (1870–1943) to "go down in bibliophilic posterity hand in hand" with him and pool their collections to form the core of the library's holdings.[81]

In 1936, after the Yale Corporation decided to go forward with the building, Atterbury presented an initial scheme detailing a freestanding structure with a large amphitheater across from the Institute of Human Relations on Davenport Avenue. School officials, however, deemed it too costly, and Cushing recommended locating the library more centrally. Atterbury's second plan—a Y-shaped two-story brick extension off the rear of the Sterling Hall of Medicine—was less expensive and easily reachable by students. With a general medical library in one arm of the wing and the historical division in the other, each section

Yale Medical Library. Interior of the historical library.
Courtesy of the Division of Rare and Manuscript Collections, Cornell University Library

was equally accessible through the central rotunda that tied the scheme together. In June 1939, the trustees of John W. Sterling's estate—who helped fund the building—approved the design; and although Cushing died four months later, he did so with the knowledge that his library would be carried out.

As one of his oldest friends, Atterbury was just the person to capture the spirit of what Cushing had envisioned. Previously, Atterbury had worked as a consultant with Charles Platt (1861–1933) on the William H. Welch Medical Library at Johns Hopkins.[82] Welch was an esteemed colleague of Cushing's and a leading pathologist instrumental in planning the university's medical school. In an attempt to personalize what Atterbury deemed an uninspired design by prolific library architect Edward Tilton (1861–1933), the architect sought out Cushing for suggestions on symbolic sentences and motifs to incorporate into

ABOVE *Yale Medical Library. Harvey Cushing Memorial Rotunda.* Courtesy of the Division of Rare and Manuscript Collections, Cornell University Library

RIGHT *Yale Medical Library. Fireplace with inscription by George Stewart in the historical library.* Courtesy of the Division of Rare and Manuscript Collections, Cornell University Library

the scheme. In 1927, he wrote, "It seems to me . . . that a library of this type, bearing the name of Welch, has a wonderful background and that it ought to be significant in its details. We ought to have, in my judgment, spaces for sculptural inserts and inscriptions on the exterior, so that any one who passes would get some stimulation from the very names and sentences . . . this same principle should be carried out in the inside."[83]

At Yale, Atterbury presented a more personal architectural statement commemorating his friend's contributions to the medical field. Cushing's colleague, Dr. John Fulton, praised the architect for bringing "into reality Dr. Cushing's dream of a great medical library, for he has caught with splendid intuition what Dr. Cushing had conceived in his mind's eye, and he has brought harmoniously together the old and the new in fitting juxtaposition."[84] While Atterbury designed the spare Georgian extension to match the other medical buildings, he created beautiful and unexpected spaces inside. The double-height historical library, with its deep-red rough plaster walls and hand-planed oak floors and beamed ceiling, was appropriately imposing. Both impressive and inviting at the same time, it resonated with a sense of gravity but also radiated a comfortable warmth more associated with a private library. Atterbury's clean lines, wood ceiling, curved roof beams, and gallery brackets gave the space an almost nautical quality while his distinctive details offered a personal and thoughtful dimension. On the flat bluestone mantel of the fireplace, the architect incorporated a stylized inscription written by George Stewart (1892–1972), Arnold Klebs's son-in-law and a Yale alumnus, designed especially for the room, and at the gallery level he innovatively integrated lights into the metal handrails, wrought with caduceus, to eliminate the need for overhead lights and floor lamps.[85] In the more utilitarian general medical library, Atterbury's detail-oriented approach was no less diminished. The smallest element was carefully thought out: for example, the manner in which he angled the lower bookshelves to facilitate the easy reading of titles was highlighted in the architectural press.

For his class's 50th reunion gift, Atterbury suggested dedicating the central rotunda in memory of Cushing. In its design, Atterbury worked with classmate and architect Egerton Swartwout (1870–1943) to develop interior details expressive of Cushing's accomplishments and endeavors, adapting new materials for decorative effect. He paired formica wall paneling in two shades of blue with metal moldings and applied hand-wrought aluminum details,

Yale Medical Library. Aluminum detail in the rotunda, 2008. Jonathan Wallen

with the patina of old silver, to create a dignified and streamlined space with a distilled classical vocabulary and proportions. Atterbury placed the crests of the fourteen universities from which Cushing had earned honorary degrees at intervals around the ground floor and applied stylized plaques symbolizing immortality and divine life on the upper level to suggest column capitals; the pattern of the formica panels evoked pilasters, wainscoting, and cornices. For the center of the red tile floor, he designed a cast-aluminum seal inlaid with blue and black tile mosaic and asked René Chambellan, by then a well-known architectural sculptor, to model it. On the balcony facia, he incorporated the bold inscription: This rotunda is dedicated to Harvey Cushing—Inspiring Teacher—Pathfinder in Neurosurgery—Master of the Science and Art of Healing. Starling Childs, a mutual friend of Atterbury and Cushing's, presented the rotunda at the library's dedication ceremony on June 15, 1941.[86]

CHAPTER SEVEN

PIONEER IN PREFABRICATION
1902–1951

According to Lewis Mumford, Atterbury, along with Frederick Ackerman (1878–1950) and John Irwin Bright (1869–1940), was one of the "first important architect[s], after Louis Sullivan, to be fully alive to the social responsibilities—and economic conditioning—of architecture."[1] Projects for tenements and low-income housing galvanized Atterbury's belief that the solution to the housing problem was scientifically based. The prefabrication and standardization of various component units and structural elements could lower construction costs and create cheaper housing for the working man. As Atterbury viewed it, only a drastic overhaul of the building profession, on par to what Henry Ford had accomplished in the automobile industry, could facilitate change. "We are still laying bricks like Babylonians," he contended, "and until we make a modern industry out of housing, we will never solve the housing problem."[2] As an inventor, Atterbury spent the better part of his fifty-year career engrossed with developing more economical building methods for low-cost housing.

With the standards of mass production just becoming more widespread, Atterbury's arguments and ideas about precast concrete construction were pioneering—so much so that they were never adopted wholesale because they were, in fact, ahead of their time and the mechanisms to set them in motion were not fully in place. While his system involved a radical rethinking and reorganization of the industry, its benefits were a logical response to the era's economic climate. Concrete was the cheapest building material available for masonry construction, and its wide use for housing during the Depression and war years, Atterbury argued, was a fitting, much-needed antidote to the housing crisis. With comprehensive efforts to systematically reorder the city's urban fabric under way, such as the *Regional Plan for New York and its Environs* (1930) underwritten by the Sage Foundation's Committee on Regional Planning, Atterbury was working at a time when it was possible to instate change. As the first major planning initiative undertaken in an American city, the committee compiled surveys, projections, and data to encourage social reform through a reorganization of the city and its suburbs. The architect resolutely strove to perfect and patent his system of hollow concrete slabs and to spread word of its benefits; however, because of intermittent funding and general public disinterest, work unfolded in a series of stops and starts. Atterbury—who also used much of his own money to finance the project—considered his quest for cheaper, better construction his life's work despite the numerous hurdles and difficulties he encountered.

As early as 1902, Atterbury independently began investigating different forms of construction—an examination that illuminated the inefficiencies plaguing the profession.

TOP *Design for a semi-detached house.*
Standardized Housing Corporation,
The Manufacture of Standardized Houses (1918): 32

BOTTOM *Design for single-family detached houses.*
Standardized Housing Corporation,
The Manufacture of Standardized Houses (1918): 31

Focusing specifically on concrete and cement, he traveled extensively to research various foreign attempts to standardize building elements to ease costs. Abroad, the recent efforts of John Alexander Brodie (1858–1934) of Liverpool and Franz Visintini of Zurich, in particular, caught the architect's interest. Brodie, Liverpool's city engineer, had made an important breakthrough with heavy prefabricated slabs, which in time would influence and inspire Walter Gropius and other members of the Bauhaus. In 1905, Brodie built Liverpool's first prefabricated tenements on Eldon Street from modular reinforced-concrete panels produced in a plant, installed dry, bolted together, and grouted with cement; his precast concrete house designed for Letchworth formed part of a widely publicized "Cheap Cottage Exhibition."[3] In his pursuit to develop efficient and less-expensive building methods, architect Visintini designed reinforced-concrete girders. Theretofore, it had been necessary to pour heavy beams in situ, but Visintini invented a technique whereby they were cast in molds offsite.[4]

At first, Atterbury began testing designs, materials, and methods in connection with the Carnegie Steel Company and Henry Phipps. Under the auspices of the Russell Sage Foundation, he started to carry out his vision of building inexpensive concrete houses with as little manpower as possible. The construction of a small shack in a backyard on East 64th Street (1908) and two cottages in Sewaren, New Jersey (1909–10), demonstrated the viability of Atterbury's fireproof system of large damp-proof prefabricated hollow concrete slabs as an alternative to brick and wood construction. Cast in steel molds and cured offsite, the panels were lifted into place by a crane. A typical eight-foot-high wall section weighed one and a half tons and consisted of two one-and-a-half-inch concrete membranes with a six-inch airspace. Compared to the shells of brick and wood houses (which cost 10 cents and 6.5 cents per cubic foot and took 27 and 21 days to build, respectively), Atterbury's concrete panel system was 7.7 cents and took a mere 15 days.

Not only was Atterbury's research the earliest instance of philanthropically supported experimentation on prefabrication, but it also predated the work of widely considered innovators in the field such as Thomas A. Edison (1908), Ernest Leslie Ransome (1911), and John E. Conzelman (1910).[5] As the period's greatest inventor, Edison attracted attention with his attempt to construct an attractive home from two sets of interlocking cast-iron molds and poured concrete in only four days. Edison's system encountered various design problems, and although more than fifty houses were built in the 1910s in Union, New Jersey,

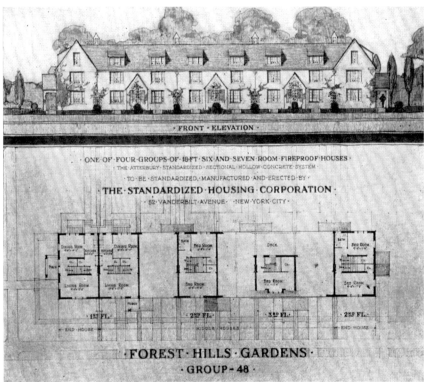

it was never a successful venture. While Ransome and Conzelman's techniques, like Atterbury's, involved precast factory-made elements swung into place by derricks, Atterbury began working on his system several years earlier, filing his first patent for "Making Constructional Sections" on December 5, 1904.

At Forest Hills Gardens, Atterbury had the opportunity to test his method on a large scale in more than forty homes (comprising Groups 2, 48, 49, and 56). In addition to its economical value—overhead notwithstanding—the prefabricated concrete construction proved to be architecturally distinguished, eminently livable, and favorably comparable to the more traditionally built houses in the development (see pages 176–80). With more houses—rather than the two that had comprised the Sewaren demonstration—the cost and speed of construction continued to decrease. Because the panels were handled only three times from manufacture to installation, the amount of

Amsterdam Houses, New York, New York. Children's playground. The LaGuardia and Wagner Archives, La Guardia Community College/The City University of New York

labor involved diminished considerably. Praising Atterbury's work, journalist Ida Tarbell noted, "Mr. Atterbury had worked out a variety of treatment of surfaces and many interesting details by which the houses [at Forest Hills] can be made individual and attractive. The results of his long, devoted, even loving experiments do more toward solving what we call the housing problem than anything else of which I know."[6] However, as much as Atterbury had manifested its possibilities, its flaws prevented a more widespread reception. Due to the high cost of the molding equipment and plant, the system was deemed more appropriate for much larger groups of houses. On top of that, the heavy panels were difficult to transport and their lengthy curing time in the molds of three days to a week impeded rates of production.

Undeterred, Atterbury filed ten patents in the 1910s upgrading his molding and casting apparatus. His paper, "How to Get Low Cost Houses," presented at the National Housing Association's Annual Meeting in Providence, Rhode Island, in 1916 called upon the organization to undertake his housing innovations in absence of a "farseeing philanthropist." Anxious to see his work progress, Atterbury offered "his rights in all such plans and inventions in their application to workingmen's homes and tenements to any association or agency [that] will properly guarantee the . . . development of this work." Patents, he described, had been taken "largely with the idea that they

might possibly be means of continuing this research work along the lines [he] was proposing."[7] After the conference, several funders seem to have materialized. As a direct outgrowth of the interest created by the National Housing Association, a group of New York businessmen organized the Standardized Housing Corporation to commercially test the system; Atterbury and John Nolen acted as consultants.[8] The American Car and Foundry Company, the country's largest railroad equipment manufacturer which was headed by Atterbury's former client William H. Woodin, continued funding the architect's work in 1919. However, due to slow production rates, it closed down the plant two years later after building three houses.

With his artistic approach, Atterbury succeeded in giving what was otherwise a bland material warmth and architectural interest. In addition to his hollow concrete-panel system, Atterbury developed a number of other innovative ways to aesthetically use concrete in construction. With Charles Pellow, a chemistry professor at Columbia University, the architect worked out a method to pre-finish the panels with mica, quartz, and muriatio acid to add a layer of color and texture to his facades. Meanwhile, the grouted interior side created smooth surfaces to receive paint, making furring, lath, and plaster unnecessary. The methods Atterbury adopted to detail his designs existed halfway between traditional building techniques and his new prefabricated system. For half-timbering, he reinforced and filled precast hollow members in situ and inserted brick panels and precast brushed-concrete grilles and relief panels. At the factory the Sage Foundation Homes Company built for Atterbury on Burns Street in Forest Hills Gardens, he also invented a damp-proof nailable concrete known as Nailcrete to use as a base for wood floors and shingles and in place of wood sleepers and mortar. As a building material, it was more readily adopted. Not only did Atterbury make extensive use of Nailcrete at Forest Hills Gardens and in numerous other projects, including the American Wing (floors and sloping roof), City Hall (roof and cupola), and Bloomingdale Hospital, but also other practitioners such as Cass Gilbert, Bertram Goodhue, Cross & Cross, Robert D. Kohn, and Mann & MacNeille incorporated it into their projects. At the same time, Atterbury began concocting a mixture of gypsum, sand, and cinder (Cinderlite) with a Portland cement waterproof coating; its faster curing time sped up his system's productivity.[9]

Without financial backing, Atterbury continued to refine his process at his own expense through the 1920s. He began espousing the idea of establishing a Research Institute for Economic Housing to stimulate and coordinate scientific solutions to the housing problem and submitted his plan, which called for a three million dollar endowment, to Clarence Stein of the State Housing Commission and James Angell of the Carnegie Corporation (later president of Yale). As he visualized it, the institute would have three arms: a research division, a demonstration sector to implement the research work, and an educational department to train practitioners and inform the public. While his proposal was well received by government officials, Secretary of Commerce Herbert Hoover suggested "[establishing] some such institution with one of the larger universities" since "the government [had] no functions for such investigations and they would be infinitely better conducted at private hands."[10]

As his contribution to the *Regional Plan for New York and its Environs*, Atterbury outlined his economical building system and housing institute in *The Economic Production of Workingmen's Homes: an Outline of a Scientific Solution of the Housing Problem and its Relation to the Development of the City* (1930). Despite the fact that Atterbury's report coincided with the onset of the Depression—the moment when the prefabrication housing movement began to gain momentum—his project stalled. "I have had terribly hard luck in the twenty five years I have been working on this problem," he wrote Harvey Cushing, "thinking more than once that it had actually been all over but what with the war and several financial setbacks, not to mention the general apathy of the public, it is only just now that it is apparently coming into its own."[11] However, as time continued to pass without any of his suggestions materializing, the architect grew increasingly frustrated and disenchanted. In 1938, he expressed to John D. Rockefeller Jr., "We seem to be stalled in the effort for a Research Institute—though I am trying to start something at Yale with the thought that it would be a great opportunity for the Institute of Human Relations to have such a man-sized problem to tackle. One hates to see 20 years work go into the discard without any opportunity to demonstrate its value or hand it on for further development. For our research actually achieved practical results which, though only a beginning, yet if applied would be at least a step in the right direction, even though the saving might be but a fraction of what will ultimately come."[12]

It was not until World War Two that Atterbury saw his research and relentless efforts gain traction. By that time, the houses at Forest Hills Gardens had sufficiently aged as successful examples of livable and durable prefabricated construction, showing "practically no structural deteriora-

Amsterdam Houses. The LaGuardia and Wagner Archives, La Guardia Community College/The City University of New York

tion and . . . demonstrating thoroughly satisfactory living qualities."[13] With his system's architectural integrity firmly established, the architect went to work on the Amsterdam Houses with Harvey Wiley Corbett (1873–1954)—one of the team that designed Rockefeller Center—and planner Arthur C. Holden (1890–1993).[14] The massive urban-renewal effort, sponsored by the New York City Housing Authority (NYCHA), provided the perfect arena for the improved Atterbury method to be tested. Begun under the auspices of Chairman Gerard Swope (1872–1957), the civic-minded former General Electric president, the project sought to revitalize the downtrodden San Juan Hill section—one of the worst slums in the city. Initially intended to house the primarily African American population resident to the area, the government-funded project would replace a series of substandard "old-law" tenements to create safer, more sanitary living conditions. By 1942, the associate architects—Corbett as chief architect and Atterbury's office as drafting support—filed their scheme for a 1,084-unit complex of thirteen buildings on a sloping superblock bound by Amsterdam Avenue, West End Avenue, 61st Street, and 64th Street. Deftly organizing ten six-story buildings and three thirteen-story towers around a central axis—the landscaped pedestrian mall—the architects created a classically composed urban space enhanced by park-like grounds laid out by Gilmore D. Clarke

Panels in the Prefabricated Building Sections, Inc., factory,
New Hyde Park, New York. Fortune (March 1921): 19

(1892–1982) and Michael Rapuano (1904–1975). With the taller structures set on the site's higher part along Amsterdam, the designers effectively walled the project off from the city and stepped the buildings down toward the Hudson River, creating unobstructed water views.

Plans for building, however, stalled with the onset on World War Two. A year after the plans were filed, Atterbury, Corbett, and Holden submitted a proposal to the New York Housing Authority outlining the benefits of the Atterbury Precast Sectional System, contending that it would save on steel (for spandrel beams), concrete, and other materials needed for waterproofing, flashing, and ties. Using one of the complex's six-story buildings as an example, Atterbury demonstrated that his sectional wall, composed of 247 units, was exponentially more economical

than standard brick and hollow tile wall construction of almost 40,000 units. Although the project's plans needed reworking to correspond to the prefabricated sections, he maintained that its architectural integrity, as exemplified by Forest Hills Gardens, would not be compromised. When the Amsterdam Houses were completed in 1948, they were done so with brick walls textured with subtle horizontal bands rather than concrete wall panels. However, according to the *New York Times*, the cost per unit was sixty-one percent above what former NYCHA commissioner Alfred Rheinstein (1889–1974) had achieved at Queensbridge (1939), the largest public housing development of its time. As encouraged by the Housing Act of 1949, the majority of Amsterdam Houses inhabitants were returning veterans.[15]

At long last, however, it appeared as though Atterbury's ideas were coming into their own with his appointment as research associate at Yale in 1943. The university drew up a contract with the War Production Board (WPB), a wartime committee established by Franklin D. Roosevelt to regulate production and spending, to manufacture Atterbury's houses. In March 1944, the Architectural League of New York held an exhibition extolling the merits of prefabrication. Nonetheless, the WPB canceled their grant for a pilot plant several months later in an attempt to concentrate on more urgent matters. Greatly disappointed, Atterbury continued to push his system. Although the factory was nowhere near completion, the Royal Engineers of Great Britain expressed interest in introducing it in England, and Atterbury's childhood friend and cousin Henry L. Stimson (1867–1950)—then secretary of war—endorsed a small test building at Camp Dix, New Jersey, in 1945. Despite severe January weather and a half-finished plant, the factory produced sixty tons of blocks. The panels were transported over one hundred miles after which five men successfully erected a sixty-by-thirty-foot hospital wing in just nine hours. As a result, the army endorsed Atterbury's system, determining that it could "be put on a favorable competitive basis with any other similar type of wall construction."[16]

By 1945, Atterbury's improvements rendered it possible to produce sections forty times faster than in 1920. The architect had continually—almost obsessively—worked to enhance what he had already established. In the late 1940s, when his health drastically deteriorated, he moved permanently to Southampton where he set up a makeshift laboratory out of corrugated Plexiglas in his back courtyard. Even after a stroke left him partly paralyzed, he persevered with his experiments and exhaustive tests. Often he would draw up ideas that other more able-bodied people would carry out.[17] Through his studies, Atterbury formulated a curing method in which the panels and inexpensive forms could be removed from their supporting cradles after a half-hour, freeing them up for the next round of blocks. Heated, set under pressure, and steam cured, the slabs—made up of lightweight, expanded slag aggregate—were durable, insulated, and unusually fireproof; their smooth finish more closely resembled limestone than concrete.

The great promise of the system's increased efficiency drew the interest of the former NYCHA chairman Alfred Rheinstein, responsible for Queensbridge (1939), and Robert Dowling (1895–1973), president of the City Investing Company. Together, they organized a small company funded by the New York Housing Trust, a nonprofit organization dedicated to developing low-income housing with private capital.[18] The corporation, Prefabricated Building Sections, Inc., constructed a plant in New Hyde Park, Long Island, capable of producing 3,000–4,000 units a day where straight-line factory methods and continuous scientific laboratory control ensured quality and consistency. "After thirty years and $500,000," announced an article in *Fortune*, "eighty-two year old inventor-architect Grosvenor Atterbury's hollow concrete building slabs [started] to come off a production line in Long Island."[19] Finally, the architect could feel some sense of gratification.

Atterbury's four-by-ten-foot concrete sections were incorporated into the design of Queensview (1951), a fourteen-building middle-income project in Astoria, Queens. The effort of the Queensview Housing Cooperative, headed by former NYCHA chairman Gerard Swope and housing reformer Louis Pink (1882–1955), the complex stood "as a public service, to bring the benefits of large-scale nonprofit planning of housing to a broader sector of New York's population."[20] Built by the Rheinstein Construction Corporation, it consisted of simple rectilinear towers designed by George Brown and Bernard Guenther on a ten-acre parcel bound by 33rd Road, Crescent Street, 34th Avenue, and 21st Street. The group took significant measures to cut expenses; they omitted basements to save on excavation and waterproofing costs and used the same floor plate or "unit plan" on each floor. As the chairman of Prefabricated Buildings Sections, Inc., and president of Rheinstein Construction Corporation, Rheinstein incorporated Atterbury's panels into the first tier of all fourteen buildings—an element that added substantially to the project's cost-cutting objective; a similar complex, Queensview West (1958), was planned for an adjacent site.[21]

With the exception of Queensview, Atterbury's struggle to change the housing industry on a widespread basis bore little fruit. Incapacitated and ill, it appears that he was pushed aside in the 1950s as the prefabrication movement rolled forward without him. From the outset, the architect had offered the results and patents to any nonprofit willing to continue his work along proper lines. As a result, he had trouble earning credit where credit was due when people finally began to grasp the system's merits. Nonetheless, Atterbury's innovative contributions to concrete and prefabrication were important and influential. As the inventor of the first precast concrete-panel system, Atterbury proved the viability of prefabrication—a key influence to later modernist prefabrication schemes such as the work of Ernst May (1886–1970) in Germany and Russia. As James Ford, author of *Slums and Housing* (1936), lamented, Atterbury's research was "too little known. Had the Research Institute of Economic Housing . . . been successfully launched, it would have provided a vitally necessary link in a real housing program."[22] During the era in which they were introduced, Atterbury's ideas were incredibly forward thinking—so much so that industry had yet to make the tremendous strides to support them well. By the time it had, the architect had been eclipsed.

Queensview, Astoria, Queens. Fortune
(March 1921): 21

CATALOGUE RAISONNÉ

Information about projects by Grosvenor Atterbury and his associates, John Almy Tompkins 2nd and Stowe Phelps, was culled from two biographical sketches (both dated May 22, 1952) in the Grosvenor Atterbury papers at Cornell University and the archives of the American Institute of Architects in Washington, DC. Although the firm's drawings have been lost, Atterbury's project lists, along with input from books, historical societies, building owners, and the architectural press, have formed the basis of this catalogue raisonné.

Buildings have been ordered chronologically by the year in which the project was begun, if known. While the firm's project lists includes more than 1,300 projects, many of them were unrealized; some were small renovations. After the retirements of Phelps (1927) and Tompkins (1937), Atterbury completed a few projects on his own, notably the Yale Medical Library and Amsterdam Houses in collaboration with Harvey W. Corbett and Arthur Holden. Despite his failing health, Atterbury focused all his energy toward further developing a panelized low-cost concrete building system. In the late 1940s, Atterbury and his wife moved permanently to Southampton.

1894
Grosvenor Atterbury house, Art Village, Southampton, New York; c. 1894; moved to the Shinnecock Hills in 1908.

Camp Uncas for William West Durant, Mohegan Lake, Adirondacks, New York; 1894–95; extant.

1895
Frank Bestow Wiborg house, The Dunes, Highway Behind the Pond, East Hampton, New York; demolished: 1941.

1896
Arthur Brigham Claflin house, Montauk Highway, Southampton, New York; 1896–98; extant: Southampton College.

1897
Ten houses for Henry Osborne Havemeyer, Bayberry Point, Islip, New York; 1897–1901; extant.

Frederick Henry Betts house, 22 East 65th Street, New York, New York; extant: stores and apartments.

Parrish Art Museum, Southampton, New York. Courtesy of the Southampton Historical Museum

Parrish Art Museum, Job's Lane, Southampton, New York; 1897–1913; extant.

York Hall, Yale University, Wall Street, New Haven, Connecticut; extant: Stoeckel Hall.

1898
Albert and Adele Herter house, Près Choisis, Route 27, East Hampton, New York; 1898–99; extant.

Robert Weeks de Forest house, Wawapek Farm, Shore Road, Cold Spring Harbor, New York; 1898–1900; extant.

Church of the Holy Communion, 49 East 20th Street, New York, New York; alteration; extant.

1899
Dr. Walter Belknap James house, Eagle's Beak, Shore Road and White Hill Road, Cold Spring Harbor, New York; demolished.

Dr. Clarence C. Rice house, East Hampton, New York. American Architect 94 (August 26, 1908)

Dr. Clarence C. Rice house, Hither Lane, East Hampton, New York; demolished by fire: 1920.

Mrs. G. H. Stanton house, The Tepee, Westerly Road, Watch Hill, Rhode Island; extant.

Mrs. G. H. Stanton house, The Bungalow, Watch Hill, Rhode Island. Watch Hill, Then and Now, Watch Hill Preservation Society, Roberta Burkhart, Michael Beddard, and Ardith Schneider

Mrs. G. H. Stanton house, The Bungalow, Westerly Road, Watch Hill, Rhode Island; extant.

John Rutledge Abney house, 15 East 86th Street, New York, New York; demolished: 1925.

Southampton Club, Southampton, New York. Courtesy of the Southampton Historical Museum

Southampton Club, First Neck Lane, Southampton, New York; extant.

1900
Charles L. Atterbury house, Sugar Loaf, Shinnecock Hills, New York; 1900–25; inherited by Grosvenor Atterbury; demolished by fire in 1929; carriage house extant.

Alanson Trask Enos house, Sowanniu, Misquamicut Road, Watch Hill, Rhode Island; and garage; extant.

William C. Gulliver house, The Box, Squabble Lane, Southampton, New York; attributed to Atterbury; demolished: 1962.

Dr. Albert Herman Ely house, Elyria, Ox Pasture Road, Southampton, New York; c. 1900; extant.

Mrs. George Hoadley and Mrs. Scarborough house, The Folly, Neptune Road, Watch Hill, Rhode Island; c. 1900; extant.

Walter George Oakman Sr. house, Oakdene, Willis Avenue, Roslyn, New York; c. 1900; demolished.

Lucien Oudin house, Cobb Road, Water Mill, New York; c. 1900; extant.

James C. Parrish house, Shinnecock Hills, New York; attributed to Atterbury; demolished.

Mrs. Benjamin Richards house, East Hampton, New York. House & Garden 3 (April 1903): 214

Mrs. Benjamin Richards house, Dunemere Lane, East Hampton, New York; extant.

Henry A. Robbins house, Dune Road, Southampton, New York; attributed to Atterbury; status unknown.

Grange Sard/Rufus Lenoir Patterson house, Southampton, New York. Architectural Record 44 (October 1918): 144

Grange Sard house, Ox Pasture Road, Southampton, New York; also known as the Rufus Lenoir Patterson house, Lenoir; extant.

Alfred H. Swayne house, Algoma, Montauk Highway, Shinnecock Hills, New York; c. 1900; extant.

Robert Waller house, Vyne Croft, First Neck Lane, Southampton, New York; c. 1900; extant.

Mrs. George Trowbridge house, 25 West 54th Street, New York, New York; demolished: 1938.

John Beach Memorial Library, Newtown, Connecticut.

John Beach Memorial Library, Main Street, Newtown, Connecticut; extant.

Misquamicut Golf Club, Watch Hill, Rhode Island, c. 1900. Watch Hill, Then and Now, Watch Hill Preservation Society, Roberta Burkhart, Michael Beddard, and Ardith Schneider

Misquamicut Golf Club, Ocean View Highway, Watch Hill, Rhode Island; extant.

1901

Edward Cushman Bodman house, Felsmere, Rowland Road, Seal Harbor, Maine; 1901–2; extant.

Dr. Christian Archibald Herter house, Miradero, New Country Road, Seal Harbor, Maine; extant.

Charles Monson house, Edgehill Road, New Haven, Connecticut; extant.

John Sanford Barnes house, 10 East 79th Street, New York, New York; extant: Greek Archdiocese of North and South America.

Henry Phipps house, 6 East 87th Street, New York, New York; 1901–4; extant: Liederkranz Foundation.

Henry Phipps house, Fifth Avenue and 87th Street, New York, New York; never built.

Sarah Jewett Robbins house, 33 East 74th Street, New York, New York; extant: owned by the Whitney Museum of American Art.

Congregational Church, Peabody Drive, Seal Harbor, Maine; 1901–2; extant.

1903

Wilbur F. Day house, Prospect Street, New Haven, Connecticut; extant: International Student Center of New Haven.

Mrs. James B. Laughlin Jr. house, Holly Road, Zellwood, Florida; addition; extant.

Rev. Dr. William Stephen Rainsford house, Savin Hill, Route 35, Lewisboro, New York; 1903–7; extant: Le Chateau.

James Russell Soley house, Shinnecock Hills, New York; demolished by fire: 1910.

Residence Realty Company, 105–7 East 73rd Street, New York, New York; extant.

Unity Chapel, Church Street, Montclair, New Jersey; 1903–4; extant.

Ernesto and Edith Fabbri house, Buonriposo, Bar Harbor, Maine. Courtesy of the Maine Historic Preservation Commission

Ernesto and Edith Fabbri house, Buonriposo, Eden Street, Bar Harbor, Maine; demolished: 1918.

Seth Low house and farm group, Broad Brook Farm, Broad Brook Road, Bedford, New York; 1904–7; extant.

Charles Sherman Haight house, 20 East 69th Street, New York, New York; alterations; extant: offices and stores.

Mrs. Sylvanus Gallup Reed house, 37 East 50th Street, New York, New York; demolished: 1940s.

Harry Payne Whitney house, 2 West 57th Street, New York, New York; alteration and addition; demolished: 1913.

Bessemer Building, 100 Sixth Street, Pittsburgh, Pennsylvania; 1904–5; demolished: 1964.

Lower East Side Music School, 53–55 East Third Street, New York, New York; 1904–5; extant: apartments.

Consulting architect for John S. Phipps house, Westbury House, Old Westbury Road, Old Westbury, New York; with George A. Crawley; 1904–7; extant: Old Westbury Gardens.

1905

Edwin A. Bradley house, Edgewood Terrace, Montclair, New Jersey. Dining room. The Brickbuilder 18 (August 1909): pl. 105

Edwin A. Bradley house, Edgewood Terrace, Upper Mountain Avenue, Montclair, New Jersey; extant.

George Dillwyn Cross house, Baricross, Douglass Avenue, Bernardsville, New Jersey; extant.

George Rudolf Mosle house, Hillandale, St. John's Drive, Peapack, New Jersey; 1905–6; extant.

Mrs. Porter Norton house, Buffalo, New York. Entrance facade. American Architect 91 (March 9, 1907)

Mrs. Porter Norton house, Gates Circle, Buffalo, New York; 1905–7; demolished: 1971.

Louis Crawford Clark house, 21 West 47th Street, New York, New York. The Brickbuilder 17 (September 1908): 188

Louis Crawford Clark house, 21 West 47th Street, New York, New York; demolished.

Phipps Model Tenement, 321–337 East 31st Street, New York, New York; 1905–7: demolished.

Fulton Building, 107 Sixth Street, Pittsburgh, Pennsylvania; 1905–6; extant: Renaissance Pittsburgh Hotel.

Connecticut Hall, alterations to 1750 building, Old Campus, Yale University, New Haven, Connecticut; extant.

1906
James Byrne house, Planting Fields, Planting Fields Road, Locust Valley, New York; demolished by fire: 1918.

Thomas Gerard Condon house, Montauk Highway, Shinnecock Hills, New York; extant.

Joseph S. Neave house, Weebetook Lane, East Walnut Hills, Ohio; extant.

Marselis Clark Parsons house, Furzen Hill, Rye, New York. General Research Division. The New York Public Library, Astor, Lenox and Tilden Foundations

Marselis Clark Parsons house, Furzen Hill, Boston Post Road, Rye, New York; demolished: 1942.

Manufacturer's Building, 530 Duquesne Way, Pittsburgh, Pennsylvania; 1906–7; demolished: 1956.

U.S. Cigar Building, 47 West 17th Street and 44 East 18th Street, New York, New York; extant.

1907
Ms. Ursula Morgan Fitz-Simmons house, Cotswold, Sisters Servants Lane, Sterlington, New York; 1907–8; demolished by fire: 1972.

Arthur C. Fraser house, Ridgefield, Connecticut. Architectural Review 8 (May 1919): pl. 70

Arthur C. Fraser house, Eleven Levels, West Mountain Road, Ridgefield, Connecticut; extant.

Henry O. Havemeyer lodge, Tomotley Plantation, Sheldon, South Carolina; c. 1907; never built.

Francis Newton house, Georgica Road, East Hampton, New York; W. W. Bosworth after Atterbury plans; 1907–10; extant.

Anna Lusk Camp, Upper St. Regis Lake, New York; extant.

Philip Kearny house, Onlya Farm, Normandie Heights, New Jersey; alterations; status unknown.

Church of All Angels, Station Road, Shinnecock Hills, New York; never built.

Natatorium, Phipps Building, 540 Duquesne Way, Pittsburgh, Pennsylvania; 1907–8; demolished: 1935.

Restoration of City Hall, New York, New York; Governor's Room, interiors and cupola; 1907–25; extant.

1908
Emma W. Harris house, Shinnecock Hills, New York; moved from the Art Village; alterations and additions; demolished.

Two precast concrete houses for the Russell Sage Foundation, Sewaren, New Jersey; 1908–9; status unknown.

162 East 74th Street, New York, New York; owned by Grosvenor Atterbury; alterations.

New Haven Country Club, Hartford Turnpike, Hamden, Connecticut; extant.

Phipps Psychiatric Clinic at Johns Hopkins Hospital, Wolfe Street, Baltimore, Maryland; 1908–13; extant.

Phipps Institute for the Treatment of Tuberculosis, Seventh and Lombard Streets, Philadelphia, Pennsylvania; 1908–13; demolished.

Rye Presbyterian Church, Rye, New York. Tympanum. Courtesy of the Division of Rare and Manuscript Collections, Cornell University Library

Rye Presbyterian Church tympanum, Boston Post Road, Rye, New York; designed by Richard Upjohn in 1870; extant.

Stable for Charity Organization Society, 514 West 28th Street, New York, New York; extant.

School house, Main Road, Isle au Haut, Maine; extant.

1909
Walter Malley house, St. Ronan Street, New Haven, Connecticut; extant: Bethesda Lutheran Parish House.

Arthur Schroeder house, Upper Mountain Avenue, Montclair, New Jersey; c. 1909; extant.

Half-timber house, Montclair, New Jersey; c. 1909; status unknown.

Charles Larned Atterbury house, 131 East 70th Street, New York, New York; 1909–11; alterations; extant: stores and apartments.

Edward H. Harriman house, 1 East 69th Street, New York, New York. Fireplace detail. American Architect 100 (August 31, 1911)

Edward H. Harriman house, 1 East 69th Street, New York, New York; alterations; demolished: 1946.

Alfonzo Rockwell Cluett Foundation, Pawling School, Pawling, New York, 1910. Courtesy of the Trinity-Pawling School

Alfonzo Rockwell Cluett Foundation, gym, field house, headmaster's house, Pawling School, Pawling, New York; 1909–36, extant.

Forest Hills Gardens, Queens, New York; 1909–22; extant.

1910

Arthur Curtiss James guest residence, Vedimar, Harrison Avenue, Newport, Rhode Island; demolished: 1975.

A. T. Loomis house, South Orange, New Jersey. The Brickbuilder 21 (December 1912): pl. 43

A. T. Loomis house, Turrell Avenue, South Orange, New Jersey; c. 1910; extant.

Charles A. Peabody Jr. house, Harbor Road and Saw Mill Road, Cold Spring Harbor, New York; 1910–12; demolished: 1978.

Henry Graff Trevor house, Coopers Neck Road, Southampton, New York; c. 1910; extant.

Harry Mighels Verrill house, Sebago Lake, Standish, Maine; never built.

George T. Bonner house, 18 East 75th Street, New York, New York. The Brickbuilder 17 (September 1908): 188

George T. Bonner house, 18 East 75th Street, New York, New York; c. 1910; demolished: 1928.

Dr. Lewis Atterbury Conner house, 119–21 East 62nd Street, New York, New York; extant: Consul General of Bulgaria.

Forest Hills Inn and Station Square, Continental Avenue, Queens, New York; 1910–11; extant.

Group II houses, 45–71 Burns Street, Forest Hills Gardens, Queens, New York; 1910–13; (I-F 28–41); extant.

1911

Grosvenor Atterbury carriage house, Little Sugar Loaf House, Shinnecock Hills, New York. Eric Woodward Collection

Grosvenor Atterbury carriage house, Sugar Loaf, Shinnecock Hills, New York; extant.

Homer A. Norris house, The Boulders, Shore Avenue, Greenwood Lake, Warwick, New York; commissioned by J. P. Morgan; extant.

Group III, 36–54 Slocum Crescent, Forest Hills Gardens, Queens, New York; (I-F 1–10); extant.

Group VI-A and B houses, Greenway Terrace, Forest Hills Gardens, Queens, New York; (I-F 11–27) extant.

1912

Rogers Model Tenement, 425–27 West 44th Street, New York, New York; 1912–15; extant.

Russell Sage Foundation building, 122–30 East 22nd Street, New York, New York; 1912–13; extant: apartments.

Group XI houses, 74–92 Beechknoll Road, Forest Hills Gardens, Queens, New York; (I-F 42–45); M. M. Allen, Clarence Arthur Perry, A. H. Flint; extant.

Group XII houses, 206 and 16 Greenway North and 9–11 Markwood Road, Forest Hills Gardens, Queens, New York; (I-F 46–49); Ketcham, Joseph W. Johnson, H. P. Jague; extant.

Group XV, Forest Hills Gardens. The Sage Foundation Homes Company, *Forest Hills Gardens* (December 1913)

Group XV houses, Forest Hills Gardens, Queens, New York; never built.

Group XVI-B, Forest Hills Gardens. The Sage Foundation Homes Company, *Forest Hills Gardens* (December 1913)

Group XVI-B houses, Forest Hills Gardens, Queens, New York; never built.

Group XVII, Forest Hills Gardens. The Sage Foundation Homes Company, *Forest Hills Gardens* (December 1913)

Group XVII houses, 33–41 Ingram Street, Forest Hills Gardens, Queens, New York; (I-F 92–95); extant.

Group XVIII-B, Forest Hills Gardens. The Sage Foundation Homes Company, *Forest Hills Gardens* (December 1913)

Group XVIII-B houses, 16–26 Ingram Street, Forest Hills Gardens, Queens, New York; (I-F 101–103); extant.

Group XIX, Forest Hills Gardens. The Sage Foundation Homes Company, *Forest Hills Gardens* (December 1913)

Group XIX houses, 187–205 Puritan Avenue, Forest Hills Gardens, Queens, New York; (I-F 104–11); extant.

Group XX, Forest Hills Gardens. The Sage Foundation Homes Company, *Forest Hills Gardens* (December 1913)

Group XX houses, Puritan Avenue, Forest Hills Gardens, Queens, New York; (I-F 112–14); never built.

Houses in Forest Hills Gardens for:

Some of the below listed houses may never have been realized; for the most part, all that were built are extant. The I-F numbers were used by the Sage Foundation Homes Company as references.

T. Commerford Martin (205 Greenway North; I-F 50);

Thomas H. Todd (167 Greenway North; I-F 51);

Robert M. Harriss (Greenway North; I-F 52);

Mrs. Carrie M. Jessup (87 Groton Street; I-F 232);

Dr. Philip G. Cole (I-F 233);

C. E. Kloetzer (Wendover Road and Ridgeway Street; I-F 234);

J. J. Crawford (I-F 235);

Mary E. Taylor (8 Shorthill Road; I-F 240);

Mrs. Will Phillip Hooper (84 Greenway South; I-F 242);

M. Worth Colewell (240 Greenway North; I-F 243);

Dr. F. R. Getz (60 Olive Place; I-F 245);

Harold Martin (140 Continental Avenue; I-F 247);

M. B. Pope (Upton Street; I-F 248);

Dr. Ralph W. Waddell (49 Groton Street; I-F 251);

F. Hagens (Slocum Crescent; I-F 252);

A. D. Anderson (I-F 253);

Frank C. Kay (93 Groton Street; I-F 255);

John Ihlder (I-F 257);

E. G. Trowbridge (63 Groton Street; I-F 258);

George Sherwood Eddy (corner of Greenway South and Union Turnpike; I-F 260);

Miss Anna G. Price (145 Greenway South; I-F 262);

Herman B. Rountree (176 Slocum Crescent; I-F 263);

J. J. Finnegan (I-F 266);

Mrs. H. L. Young (I-F 268);

William Roswell Hulbert (52 Deepdene Road; I-F 269);

Mrs. J. R. Woodrough (Greenway South; I-F 272);

A. C. Weil (Greenway South; I-F 272);

Austin K. Hanks (101 Slocum Crescent; I-F 273);

Miss M. E. Oehler (I-F 275);

P. J. Eder (I-F 276);

Israel A. Washburne (55 Olive Place; I-F 283);

H. H. Buckley (8 Markwood Road; I-F 286);

Miss Lillian Dynevor Rice (120 Puritan Avenue; I-F 301);

Charles Edward Stowe (35 Slocum Crescent; I-F 302);

Albert Stotler (I-F 303);

C. H. Schammell (Slocum Crescent; I-F 304);

Arthur E. McFarlane (84 Puritan Avenue; I-F 305);

Dr. A. Latham Baker (41 Slocum Crescent; I-F 306);

John A. Meeker (Olive Place; I-F 307);

J. E. Cox (I-F 312);

Frederic W. Goudy (40 Deepdene Road; I-F 313);

John A. Tompkins 2nd (41 Deepdene Road; I-F 320);

Guyon Locke Crocheron Earle (37 Greenway South; I-F 321);

John A. Meeker house, Forest Hills Gardens.
American Homes & Gardens 12 (February 1915): 43

James Rea (75 Ascan Avenue; I-F–324);

G. H. Brainard house (I-F 330);

Mrs. A. D. Miller (I-F 420);

Rufus Angell (Shorthill Road; I-F 421);

J. M. Dearest (I-F 595);

Chase Bishop garage (I-F 800);

Reutermann (I-F 948);

Fred Stone house, Forest Hills Gardens. Samuel H. Gottscho. Architectural Record 59 (April 1925): 347

Fred Stone (Greenway North);

T. C. Jones; Robert J. Cole (Wendover Road);

Dr. Edward L. Keyes (Greenway South);

R. C. McGirr (Slocum Crescent);

W. Leslie Harriss (80 Slocum Crescent);

Brown (Greenway South);

J. O. Morris (Overhill Road);

Company houses (I-F 449, 665, 666, 669, 930–33, 937).

1913

Mrs. G. H. Stanton house, Chenowith, Watch Hill, Rhode Island. Watch Hill, Then and Now, Watch Hill Preservation Society, Roberta Burkhart, Michael Beddard, and Ardith Schneider

Mrs. G. H. Stanton house, Chenowith, Westerly Road, Watch Hill, Rhode Island; 1913–14; extant.

West Side Tennis Club, Tennis Place, Forest Hills Gardens, New York; 1913–14; extant.

Mrs. W. R. Thompson house, Sunset Hill, Aquidneck Avenue. Watch Hill, Rhode Island; 1913–15; extant.

Ernesto G. and Edith S. Fabbri house, 7 East 95th Street, New York, New York; with Egisto Fabbri; 1913–17: extant: House of the Redeemer.

1914

Arthur Curtiss James estate, Surprise Valley Farm, Harrison Avenue, Newport, Rhode Island; extant: SVF Foundation.

Morgan cottage, Stone House, Montauk, New York; c. 1914; extant.

Gertrude Vanderbilt Whitney studio, 8 West 8th Street, New York, New York.

Group XXXIII houses, Middlemay Place and Bow Street, Forest Hills Gardens, Queens, New York; 1914–16; extant.

Design for courthouse and prison, Inferior Jurisdiction, New York, New York; never built.

1915

Edwin Cornell Jameson house, 9 East 69th Street, New York, New York; 1915–17; extant.

Church-in-the-Gardens, Ascan Avenue, Forest Hills Gardens, Queens, New York; extant.

Indian Hill, industrial village for Norton Company, Worcester, Massachusetts; 1915–16; extant.

Industrial village for Holston Corporation, Erwin, Tennessee; 1915–16; extant.

Jeppson Monument, Worcester, Massachusetts; c. 1915; status unknown.

1916

William Hartman Woodin house, Dune House, Lily Pond Lane, East Hampton, New York; attributed to Atterbury; added gardener's cottage in 1925; extant.

Caspar Wistar Hodgson house, Kanyonkrag, Yonkers, New York. Arts and Decoration 32 (April 1930): 49

Caspar Wistar Hodgson house, Kanyonkrag, Park Hill Avenue, Yonkers, New York; c. 1916; extant.

1917

Harold H. Weekes house, Wereholme, South Bay Avenue, Islip, New York; extant: Seatuck Environmental Association and Suffolk County Nature Center.

Houses for Kingsport Improvement Corporation, Kingsport, Tennessee; with John Nolen; 1917–19; extant.

1918

Dr. Albert Herman Ely house, Fort Hill, Shinnecock Hills, New York. Living room. Courtesy of the Winterthur Library: Joseph Downs Collection of Manuscripts and Printed Ephemera, no. 99 x 71.15

Dr. Albert Herman Ely house, Fort Hill, Shinnecock Hills, New York; demolished: 1968.

William Adams Walker Stewart house, Edgeover, Cold Spring Harbor, New York. Architectural Catalog (April 1918)

William Adams Walker Stewart house, Edgeover, Shore Road, Cold Spring Harbor, New York; c. 1918; demolished.

Miners' village, West End Coal Company, Italy Street, Mocanaqua, Pennsylvania; 1918–24; extant.

Group XLVIII houses, 4–18 Park End Place, Forest Hills Gardens, Queens, New York; extant.

1919

Richard E. Forrest house, Altadena, Harrison, New York. American Architect 121 (February 15, 1922)

Richard E. Forrest house, Altadena, Hilltop Place, Harrison, New York; extant.

American Wing, Metropolitan Museum of Art, 1000 Fifth Avenue, New York, New York; 1919–24; extant.

Remodeling of First Presbyterian Church, 12 West 12th Street, New York, New York; extant.

Group XLIX houses, Burns Street, Forest Hills Gardens, Queens, New York; extant.

1920

Hubert Vos studio, Zee Rust, Brenton Road, Newport, Rhode Island; commissioned by Arthur Curtiss James; c. 1920; extant.

Grosvenor Atterbury office, 139 East 53rd Street, New York, New York; alterations; demolished.

Group LVI houses, Burns Street and Underwood Road, Forest Hills Gardens, Queens, New York; extant.

1921

Bloomingdale Hospital, White Plains, New York. Sturgis Hall. Richard S. Grant. *The Architect* 5 (January 1926): pl. 81

Bloomingdale Hospital, Sturgis Hall (1921–22), Rogers Gymnasium (1922–24), Taylor Building (1924–25), Bard and Bruce houses (1930–31), staff house (1921–25), six physicians' cottages (1922–23; 1930–31), student nurses' residence (1925), Bloomingdale Road, White Plains, New York; 1921–31; extant: New York Hospital–Payne Whitney Westchester.

First Methodist Episcopal Church, Church Circle, Kingsport, Tennessee; 1921–26; extant.

1922

Lytle J. Hunter house, Greenway Terrace, Forest Hills Gardens. Courtesy of Elizabeth Seeler

Lytle J. Hunter house, Greenway Terrace, Forest Hills Gardens, Queens, New York; extant.

Russell Sage Foundation building annex, 122–30 East 22nd Street, New York, New York; 1922–23; extant: apartments.

1925

Aldus Chapin Higgins house, John Wing Road, Worcester, Massachusetts; extant: Worcester Polytechnic Institute.

Mrs. William Horace Schmidlapp house, Ca Sole, East Walnut Hills, Ohio; 1925–27; extant.

Cornelia Connelly Hall, Rosemont College, Rosemont, Pennsylvania. Rosemont College Archives

Ten residences, Sheldon Close and Crystal Springs Road, Mariemont, Ohio; with John Nolen; extant.

Cornelia Connelly Hall, Rosemont College, Montgomery Avenue, Rosemont, Pennsylvania; extant.

Hartford Orphan Asylum and Children's Village, Albany Avenue, Hartford, Connecticut; 1925–28; extant: Child & Family Services of Connecticut.

1926

Efrem Zimbalist house, 225–27 East 49th Street, New York, New York; alterations; extant: apartments.

Nassau Shores Country Club, Massapequa, New York. Samuel H. Gottscho. *Architectural Record* 69 (June 1931): 463

Nassau Shores Country Club, East Shore Drive, Massapequa, New York; 1926–27; extant: Riviera Waterfront Caterers.

Study for the Union Club, street to street with interior court, New York, New York; never built.

1927

C. P. Lineaweaver house, Rose Lane, Haverford, Pennsylvania; status unknown.

Paul Salembier house, Lily Pond Lane, East Hampton, New York; designed by Roger Bullard; alterations; extant.

Tenney Memorial Chapel, Methuen, Massachusetts. Courtesy of the Methuen Historical Commission

Tenney Memorial Chapel, Grove and Railroad Streets, Methuen, Massachusetts; extant.

Holy Trinity Church rectory, 341 East 87th Street, New York, New York; extant.

1928
Starling W. Childs house, Yeamans Hall Club, Charleston, South Carolina; extant.

Frank A. Dillingham garden, Beechcroft Farm, Old Short Hills Road, Short Hills, New Jersey; c. 1928; extant.

Commercial buildings, Job's Lane, Southampton, Long Island. Courtesy of the Southampton Historical Museum

Commercial buildings, Main Street and Job's Lane, Southampton, New York; c. 1928; extant.

Gotham Hospital, New York, New York. Architecture 62 (July 1930): 14

Gotham Hospital, Central Park West between 107th and 108th Streets, New York, New York; 1928–30; never built.

Proposal for addition to Fraunces Tavern, 101 Broad Street, New York, New York; never built.

Competition entry for the Museum of the City of New York; New York, New York; never built.

1929

Charles P. Cooley house, Hartford, Connecticut. Charles E. Knell. Country *Life in America* 70 (July 1936): 22

Charles P. Cooley house, Prospect Avenue, Hartford, Connecticut; extant.

Harry L. Linch house, Avondale Avenue, Avondale, Ohio; extant.

Institute of Human Relations and Dr. Gesell's Children's Psychiatric Ward, Yale University, New Haven, Connecticut; 1929–30; extant.

1930
Barns for John D. Rockefeller Jr., Bedford Road, Pocantico Hills, New York; 1930–33; extant: Stone Barns Center for Food and Agriculture.

Six houses for Rockefeller employees, Bedford Road, Coprock Road and Willard Avenue, Pocantico Hills, New York; extant.

Gate lodge, Brown Mountain, Northeast Harbor, Maine; 1930–32; extant.

Gate lodge, Jordan Pond, Seal Harbor, Maine; 1930–32; extant.

1933
Joseph Spencer Graydon house, Cobble Court, Drake Road, Indian Hill, Ohio; 1933–34; extant.

National Park Service station headquarters building, apartment building for housing personnel, Schoodic Point, Maine; 1933–35; extant: Schoodic Education and Research Center.

1934
Miss Florence L. Pond house, Stone Ashley, East El Dorado Circle, Tucson, Arizona; extant: Mountain Oyster Club.

1937
H. Rowland Vermilye house, Woodwinds, Wawapek Road, Cold Spring Harbor, New York; c. 1937; extant.

Alexander Chapel, First Presbyterian Church, 12 West 12th Street, New York, New York; extant.

St. James Episcopal Church, Parish House, 865 Madison Avenue, New York, New York; extant.

1939
Yale Medical Library and Harvey Cushing Memorial Rotunda, Yale University; New Haven, Connecticut; 1939–41; extant.

1942
Amsterdam Houses, West 61st Street to West 64th Street and Amsterdam to West End Avenues; New York, New York, with Harvey W. Corbett and Arthur Holden; 1942–48; extant.

1945
John D. Rockefeller Jr. garage, 163 East 70th Street, New York, New York; originally designed by C. P. H. Gilbert in 1902; extant.

1951
Queensview, 33rd Road, Crescent Street, 34th Avenue and 21st Street, Astoria, Queens, New York; extant.

APPENDIX

Gardner Abbott (1873–1904)

Walter Frederick Anderson (1875–1948)

Roger H. Bullard (1884–1935)

William E. Butler

Raymond Cherubini Celli (1906–1959)

G. Harloe Chichester (1877–1950)

Elisabeth Coit (1897–1987)

Frank Dvorak

Charles H. Eckert

Anne Grant

Henry Higby Gutterson (1884–1954)

G. K. Johnson

E. G. Kingston

Philip E. Langworthy (1896–1967)

F. W. Magdeburg

Joseph P. Marshall

Charles C. May (1882–1937)

Irving L. Osgood

Edward Thomas Parker (1878–1930)

Julian L. Peabody (1881–1935)

Stowe Phelps (1869–1952)

Walter Rossberg

John Almy Tompkins 2nd (1871–1941)

Gordon Manfred Trautschold (b. 1883)

W. Leslie Walker (1877–1937)

Albert E. Wilson (1879–1955)

William Wilson (1880–1965)

MUSEUM LIST

The following are Atterbury buildings that are open to the public as museums, memorials, and houses.

ACADIA NATIONAL PARK
Mount Desert Island, Maine
(207) 288-3338
www.nps.gov/acad

FIRST PRESBYTERIAN CHURCH
12 West 12th Street
New York, New York 10011
(212) 675-6150
info@fpcnyc.org
www.fpcnyc.org

THE AMERICAN WING, METROPOLITAN MUSEUM OF ART
1000 Fifth Avenue
New York, New York 10028
(212) 535-7710
www.metmuseum.org

NEW YORK CITY HALL
Park Row
New York, New York 10007
(212) 788-3077
JBright@cityhall.nyc.gov
www.nyc.gov

OLD WESTBURY GARDENS
71 Old Westbury Road
Old Westbury, New York 11568
(516) 333-0048
webmaster@oldwestburygardens.org
www.oldwestburygardens.org

PARRISH ART MUSEUM
25 Job's Lane
Southampton, New York 11968
(631) 283-2118
info@parrishart.org
www.parrishart.org

SEATUCK ENVIRONMENTAL ASSOCIATION
AND SUFFOLK COUNTY NATURE CENTER
South Bay Avenue
Islip, New York 11751
(631) 581-6908
staff@seatuck.org
www.seatuck.org

STONE BARNS CENTER FOR FOOD AND AGRICULTURE
630 Bedford Road
Pocantico Hills, New York 10591
(914) 366-6200
info@stonebarnscenter.org
www.stonebarnscenter.org

NOTES

CHAPTER 1
Introduction

1 A discussion of the age of metropolitanism, which stretched from after the Civil War to 1940, can be found in Robert A. M. Stern, Gregory Gilmartin, and John Massingale, *New York 1900: Metropolitan Architecture and Urbanism, 1890–1915* (New York: Rizzoli, 1983): 11–25.

2 James Ford, *Slums and Housing*, vol. I (Cambridge, MA: Harvard University Press, 1936): 13.

3 John L. Fox, *Housing for the Working Classes: Henry Phipps, from the Carnegie Steel Company to Phipps Houses* (Larchmont, NY: Memorystone Publishing, 2007): 36.

4 Grosvenor Atterbury, "Our Monster City and its Life," *New York Times* (January 13, 1929): 80.

5 Grosvenor Atterbury, "The Community and the Home: A Preface to the Discussion of City Planning and Housing," Army Educational Commission (March 31, 1919): 16; Manuscripts and Archives, Yale University Library.

6 Grosvenor Atterbury, "Modernism in our Architecture," *New York Herald* (May 8, 1938).

7 "Honors," *Journal of the AIA* 19 (June 1953): 260.

CHAPTER 2
Grosvenor Atterbury and His Office

1 John Quillin Tilson, ed., *Yale '91 Class Book* (New Haven, CT: Price, Lee and Atkins, Co., 1891): 16. Atterbury was descended from the Boudinots, a French Huguenot family who settled in America in the 1680s, as well as from Job Atterbury of England, who immigrated to the United States in the 1790s. Since all Atterburys in this country descended from Job Atterbury, the family was fairly small and the last name infrequent. Atterbury's father, Charles, was a direct descendant of merchant Lewis Atterbury of Pittsburgh and Baltimore, Elisha Boudinot of New Jersey, and William Peartree Smith of Connecticut. Elisha Boudinot (Charles Atterbury's great-grandfather) was a lawyer and New Jersey Supreme Court justice (1798–1804), while his brother, Elias Boudinot, was the first president of the Continental Congress and, later, the director of the Mint.

2 Many family members sought out the ministry while others rose to prominence as lawyers, doctors, stockbrokers, government officials, and railroad presidents. One of Atterbury's cousins, Rev. Dr. Anson Phelps Atterbury (1855–1931), was the pastor of the West Park Presbyterian Church, while another, Henry L. Stimson (1867–1950), served as secretary of war under President Taft and President Roosevelt as well as secretary of state under President Hoover. His uncle, William Wallace Atterbury (1866–1935), headed the Pennsylvania Railroad from 1925 to 1935.

3 Charles Atterbury had a long and successful career as a lawyer. He was also the general counsel for the Erie Railway, the Chicago & Atlantic Railway Company, the Pullman Palace Car Company, and the National Cordage Company as well as the consulting lawyer for the United Railroads of San Francisco, the United Railroads Investment Company, the Sierra & San Francisco Power Company, the Railroads and Development Power Company, and Pittsburgh Railway, Light and Power Company.

4 Louis Effingham de Forest and Anne Lawrence de Forest, *The Descendants of Job Atterbury* (New York: de Forest Publishing Co., 1933): 65. The club consisted of sculptor Olin Levi Warner (1844–1896), painter Albert Pinkham Ryder (1847–1917), art dealer Daniel Cottier (1838–1891), and architects Stanford White (1853–1906), Charles McKim (1847–1909), and William Mead (1846–1928).

5 As quoted in an issue of the *Forest Hills Gardens Bulletin* from 1921 and from notes made following a conversation with Mr. Arthur Flint concerning the history of the Church-in-the-Gardens, February 16, 1938, courtesy of William E. Coleman. Katharine Mitchell Dow descended from the Dows of Thompson, Connecticut, and Sylvanus Miller of East Hampton.

6 The Berkeley School moved into a new building at 20 West 44th Street in 1891, which became the Society of Mechanics and Tradesmen in 1899. The school's playing fields in the Bronx, the Berkeley Oval, were designed by Vaux & Company.

7 Upon entering college, Atterbury was 65 inches tall and weighed 111 pounds. At graduation, he was 66.5 inches and 118 pounds. Tilson, *Yale '91 Class Book*, 96.

8 Tilson, *Yale '91 Class Book*, 86, 108, 114.

9 From a letter Cushing wrote to Bryson Delavan in 1891; referenced in "Inspiration and Epiphanies," *Bulletin of the American Association of Neurological Surgeons* 16 (2007); Peter McL. Black, Matthew R. Moore, and Eugene Rossitch Jr., eds., *Harvey Cushing at the Brigham* (Park Ridge, IL: American Association of Neurological Surgeons, 1993): 78.

10 William Adams Delano to Leopold Arnaud, Columbia University, School of Architecture, October 11, 1949. William Adams Delano Papers, Manuscripts and Archives, Yale University Library. Like many of his generation, Atterbury apprenticed in the offices of McKim, Mead & White—a position that likely came out of his father's connections with Stanford White. Part of the legacy of a Beaux-Arts education was membership in the close group of practitioners who supported one another in fostering new careers. Atterbury was not listed in the firm's roster of employees.

11 Atterbury to Harvey Cushing, February 23, 1892, Cairo; Harvey Williams Cushing Papers, Manuscripts and Archives, Yale University Library. In 1898, Atterbury prepared plans for alterations and additions to the Scroll and Key building that were to cost $30,000.

12 Atterbury to Harvey Cushing, November 11, 1894, Paris; Harvey Williams Cushing Papers.

13 Atterbury is not listed in David De Penanrun, Roux, and Delaire, *Les Architectes: Élèves de l'École des Beaux-Arts* (Paris: Librarie de la Construction Moderne, 1907).

14 Ernest Flagg, "The École des Beaux-Arts," *Architectural Record* 3 (April–June 1894): 422.

15 Ibid., 422–23.

16 Atterbury to William Adams Delano, February 15, 1953; William Adams Delano Papers.

17 Letters from the Visiting Committee of Architects Relating to the Reorganization of the School of Architecture, Columbia University in the City of New York, January 1904; University Archives and Columbiana Library.

18 Atterbury moved to 18–20 West 34th Street in 1899 and to 25 West 33rd Street in 1901. From 1903 to 1920, the office was located at 20 West 40th Street, after which it moved to 139 East 53rd Street. The 53rd Street office consisted of two seventeen-foot-wide houses that Atterbury joined into one building in 1920 for $3,000.

19 Helen Minerva Stowe's ancestors were related to Harriet Beecher Stowe and the Stowes of Vermont.

20 Edith Catlin Phelps studied under Charles Hawthorne and William Merritt Chase and at the Académie Julian in Paris. Phelps designed a pro bono beach house for the Cate School in Santa Barbara upon his move to California. He also designed the family's summer house in Provincetown and his wife's studio on the top floor of their house at 161 East 74th Street. Taking advantage of a robust economy, architects frequently dabbled in real estate; Phelps and Atterbury renovated, rented, and sold houses at 160 and 162 East 74th Street.

21 Elisabeth Coit to John Moore, New York Committee of Preservation of Architectural Records, April 16, 1982; Elisabeth Coit Papers, Schlesinger Library, Radcliffe Institute, Harvard University.

22 Ibid.

23 John Almy Tompkins 2nd, Form of Proposal for Fellowships, American Institute of Architects, 1928; the American Institute of Architects, Washington, DC.

24 Roger H. Bullard worked for Atterbury for six years before forming his own firm,

Goodwin, Bullard, & Woolsey, in 1916. He designed the Maidstone Club in East Hampton, Long Island, the Plainfield Country Club in Plainfield, New Jersey, the Oakland Golf Club in Bayside, Long Island, and the chapel at Kent School in Connecticut as well as a number of private estates. Henry Higby Gutterson worked briefly for Atterbury before moving to California to join the office of John Galen Howard. Gutterson also taught at the University of California and was the cofounder and president of the Berkeley Planning and Housing Association. Julian Peabody was associated with several architects in New York, including Atterbury, before establishing his own firm, Peabody, Wilson & Brown, in 1911. Edward T. Parker and Albert E. Wilson also joined Julian Peabody at his new firm. Associate Charles C. May, a former associate editor at *Reader's Digest*, worked for Atterbury before opening his own office in New York. May was active in town planning during World War One and also designed the YMCA buildings in Pleasantville, New York, Norwalk, Connecticut, and on Governors Island, New York. Associate W. Leslie Walker later designed the town of Coatesville, Pennsylvania, for the Midland Steel Company and the Montclair Women's Club. Associate William Wilson worked with Atterbury on such commissions as Forest Hills Gardens, the American Wing of the Metropolitan Museum of Art, and City Hall. Wilson later became the commissioner of Housing and Building for New York. Raymond C. Celli, born in Arezzo, Italy, was a project head for Atterbury from 1929 to 1933; he later established Beall & Celli, with partner S. Lloyd Beall, in Pennsylvania.

25 Elisabeth Coit to John Moore, New York Committee of Preservation of Architectural Records, April 16, 1982; Elisabeth Coit Papers.

26 Atterbury to Harvey Cushing, February 23, 1892, Cairo; Harvey Williams Cushing Papers.

27 Mary Cummings, Joanne Englehardt, Graydon Topping, Michael Zarrow, Janet Lavinio, and Richard Barnes, Oral History on Grosvenor Atterbury, May 15, 2004, transcript from audiotape, Southampton Historical Museum, Southampton, New York. In the accident, Johnstone suffered brain damage and was unable to work, and his sixteen-year-old daughter essentially became responsible for the household. Her mother was an invalid. Marrying Atterbury offered some financial security.

28 W. A. Swanberg, *Whitney Father, Whitney Heiress* (New York: Scribner's, 1980): 243.

29 Future client John D. Rockefeller Jr., whom Atterbury fondly referred to as "Doctor," frequently gave the architect money to pay his doctor's bills.

30 Cummings, Englehardt, Topping, Zarrow, Lavinio, and Barnes, Oral History on Grosvenor Atterbury, May 15, 2004. A fire in 1929 destroyed the Atterburys' main house and the couple moved into a remodeled carriage house on the property known as Little Sugar Loaf House. Atterbury is buried in Greenwood Cemetery in Brooklyn.

31 Mariana Griswold Van Rensselaer was an important American author and architectural critic. Her article in *Century Magazine*

(1899) about the Churches of Auvergne and the Cathedral of Le Puy, illustrated by Joseph Pennell, inspired Atterbury to visit the region; Pennell and his wife, Elizabeth Robins Pennell, also illustrated an article called "The Most Picturesque Place in the World" in *Century Magazine* (1893).

32 Harvey Cushing, *A Visit to Le Puy-en-Velay* (Cleveland: The Rowfant Club, 1986): 7, 17–19.

33 A lifelong member, Atterbury was elected to the Century Association in 1900, having been proposed by Robert W. de Forest and architect Edward H. Kendall. His father had been a member from 1894 to 1911.

34 Atterbury excelled at tennis and was known to play with William Bell Dinsmoor (1886–1973), chairman of Columbia University's Department of Art History and noted classicist and archaeologist. Mosette Glaser Broderick, "McKim, Mead & White: The South Shore of Long Island," in Helen Searing, ed., *In Search of Modern Architecture: A Tribute to Henry-Russell Hitchcock* (New York: Architectural History Foundation, 1982): 205.

35 The original members of the committee also included Allen B. Pond (1858–1929) of Chicago, Frank C. Baldwin (1869–1945) of Detroit, Frank W. Ferguson (1861–1926) of Boston, and William A. Boring (1859–1937) of New York. They collected copies of general clauses and contracts from some twenty-five leading firms throughout the country, from which they created standardized documents. "Report on the Committee of Specifications," *American Architect and Building News* 91 (January 19, 1907): 43.

36 Atterbury to Prof. John F. Weir, October 31, 1909; John Ferguson Weir Papers, Manuscripts and Archives, Yale University Library.

37 Letters from the Visiting Committee of Architects Relating to the Reorganization of the School of Architecture; Columbia University, January 1904.

38 Grosvenor Atterbury, "The Community and the Home: A Preface to the Discussion of City Planning and Housing," Army Educational Commission (March 31, 1919), Manuscripts and Archives, Yale University Library; Henry H. Saylor, "The AIA's First Hundred Years," *Journal of the AIA* (May 1957): 115–16; Mark Meigs, "Crash-Course Americanism: The A. E. F. University, 1919," *History Today* 44 (August 1994): 36–43; Alfred Emile Cornebise, *Soldier-Scholars: Higher Education in the A. E. F., 1917–19* (Philadelphia: American Philosophical Society, 1997).

39 Atterbury became a member in 1897; in 1916, his friend Lloyd Warren—Whitney Warren's brother—incorporated the Beaux-Arts Institute of Design, an accredited program born out of the society's informal ateliers.

40 A member of the Architectural League since 1901, Atterbury was preceded by Cass Gilbert as president. Other members in the office included Charles C. May (1914), Stowe Phelps (1902), John Almy Tompkins 2nd (1908), and W. F. Anderson (1918).

41 "Honors," *Journal of the AIA* 19 (June 1953): 259–60.

42 Atterbury to Robert W. McLaulin, Director, School of Architecture, Princeton, New Jersey, March 2, 1955; William Adams Delano Papers.

43 Grosvenor Atterbury, "What Can be Done to Bring Art Closer to the People and Increase their Love for It?" Republican Club of the City of New York, Saturday Discussions Committee, March 4, 1916.

CHAPTER 3
Establishing a Practice: 1895–1917

COUNTRY HOUSES, CLUBS, AND CHAPELS

1 Elisabeth Coit to John Moore, New York Committee of Preservation of Architectural Records, April 16, 1982; Elisabeth Coit Papers, Schlesinger Library, Radcliffe Institute, Harvard University.

2 Mrs. John King Van Rensselaer, *The Social Ladder* (New York: H. Holt, 1924): 278.

3 As quoted in Ronald G. Pisano, *The Students of William Merritt Chase* (Huntington, NY: Heckscher Museum, 1973): 4. According to Mary Cummings, Atterbury designed several buildings in the village to give it a distinct look, including the picturesque tower at the corner of Job's Lane and South Main Street and the Colonial Revival building formerly occupied by Saks.

4 Charles Atterbury sold his property near Lake Agawam to J. Hampden Robb. The Long Island Improvement Company had intended to convert the Hills into a development with villas, walks, and streets, but the company collapsed in 1893, having sold 810 acres. Other buyers included William S. Hoyt, General Wager Swayne, Austin Corbin, Samuel and James C. Parrish, R. C. Hoyt, Francis Key Pendleton, Herbert E. Dockson, and the Shinnecock Hills Golf Club. As reported by the *New York Times* in 1906, the Shinnecock Land Company consisted of Charles Atterbury, John Claflin, General Wager Swayne, James C. Parrish, and F. K. Pendleton.

5 In November 1929, a fire started by a plumber winterizing the home destroyed the main house and windmill. Atterbury and his wife moved into the remodeled carriage house, which he had designed in 1911. Another house, known as Brooks House, originally owned by Atterbury's cousin Dr. Lewis Atterbury Conner, was also located on Sugar Loaf but was torn down for a motel complex. *Pittsburgh Architectural Club Exhibition*, Carnegie Galleries (1903): 29; "House, Mr. Grosvenor Atterbury, Shinnecock Hills, Long Island," *The Architect* 9 (January 1928): 475–79; Harriet Sisson Gillespie, "Grosvenor Atterbury's Own Home, the House on the Hills," *Arts and Decoration* 26 (March 1926): 35–37; Donald Dwyer, "Grosvenor Atterbury," in Robert B. MacKay, Anthony K. Baker, and Carol A. Traynor, eds., *Long Island Country Houses and Their Architects, 1860–1940* (New York: W. W. Norton, 1997): 50.

6 C. Matlack Price, "The Development of a National Architecture: the Work of Grosvenor Atterbury," *Arts and Decoration* 2 (March 1912): 176.

7 John Taylor Boyd Jr., "Personality in Architecture," *Arts and Decoration* 32 (April 1930): 49.

8 Ibid.

9 Atterbury to Harry L. Linch, December 28, 1927; from the collection of the current owners of the Harry L. Linch house, Cincinnati, Ohio.

10 According to Craig A. Gilborn, *Durant: The Fortune and Woodland Camps of a Family in the Adirondacks* (Sylvan Beach, NY: North Country Books, 1981), Atterbury visited Camp Pine Knot on April 15, 1893. His later sketches of a gate at Camp Sagamore and an unidentified lodge and fireplace were shown in the Architectural League's annual exhibition of 1906; Durant began developing Sagamore in 1895 and later sold it to Alfred G. Vanderbilt.

11 The rusticity of Camp Uncas, like all other great camps, was a facade; the Morgans lived in relative luxury with a year-round staff of thirty. Gilborn, *Durant: The Fortune and Woodland Camps of a Family in the Adirondacks*, 100–103; Barbara Plumb, "How the Morgans Roughed It," *New York Times* (August 21, 1966): 248; Patricia Leigh Brown, "Preserving Adirondacks Great Camps," *New York Times* (June 11, 1992): C, 1, 6; Craig A. Gilborn, *Adirondack Camps: Homes Away from Home, 1850–1950* (Syracuse, NY: Syracuse University Press, 2000): 222–23.

12 According to Wesley Hayne's *Adirondack Camps Theme Study*, Atterbury designed a camp for Anna Lusk in 1907 on Upper St. Regis Lake adjoined to Camp Comfort, owned by Prof. Graham Lusk and his wife, Mary Woodbridge Tiffany Lusk, Louis Comfort Tiffany's daughter. According to the *New York Times*, "This camp [was to] be one of the most elaborate and extensive of the entire chain of lakes" (July 14, 1907). It featured a two-story living hall with a monumental fieldstone fireplace.

13 The cottage that Atterbury designed on lot 13 in the Art Village was moved to the northwesterly portion of Sugar Loaf in 1908. At that time, he enlarged and renovated it for Mrs. Emma W. Harris. It is possible that Atterbury also designed The Honeysuckles for Parrish's nieces, the Misses Lee. According to Samuel G. White, *The Houses of McKim, Mead & White* (New York: Rizzoli, 1998): 157, William Merritt Chase's house in the Shinnecock Hills (1892) was possibly designed for Charles Atterbury and then later modified for Chase. A flurry of letters from 1889 to 1892 from Charles Atterbury to Stanford White in the Stanford White Papers at the New-York Historical Society discuss locations and a piece of property for rent/sale.

14 The Church of All Angels was built around 1894 in the Shinnecock Hills on the east side of Station Road. As described by Helen Wetterau, *Shinnecock Hills* (East Patchogue, NY: Searles Graphics, 1991), McKim, Mead & White possibly designed it; however, the attribution is unclear. After it burned in 1905, Atterbury designed a new building for the church, which was never built. His dull redbrick chapel with leaded casements, steeply pitched roof, and entrance framed with a light Gothic arch of wood was described by Gustav Stickley's magazine *The Craftsman* as "particularly suited to a landscape of dull color and light broken contour." "The Theory of Grosvenor Atterbury, Who Bases All of His Work Upon the Principle That Originality in Architecture Springs Only from the Direct Meeting of Material Conditions," *The Craftsman* 3 (June 1909): 301, 309.

15 *Pittsburgh Architectural Club Exhibition*, Carnegie Galleries (1903): 29, 60; "House for J. R. Soley, Esq., and House for W. Swayne, Esq., Shinnecock Hills, Long Island, N.Y.," *American Architect and Building News* 94 (August 26, 1908): pls.

16 "House for Lucien Oudin, Watermill, Long Island," *Architectural League of New York Yearbook* (1907): pl.; Samuel Ward, "The Summer Home of Lucien Oudin, Esq.," *American Homes and Gardens* 5 (April 1908): 147–50; "House of Mr. Lucien Oudin, Long Island, N.Y.," *American Architect and Building News* 94 (September 2, 1908); MacKay, Baker, and Traynor, *Long Island Country Houses and Their Architects, 1860–1940*, 54–55.

17 According to Wetterau, *Shinnecock Hills*, Claflin had desired a Spanish design, which irked Atterbury; as a result, Atterbury never liked the residence. *Pittsburgh Architectural Club Exhibition*, Carnegie Galleries (1903): 41; "House of A. B. Claflin, Southampton L.I., N.Y.," *American Architect and Building News* 94 (August 26, 1908): pls.; Byron Porterfield, "Southampton Group to Raise Funds for Four-Year College," *New York Times* (January 26, 1962): 18; Lisa and Donald Sclare, *Beaux-Arts Estates: A Guide to the Architecture of Long Island* (New York: Viking Press, 1979): 223–28; MacKay, Baker, and Traynor, *Long Island Country Houses and Their Architects, 1860–1940*, 50–51. Claflin's daughter Beatrice married Robert P. Breese, son of photographer James L. Breese, who summered in Southampton at The Orchard, designed by Stanford White; she later married the fifth Earl of Gosford in 1928. Claflin's estate in New Jersey is now the Lakewood Country Club.

18 This property was renamed Andros Hills in the 1950s. The water tower, laundry, and servants' quarters were burned.

19 The Elys' first house was named after Elyria, Ohio—the town Dr. Ely's grandfather had founded in 1817. According to Wetterau, *Shinnecock Hills*, carpenters were brought over from England to construct the special roof on Fort Hill. Dr. Ely was President Harding's physician, and Fort Hill was known as the "summer white house" because Harding visited frequently. "The Carriage House and Stable of Shingled Exterior," *Building Age* 34 (November 1912): 595–96; "Garden View, House of Dr. Albert H. Ely, Southampton, L.I.," *Inland Architect* 52 (November 1907): 66; "House for Dr. A. H. Ely, Southampton, Long Island," *Architectural League of New York Yearbook* (1907): pl.; MacKay, Baker, and Traynor, *Long Island Country Houses and Their Architects, 1860–1940*, 53.

20 MacKay, Baker, and Traynor, *Long Island Country Houses and Their Architects, 1860–1940*, 53–54.

21 The Trevors owned a number of properties in Southampton. The collections of the Southampton Historical Museum include a sketch of a lodge by Atterbury for Trevor, dated March 4, 1893. "House at Southampton, Long Island, N.Y.," *The Brickbuilder* 22 (November 1913): 175–76; MacKay, Baker, and Traynor, *Long Island Country Houses and Their Architects, 1860–1940*, 55–56. According to Guy Lawrance and Anne Surchin,

Houses of the Hamptons, 1880–1930 (New York: Acanthus Press, 2007): 319, Atterbury also designed another residence, Meadowmere, for Trevor, across the street.

22 Van Rensselaer, *The Social Ladder*, 281.

23 It is unclear how Atterbury initially won this commission. According to his project list, the architect did design several early houses in Cincinnati for Joseph Neave and Jacob Schmidlapp but they did not predate the Wiborg house. Wendy Goodman, "A South Fork Story," *New York* (July 17, 2006): 46–52; Robert A. M. Stern, "One Hundred Years of Resort Architecture in East Hampton: The Power of the Provincial," *East Hampton's Heritage* (New York: W. W. Norton, 1982): 113.

24 "Country House, D. W. McCord, East Hampton, Long Island," *Architecture* 24 (October 1911): 164.

25 "Villas All Concrete," *Architectural Record* 17 (February 1905): 86–87; "House of Albert Herter, Esq., East Hampton, Long Island, N.Y.," *American Architect and Building News* 94 (September 2, 1908): pls; Charles de Kay, "Eastern Long Island—Its Architecture and Art Settlements," *The American Architect* 93 (April 1, 1908): 110; *Country Life* 32 (May 1917): 36–37; Amy L. Barrington, "A Fielde of Delite," *The House Beautiful* 45 (April 1919): 188–91; "Country Estate, Albert Herter, East Hampton, Long Island," *Architecture* 40 (September 1919): pls. 135–39; "Ossorio," *Architecture Plus* (January–February 1974): 64–73; MacKay, Baker, and Traynor, *Long Island Country Houses and Their Architects, 1860–1940*, 52–53; Stern, "One Hundred Years of Resort Architecture in East Hampton," 108–10, 176; Lawrance and Surchin, *Houses of the Hamptons*, 100–109. The Herters occupied the house up until Albert Herter's death in 1950; their son Christian Herter, who later became Eisenhower's secretary of state, sold it to artist Alfonso Ossorio in 1952. At that time, Ossorio stripped and painted the interiors white and the exterior of the house black. The Herters also commissioned Delano & Aldrich in 1909 to design El Mirasol in Santa Barbara.

26 This house was later owned by tobacco manufacturer and inventor Rufus Lenoir Patterson (1872–1943) and his wife Margaret Morehead Patterson (1875–1968) and known as Lenoir. "House of R. L. Patterson, Southampton L.I.," *Architectural Record* 44 (October 1918): 335, 372–73; MacKay, Baker, and Traynor, *Long Island Country Houses and Their Architects, 1860–1940*, 56–57; Lawrance and Surchin, *Houses of the Hamptons, 1880–1930*, 314. Lenoir's wood paneled living room, with a fireplace surround carved with crests and molded tracery ceiling, displayed Atterbury's characteristic attention to detail.

27 Grace Wickham Curran, *American Magazine of Art* (June 1927), as quoted in Patricia Trenton and Sandra d'Emilio, *Independent Spirits: Women Painters of the American West, 1890–1945* (Berkeley, CA: University of California Press, 1995): 51.

28 Charles de Kay, "Summer Houses at East Hampton," *Architectural Record* 13 (January 1903): 32; *Pittsburgh Architectural Club Exhibition*, Carnegie Galleries (1903): 41; "Villas

All Concrete," 86–87; "House of Dr. C. C. Rice, East Hampton, Long Island, N.Y.," *American Architect and Building News* 94 (August 1908): pls.; de Kay, "Eastern Long Island—Its Architecture and Art Settlements," 110; "Country House, D. W. McCord, East Hampton, Long Island," 164, pls. 98–101; MacKay, Baker, and Traynor, *Long Island Country Houses and Their Architects, 1860–1940*, 53; Stern, "One Hundred Years of Resort Architecture in East Hampton," 110–11.

29 "Country House, D. W. McCord, East Hampton, Long Island," 164.

30 "A Cottage and Garden at East Hampton, L.I.," *House & Garden* 3 (April 1903): 213–14; *Pittsburgh Architectural Club Exhibition*, Carnegie Galleries (1903): 41; "Villas All Concrete," 88; Stern, "One Hundred Years of Resort Architecture in East Hampton," 111, 180.

31 Stern, "One Hundred Years of Resort Architecture in East Hampton," 112–13, 192, 198; MacKay, Baker, and Traynor, *Long Island Country Houses and Their Architects, 1860–1940*, 56–57; Lawrance and Surchin, *Houses of the Hamptons, 1880–1930*, 320.

32 Tiffany built his first country house, The Briars, in Cold Spring Harbor in 1889 before moving to Laurelton Hall across the harbor in the early 1900s. While Atterbury's house for the de Forests, Wawapek Farm, was not completed until 1900, the de Forests had lived off and on in Cold Spring Harbor in a white Colonial farmhouse off of Shore Road on land owned by de Forest's father since the late 1870s. Tiffany and his wife spent the first weekend of their honeymoon at Julia de Forest's cottage (Robert de Forest's sister) in Laurel Hollow. Atterbury also designed a scheme for a shooting lodge at Tomotley, South Carolina, for Havemeyer in the early 1900s, a rendering of which was displayed at the Pittsburgh Architectural Club's exhibit of 1907. James Pooton Jr., "Henry O. Havemeyer's Venice," *New York Times Supplement* (May 23, 1897): 14; *Moorish Houses at Bayberry Point, Islip, L.I., Built for Mr. H. O. Havemeyer* (1897); *Pittsburgh Architectural Club Exhibition*, Carnegie Galleries (1900): 20; *Pittsburgh Architectural Club Exhibition*, Carnegie Galleries (1903): 29, 70; "The Pittsburgh Architectural Club's Exhibition," *American Architect and Building News* 92 (November 30, 1907): pl.; Aymar Embury II, *One Hundred Country Houses* (New York: The Century Co., 1909): 96–98; "Some Work at Bayberry Point, L.I., by Grosvenor Atterbury," *The American Architect* 96 (September 8, 1909): 94–96, pls.; Russell F. Whitehead, "American Seaside Homes," *Architectural Record* 28 (August 1910): 79–87, *Pittsburgh Architectural Club Exhibition*, Carnegie Galleries (1910); Oswald C. Hering, *Concrete and Stucco Houses* (New York: McBride, Nast and Company, 1912): 78–79; Grosvenor Atterbury, Stowe Phelps, and John A. Tompkins, Architects, *Architectural Catalog* (April 1918): pls.; "Bayberry Point Homes," *New York Times* (July 7, 1930): 39; MacKay, Baker, and Traynor, *Long Island Country Houses and Their Architects, 1860–1940*, 51; Harry W. Havemeyer, *Along the Great South Bay: From Oakdale to Baby-*

lon, the Story of a Summer Spa, 1840–1940 (Mattituck, NY: Amereon Ltd., 1996): 227–31.

33 According to Harry W. Havemeyer, H. O. Havemeyer organized the Bayberry Point Corporation to sell the houses and an additional 117 lots that comprised his property in 1929. At that time, a third canal was dug. By 1950, all of the original houses and lots had been sold.

34 "Interlocking Directors in Charities and Good Works," *New York Times* (December 12, 1912): 44. Also: James A. Hijiya, "Four Ways of Looking at a Philanthropist: A Study of Robert Weeks de Forest," *Proceedings of the American Philosophical Society* 124 (December 1980): 404–18.

35 Atterbury went on to design several houses in Cold Spring Harbor for de Forest's children, including Edgeover (c. 1918) for Frances de Forest Stewart (1879–1957) and William Adams Walker Stewart (1876–1960) and Woodwinds (c. 1937) for Ethel de Forest Vermilye and H. Rowland Vermilye.

36 "The Story of Wawapek, 1898–1998," courtesy of Mrs. Douglas Williams, Department of American Decorative Art, Metropolitan Museum of Art; MacKay, Baker, and Traynor, *Long Island Country Houses and Their Architects, 1860–1940*, 51–52. As an artist and importer, Lockwood de Forest had started a decorating business with Tiffany and textile designer Candice Wheeler (1827–1923) during the 1880s, known as Louis C. Tiffany and Company, Associated Artists. Before the partnership dissolved in 1883, the group worked on interiors in the White House and in the Mark Twain house in Hartford, Connecticut. De Forest commissioned Frederick Law Olmsted Jr. to design various aspects of the landscape and gardens in 1910.

37 *Pittsburgh Architectural Club Exhibition*, Carnegie Galleries (1903): 29; MacKay, Baker, and Traynor, *Long Island Country Houses and Their Architects, 1860–1940*, 53. In 1901, he also slightly altered James's house at 17 West 54th Street.

38 "House at Cold Spring Harbor, Long Island, N.Y.," *The Brickbuilder* 22 (May 1913): pls. 69–71; Atterbury, Phelps, and Tompkins, *Architectural Catalog*, pls.; MacKay, Baker, and Traynor, *Long Island Country Houses and Their Architects, 1860–1940*, 56.

39 In 1913, William Robertson Coe and his wife, Mary Rogers Coe, purchased the property from the Byrnes and hired Guy Lowell and Andrew Robeson Sargent to design extensive gardens. They also commissioned Walker & Gillette to design a hay barn, superintendent's house, and laundry to harmonize with Atterbury's lammie-brick construction. In 1918, the main house burned to the ground in six hours. The fire occurred in the sun parlor located in the west wing of the house, where workers were waterproofing a large imported stained-glass window. A blow torch fell and ignited combustible materials, spreading quickly to other parts of the house. Loss to property and content damage, which included James Byrne's personal collection of art and furniture, was estimated to be over seven hundred thousand dollars. The Coes commissioned Walker & Gillette to design

another house on its foundation. In 1901, Atterbury also worked on the Byrnes' house at 51 West 58th Street. "House at Locust Valley, Long Island, N.Y.," *The Brickbuilder* 17 (January 1908): 13–14, pls. 9–14; "House at Locust Valley, L.I.," *Architectural League of New York Yearbook* (1908): pl.; Embury, *One Hundred Country Houses*, 144–46; Atterbury, Phelps, and Tompkins, *Architectural Catalog*, pls.; "The Former Residence of Mr. James Byrne at Locust Valley, L.I., by Grosvenor Atterbury," *Country Life* 37 (November 1919): 34–35; Mac Griswold and Eleanor Weller, *The Golden Age of American Gardens, Proud Owners, Private Estates, 1890–1940* (New York: Abrams, 1991): 95–96; MacKay, Baker, and Traynor, *Long Island Country Houses and Their Architects, 1860–1940*, 55.

40 Embury, *One Hundred Country Houses*, 144–46.

41 Ibid.

42 G. M. Clapham, "An Art Lover's Country Villa," *Town & Country* 63 (June 27, 1907): 10–12. Also: Welles Goodrich, "Waldene, the Henry D. Walbridge Place, at Roslyn, Long Island," *The Spur* 36 (September 1, 1925): 55–58, 100; MacKay, Baker, and Traynor, *Long Island Country Houses and Their Architects, 1860–1940*, 54.

43 Atterbury's original design for the building was larger and more expensive, but at the urging of Albert Herter the architect redesigned the chapel to conform to the church's small budget. Isabel K. Bechtle, *A History of the Congregational Church, Seal Harbor, Maine* (Bangor, ME: Northeast Reprographics, 2002): 4–7, 25.

44 "The Theory of Grosvenor Atterbury, Who Bases All of His Work Upon the Principle That Originality in Architecture Springs Only from the Direct Meeting of Material Conditions," 301, 304, 309.

45 Herter and Bodman houses: Jane Brown, *Beatrix: The Gardening Life of Beatrix Jones Farrand, 1872–1959* (New York: Viking, 1995): 206–7; Earl Shettleworth Jr. and Lydia Vanderbergh, *Revisiting Seal Harbor and Acadia National Park* (Charleston, SC: Arcadia, 1997): 40–41.

46 *Bar Harbor Times* (January 26, 1918): 1; "House of Ernesto G. Fabbri, Esq. at Bar Harbor, Maine," *Academy of Architecture and Architectural Review* 24 (1903): 90–91; "Sketch, Country House, E. G. Fabbri, Bar Harbor," *Architectural League of New York Yearbook* (1904): pl.; Brown, *Beatrix: The Gardening Life of Beatrix Jones Farrand, 1872–1959*, 65, 206, pl. This house burned in 1918 and was rebuilt in 1919 by Ernesto Fabbri's brother Egisto on the foundations of the original house.

47 Tompkins's mother was originally from Providence and Westerly; this connection with Rhode Island may have led to the Watch Hill commissions. Roberta Burkhardt, *Watch Hill, Then and Now* (Watch Hill, RI: Watch Hill Preservation Society, 1988): 244–47; "Works by Grosvenor Atterbury and his Associates; Stowe Phelps, John Almy Tompkins 2nd, Leslie Walker," *The New York Architect* 3 (August 1909); Rupert O. Jones Jr., *National Register of Historic Places, Watch Hill, Rhode Island* (Watch Hill: The Boot and Tackle Shop, 1998): 53.

48 Enos house: "Works by Grosvenor Atterbury and his Associates; Stowe Phelps, John Almy Tompkins 2nd, Leslie Walker," pl.; Burkhardt, *Watch Hill, Then and Now*, 146, 272–73: Jones, *National Register of Historic Places, Watch Hill, Rhode Island*, 41–42. Stanton house: "Bungalow for Mrs. Stanton, Watch Hill, Rhode Island," *Architectural League of New York Yearbook* (1913): 113; "Works by Grosvenor Atterbury and his Associates; Stowe Phelps, John Almy Tompkins 2nd, Leslie Walker," pl.; Jones, *National Register of Historic Places, Watch Hill, Rhode Island*, 65–67; Burkhardt, *Watch Hill, Then and Now*, 194, 338, 341, 344–45. According to Jones, many of Mrs. Clara Stanton's rental properties were also attributed to Atterbury and Tompkins.

49 "An Informal Garden at Watch Hill," *Architectural League of New York Yearbook* (1917): pl.; W. F. Anderson, "Noteworthy Houses by Well-Known Architects—II," *The House Beautiful* 46 (August 1919): 69–71, 110; Jones, *National Register of Historic Places, Watch Hill, Rhode Island*, 20; Burkhardt, *Watch Hill, Then and Now*, 21–22.

50 W. F. Anderson, "Farm Buildings of Arthur Curtiss James, Esq., Newport, Rhode Island," *Architectural Forum* 34 (February 1921): 56–58, pls.; Augusta Owen Patterson, *American Homes of To-Day* (New York: MacMillan Company, 1924): 337–40, 343–45; Lida Rose McCabe, "Surprise Valley Farm: On the Estate of Arthur Curtiss James, Esq., at Newport, R.I.," *Country Life* 45 (April 1924): 51–53; "Farm Group, Estate of Mr. Arthur Curtiss James, Newport, R.I.," *The Architect* 9 (March 1928): 713–15, pls.; "Picturesque Farm Architecture on Newport Estate," *Arts and Decoration* 30 (March 1929): 60–61, 100, 125; "Surprise Valley Farm for Arthur Curtiss James, Esq., Newport, Rhode Island," *Pencil Points* 14 (July 1933): 314; Tom Christopher, "The Peaceable Kingdom," *Town & Country* 172 (November 2003): 156–63.

51 "Arthur Curtiss James, 74, Rail Titan, Is Dead," *New York Times* (June 5, 1941): 23. The farm fed the two James household staffs, one hundred farm hands, and the crew of his yacht. Stowe Phelps was distantly related, if at all, to the Phelpses of the Phelps Dodge empire, which included I. N. Phelps Stokes.

52 Patterson, *American Homes of To-Day*, 337.

53 Ibid., 340.

54 Grosvenor Atterbury File, Architect and Engineer's File (PR-003-01), New-York Historical Society; "Tracts and Homes in Westchester Sales," *New York Times* (January 12, 1926): 55; Robert Hammer, "The Search for Seth Low," *Bedford Hills Historical Museum Newsletter* 5 (July 2006): 2–3.

55 The Savin Hill property also included a large barn, three frame cottages, a garage, and an ice house. *Pittsburgh Architectural Club Exhibition*, Carnegie Galleries (1907): 17; "Garden and House at Ridgefield, Connecticut," *Academy of Architecture and Architectural Review* 33 (1908): 134; "House at Ridgefield, Connecticut," *The American Architect* 93 (April 22, 1908): pl.; "Detail, House of Dr. W. S. Rainsford, Ridgefield, Conn.," *The American Architect* 113 (February 20, 1918): 210; "House for Dr. W. S. Rainsford at Ridgefield, Conn.," *Architectural Review* 9 (July 1919): 11–12,

pls. 7–9; "Savin Hill, Country Estate of Late Rev. Dr. W. S. Rainsford, Sold," *New York Times* (July 21, 1935): 1; "Detail in Garden of Dr. W. S. Rainsford," *Architectural League of New York Yearbook* (1918): pl.

56 In 1911, J. P. Morgan also commissioned Atterbury to design a house on Greenwood Lake in Warwick, New York, for Homer A. Norris, the organist and choirmaster at St. George's.

57 John K. Turpin and W. Barry Thomson, *New Jersey Country Houses: The Somerset Hills*, Vol. I (Far Hills, NJ: Mountain Colony Press, 2004): 108–11; 200–201.

58 W. Leslie Walker's hollow tile house was located at 190 Gates Avenue in Montclair. H. W. Frohne, "Hollow Tile in Construction and Design," *Building Progress* 1 (April 1911): 123–24.

59 "House for E. Bradley, Montclair, N.J.," *Architectural League of New York Yearbook* (1909): pl.; "House at Montclair, N.J.," *The Brickbuilder* 18 (August 1909): pl. 104–5; "Residence at Montclair, N.J.," *The New York Architect* 3 (August 1909): pl.; Richard K. Cacioppo, *The Glory of Montclair: Past and Present* (Montclair, New Jersey: Dream City Publishing, 1995): 43–48. Unity Chapel: *The Unitarian Church, Montclair: An Effective Suburban Church, Celebrating 100 Years* (Montclair: The Unitarian Church, 1997): 7. In style and massing, the Unity Chapel closely resembled Atterbury's design for the Seal Harbor Congregational Church.

60 According to Elizabeth Mills Brown, *New Haven: A Guide to Architecture and Design* (New Haven: Yale University Press, 1976), Atterbury designed houses at 64 Edgehill Road (1901) for Charles Monson, 406 Prospect Street (1903) for Wilbur F. Day, and 305 St. Ronan Street (1909) for Walter Malley.

61 The club (then known as the New Haven Golf Club) and its nine-hole course (1895), originally located on Prospect Street and Winchester Avenue, was quickly overrun by Yale students. This prompted the club to move and limit its membership. "New Haven Country Club, New Haven, Connecticut," *American Architectural and Building News* 96 (September 2, 1908): pls.; "Sketch for a Country Club, Lake Whitney, New Haven, Connecticut," *Architectural League of New York Yearbook* (1906): pl.

CITY HOUSES

62 Price, "The Development of a National Architecture," 176.

63 Additional houses Atterbury designed in the Georgian idiom included those for John Rutledge Abney at 15 East 86th Street (1899) and George T. Bonner at 18 East 75th Street (1910), both demolished. In 1905, Atterbury also transformed a brownstone into a Georgian Revival American basement house at 21 West 47th Street for Marion de Forest Cannon Clark and her husband, Louis Crawford Clark, a member of the New York Stock Exchange. Marion de Forest Clark was the daughter of Col. Le Grand B. Cannon, a banker and railroad builder, and a sister of Miss Caroline de Forest.

64 "The Fashionable Residential District, No. One," *Real Estate Record and Builder's Guide* 76 (December 16, 1905): 950.

65 For Gertrude Vanderbilt Whitney and her husband, Harry Payne Whitney, Atterbury designed a five-story addition (1904) to their house at 2 West 57th Street. The house was designed by George E. Harney in 1875 and previously owned by William C. Whitney. In 1914, Atterbury remodeled the ground floor of a building at 8 West 8th Street into two exhibition rooms to form the Whitney Studio, adjoining Mrs. Whitney's artist's studio at 19 MacDougal Alley. Atterbury and Whitney had caused somewhat of a scandal with their study for a pool and garden pavilion with mural painter Hugo Ballin (1879–1956) that they entered in the Architectural League's 1908 competition. They received first rank for the special collaborative prize; however, since Atterbury sat on the prize committee, the award stirred up a controversy within the artistic community. Working with associate Julian Peabody, Atterbury also remodeled Edward and Mary Harriman's house at 1 East 69th Street in 1909. The mansard roof was replaced with a fifth-floor sun parlor, which contained a beautiful faience mantel with sculpture by A. Stirling Calder of children playing among beanstalks, vines, and sunflowers.

66 A Tiffany window in memory of Betts was installed at St. Andrew's Dune Church in Southampton in 1906. Betts and his brother C. Wyllys Betts were founders of the church in 1879 and owned a number of properties in the village that they rented to friends. The Betts's house was located on the west shore of Lake Agawan, and Mrs. Betts was known to have been delivered to church via a gondola guided by four footmen.

67 Landmarks Preservation Commission, *Upper East Side Historic District Designation Report* (New York: The Commission, 1981): 227.

68 Mrs. Trowbridge was the widow of Dr. George Trowbridge (d. 1898); her daughter married the well-known realtor Douglas Elliman. Like Atterbury, John Sanford Barnes was a member of Scroll and Key. His father had been a Civil War naval officer and a railroad financier as president of Texas's International Railroad Company and the St. Paul & Pacific Railroad. Barnes house: Landmarks Preservation Commission, *Metropolitan Museum Historic District Designation Report* (New York: The Commission, 1977): 80–81.

69 "33 East 74th Street, Grosvenor Atterbury, Architect," *The Brickbuilder* 17 (September 1908): 200; Landmarks Preservation Commission, *Upper East Side Historic District Designation Report*, 722; "Residence, J. W. Robbins, 33 East 74th Street, New York," *Architecture* 9 (January 1904): pl. 6; Herbert Croly, "Renovation of the New York Brownstone District," *Architectural Record* 13 (June 1903): 560, 562, 566; "No. 35 East 74th Street, Grosvenor Atterbury, Architect," *Real Estate Record and Guide* 73 (June 11, 1904): 1459.

70 "Renovation of the New York Brownstone District," *Architectural Record* 13 (June 1903): 562, 566.

71 Edwin O. Holter (1871–1964), lawyer and president of the Residence Realty Company, resided at 105 East 73rd Street. "105–7 East 73rd Street, New York," *Architecture* 13 (January 1906): pl. 8; "105 and 107 East

73rd Street, Grosvenor Atterbury, Architect," *The Brickbuilder* 17 (September 1908): 189; Montgomery Schuyler, "The New New York House," *Architectural Record* 19 (February 1906): 97; "Architectural Criticism," *Architecture* 21 (February 1910): 17–18; Landmarks Preservation Commission, *Upper East Side Historic District Designation Report*, 679.

72 Montgomery Schuyler, "New New York Houses, East Side," *Architectural Record* 30 (November 1911): 465; Landmarks Preservation Commission, *Upper East Side Historic District Designation Report*, 80.

73 "$60,000 Residence in East 69th Street," *New York Times* (August 6, 1915): 16; "Residence of Mr. Edwin C. Jameson, New York City," *Architecture and Building* 49 (December 1917): pl. 30; "Residence of Edwin Jameson, 9 East 69th Street, New York," *Architecture* 44 (September 1921): 276–77; Landmarks Preservation Commission, *Upper East Side Historic District Designation Report*, 408.

74 "Homes of Well-Known Architects, the Home of Mr. Atterbury, New York City," *The House Beautiful* 39 (May 1916): 169–71; "The Living Room, House, Mr. Grosvenor Atterbury, 131 East 70th St., New York," *The Architect* 6 (September 1926): pls. 131–32; Janet Howison Marsh, "City Home Problem Solved by Triplex Apartment," *Arts and Decoration* 27 (October 1927): 58–60, 100; Landmarks Preservation Commission, *Upper East Side Historic District Designation Report*, 511; Christopher Gray, "Streetscapes: 131 East 70th Street—Architect's Own Brownstone Doesn't Fit the Mold," *New York Times* (April 23, 2006): 11, 13. In the 1920s, the house was divided into two apartments—Atterbury's on the first three floors and another, accessed from Lexington Avenue, on the fourth, fifth, and sixth floors.

75 By 1916, the city building laws had outlawed the direct communication between house and garage.

76 Marsh, "City Home Problem Solved by Triplex Apartment," 100.

77 "Homes of Well-Known Architects, the Home of Mr. Atterbury, New York City," 171.

78 Correspondence from Jane Dow Bromberg, October 23, 1994, Grosvenor Atterbury File, Stanford White Collection, Avery Architectural and Fine Arts Library, Columbia University.

79 "City Residence of Mr. E. G. Fabbri," *Architecture and Building* 49 (April 1917): pls. 15–18; "The Home of Ernesto Fabbri, New York City," *Arts and Decoration* 12 (December 1919): 104–5; Mabel La Farge, *Egisto Fabbri, 1866–1933* (New Haven: Yale University Press, 1937); Bonnie Farber, "Two Problems in Stained Glass Window Chapel Design," *Faith and Form* 18 (Spring 1985): 14–18; Landmarks Preservation Commission, *Expanded Carnegie Hill Historic District Designation Report* (New York: The Commission, 1993): 257–58; Christopher Gray, "Streetscapes: 7 East 95th Street—at 1916 Fabbri house, Artisanship of Bygone Era," *New York Times* (April 25, 2004): 11, 7; Michael C. Kathrens, *Great Houses of New York: 1880–1930* (New York: Acanthus Press, 2005): 316–20.

80 Gray, "Streetscapes: 7 East 95th Street— at 1916 Fabbri house, Artisanship of Bygone Era," 7.

81 La Farge, *Egisto Fabbri, 1866–1933*, 32.

82 "The Nailcrete Corporation: Manufacturing of the Original Nailing Concrete," *Sweet's Architectural Catalogue*, 1922.

83 "The Home of Ernesto Fabbri, New York City," 104.

PHIPPS COMMISSIONS

84 *An Account of the Exercises on the Occasion of the Opening of the New Building of the Henry Phipps Institute* (Philadelphia: University of Pennsylvania, 1913): 49.

85 "Works by Grosvenor Atterbury and his Associates, Stowe Phelps, John Almy Tompkins 2nd, Leslie Walker."

86 "Residence, John S. Phipps, 6 East 87th Street, New York," *Architecture* 9 (January 1904): pls. 4–5; Landmarks Preservation Commission, *Expanded Carnegie Hill Historic District Designation Report*, 127–28; Christopher Gray, "Streetscapes: Henry Phipps and Phipps House—Millionaire's Effort to Improve Housing for the Poor," *New York Times* (November 23, 2003): 11, 7. In 1916, the Phipps family sold 6 East 87th Street to Walter P. Bliss; he in turn sold it to the German singing society, Liederkranz Club, in 1949. Peggie Phipps Boegner and Richard Gachot, *Halcyon Days: An American Family Through Three Generations* (New York: Abrams, 1986): 86–88.

87 The Beaux-Arts–trained architects S. Breck Parkman Trowbridge and Goodhue Livingston formed their partnership in 1894 and were fashionable residential designers. While they were working on the Phipps mansion, they were also designing the St. Regis Hotel (1902–3), one of their best-known commissions. Henry Phipps met George Crawley in Scotland where the family had rented an estate and showed the designer Trowbridge & Livingston's plans. Impressed by his suggestions and taste, Phipps asked Crawley to improve upon the scheme; to do so, Crawley called upon various craftsmen, sculptors, and painters to help him, including the neophyte architect Alfred C. Bossom. MacKay, Baker, and Traynor, *Long Island Country Houses and Their Architects, 1860–1940*, 119.

88 Boegner and Gachot, *Halcyon Days: An American Family Through Three Generations*, 86–92.

89 The Bessemer Building housed the Pittsburgh office of the Bessemer Trust Company, which Phipps founded in 1907 as his family office to reinvest the proceeds of his sale of Carnegie Steel for the benefit of his descendants. *The Brickbuilder* 13 (January 1904): 131; *The Brickbuilder* 14 (October 1905): 236; *Pittsburgh Architectural Club Exhibition*, Carnegie Galleries (1905): 49, 120; "Works by Grosvenor Atterbury and his Associates; Stowe Phelps, John Almy Tompkins 2nd, Leslie Walker," pls.; "Corridor, Bessemer Building, Pittsburgh, PA," *The Ohio Architect and Builder* 14 (December 1909): 42; James D. Van Trump, "Henry Phipps and the Phipps Conservatory," *Carnegie Magazine* 50 (January 1976): 26–35; Albert M. Tannler, "Renaissance Man," *Pittsburgh Tribune-Review Focus* 29 (April 11, 2004): 8–11.

90 "Works by Grosvenor Atterbury and his Associates, Stowe Phelps, John Almy Tompkins 2nd, Leslie Walker."

91 James D. Van Trump and Arthur P. Ziegler Jr., *Landmark Architecture of Allegheny County, Pennsylvania* (Pittsburgh: Pittsburgh History and Landmark Foundation, 1967): 53; Van Trump, "Henry Phipps and the Phipps Conservatory," 26–35; Patricia Lowry, "Renovated Fulton Building Opening as Renaissance Pittsburgh Hotel," *Pittsburgh Post-Gazette* (March 13, 2001); Tannler, "Renaissance Man," 8–11.

92 Manufacturer's Building: "Works by Grosvenor Atterbury and his Associates; Stowe Phelps, John Almy Tompkins 2nd, Leslie Walker"; Van Trump, "Henry Phipps and the Phipps Conservatory," 26–35; Tannler, "Renaissance Man," 8–11. 44 West 18th Street: *Pittsburgh Architectural Club Exhibition*, Carnegie Galleries (1907): 17; "Loft Building, West 18th St., N.Y.C.," *The New York Architect* 3 (August 1909): pls. Next door to the West 18th Street loft at 42 West 18th Street (1907), Phipps commissioned George Crawley to design a six-story brick and stone loft.

93 *Pittsburgh Architectural Club Exhibition*, Carnegie Galleries (1907): 17; "Natatorium in Phipps Building, Pittsburgh, Pennsylvania," *The Brickbuilder* 18 (March 1909): pl. 30; Atterbury, Phelps, and Tompkins, *Architectural Catalog*, pl.; Van Trump, "Henry Phipps and the Phipps Conservatory," 26–35; Tannler, "Renaissance Man," 8–11; Janet Parks and Alan G. Neumann, *The Old World Builds the New* (New York: Avery Architectural and Fine Arts Library, 1996): 93.

94 "Works by Grosvenor Atterbury and his Associates, Stowe Phelps, John Almy Tompkins 2nd, Leslie Walker."

95 "Some Strong Contrasts in Tenement House Life," *New York Tribune* (February 25, 1906): C3; "Phipps Model Tenement," *The Craftsman* 10 (April 1906); Grosvenor Atterbury, "The Phipps Model Tenement House," *Survey Mid-Monthly* 16 (October 6, 1906): 49–65; "Phipps House, Tenement No. 1, Study for Interior Court," *Architectural League of New York Yearbook* (1906): pl.; *Pittsburgh Architectural Club Exhibition*, Carnegie Galleries (1907): 17; "The Phipps Model Tenement Houses," *The Brickbuilder* 16 (September 1907): 165–66, pls. 129–33; Louise E. Dow, "Money-Making Model Tenements," in Walter Hines Page and Arthur Wilson Page, *The World's Work: A History of Our Time*, vol. XV (New York: Doubleday, Page, 1908): 9998–10004; H. W. Frohne, "The Planning of Fireproof Apartment Houses in New York," *The American Architect* 100 (November 29, 1911): 213–14; Atterbury, Phelps, Tompkins, *Architectural Catalog*, pls.

96 *New York World*, 1905, as quoted in John L. Fox, *Housing for the Working Classes: Henry Phipps, from the Carnegie Steel Company to Phipps Houses* (Larchmont, NY: Memorystone Publishing, 2007): 53.

97 As described by Fox, *Housing for the Working Classes*, Phipps's former partner, Andrew Carnegie, had served on the New York State Tenement House Committee with de Forest and Gould and most likely made the introduction. Other board members, such as Myles Tierney and Charles S. Brown,

founder of Brown, Harris, Stevens, had also served on the committee. By the time the first Phipps tenement was constructed, the Peabody Trust, established fifty years earlier, had set a strong precedent, providing accommodations for nearly six thousand families and earning 2.41 percent on the capital invested.

98 Today, the Phipps Houses is the oldest and largest not-for-profit developer of housing for low- and moderate-income families. As of 2004, they owned and/or managed 12,600 units and 42 properties.

99 Fox, *Housing for the Working Classes*, 67.

100 Atterbury, "The Phipps Model Tenement House," 50.

101 Ibid., 57.

102 Ibid., 57.

103 Ibid., 50.

104 James Ford, *Slums and Housing* (Cambridge, MA.: Harvard University Press, 1936): 684.

105 Phipps Tenement #2 (1906), designed by Whitfield & King, was located at 233–47 West 63rd Street. Henry Whitfield was the brother of Louise Whitfield Carnegie, Andrew Carnegie's wife. Phipps Tenement #3 (1912) at 234–48 West 64th Street, designed by City and Suburban Homes' architectural staff, headed by Philip Ohm, backed against it. The Phipps Houses' next project materialized in 1931 with the Phipps Garden Apartments in Sunnyside, Queens.

106 Dennis Sharp, ed., *Alfred C. Bossom's American Architecture, 1903–1926* (London: Book Art, 1984); Bossom immigrated to the United States in 1903 to work for Carnegie Steel. The tenements, razed in the 1960s, were located on Shore Avenue.

107 "Notes and News," *Journal of Philosophy, Psychology, and Scientific Methods* 5 (July 2, 1908): 391–92; "Phipps Hospital: A World's Model," *New York Times* (July 9, 1909): 6; "Thirty-First Annual Exhibition, Architectural League of New York," *The American Architect* 109 (February 23, 1916): 115; Grosvenor Atterbury, "Hospitals and Esthetics: The Architectural Problem, with Particular Reference to Esthetics and the Art of Architecture," *American Medical Association Journal* 65 (September 25, 1915): 1080–85; "The Psychiatric Clinic and the Community," *Science* 33 (June 6, 1913): 856–58; Atterbury, Phelps, and Tompkins, *Architectural Catalog*, pls.; Anne Bennett Swingle, "Where a Mind Could Find Itself Again," *Hopkins Medical News* (Winter 2003); Janet Farrer Worthington, "When Psychiatry Was Very Young," *Hopkins Medicine* (Winter 2008).

108 Atterbury later served on the university's advisory board with Charles Platt and John Russell Pope to supervise the development of Johns Hopkins's Homewood campus between the years 1919 and 1933.

109 "Phipps Hospital: A World's Model," *New York Times* (July 9, 1909): 6.

110 Swingle, "Where a Mind Could Find Itself Again."

111 Atterbury, "Hospitals and Esthetics," 1081.

112 As described by Swingle, Atterbury was upset by the administration's criticisms and strove to justify his design in his lengthy paper, "Hospitals and Esthetics."

113 Dr. Lawrence F. Flick, "An Historical Sketch of the Henry Phipps Institute," *An Account of the Exercises on the Occasion of the Opening of the New Building of the Henry Phipps Institute* (Philadelphia: University of Pennsylvania, 1913): 24. Flick worked exhaustively to educate the public about tuberculosis. He also founded the Pennsylvania Society for the Prevention of Tuberculosis with Phipps's support, the Free Hospital for Poor Consumptives, and a sanatorium in White Haven, Pennsylvania. The Phipps Institute was integral to bringing the International Congress on Tuberculosis to the United States in 1908.

114 Flick, "An Historical Sketch of the Henry Phipps Institute," 25.

115 *An Account of the Exercises on the Occasion of the Opening of the New Building of the Henry Phipps Institute*; "The Henry Phipps Institute for the Treatment of Tuberculosis, Philadelphia, Pennsylvania," *The Brickbuilder* 23 (September 1914): pls. 129–31; "Endowment for the Henry Phipps Institute," *Science* 63 (March 5, 1926): 250; "The Henry Phipps Institute," *Science* 51 (March 12, 1920): 265.

MUSEUMS, RESTORATIONS,
AND SCHOOLS

116 "Biographical Sketch, May 22, 1953," Grosvenor Atterbury Papers, #3762, Division of Rare and Manuscript Collections, Carl A. Kroch Library, Cornell University; Samuel L. Parrish, *Historical, Bibliographical and Descriptive Catalogue of the Objects Exhibited at the Southampton Art Museum, Established at Southampton, N.Y.* (New York: B. H. Tyrrel, 1898); Charles C. May, "The Parrish Art Museum, Southampton, Long Island," *Architectural Record* 38 (November 1915): 524–39; Atterbury, Phelps, and Tompkins, *Architectural Catalog*, pls.; Samuel L. Parrish, *Early Reminiscences* (New York: B. H. Tyrrel, 1927): 62–76; Phyllis Braff, "The Parrish Marks a Century," *New York Times* (May 17, 1988): 112; Donna M. De Salvo, ed., *Past Imperfect: A Museum Looks at Itself* (Southampton, NY: Parrish Art Museum, 1993).

117 In 1880, Parrish formed a partnership with his Harvard classmate Francis Key Pendleton (1850–1930), also a Southampton resident. Their practice, Parrish & Pendleton, represented railroad interests, such as the Norfolk & Western and the Denver & Pacific; Pendleton went on to become a State Supreme Court justice.

118 Samuel L. Parrish, *Early Reminiscences*, 65.

119 Both additions were endowed by Parrish's brother, James Cresson Parrish. The large 1902 hall, inspired by the Louvre's Hall of Augustus, originally housed the marble busts of the first eighteen emperors, modeled after originals in Europe, that now decorate the grounds. In contemplating this space, Parrish consulted with Augustus Saint-Gaudens at the Hall of Augustus in June 1900.

120 May, "The Parrish Art Museum, Southampton, Long Island," 524.

121 Ibid., 536.

122 "York Hall, New Haven, Connecticut," *American Architect and Building News* 56 (June 12, 1897): 86, pls.; Brown, *New Haven: A Guide to Architecture and Design*, 131; "The Twelfth League Exhibition," *American Architect and Building News* 55 (March 27, 1987): 99;

Patrick Pinnell, *The Campus Guide: Yale University* (New York: Princeton Architectural Press, June 1999): 123–25.

123 Trumbull later sold a collection of his paintings to Yale. They were originally housed in a neoclassical art gallery—America's first university art collection—that the artist designed on Old Campus, no longer extant.

124 Harold B. Davis, "Connecticut Hall, Yale University, New Haven, CT," Historic American Buildings Survey, Library of Congress, 1936; Brown, *New Haven: A Guide to Architecture and Design*, 122; Judith Ann Schiff, "Nathan Hale Slept Here," *Yale Alumni Magazine* (February 2001).

125 "Pawling School Cornerstone Laid," *New York Times* (June 10, 1909): 4; "Pawling School Dedicated," *New York Times* (June 10, 1910): 7; John M. Benson, "Trinity-Pawling History Interwoven with the Pawling Community," *Pawling News Chronicle* (September 29, 2006). The school closed during World War Two and reopened as the Trinity-Pawling School in 1947.

126 The Cluett properties in Troy later became part of the Emma Willard School—a campus funded by Mrs. Russell Sage in 1910. Mrs. Sage had attended the school, formerly known as the Troy Female Seminary.

127 In 1925, Atterbury designed Cornelia Connelly Hall at Rosemont College in Rosemont, Pennsylvania, in a collegiate Gothic style. The college's first freestanding dormitory featured facades of local gray stone, a green slate roof, and steel casement windows framed in brick. Atterbury also designed a scheme for the campus's development which included a chapel, administration buildings, library, gymnasium, and other residence halls; however, none of these buildings were carried out.

128 Grosvenor Atterbury and Frederick Law Olmsted, "Report on the Physical Development of St. Paul's School, Concord, New Hampshire," Boston, 1923; Robert A. M. Stern, "The Architecture of St. Paul's School and the Design of the Ohrstrom Library," http://library.sps.edu/exhibits/stern/olmsted.shtml.

129 "Mrs. Sage Saves Governor's Room," *New York Times* (December 31, 1907): 1; "The Governor's Room in The City Hall, New York," *The American Architect* 96 (July 7, 1909): 1–3, pls.; John Quincy Adams Jr., *The Governor's Room in the City Hall, New York City* (New York: Privately Printed, 1909); "The Court House Site," *New York Times* (March 14 1910): 6; "Restoration of City Hall Is Almost Complete," *New York Times* (January 12, 1913): 5, 4; "Dispute over Share in City Hall's Fame," *New York Times* (September 25, 1915): 15; Charles C. May, "The New York City Hall," *Architectural Record* 39 (April–June 1916): 229–319, 474–90, 513–35; "Restored City Hall Aim of Architects," *New York Times* (October 15,1916): 3, 5; "City Hall Cupola Ruined by Fire," *New York Times* (May 11, 1917): 13; John Walker Harrington, "New Cupola of the New York City Hall," *The American Architect* 112 (September 12, 1917): 177–80; Atterbury, Phelps, and Tompkins, *Architectural Catalog*, pls.; "The Restored Tower of New York's City Hall," *Architecture and Building* 51 (January 1919): 6, 18, pls. 26–27; Art Commission of the City of New York, *The*

Governor's Room in the City Hall, New York City (March 12, 1970); Clay Lancaster, "New York City Hall Stair Rotunda Reconsidered," *Journal of the Society of Architectural Historians* 29 (March 1970): 33–39; Mary Beth Betts, *The Governor's Room, City Hall, New York* (New York: Art Commission of the City of New York, 1983): 2–14; Art Commission of the City of New York, *On City Hall, in City Hall* (New York: The Commission, 1984).

130 According to Betts, *The Governor's Room, City Hall, New York*, McComb and Mangin won the competition together and were both responsible for the initial scheme for the building and drawings. As supervisor, McComb saw the design carried out and selected details unspecified in the drawings and only his name appears on the cornerstone of the building. As sole practitioner, McComb also designed the James Watson House on State Street (1806), the Alexander Hamilton house—the Grange—on Convent Avenue (1801–2), the front of the Government House in New York (1790), St. John's Chapel, Washington Hall, and churches on Murray Street and Bleecker Street. Mangin designed St. Patrick's Old Cathedral on Mott Street (1809–15) and worked as the city surveyor in 1795. City Hall is the only building the two men designed in partnership.

131 An extended discussion of the threats posed to City Hall is in Robert A. M. Stern, Gregory Gilmartin, and John Massengale, *New York 1900: Metropolitan Architecture and Urbanism, 1890–1915* (New York: Rizzoli, 1983): 61–67.

132 "Mrs. Sage Saves Governor's Room," 1. The Art Commission was founded in 1898 as a steward to city-owned property. In addition to de Forest, other members of the committee who oversaw Atterbury's restoration were architect I. N. Phelps Stokes, painter Francis C. Jones, and R. T. Haines Halsey.

133 An excerpt from the *Daily Tribune* as quoted in Betts, *The Governor's Room, City Hall, New York*, 16.

134 On the wood panels over the doors, the state seal was flanked by liberty and justice, the national seal by emblems of war and peace (battle axe and olive branch), the seal of the province by emblems of native weapons and food (arrows and corn), and the seal of New Amsterdam by figures of sailors and Native Americans.

135 May, "The New York City Hall," 480.

136 According to Betts, *The Governor's Room, City Hall, New York*, Atterbury supervised the replacement of the wooden doors connecting the rotunda to the Governor's Room with glass doors (1910–11), the re-covering of some furniture (1926), and a larger restoration (1937–39) that involved both cosmetic and structural repairs.

137 The wooden benches in the halls of the building were originally designed by Atterbury for the Board of Estimate chamber.

138 Harrington, "New Cupola of the New York City Hall," 180.

139 "City Hall Cupola Ruined by Fire," 13.

140 Harrington, "New Cupola of the New York City Hall," 180.

141 Atterbury to Mr. T. Rousseau, secretary to the mayor, October 9, 1919; Municipal Archives, New York, NY.

142 Harrington, "New Cupola of the New York City Hall," 180.

CHAPTER 4
The Russell Sage Foundation and Forest Hills Gardens: 1909–1940

1 In 1907, there were only eight foundations in the United States, two of which had an endowment equivalent to that of the Russell Sage Foundation. John M. Glenn, Lilian Brandt, and F. Emerson Andrew, *Russell Sage Foundation, 1907–1946* (New York: Russell Sage Foundation, 1947): 13.

2 "Forest Hills Gardens, Long Island," *Construction News* 4 (October 4, 1913): 9; according to the "Background and Examples of Work, Grosvenor Atterbury, June 1948," he had gone on "numerous trips for special study of model tenements, industrial housing, town planning and cement construction," Grosvenor Atterbury Papers, #3762, Division of Rare and Manuscript Collections, Carl A. Kroch Library, Cornell University.

3 Cleveland H. Dodge, Robert C. Ogden, and Helen M. Gould were Mrs. Sage's personal friends. Dodge was involved in the American National Red Cross, the International Young Men's Christian Association, and the American Museum of Natural History; Ogden worked to improve educational opportunities in the South; and Gould donated generously to charitable organizations. De Forest chose the other board members. Mrs. William Rice was one of the founders of the Charity Organization Society; Louisa Lea Schuyler was founder of the State Charities Aid Association and the Bellevue Hospital training school for nurses; Daniel Coit Gilman, an educator and administrator, was the first president of Johns Hopkins University and had also served as president of the Carnegie Institute in Washington. Alfred Tredway White, builder of model tenements, replaced Gilman after his death in 1908.

4 The first meeting of the Sage Foundation Home Company's executive committee was held on July 15, 1909, at the Downtown Association to elect officers and authorize the issue of capital stock. Shareholders were de Forest, Alfred T. White, Cleveland H. Dodge, John M. Glenn, and Robert C. Ogden. De Forest was elected president, John M. Glenn secretary and vice president, and Cleveland H. Dodge treasurer.

5 Susan L. Klaus, *A Modern Arcadia: Frederick Law Olmsted Jr. and the Plan for Forest Hills Gardens* (Amherst: University of Massachusetts Press, 2002): 13–15.

6 These projects included de Forest's brother Henry's estate, Nethermuir, and the neighboring property of his sister Julia. Olmsted Jr. later did work at Wawapek Farm for de Forest.

7 Olmsted to de Forest, December 20, 1908; Series 3, Box 23, Folder 182, Russell Sage Foundation Records, Rockefeller Archive Center, Sleepy Hollow, New York (hereafter cited as RSF). Olmsted was particularly interested in German planning, inquiring of the director of land surveying in Cologne, Germany, as to how new city quarters were planned and what ratios existed between streets, traffic facilities, parks, and building lots. Olmsted to Herm Halbach, Vermessungs Direktor, Cologne, Germany, March 15, 1909; Series B, #3586, Folder 1,

Records of the Olmsted Associates, Manuscript Division, Library of Congress, Washington, DC (hereafter cited as OA).

8 De Forest to Olmsted, January 4, 1909; Series 3, Box 23, Folder 182, RSF.

9 Robert W. de Forest, "Forest Hills Gardens: What it is, Why it is, and What it is not," in Sage Foundation Homes Company, *Forest Hills Gardens*, New York, 1910.

10 De Forest to Olmsted, December 7, 1908; Series 3, Box 23, Folder 182, RSF.

11 De Forest to Olmsted, January 4, 1909; Series 3, Box 23, Folder 182, RSF.

12 Howard's *To-morrow: A Peaceful Path to Real Reform* (1898) was republished in 1902 as *Garden Cities of To-morrow*.

13 Parker & Unwin's partnership continued until 1914 when Unwin became chief town planning inspector of the Ministry of Health.

14 Frederick Law Olmsted, "Through American Spectacles: An Expert's View of English 'Garden City' Schemes," *Garden Cities and Town Planning* 4 (May 1909): 199.

15 Frederick C. Howe, "The Garden Cities of England," *Scribner's Magazine* 52 (July 1912): 3–4.

16 Barnet, a disciple of Octavia Hill, also founded several charitable and educational institutions, including Whitechapel Art Gallery and the East End settlement house, Toynbee Hall, with her husband Canon Barnet.

17 www.hgs.org.uk/history/index.html.

18 Elsa Rehmann, "Margarethenhöhe bei Essen: the Krupp Foundation Suburb," *Architectural Record* 36 (October 1914): 375.

19 Quote of Unwin's from Walter L. Creese, *The Search for Environment: The Garden City, Before and After*. Esteem of German city planning diminished considerably with the onset of the war.

20 Richard E. Foglesong, *Planning the Capitalist City: The Colonial Era to the 1920s* (Princeton: Princeton University Press, 1986): 189.

21 De Forest to Olmsted, January 4, 1909; Series 3, Box 23, Folder 182, RSF.

22 Grosvenor Atterbury, "The Architectural Work," in Sage Foundation Homes Company, *Forest Hills Gardens*, New York, 1910.

23 De Forest, "Forest Hills Gardens: What it is, Why it is, and What it is not."

24 Grosvenor Atterbury, "Forest Hills Gardens," *The Survey* 25 (January 7, 1911): 565.

25 Later that evening, the men met at de Forest's house at 7 Washington Square North with John M. Glenn, manager of the foundation. Minutes of the First Meeting of the Sage Foundation Development Committee, April 29, 1909; Series 3, Box 21, Folder 167, RSF.

26 As manager of Roland Park, the Kansas City, Missouri, native was responsible for creating the first planned shopping center (1896). In addition, Boutan included land-use restrictions into the individual property deeds to retain the neighborhood's architectural integrity and instated annual dues for the maintenance of the property. An architectural review board was also created under his management. www.rolandpark.org/rp history.html.

27 At the Development Committee's May 13, 1909, meeting, Harmon, Olmsted, and Atterbury recommended purchasing additional property south of the railroad station

because "in its present shape [its] immediate development . . . could not be successfully undertaken." By the next meeting on May 20th, de Forest had reached an arrangement with Meyer. Minutes of the Fourth, Fifth, and Sixth Meetings of the Sage Foundation Development Committee, May 13, May 20, and May 27, 1909; Series 3, Box 21, Folder 167, RSF.

28 Minutes of the Seventh Meeting of the Sage Foundation Development Committee, June 3 and 4, 1909; Series 3, Box 21, Folder 167, RSF.

29 Olmsted to Atterbury, June 15, 1909; Series B, #3586, Folder 1, OA.

30 Atterbury to Olmsted, June 19, 1909; Series B, #3586, Folder 1, OA.

31 At the February 24, 1910, Development Committee meeting, it was estimated that the cost of building the station, platforms, shelters, and stairs as designed by Atterbury would cost from $25,000 to $35,000. The final cost of the station was $50,000, of which the Russell Sage Foundation paid $20,000, Cord Meyer $20,000, and the LIRR $10,000.

32 Minutes of the Eighth Meeting of the Sage Foundation Development Committee, June 10, 1909; Series 3, Box 21, Folder 167, RSF.

33 Atterbury carefully looked at his designs for the square's buildings, and in October 1909 resubmitted plans; however, in January he deemed it necessary to enlarge them, a change balanced by reducing the volume of houses elsewhere on the property. Minutes of the Eighteenth and Twenty-Fourth Meetings of the Sage Foundation Development Committee, October 14, 1909, and January 27, 1910; Series 3, Box 21, Folder 167, RSF.

34 Olmsted to Atterbury, December 28, 1920; Series B, #3586, Folder 6, OA.

35 The development committee had originally determined that the least expensive house of five to six rooms would be offered at $3,000 and the most expensive of thirteen to fifteen rooms at $8,000. However, at the July 8, 1909, meeting, the committee decided that these numbers would be inaccessible due to the price of the land.

36 Atterbury, "The Architectural Work."

37 Frederick Law Olmsted, "The Landscape Work," in Sage Foundation Homes Company, Forest Hills Gardens, New York, 1910.

38 Olmsted planned interior parks for blocks 3, 16, 21, 23, 30, and 33; only the parks on blocks 3, 30, and 33 were carried out.

39 Olmsted, "The Landscape Work."

40 Forest Hills Gardens, Preliminary Information for Buyers, April 1914; Forest Hills Gardens Records, #3495, Box 1, Division of Rare and Manuscript Collections, Carl A. Kroch Library, Cornell University.

41 Characterization List of Purchasers, February 1, 1912; Series 3, Box 20, Folder 161, RSF. The development committee strategically advertised Forest Hills Gardens in the more important New York newspapers for a period of six weeks and kept careful records of the purchasers. As sales began, de Forest cautioned John Glenn to "watch especially what is done in relation to selection of first purchasers. Upon the personnel of those who buy at first depends in my judgment very largely the success of the enterprise." De Forest to Glenn, June 24, 1911; Series 3, Box 23, Folder 182, RSF.

42 Klaus, A Modern Arcadia, 118. Vacant lots required five percent down and houses with land required ten. The balance could be paid off in 120 equal installments with 4.5 percent interest.

43 A substantial savings, plans and specifications normally cost six to ten percent of the cost of the building and other improvements. This offer was good for houses completed before November 20, 1912. The Homes Company continued to offer a discount of 2.5 percent after that date to stimulate improvement of vacant lots.

44 As originally approved in November 1909, Station Square had only two bridges. Atterbury and Olmsted later added a third bridge, considering it necessary to the design. Report of the General Manager, October 28, 1910; Series 3, Box 21, Folder 167, RSF.

45 Samuel Howe, "Town Planning on a Large Scale," The House Beautiful 36 (October 1914): 134.

46 Advertisement in the New York Times from June 19, 1912. As originally approved in November 1909, the inn was not a fireproof building. However, in 1910, Atterbury and Bouton urged the development committee to approve a fireproof structure, an increase of $15,000–$20,000 because "the difference in depreciation alone . . . would more than justify the added cost." Report of the General Manager, October 28, 1910; Series 3, Box 21, Folder 167, RSF. In August 1920, the Homes Company sold the inn to the Forest Hills Inn Corporation, headed by John M. Demarest, for $1,250,000.

47 Louis Graves, "A 'Model Village' Under Way," Building Progress 2 (January 1912): 20.

48 Grosvenor Atterbury, "Model Towns in America," Scribner's Magazine 52 (July 1912): 29.

49 W. F. Anderson, "Forest Hills Gardens—Building Construction," The Brickbuilder 21 (December 1912): 320.

50 Clarence True to Robert W. de Forest, June 24, 1911; Series 3, Box 21, Folder 167, RSF.

51 Report of Special Committee on Building Restrictions, December 30, 1910; Series 3, Box 23, Folder 183, RSF.

52 Aymar Embury II, "Cooperative Building," The House Beautiful 38 (March 1913): 117.

53 Charles C. May, "Forest Hills Gardens from the Town Planning Viewpoint," Architecture 34 (August 1916): 170.

54 May, "Forest Hills Gardens from the Town Planning Viewpoint," 171.

55 Carlyle Ellis, "Houses that Fit their Neighbors," Delineator 83 (November 1913): 13.

56 "Forest Hills Gardens: An Example of Collective Planning, Development and Control," The Brickbuilder 21 (December 1912): pl; Paul Carey Maxwell, "Using Brick to Advantage," Suburban Life 18 (February 1914): 62; "Home of H. H. Doehler," Forest Hills Gardens Bulletin 5 (June 12, 1920): 1; "Home of N. S. Jonas," Forest Hills Gardens Bulletin 7 (March 4, 1922): 1.

57 "Forest Hills Gardens: An Example of Collective Planning, Development and Control," pl; Maxwell, "Using Brick to Advantage," 62–63; "What the Suburban-Dweller May Learn from a Model Town," American Homes and Gardens 12 (February 1915): 40; "The Architect's Scrapbook—Houses at Forest Hills, Long Island," Archi-

tecture 32 (August 1915): 212; "Home of Thomas Todd," Forest Hills Gardens Bulletin 1 (April 22, 1916): 1.

58 "Home of Robert Harriss," Forest Hills Gardens Bulletin 3 (June 1, 1918): 1. Later, Harriss became the owner of block twelve and attempted to build an apartment building, to much controversy.

59 Klaus discusses Olmsted's site and garden plans for the Todd and Harriss houses (I-F 51 and I-F 52) in A Modern Arcadia, 107–9.

60 "The Architect's Scrapbook—Houses at Forest Hills, Long Island," 212; "Recent Houses at Forest Hills Gardens, Long Island," The Brickbuilder 25 (June 1916): 139; "Brick as Building Material for Small Houses," The Touchstone 1 (June 1917): 210; "Home of Miss Mary E. Taylor," Forest Hills Gardens Bulletin 2 (September 8, 1917): 1; "Home of H. H. Buckley," Forest Hills Gardens Bulletin 3 (January 26, 1918): 1.

61 "A Cottage Designed to Become a Garage," Country Life in America 43 (December 1922): 72–73; "Studio at Forest Hills Gardens, L.I., John Tompkins, Architect and Owner, New York," Architectural League of New York Yearbook (1922): pls.; "The Home of John Almy Tompkins," Forest Hills Gardens Bulletin 9 (October 13, 1923): 1.

62 In 1913, the Homes Company bought a 32-acre plot from the Cord Meyer Company, 22 acres of which it kept for the development of Forest Hills Gardens and 10 acres of which the West Side Tennis Club purchased. The United States Lawn Tennis Association National Championship (or U.S. Open) was played at the club for six decades, beginning in 1915. "The West Side Tennis Club, Forest Hills Gardens, Long Island," Architectural League of New York Yearbook (1914): pl.; "West Side Tennis Club, Forest Hills, Long Island, N.Y., Grosvenor Atterbury and John A. Tompkins, Associated Architects," Architectural Forum 28 (June 1918): pls. 72–73; Edwin Clarkson Potter, The West Side Tennis Club Story, 60th Anniversary, 1892–1952 (New York, 1952).

63 "To Spend $300,000 on Tennis Grounds," New York Times (January 11, 1914): 4, 2.

64 The Church-in-the-Gardens was formally organized in 1913 with thirty-eight members and originally operated out of a store on Station Square and a portable church until Mrs. Sage's building was completed in 1915. "The Church in the Gardens, Forest Hills, L.I.," Architectural League of New York Yearbook (1914): pl.; "The Story of the Church," Forest Hills Gardens Bulletin 1 (October 9, 1915): 1; "The Church in the Gardens, Forest Hills, L.I.," Architectural League of New York Yearbook (1918): pl.; "The Church in the Gardens at Forest Hills, N.Y.," Architectural Review 9 (August 1919): 37–40, pls. 24–25.

65 Notes on Talk with Mr. John Almy Tompkins, February 19, 1938; courtesy of William W. Coleman. According to Tompkins, he got the idea for the chancel screen from an old portiere he bought at auction. They bought an old wrought-iron lantern and added brackets, in the form of thistles; the ironwork in the bell tower also includes thistles. According to notes made following a conversation with Mr. Arthur Flint, February 16, 1938, courtesy of William E. Cole-

man, Atterbury "and his mother used to come out when the church was being built, and personally pick out stones of the right color to use together in the interior. It had been planned to put gold stars in the blue ceiling over the choir, but they decided they were too conspicuous, and eliminated them."

66 Atterbury to Olmsted, December 31, 1920; Series B, #3586, Folder 6, OA.

67 Olmsted to Atterbury, December 20, 1920; Series B, #3586, Folder 6, OA.

68 When the foundation sold its interest in 1922, it consented to modify the restrictions in the Declarations booklet #3 from April 18, 1913, to include an apartment building on block twelve. After W. Leslie and Robert M. Harriss purchased the block in 1924 and proposed building Atterbury's three-tower apartment building, the community responded by filing a lawsuit. In 1929, the Supreme Court determined that an apartment building could not be constructed on the site; however, the decision was reversed in 1933 by the Court of Appeals in the Appellate Division.

69 "A Problem of Pressures in Planning," *Architectural Record* 95 (January 1944): 87–92. Wagner, a director of the Forest Hills Gardens Corporation, also designed the New Jersey Turnpike, railroad terminals in Cincinnati and Buffalo, the Farragut and Albany housing projects in Brooklyn, and several plants and factories in New Jersey with his partner Alfred Fellheimer, also a Gardens resident. Fellheimer & Wagner was the successor firm to Reed & Stem, associated architects of Grand Central Terminal.

70 Grosvenor Atterbury, "Garden Cities," Proceedings of the Second National Conference on Housing, *Housing Problems in America*, Philadelphia, December 4–6, 1912 (Cambridge: University Press, 1912): 107.

71 Emily de Forest's father, John Taylor Johnston, had purchased stock in the rail lines between Elizabeth and Perth Amboy, New Jersey, in 1873. The Sage Foundation continued to own the houses and the Sewaren Improvement Company the land until 1919, when the houses were sold back to the Sewaren Company for $1,000 each.

72 William B. Fuller, Report on Standard Sectional Building Construction, April 22, 1909; Series 3, Box 24, Folder 185, RSF.

73 Concrete Block Committee to the Real Estate Development Committee, January 10, 1910; Series B, #3586, Folder 2, OA.

74 "The Nailcrete Corporation: Manufacturer of the Original Nailing Concrete," *Sweet's Architectural Catalogue*, 1922.

75 Engineer William B. Fuller determined that Atterbury's "standardized sectional construction method when applied to groups of houses exceeding fifty houses in any locality easily accessible to cheap concrete aggregates will produce a more economical house than any other type investigated, with the single exception of the cheap wood frame construction which is neither sanitary, fireproof or of durable construction." Report on Standard Sectional Building Construction, April 22, 1909; Series 3, Box 24, Folder 185, RSF; Frederick Squires, "Houses at Forest Hills Gardens—Pre-cast Hollow Concrete Floor, Wall and Roof Units and Exposed Aggre-

gates," *Concrete-Cement Age* 6 (January 1915): 8.

76 Squires, "Houses at Forest Hills Gardens—Pre-cast Hollow Concrete Floor, Wall and Roof Units and Exposed Aggregates," 54.

77 Groups and Houses Authorized by the Committee, January 24, 1913; Series 3, Box 23, Folder 183, RSF.

78 Report of the General Manager, April 24, 1915; Series 3, Box 20, Folder 163, RSF.

79 Atterbury to Demarest, Sept. 18, 1914; Series B, #3586, Folder 5, OA.

80 Draft of Statement about Approval of Plans to Accompany Letter of June 6th, 1921, F. L. Olmsted; Series 3, Box 20, Folder 158, RSF.

81 Sale of Forest Hills Gardens by the Russell Sage Foundation to a Syndicate Organized by John M. Demarest, Vice-President and General Manager, of the Sage Foundation Homes Company, 1922; Series 3, Box 17, Folder 146, RSF.

82 Atterbury to Lawrence Abbott, December 27, 1922; Forest Hills Gardens Corporation Records, #2775, Box 20, Division of Rare and Manuscript Collections, Carl A. Kroch Library, Cornell University.

83 Atterbury to B. D. Seeley, September 19, 1922; Series B, #3586, Folder 7, OA.

84 As supervising architect, Atterbury received $25 for each design he oversaw in the 1920s.

85 Atterbury to Lawrence Abbott, September 12, 1924; Forest Hills Gardens Corporation Records, #2775, Box 20.

86 Two tracts of land (Van Siclen and Vanderveer tracts) were added to the original 142 acres. The Gardens Corporation was responsible for overseeing the architectural development of these sections, which tended to be shoddier than in Forest Hills Gardens proper.

87 Executive Secretary to W. D. Teague, December 18, 1936; Forest Hills Gardens Corporation Records, #2775, Box 5.

88 "Sage Foundation Plans Disclosed," *New York Times* (September 4, 1911): 7.

89 Atterbury, "Model Towns in America," 32.

90 John M. Glenn to Atterbury, June 5, 1939; Series 3, Box 8, Folder 71, RSF.

91 De Forest to Atterbury, April 13, 1922; Series 3, Box 23, Folder 183, RSF.

92 As chairman of the National Housing Association's Committee on Wartime Housing, Atterbury, with John Nolen and Lawrence Veiller, urged the federal government and President Woodrow Wilson to establish a housing administration that would instate an administrator with direct charge over workers' housing related to war industries. In 1918, Otto M. Eidlitz, one of New York's leading builders, was appointed housing administrator under the Labor Department and was given the power and funding to initiate a definitive war housing program (see page 190).

93 Electus D. Litchfield, "Yorkship Village," *American Review of Reviews* 6 (December 1919): 599–602; Electus D. Litchfield, "The Model Village That Is: The Story of Yorkship Village, Planned and Completed in Less than Two Years," *The House Beautiful* 51 (June 1922): 533–36. In 1914, Litchfield also designed a small middle-class development in Jamaica, Queens, that encompassed individual houses, semi-detached dwellings,

and row houses, similarly carried out in the Federal style.

94 Richard M. Candee and Greer Hardwicke, "Early Twentieth Century Reform Housing by Kilham & Hopkins, Architects of Boston," *Winterthur Portfolio* 22 (Spring 1987): 47–80.

95 Glenn, Brandt, and Andrew, *Russell Sage Foundation*, 1907–1946, 52.

96 In 1908, Atterbury filed a building permit for a brick and stone stable and concrete and iron shed for the Charity Organization Society—also located in the United Charities Building—at 514–16 West 28th Street.

97 "Sage Foundation Building," *New York Times* (December 8, 1912): 3, 4; Russell Sage Foundation Building, No. 130 East 22nd Street, New York," *The American Architect* 108 (October 20, 1915): 267–69, pls.; "Russell Sage Foundation," *Architecture and Building* 47 (November 1915): 390–95; Rudolf Hempel, "The Russell Sage Foundation Office Building," *The American Architect* 108 (October 20, 1915): 267–69; Grosvenor Atterbury, Stowe Phelps, and John A. Tompkins, *Architectural Catalog* (April 1918): pls.; "Study for Decorative Panel and Entrance, Sage Foundation Building, New York," *The Architect* 8 (April 1927): 38; "Sage Fund to Build a 15-Story Annex," *New York Times* (April 14, 1930): 42; "Russell Sage Annex under Construction," *New York Times* (October 26, 1930): 11, 1; Glenn, Brandt, and Andrew, *Russell Sage Foundation, 1907–1946*, 51–54; Landmarks Preservation Commission, *Russell Sage Foundation Building and Annex* (New York: The Commission, 2000).

98 Hempel, "The Russell Sage Foundation Office Building," 269.

99 One of the leading architectural sculptors of his time, Chambellan was also responsible for decorative sculpture in such buildings as Radio City Music Hall, Rockefeller Center (with Lee Lawrie), the Chanin Building, the American Radiator Building, Stewart & Company (Bonwit Teller), and Sterling Library at Yale.

100 "Symbolic Panels Tell Foundation's Purpose," *New York Evening Post* (May 1, 1923).

101 Atterbury to John Glenn, March 17, 1930; John Glenn to de Forest, October 10, 1930; Series 3, Box 10, Folder 96, RSF.

CHAPTER 5
Specialist in Town Planning and
Affordable Housing: 1909–1925

1 Robert A. M. Stern, Gregory Gilmartin, and John Massengale, *New York 1900: Metropolitan Architecture and Urbanism, 1890–1915* (New York: Rizzoli, 1983): 32.

2 "Assails Tax System," *New York Times* (February 16, 1910): 9.

3 Grosvenor Atterbury, "Garden Cities," Proceedings of the Second National Conference on Housing, *Housing Problems in America*, Philadelphia, December 4–6, 1912 (Cambridge: Cambridge University Press, 1912): 106–13; Grosvenor Atterbury, "How to Get Low Cost Houses: The Real Housing Problem and the Arts of Construction Illustrated from Research Work Done under the Auspices of the Russell Sage Foundation," Pro-

ceedings of the National Housing Association, Volume 5, *Housing Problems in America*, Providence, October 9–10, 1916 (Cambridge: Cambridge University Press, 1916): 91–101.

4 Grosvenor Atterbury, "Model Towns in America," *Scribner's Magazine* 52 (July 1912): 33.

5 National Housing Association, A Symposium on War Housing Held Under the Auspices of the National Housing Association, February 25, 1918, Philadelphia, Pennsylvania.

6 *Reminiscences of Lawrence Veiller, 1949*, page 110 in the Columbia University Oral History Research Office Collection.

7 In addition, Atterbury was on the Community Service Committee on Housing and in the National Institute of Social Sciences. In 1910, he sat on the awards committee of the Building Trades Employer's Association to determine a competition for the best designs for houses of moderate cost.

8 Olmsted's involvement in the planning of Forest Hills, Massachusetts (Woodbourne), led to Atterbury's participation in the project, along with the Boston firm of Kilham & Hopkins. However, the project funders, which included Robert Winsor, a director of the Boston elevated railroad, deemed Olmsted's proposal—much like Forest Hills Gardens, Queens—too expensive and asked Robert Anderson Pope of New York to prepare another scheme. In effect pushed off the project, Olmsted resigned, which canceled out Atterbury's involvement. Richard M. Candee and Greer Hardwicke, "Early Twentieth Century Reform Housing by Kilham and Hopkins, Architects of Boston," *Winterthur Portfolio* 22 (Spring 1987): 51–54.

9 The houses at Roland Park were designed under the immediate direction of an advisory board that consisted of Frederick Law Olmsted Jr., Grosvenor Atterbury, and Baltimore architects J. B. Noel Wyatt, Howard Sill, and Edward L. Palmer Jr.; "Background and Examples of Work, Grosvenor Atterbury, June 1948," Grosvenor Atterbury Papers, #3762, Division of Rare and Manuscript Collections, Carl A. Kroch Library, Cornell University.

TENEMENTS

10 "Rent Model Flats After Rigid Test," *New York Times* (August 8, 1913): 14; "Rogers Model Dwellings," *The American Architect* 104 (October 29, 1913): pls.; "Tenements to Live In," *The Independent* 78 (April 13, 1914): 2. "The Current Architectural Press," *The American Architect* 108 (July 14, 1915): 23; "Roger Tenements, West 44th Street, New York, N.Y.," *The Brickbuilder* 24 (May 1915): pls. 64–65. When the building opened in August 1913, the front and back apartments rented for twenty and twenty-two dollars a week, approximately half the price demanded by other new buildings in the area.

11 Roy Lubove, *The Progressives and the Slums: Tenement House Reform in New York City, 1890–1917* (Pittsburgh: University of Pittsburgh Press, 1962): 175.

12 Richard Plunz, *A History of Housing in New York City* (New York: Columbia University Press, 1990): 106.

TOWN PLANNING AND AFFORDABLE HOUSING

13 W. E. Freeland, "New Housing Development at Worcester," *The Iron Age* 97 (May 18, 1916): 1187. Also: Charles C. May, "Indian Hill: An Industrial Village at Worcester, Mass., Grosvenor Atterbury, Town Planner and Architect," *Architectural Record* 41 (January 1917): 21–35; George B. Ford, "Indian Hill—A Garden Village Near Worcester, Mass.," *Journal of the AIA* 5 (January 1917): 28–29; "Giving the People What They Want: Number Two: Beautiful Homes for Working People Designed by Grosvenor Atterbury," *The Touchstone* 1 (June 1917): 179–87, 209–10; Ida M. Tarbell, *New Ideals in Business: An Account of their Practice and their Effect upon Men and Profit* (New York: The Macmillan Co., 1917): 155–62; Arthur C. Comey and Max Wehrly, "Planned Communities," in *Supplementary Report of the Urbanism Committee*, part 1, vol. 2 (Washington, DC: Government Printing Office, 1938): 53–55; *Indian Hill: An Ideal Village*, (Worcester, MA: Norton Co., 1953); Clifford S. Anderson, *Indian Hill: An Industrial Village* (Worcester, MA: Norton Co., n.d.); Mildred McClary Tymeson, *The Norton Story* (Worcester, MA: Norton Co., 1953); Margaret Crawford, *Building the Workingman's Paradise: The Design of American Company Towns* (New York: Verso, 1995): 101–28.

14 H. Daniels, Memorandum, Indian Hill Homes, Norton Company, July 16, 1915; as quoted in Harriet V. Relman, *A Village of Promise on Indian Hill in Worcester, Mass.* (Lincoln, MA: privately printed, 1990).

15 *Norton Spirit* (May 1915 and June 1915), as quoted in Crawford, *Building the Workingman's Paradise*, 116.

16 Atterbury, "Model Towns in America," 23.

17 "Beautiful Homes for Working People Designed by Grosvenor Atterbury," 185.

18 May, "Indian Hill: An Industrial Village at Worcester, Mass.," 25.

19 Crawford, *Building the Workingman's Paradise*, 117.

20 Tarbell, *New Ideals for Business*, 159.

21 Crawford, *Building the Workingman's Paradise*, 121.

22 Tarbell, *New Ideals in Business*, 155–6.

23 Lawrence Veiller, "Industrial Housing Developments in America. I. Beloit, Wis., Eclipse Park," *Architectural Record* 43 (March 1918): 256; also: Ralph F. Warner, "A Wage Earner's Community Development at Beloit, Wisconsin," *The American Architect* 113 (May 22, 1918): 657–66.

24 William B. Rhoads, "The Colonial Revival and American Nationalism," *Journal of the Society of Architectural Historians* 35 (December 1976): 239–54.

25 Lawrence Veiller, "A Colony in the Blue Ridge Mountains of Erwin, Tenn., Grosvenor Atterbury, Architect and Town Planner," *Architectural Record* 43 (June 1918): 547–59; Grosvenor Atterbury, Stowe Phelps, and John A. Tompkins, *Architectural Catalog* (April 1918): pls.; Margaret Duncan Binnicker, "A Garden City in Appalachia Tennessee: Grosvenor Atterbury's Design for Erwin," *Tennessee Historical Quarterly* 59 (Winter 2000): 274–89.

26 Veiller, "A Colony in the Blue Ridge Mountains of Erwin, Tenn.," 559.

27 In 1920, the Holston Corporation sold one third of its houses to their occupants and the remaining two thirds to Southern Potteries, a company specializing in hand-painted china. Having located to Erwin in 1916, Southern Potteries grew into the city's leading industry. In spite of the fact that Southern Potteries closed in the 1950s, Atterbury's houses continue to be known as the "pottery houses."

28 Comey and Wehrly, "Planned Communities," 35–39; Margaret Ripley Wolfe, *Kingsport, Tennessee: A Planned American City* (Lexington, KY: University Press of Kentucky, 1987): 44–54; John Nolen with Introduction by Charles D. Warren, *New Towns For Old* (Boston, MA: Marshall Jones Company, 1927; Amherst, MA: University of Massachusetts Press, 2005): xvii–xxiii, 50–65; Edward L. Ayers, "Northern Business and the Shape of Southern Progress: the Case of Tennessee's 'Model City,'" *Tennessee Historical Quarterly* 39 (1980): 208–22.

29 "Capacity Audiences in Attendance Yesterday for Church Dedication," *Kingsport Times News* (October 18, 1926): 1, 3; J. H. Osborne, "Kingsport Church Replacing Old Steeple," *Kingsport Times News* (July 8, 2005).

30 Crawford, *Building the Workingman's Paradise*, 229; Archaeological and Historical Consultants, *Pennsylvania Historical Resource Form: Mocanaqua Historic District* (Pennsylvania Historical and Museum Commission, 1989).

31 "Mariemont—A New Town," *Architecture* 54 (September 1926): 247–74, pls. 171–75; Mariemont Company, *Mariemont: The New Town* (Cincinnati: Mariemont Company, 1925); Comey and Wehrly, "Planned Communities," 92–97; Millard F. Rogers, *John Nolen and Mariemont: Building a New Town in Ohio* (Baltimore: Johns Hopkins University Press, 2001); John Clubbe, *Cincinnati Observed: Architecture and History* (Columbus: Ohio State University Press, 1992): 453, 456; Warren Wright Parks, *The Mariemont Story: A National Exemplar in Town Planning* (Cincinnati: Creative Writers and Publishers, 1967).

32 Livingood traveled extensively to familiarize himself with the garden cities that would serve as inspiration for Mariemont. In addition to Letchworth, Port Sunlight, and Hampstead Garden Suburb, he visited the Krupp projects in Germany and most likely developments on the East Coast, including Forest Hills Gardens and Indian Hill. Rogers, *John Nolen and Mariemont*, 10–15.

33 Mariemont Company, *Mariemont: The New Town*, 19.

34 "Mariemont—A New Town," pl. 185; Rogers, *John Nolen and Mariemont*, 165–68.

35 Atterbury, "Garden Cities," 107.

CHAPTER SIX
Late Projects: 1917–1941

ESTATES AND CITY HOUSES

1 Louisine Peters Weekes had divorced Harold Weekes by 1923 and remarried Russian composer and pianist Alexander Tcherepnine in 1926. "House of Harold H. Weeks, Islip, L.I., N.Y.," *The American Architect—Architectural*

Review 121 (February 15, 1922): pls; Harry W. Havemeyer, *Along the Great South Bay: From Oakdale to Babylon, the Story of a Summer Spa, 1840–1940* (Mattituck, NY: Amereon Ltd., 1996): 388; Donald Dwyer, "Grosvenor Atterbury," in Robert B. MacKay, Anthony K. Baker, and Carol A. Traynor, eds., *Long Island Country Houses and Their Architects, 1860–1940* (New York: W. W. Norton, 1997): 57; "Wereholme," National Register of Historic Places Registration Form, United States Department of the Interior, National Parks Service.

2 "The Residence of Aldus C. Higgins, Esq., at Worcester, Massachusetts," *Country Life* 49 (March 1926): 57–59; "House, Mr. Aldus C. Higgins, Worcester, Mass.," *The Architect* 5 (October 1925): 40, pls. 1–9; "A Tudor Gothic House of Rare Distinction," *Arts and Decoration* 26 (February 1927): 41–43.

3 "A Tudor Gothic House of Rare Distinction," 43.

4 Ibid., 41.

5 In Atterbury's biographical sketch, a house for Jacob Schmidlapp is listed; however, there is no information about it. It is possible that Schmidlapp may have commissioned a house in East Walnut Hills where he owned a large amount of property and his estate Kirchheim was located.

6 By the time Ca Sole was built, Jean Maxwell Schmidlapp and her husband William Horace Schmidlapp (1883–1929) were separated. "House for Mrs. Jean M. Schmidlapp, Cincinnati, Ohio," *Architectural League of New York Yearbook* (1928): pl.; Mac Griswold and Eleanor Weller, *The Golden Age of American Gardens, Proud Owners, Private Estates, 1890–1940* (New York: Abrams, 1991): 283–84; "Architecture Comes into the Garden," *House & Garden* 63 (April 1933): 25; "The Residence of Mrs. Jean Schmidlapp, Cincinnati, Ohio," *Country Life* 33 (April 1928): 46–49; R. Terry Schnadelbach, *Ferruccio Vitale: Landscape Architect of the Country Place Era* (New York: Princeton Architectural Press, 2001): 214–17.

7 Alfred Geiffert Jr. was originally from Cincinnati; the firm of Vitale & Geiffert also designed the grounds of the estate of W. H. Schmidlapp's brother, Carl J. Schmidlapp, in Mill Neck, New York. Around 1928, Atterbury also executed a charming walled garden for lawyer and Yale classmate Frank A. Dillingham (1870–1941) at Beechcroft Farm in Short Hills, New Jersey.

8 Virginia S. White, ed., *From Camargo to Indian Hill* (Indian Hill, OH: Indian Hill Historical Museum Association, 1983): 144–46; "Cobble Court in Cincinnati: The Indian Hill Home of Mrs. Joseph S. Graydon," *Country Life* 73 (February 1938): 41–46, 112.

9 "House for Harry L. Linch, Esq., Cincinnati, Ohio," *The Architect* 11 (January 1929): 400.

10 "Desert Country: Stone Ashley, Miss Florence L. Pond's Estate Rises from the Sandy Mesa Near Tucson, Arizona," *House & Garden* 74 (December 1938): 58–61; Anne M. Neguette and R. Brooks Jeffery, *A Guide to Tucson Architecture* (Tucson: University of Arizona Press, 2002): 211; "Grosvenor Atterbury, Architect, John Tompkins, Associated, Stone Ashley," *Architectural League of New York Yearbook* (1938): pl.; Grosvenor Atterbury, "The Cooling Fountains of Stone

Ashley," *Bulletin of the Garden Club of America* 23 (September 1936): 40–48.

11 Atterbury to John D. Rockefeller Jr., March 3, 1947; Record Group 2, Friends and Services, Box 43, Folder 326, Rockefeller Family Archive, Rockefeller Archive Center, Sleepy Hollow, New York (hereafter cited as RFA).

12 Atterbury, "The Cooling Fountains of Stone Ashley," 43.

13 "Miss Florence L. Pond," *New York Times* (July 20, 1955): 27.

14 John D. Rockefeller Jr. to Atterbury, February 27, 1947; Record Group 2, Friends and Services, Box 43, Folder 326, RFA.

15 Atterbury to Harry L. Linch, December 28, 1927; from the collection of the current owners of the Harry L. Linch house, Cincinnati, Ohio.

16 Augusta Owen Patterson, "Why the North Goes South to Carolina," *Town & Country* 86 (January 15, 1932): 29, 32–34.

17 "Study for Alteration to 225 and 227 East 49th Street, New York City, for Efrem Zimbalist," *The American Architect* 131 (March 5, 1927): 325; "20-Room Mansion on East Side Becomes a Gilded Police Station," *New York Times* (December 11, 1957): 33; Roy Malan and Efrem Zimbalist, *Efrem Zimbalist: A Life* (Pompton Plains, NJ: Amadeus Press, 2004): 169. Atterbury's extensive alteration to the house cost $75,000. According to the *Forest Hills Gardens Bulletin*, the Zimbalists also owned a house in Forest Hills Gardens at 86 Beechknoll Road.

18 "Efrem Zimbalist, Violinist, Dies at 94," *New York Times* (February 23, 1985): 1.

ROCKEFELLER COMMISSIONS

19 "A Westchester Farm Group," *The Sportsman* 17 (February 1935): 34–36; Todd Shapera, "Designing the Stone Barns," *New York Times* (July 4, 1999): 388; "Stone Barns Center," *Architectural Record* 193 (March 2005): 122–27; "Planters Potluck," *Country Home* (March 2006): 106–11.

20 Atterbury to John D. Rockefeller Jr., July 3, 1931; Record Group 2, Home Series-Pocantico Hills, Box 47, Folder 139, RFA.

21 "A Westchester Farm Group," 35.

22 Nelson A. Rockefeller to Mr. Tompkins, February 15, 1932; Record Group 2, Home Series-Pocantico Hills, Box 47, Folder 139, RFA.

23 Nelson A. Rockefeller to Atterbury, February 2, 1932; Record Group 2, Home Series-Pocantico Hills, Box 47, Folder 139, RFA.

24 Nelson A. Rockefeller to Atterbury, March 4, 1932; Record Group 2, Home Series-Pocantico Hills, Box 47, Folder 139, RFA.

25 Nelson A. Rockefeller to Mr. Tompkins, March 26, 1932; Record Group 2, Home Series-Pocantico Hills, Box 47, Folder 139, RFA.

26 Nelson A. Rockefeller to Mr. Tompkins, February 15, 1932; Atterbury to John D. Rockefeller Jr., February 18, 1932; Record Group 2, Home Series-Pocantico Hills, Box 47, Folder 139, RFA.

27 Atterbury to John D. Rockefeller Jr., May 4, 1933; Record Group 2, Home Series-Pocantico Hills, Box 47, Folder 139, RFA.

28 John D. Rockefeller Jr. to Atterbury, July 6, 1933; Record Group 2, Home Series-Pocantico Hills, Box 47, Folder 139, RFA.

29 Charles W. Eliot was the father of landscape architect Charles Eliot (1859–1897), Frederick L. Olmsted Jr.'s colleague and former partner. Eliot's early death spurred his father, as Harvard's president, to establish the landscape architecture program in 1900 and to espouse the principles of landscape preservation that his son had embraced.

30 John D. Rockefeller Jr. to Mr. Gordon, October 30, 1933; Record Group 2, Home Series-Seal Harbor, Box 73, Folder 755, RFA.

31 "Working on the New Gate Lodges," *Bar Harbor Times* (November 25, 1931); "Lodge and Gate, Brown Mountain Entrance, Acadia National Park, Mount Desert, Maine, Grosvenor Atterbury, Architect, John Tompkins, Associated," *Architecture* 71 (March 1935): 127–32; Ann Rockefeller Roberts, *Mr. Rockefeller's Roads: The Untold Story of Acadia's Carriage Roads and Their Creator* (Camden, ME: Down East Books, 1990): 123–33; Jane Brown, *Beatrix: The Gardening Life of Beatrix Jones Farrand, 1872–1959* (New York: Viking, 1995): 208; William D. Rieley and Roxanne S. Brouse, *Historic Resource Study for the Carriage Road System, Acadia National Park, Mount Desert Island, Maine* (U.S. Department of the Interior, National Park Service, 1989). Rockefeller gave the Brown Mountain Lodge and its accompanying land to the National Park Service in 1933 and the Jordon Pond Lodge in 1940. Olmsted was a steadfast supporter of landscape preservation. He had toured the western parks and been asked to serve on Yosemite's advisory committee. In addition to having collaborated on Forest Hills Gardens, he and Atterbury worked on a number of additional projects together, including a development plan for St. Paul's School in Concord, New Hampshire, in 1923.

32 Horace M. Albright, Director, Department of the Interior, National Park Service, to Atterbury, June 19, 1930; Record Group 2, Home Series-Seal Harbor, Box 73, Folder 755, RFA.

33 Grosvenor Atterbury, "Notes on the Architectural and Other Esthetic Problems Involved in the Development of our Great National Parks" (Department of the Interior, National Park Service, 1929): 53.

34 Atterbury to John D. Rockefeller Jr., May 16, 1930; Record Group 2, Home Series-Pocantico Hills, Box 16, Folder 156, RFA.

35 John D. Rockefeller Jr. to Atterbury, May 23, 1930; Record Group 2, Home Series-Pocantico Hills, Box 16, Folder 156, RFA.

36 "J. D. Rockefeller Jr. Drops Park Project," *New York Times* (January 29, 1931): 20.

37 Atterbury, "Notes on the Architectural and Other Esthetic Problems Involved in the Development of our Great National Parks," 51.

38 Office of John D. Rockefeller Jr. to Atterbury, November 9, 1931; Record Group 2, Home Series-Seal Harbor, Box 73, Folder 755, RFA.

39 Atterbury, "Notes on the Architectural and Other Esthetic Problems Involved in the Development of our Great National Parks," 51.

40 Ibid., 13.

41 Atterbury to John D. Rockefeller Jr., October 1, 1931; Record Group 2, Home Series-Seal Harbor, Box 73, Folder 755, RFA.

42 John D. Rockefeller Jr. to Atterbury, September 3, 1931; Record Group 2, Home Series-Seal Harbor, Box 73, Folder 755, RFA.

43 Atterbury, "Notes on the Architectural and Other Esthetic Problems Involved in the Development of our Great National Parks," 14.

44 Ibid., 12.

45 Atterbury to John D. Rockefeller Jr., November 29, 1932; Personal collection of Mr. and Mrs. Charles P. Simpson as found in Rieley and Brouse, *Historic Resource Study for the Carriage Road System, Acadia National Park, Mount Desert Island, Maine*, 207.

46 John D. Rockefeller Jr. to Atterbury, May 27, 1932; Record Group 2, Home Series-Seal Harbor, Box 73, Folder 755, RFA.

47 Welles Bosworth to Miss Janet M. Warfield, June 21, 1935; Record Group 2, Home Series-Pocantico Hills, Box 47, Folder 139, RFA.

48 The Schoodic Point naval base eventually grew into a small village with multiple family housing units, restaurant, bar, mess hall, tennis courts, commissary, medical facility, and firehouse. In 2002, the navy closed the station and it now serves as the Schoodic Education and Research Center (SERC), part of a network of National Park Service research learning centers. The National Park Service jointly manages SERC with the nonprofit organization Acadia Partners for Science and Learning.

49 Atterbury to John D. Rockefeller Jr., August 22, 1934; Record Group 2, Home Series-Pocantico Hills, Box 16, Folder 156, RFA.

50 John D. Rockefeller Jr. to Atterbury, August 19, 1935; Record Group 2, Home Series-Pocantico Hills, Box 47, Folder 139, RFA.

51 John D. Rockefeller Jr. to Atterbury, June 11, 1935; Record Group 2, Home Series-Pocantico Hills, Box 47, Folder 139, RFA.

MUSEUMS, CHURCHES, AND CLUBS

52 "$2,000,000 Building Gift to Art Museum," *New York Times* (November 18, 1922): 1; "An American Wing of the Metropolitan Museum of Art," *Bulletin of the Metropolitan Museum of Art* 17 (November 1922); Gardner Teall, "A Gift of National Importance," *The Independent* 109 (December 9, 1922): 337; "The American Wing," *Bulletin of the Metropolitan Museum of Art* 19 (November 1924); Royal Cortissoz, "The American Wing of the Metropolitan Museum of Art of New York," in R. T. Haines Halsey, *The Homes of our Ancestors Shown in the American Wing on the Metropolitan Museum of Art* (Garden City, NY: Doubleday, Page and Company, 1925): vii–x; "The American Wing of the Metropolitan Museum of Art, New York City," *The American Architect* 126 (November 12, 1924): 489–94; "Wood Trusses," *Pencil Points* 16 (November 1935): 58–59; "The American Wing of the Metropolitan Museum of Art," *Architecture and Building* 56 (November 1942): 103–6; Morrison H. Heckscher, "The Metropolitan Museum of Art: An Architectural History," *Bulletin of the Metropolitan Museum of Art* 53 (Summer 1995): 54–55; Alice Cooney Frelinghuysen, "Emily Johnston de Forest," *Magazine Antiques* 157 (January 2000): 192–97; Amelia Peck, "Robert de Forest and the Founding of the American Wing," *Magazine Antiques* 157 (January 2000): 176–81.

53 "De Forest, a Leader in Charities Here," *New York Times* (May 7, 1931): 14; John Taylor Johnston, president of the Central Railroad of New Jersey, was president of the Metropolitan Museum from 1870 to 1889.

54 Robert W. de Forest, Address on the Occasion of the Opening of the American Wing, The Metropolitan Museum of Art, New York, November 10, 1924.

55 Peck, "Robert de Forest and the Founding of the American Wing," 179. According to Peck's article, the official museum architects, McKim, Mead & White, had turned down the commission.

56 De Forest, Address on the Occasion of the Opening of the American Wing.

57 Grosvenor Atterbury, Address on the Occasion of the Opening of the American Wing, The Metropolitan Museum of Art, New York, November 10, 1924.

58 These plans (c. 1920) are attributed to Charles Over Cornelius.

59 Norman Isham, an antiquarian architect from Providence, consulted on the installation of old interiors and restorations, while George Francis Dow of Topsfield, Massachusetts, designed and executed the reproduction rooms from the seventeenth century. For the seventeenth-century exhibition gallery, William W. Cordingly of Chestnut Hill, Massachusetts, suggested following the model of the Old Ship Meeting House (1681) in Hingham, Massachusetts, and provided drawings and models of the roof trusses.

60 De Forest, Address on the Occasion of the Opening of the American Wing.

61 Cortissoz, "The American Wing of the Metropolitan Museum of Art of New York," x.

62 Atterbury, Address on the Occasion of the Opening of the American Wing.

63 "Competition for the Museum of the City of New York," *American Architect* 133 (May 5, 1928): 619–24; Robert A. M. Stern, Gregory Gilmartin, and Thomas Mellons, *New York 1930: Architecture and Urbanism Between the Two World Wars* (New York: Rizzoli, 1987): 131–34. The three-story brick Fraunces Tavern, which was originally constructed as a private residence in 1719, once housed Samuel Fraunces's Queens Head Tavern, where George Washington delivered his famous farewell speech in December 1783. Like so many buildings of its era, the building fell into disrepair; the Sons of the Revolution in the State of New York saved it from demolition and restored it to a more Colonial appearance in 1907 from the designs of William Mersereau. During the 1920s and 1930s, the organization acquired additional buildings to the north, which became part of the Fraunces Tavern complex.

64 "The Tenney Memorial Chapel is a Period Piece," *Lawrence Telegram* (April 3, 1928), as quoted in "Tenney Memorial Chapel, Grove Street, Methuen, Massachusetts," Massachusetts Historical Commission, Boston, Massachusetts.

65 Atterbury designed the Holy Trinity Church Rectory at 341 East 87th Street (1927) and the St. James Episcopal Church's Parish House at 865 Madison Avenue (1937). In 1908, he also designed a tympanum for the Rye Presbyterian Church (Richard Upjohn, 1870) as a gift of Marselis C. Parsons (1865–1941), former president of the Rye National Bank. Atterbury artistically developed the details, which depicted the church's history and the community's early settlement.

66 Dorothy Ganfield Fowler, *A City Church: The First Presbyterian Church in the City of New York, 1716–1976* (New York: The First Presbyterian Church, 1981); "Gate and Choir Screen, First Presbyterian Church of New York," *Architectural League of New York Yearbook* (1921): pl.; "First Presbyterian Church of New York City," *The Western Architect* 32 (June 1923): pl. 7. Taber Sears was also responsible for the ceiling murals in what is now City Hall's City Council Chamber: "New York Receiving the Gifts of the Nation."

67 "Special Report of the Governors of the Union Club to the Members, 1926," Delano & Aldrich Collection, Avery Architectural and Fine Arts Library, Columbia University in the City of New York; Peter Pennoyer and Anne Walker, *The Architecture of Delano & Aldrich* (New York: W. W. Norton, 2003): 148–50.

HOSPITALS, ORPHANAGES, AND MEDICAL BUILDINGS

68 Grosvenor Atterbury, "Hospitals and Esthetics: the Architectural Problem with Particular Reference to Esthetics and the Art of Architecture," *The Architect* 5 (January 1926): 379.

69 William Logie Russell, *The New York Hospital: A History of Psychiatric Service: 1771–1936* (New York: Columbia University Press, 1945): 343.

70 "Hospital Receives Whitney $1,250,000," *New York Times* (October 16, 1930): 24; "Staff House, Bloomingdale Hospital, White Plains, New York," *Architectural League of New York Yearbook* (1926): pl.; Atterbury, "Hospitals and Esthetics," 379–86, pls. 81–86; Andrew S. Dolkart and Karin G. Lucas, "New York Hospital, White Plains, Westchester County, New York," State Register of Historic Places, United States Department of the Interior, National Park Service. The hospital, established in 1821, was originally known as the Bloomingdale Asylum for the Insane. In 1936, the name was changed to the New York Hospital–Westchester Division.

71 Atterbury, "Hospitals and Esthetics," 381.

72 Ibid., 381.

73 Hartford Orphan Asylum, *100th Anniversary: 1833–1933* (Hartford, CT: Case, Lockwood & Brainard Co., 1933); Hartford Orphan Asylum, *Children's Village of the Hartford Orphan Asylum* (Hartford, CT: The Asylum, 1945); George E. Andrews and David F. Ranson, *Structure and Styles, Guided Tour of Hartford* (Hartford, CT: Connecticut Historical Society and Connecticut Architectural Foundation, 1988): 191.

74 "Charles P. Cooley Residence, Hartford, Conn.," *Country Life in America* 70 (July 1936): 22–23; Andrews and Ranson, *Structure and Styles*, 189.

75 Hartford Orphan *Asylum, 100th Anniversary: 1833–1933*, 16.

76 Diana Rice, "Hospital to Cut the Cost of Illness," *New York Times* (July 8, 1928): 98; "$6,000,000 Sought for New Hospital," *New York Times* (October 3, 1929): 19; "Aid Gotham Hospital," *New York Times* (December 23, 1929): 8; "Architectural News in Photographs," *Architecture* 62 (July 1930): 14; "Hospital Designed for Group Nursing," *New York Times* (March 23, 1930): 2, 5;

"Gen. Atterbury Lauds New Hospital System," *New York Times* (April 5, 1930): 25.

77 "Hospital Designed for Group Nursing," 5.

78 Gerard N. Burrow, M.D., *A History of Yale's School of Medicine: Passing Torches to Others* (New Haven: Yale University Press, 2002): 124.

79 "$7,500,000 Yale Fund for Study of Man," *New York Times* (February 15, 1929): 1; C. G. Poore, "Yale is Now to Study Mankind," *New York Times* (February 24, 1929): 133; "Yale Research Unit Gets $500,000 Gift," *New York Times* (September 30, 1929): 12; "Yale is Given $500,000 More; Starts Today on 'Humanity' Building," *New York Times* (September 30, 1929): 37; "Construction of Yale's Institute of Human Relations Building Commences Today, Additional Gift of $500,000 Announced," *Yale University News Statement* (September 30, 1929); "The Yale Institute of Human Relations," *Science* 70 (October 4, 1929): 322; Patrick Pinnell, *The Campus Guide: Yale University* (New York: Princeton Architectural Press, 1999): 122–23; Burrow, *A History of Yale's School of Medicine*; Catherine Lynn, "Building Yale and Razing It from the Civil War to the Great Depression," in *Yale in New Haven: Architecture and Urbanism* (New Haven: Yale University, 2004): 217–19.

80 *Yale University News Statement* (October 18, 1939); "Library for the History of Medicine at Yale University," *Science* 90 (October 27, 1939): 389; "The Yale Medical Library," *Pencil Points* 23 (January 1942): 31–42; Burrow, *A History of Yale's School of Medicine*; Pinnell, *The Campus Guide: Yale University*, 122–23.

81 Harvey Cushing to Arnold Klebs, October 4, 1934, from *The Making of a Library: Extracts from Letters, 1934–1941, of Harvey Cushing, Arnold C. Klebs [and] John F. Fulton* (New Haven, CT: Yale University Press, 1959): 11.

82 "The William H. Welch Medical Library in Baltimore," *Through the Ages* 7 (August 1929): 7–11.

83 Atterbury to Harvey Cushing, May 17, 1927; Harvey Williams Cushing Papers, Manuscripts and Archives, Yale University.

84 Excerpt from report of J. F. Fulton, M.D., Chairman, Advisory Board, from "The Yale Medical Library," *Pencil Points* 23 (January 1942): 31.

85 Stewart's inscription reads: "Here, silent, speak the great of other years, the story of their steep ascent from the unknown to the known, erring perchance in their best endeavor, succeeding often, where to their fellows they seemed most to fail. Here, the distilled wisdom of the years, the slow deposit of knowledge gained and writ by weak yet valorous men, who shirked not the difficult emprize; Here is offered you the record of their days and deeds, their struggle to attain that light which God sheds on the mind of men, and which we know as Truth. Unshared must be their genius; it was their own; but you, be you but brave and diligent, may freely take and know the rich companionship of others' ordered thought."

86 One of Cushing's daughters, Betsy Cushing Roosevelt Whitney, widow of John Hay Whitney, donated eight million dollars in the 1980s to enlarge and renovate the Medical Library.

CHAPTER SEVEN
Pioneer in Prefabrication: 1902–1951

1 Lewis Mumford, *Roots of Contemporary Architecture*, as quoted in Richard Plunz, *A History of Housing in New York City* (New York: Columbia University Press, 1990): 219. Ackerman served as a consultant to the New York City Housing Authority and the housing division of the Public Works Administration. In addition to designing two hundred houses in Sunnyside, Queens, he consulted on many other housing developments and acted as chief of the division of housing and town planning design of the U.S. Shipping Board, Emergency Fleet Corporation, during World War One. Bright was a Philadelphia architect. As a member of the city's planning commission, he was concerned primarily with housing developments and urban congestion and was instrumental in the creation of the Port of Philadelphia.

2 "House Building Needs Revolution Says Atterbury," unidentified newspaper article, c. 1930, Southampton Historical Museum.

3 In addition to his role as city engineer, Brodie was the associate professor and lecturer in civil engineering at Liverpool's experimental School of Architecture and Applied Arts. Quentin Hughes, "Before the Bauhaus: The Experiment at the Liverpool School of Architecture," *Architectural History* 25 (1982): 109.

4 "Armed Concrete Lattice-Girders," *American Architect and Building News* 81 (September 26, 1903): 99–101.

5 Burnham Kelly, *The Prefabrication of Houses: A Study by the Albert Farwell Bemis Foundation* (Cambridge: Technology Press of the Massachusetts Institute of Technology, 1951): 13.

6 *The Manufacture of Standardized Houses: A New Industry* (New York: Standardized Housing Corporation, 1918): 24.

7 Grosvenor Atterbury, "How to Get Low Cost Houses: The Real Housing Problem and the Arts of Construction Illustrated from Research Work Done under the Auspices of the Russell Sage Foundation," *Proceedings of the National Housing Association, Volume 5, Housing Problems in America*, Providence, October 9–10, 1916 (Cambridge: Cambridge University Press, 1916): 101.

8 The group of businessmen included Harry P. Robbins (president), Allan Robinson (vice president), Charles H. Conner (treasurer), and James W. Pryor (secretary).

9 Albert Farwell Bemis and John Burchard II, *The Evolving House* (Cambridge, MA: The Technology Press, 1936): 350.

10 "Proposal to End Housing Shortage," *New York Times* (February 14, 1926): 8, 17.

11 Atterbury to Harvey W. Cushing, February 21, 1930; Harvey Williams Cushing Papers, Manuscripts and Archives, Yale University.

12 Atterbury to John D. Rockefeller Jr., May 11, 1938; Record Group 2, Friends and Services, Box 43, Folder 326, Rockefeller Family Archive, Rockefeller Archive Center, Sleepy Hollow, New York (hereafter cited RFA).

13 Various representatives of the New York City Housing Authority and the offices of the State Commissioner of Housing and Federal Housing Authority confirmed the structural integrity of the houses at Forest Hills Gardens when Atterbury put together his report for Amsterdam Houses. Atterbury, Corbett, and Holden, *Report on the Use of Prefabricated Fireproof Construction as Exemplified by the Atterbury Precast Sectional System as Proposed in Concrete for a Typical Six-Story Unit of the Amsterdam Houses* (New York: Housing Authority, May 1943): 3.

14 "Board Approves New Housing Unit," *New York Times* (October 11, 1940): 23; "More City Housing Voted After Row," *New York Times* (June 20, 1941): 23; "Plans for Housing on West Side Field," *New York Times* (July 11, 1942): 23; Atterbury, Corbett, and Holden, *Report on the Use of Prefabricated Fireproof Construction as Exemplified by the Atterbury Precast Sectional System as Proposed in Concrete for a Typical Six-Story Unit of the Amsterdam Houses*; Lee E. Cooper, "Large-Scale Housing Leads Building Activity in City," *New York Times* (August 3, 1947): 1.

15 Under the Housing Act of 1949, veterans were given priority for low-rent public housing.

16 Memorandum of Progress of a Sectional System since 1944, February 15, 1946; Record Group 2, Home Series-Friends and Services, Box 43, Folder 326, RFA.

17 Mary Cummings, Joanne Englehardt, Graydon Topping, Michael Zarrow, Janet Lavinio, and Richard Barnes, Oral History on Grosvenor Atterbury, May 15, 2004, transcript from audiotape, Southampton Historical Museum, Southampton, New York.

18 Members of the New York Housing Trust included Mrs. Benjamin J. Buttenwieser, Ward Cheney, Kenneth A. Ives, William G. Lord, and Frank K. White; also Robert Dowling's City Investing Company and Floyd Odlum's Atlas Corporation.

19 "Business Roundup," *Fortune* 43 (March 1951): 19–21.

20 Lee E. Cooper, "$8,000,000 Private Project to Offer Non-Profit Homes," *New York Times* (September 19, 1948): 1.

21 Rheinstein agreed to build the apartments on a cost plus fixed fee basis and guaranteed to return any savings to the owners below a maximum set price. Cooper, "$8,000,000 Private Project to Offer Non-Profit Homes," 1, 67; "Design for Queensview Omits Basements; other Innovations to Cut Housing Costs," *New York Times* (May 15, 1949): 1; M. S. Shepard, "Pre-Cast Blocks Used in Housing," *New York Times* (November 12, 1950): 241.

22 James Ford, *Slums and Housing*, Volume One (Cambridge, MA: Harvard University Press, 1936): 819.

BIBLIOGRAPHY

"Adaptation of Public Architecture to American Needs, with Promise of the Development of a National Style." *The Craftsman* 10 (April 1906): 23–39.

Anderson, Clifford S. *Indian Hill: An Industrial Village*. Worcester, MA: The Norton Company, n.d.

Atterbury, Grosvenor, Stowe Phelps, and John A. Tompkins, Architects. *Architectural Catalogue*. New York: Architectural Catalogue Co., 1918.

Bacon, Mardges. *Ernest Flagg: Beaux-Arts Architect and Urban Reformer*. New York: The Architectural History Foundation, 1986.

Bemis, Albert Farwell, and John Burchard II. *The Evolving House*. Cambridge, MA: The Technology Press, MIT, 1936.

Betsky, Aaron. *James Gamble Rogers and the Architecture of Pragmatism*. New York: The Architectural History Foundation, 1994.

Betts, Mary Beth. *The Governor's Room, City Hall, New York*. New York: Art Commission of the City of New York, 1983.

Boegner, Peggie Phipps, and Richard Gachot. *Halcyon Days: An American Family Through Three Generations*. New York: Abrams, 1986.

Boyd Jr., John Taylor. "Personality in Architecture." *Arts and Decoration* 32 (April 1930): 49–52, 92.

Brown, Elizabeth Mills. *New Haven: A Guide to Architecture and Design*. New Haven, CT: Yale University Press, 1976.

Brown, Jane. *Beatrix: The Gardening Life of Beatrix Jones Farrand, 1872–1959*. New York: Viking, 1995.

Bruce, Alfred, and Harold Sandbank. *A History of Prefabrication*. Raritan, NJ: J. B. Pierce Foundation, 1945.

Burkhardt, Roberta. *Watch Hill, Then and Now*. Watch Hill, RI: Watch Hill Preservation Society, 1988.

Burrow, Gerard N., M.D. *A History of Yale's School of Medicine: Passing Torches to Others*. New Haven, CT: Yale University Press, 2002.

Crawford, Margaret. *Building the Workingman's Paradise: The Design of American Company Towns*. New York: Verso, 1995.

Cushing, Harvey. *A Visit to Le Puy-en-Velay*. Cleveland: The Rowfant Club, 1986.

De Forest, Louis Effingham, and Anne Lawrence de Forest. *The Descendants of Job Atterbury*. New York: de Forest Publishing Co., 1933.

Embury, Aymar II. *One Hundred Country Houses*. New York: The Century Company, 1909.

Foglesong, Richard E. *Planning the Capitalist City: The Colonial Era to the 1920s*. Princeton: Princeton University Press, 1986.

Ford, James. *Slums and Housing*. Cambridge, MA: Harvard University Press, 1936.

Fox, John L. *Housing for the Working Classes: Henry Phipps, from the Carnegie Steel Company to Phipps Houses*. Larchmont, NY: Memorystone Publishing, 2007.

Frelinghuysen, Alice Cooney. *Louis Comfort Tiffany and Laurelton Hall: An Artist's Country Estate*. New Haven, CT: Yale University Press, 2006.

Gilborn, Craig. *Adirondack Camps: Homes Away from Home, 1850–1950*. Syracuse, NY: Syracuse University Press, 2000.

———. *Durant: The Fortune and Woodland Camps of a Family in the Adirondacks*. Sylvan Beach, NY: North Country Books, 1981.

Glenn, John M., Lilian Brandt, and F. Emerson Andrew. *Russell Sage Foundation, 1907–1946*. New York: Russell Sage Foundation, 1947.

Griswold, Mac, and Eleanor Weller. *The Golden Age of American Gardens, Proud Owners, Private Estates, 1890–1940*. New York: Abrams, 1991.

Halsey, R. T. Haines. *The Homes of our Ancestors Shown in the American Wing of the Metropolitan Museum of Art*. Garden City, NY: Doubleday, Page and Company, 1925.

Handlin, David P. *The American Home: Architecture and Society, 1815–1915*. Boston: Little, Brown, 1979.

Havemeyer, Harry W. *Along the Great South Bay: From Oakdale to Babylon, the Story of a Summer Spa, 1840–1940*. Mattituck, NY: Amereon Ltd., 1996.

Hering, Oswald C. *Concrete and Stucco Houses*. New York: McBride, Nast and Company, 1912.

Jackson, Anthony. *A Place Called Home: A History of Low-Cost Housing in Manhattan*. Cambridge, MA: MIT Press, 1976.

Jones Jr., Rupert O. *National Register of Historic Places, Watch Hill, Rhode Island*. Watch Hill, RI: The Boot and Tackle Shop, 1998.

Kathrens, Michael C. *Great Houses of New York: 1880–1930*. New York: Acanthus Press, 2005.

Kelly, Burham. *The Prefabrication of Houses: A Study by the Albert Farwell Bemis Foundation*. Cambridge, MA: Technology Press, MIT, 1951.

Klaus, Susan L. *A Modern Arcadia: Frederick Law Olmsted Jr. and the Plan for Forest Hills Gardens*. Amherst, MA: University of Massachusetts Press, 2002.

Kurland, Gerald. *Seth Low: The Reformer in an Urban and Industrial Age*. New York: Twayne, 1971.

Lawrance, Gary, and Anne Surchin. *Houses of the Hamptons*. New York: Acanthus Press, 2007.

Lubove, Roy. *The Progressives and the Slums: Tenement House Reform in New York City, 1890–1917*. Pittsburgh: University of Pittsburgh Press, 1962.

MacKay, Robert B., Anthony K. Baker, and Carol A. Traynor, eds. *Long Island Country Houses and Their Architects, 1860–1940*. New York: W. W. Norton & Company, 1997.

Madge, John, ed. *Tomorrow's Houses: New Building Methods, Structures and Materials*. London: Pilot Press Limited, 1946.

Morris, A. E. J. *Precast Concrete in Architecture*. New York: Whitney Library of Design, 1978.

Mumford, Lewis. *City Development: Studies in Disintegration and Renewal*. New York: Harcourt, Brace & Company, 1945.

Oliver, Richard, ed. *The Making of an Architect, 1881–1981: Columbia University in the City of New York*. New York: Rizzoli, 1981.

Page, Walter Hines, and Arthur Wilson Page. *The World's Work: A History of Our Time*, Vol. XV. New York: Doubleday, Page, 1908.

Parks, Janet, and Alan G. Neumann. *The Old World Builds the New*. New York: Avery Architectural and Fine Arts Library, 1996.

Patterson, Augusta Owen. *American Homes of To-Day*. New York: MacMillan Company, 1924.

Pennoyer, Peter, and Anne Walker. *The Architecture of Delano & Aldrich*. New York: W. W. Norton & Company, 2003.

Pinnell, Patrick. *The Campus Guide: Yale University*. New York: Princeton Architectural Press, 1999.

Plunz, Richard. *A History of Housing in New York City*. New York: Columbia University Press, 1990.

Price, C. Matlock. "The Development of National Architecture: The Work of Grosvenor Atterbury." *Arts and Decoration* 2 (March 1912): 176–79.

Relman, Harriet V. *A Village of Promise on Indian Hill in Worcester, Mass*. Lincoln, MA: privately printed, 1990.

Reps, John William. *The Making of Urban America: A History of City Planning in the United States*. Princeton, NJ: Princeton University Press, 1965.

Rieley, William D., and Roxanne S. Brouse. *Historic Resource Study for the Carriage Road System, Acadia National Park, Mount Desert Island, Maine*. United States Department of the Interior, National Park Service: The Associates, 1989.

Roberts, Ann Rockefeller. *Mr. Rockefeller's Roads: The Untold Story of Acadia's Carriage Roads and Their Creator*. Camden, ME: Down East Books, 1990.

Rogers, Millard F. *John Nolen and Mariemont: Building a New Town in Ohio*. Baltimore: Johns Hopkins University Press, 2001.

Schnadelbach, Terry. *Ferruccio Vitale: Landscape Architect of the Century Place Era*. New York: Princeton Architectural Press, 2001.

Sclare, Lisa, and Donald Sclare. *Beaux-Arts Estates: A Guide to the Architecture of Long Island*. New York: Viking Press, 1979.

Scott, Mel. *American City Planning Since 1890*. Chicago, Illinois: American Planning Association, 1969; 1995.

Scully, Vincent, Catherine Lynn, Erik Vogt, and Paul Goldberger. *Yale in New Haven: Architecture and Urbanism*. New Haven, CT: Yale University, 2004.

Shettleworth Jr., Earl, and Lydia Vanderbergh. *Revisiting Seal Harbor and Acadia National Park*. Charleston, SC: Arcadia, 1997.

Spinzia, Raymond E., and Judith A. *Long Island's Prominent North Shore Families: Their Estates and Their Country Houses*. College Station, TX: Virtual Bookworm, 2006.

Standardized Housing Corporation. *The Manufacture of Standardized Houses: A New Industry*. New York: privately printed, 1918.

Stern, Robert A. M. "One Hundred Years of Resort Architecture in East Hampton: The Power of the Provincial," in *East Hampton's Heritage*. New York: W. W. Norton & Company, 1982.

Stern, Robert A. M., Gregory Gilmartin, and John Massengale. *New York 1900: Metropolitan Architecture and Urbanism, 1890–1915*. New York: Rizzoli, 1983.

Stern, Robert A. M., Gregory Gilmartin, and Thomas Mellins. *New York 1930: Architecture and Urbanism Between the Two World Wars*. New York: Rizzoli, 1988.

Stern, Robert A. M., and John Massengale. *The Anglo-American Suburb*. New York: St. Martin's Press, 1981.

Tarbell, Ida M. *New Ideals in Business: An Account of Their Practice and Their Effect upon Men and Profit*. New York: The Macmillan Company, 1917.

"The Theory of Grosvenor Atterbury, Who Bases All of His Work upon the Principle That Originality in Architecture Springs Only from the Direct Meeting of Material Conditions." *The Craftsman* 3 (June 1909): 300–312.

Tilson, John Quillin, ed. *Yale '91 Class Book*. New Haven, CT: Price, Lee and Atkins Co., 1891.

Turpin, John K., and W. Barry Thomson. *New Jersey Country Houses: The Somerset Hills*, Vol. I. Far Hills, NJ: Mountain Colony Press, 2004.

Tymeson, Mildred McClary. *The Norton Story*. Worcester, MA: Norton Company, 1953.

Van Rensselaer, Mrs. John King. *The Social Ladder*. New York: H. Holt, 1924.

Van Trump, James D., and Arthur P. Ziegler Jr. *Landmark Architecture of Allegheny County, Pennsylvania*. Pittsburgh: Pittsburgh History and Landmark Foundation, 1967.

Warren, Charles D. *New Towns For Old*. Boston, MA: Marshall Jones Company, 1927; Amherst, MA: University of Massachusetts Press, 2005.

Warren, Wright Parks. *The Mariemont Story: A National Exemplar in Town Planning*. Cincinnati: Creative Writers and Publishers, 1967.

Waters, Margaret. "Presenting . . . Grosvenor Atterbury." *Hamptonian* (August 25, 1955): 9–10.

Wetterau, Helen M. *Shinnecock Hills*. East Patchogue, NY: Searles Graphics, Inc.: 1991.

White, Samuel G. *The Houses of McKim, Mead & White*. New York: Rizzoli, 1998.

White, Virginia S., ed. *From Camargo to Indian Hill*. Indian Hill, OH: Indian Hill Historical Museum Association, 1983.

Wolfe, Margaret Ripley. *Kingsport, Tennessee: A Planned American City*. Lexington, KY: University Press of Kentucky, 1987.

"Works by Grosvenor Atterbury and his Associates; Stowe Phelps, John Almy Tompkins 2nd, Leslie Walker," *The New York Architect* 3 (August 1909).

UNPUBLISHED SOURCES

Architect and Engineer's File, New-York Historical Society, New York, NY.

Archives of the American Institute of Architects, Washington DC.

Department of American Decorative Art, Metropolitan Museum of Art, New York, NY.

Elisabeth Coit Papers, Schlesinger Library, Radcliffe Institute, Harvard University.

Forest Hills Gardens Corporation, #2775, Rare and Manuscript Collection, Carl A. Kroch Library, Cornell University.

Forest Hills Gardens Records, #3495, Rare and Manuscript Collection, Carl A. Kroch Library, Cornell University.

Grosvenor Atterbury File, Stanford White Collection, Avery Architectural and Fine Arts Library, Columbia University.

Grosvenor Atterbury Papers, #3762, Rare and Manuscript Collection, Carl A. Kroch Library, Cornell University.

Grosvenor Atterbury Student File, Manuscript and Archives, Yale University.

Harvey William Cushing Papers, Manuscripts and Archives, Yale University.

John Ferguson Weir Papers, Manuscripts and Archives, Yale University.

John Nolen Papers, #2903, Rare and Manuscript Collection, Carl A. Kroch Library, Cornell University.

Maine Historical Commission, Augusta, ME.

Mary Cummings, Joanne Englehardt, Graydon Topping, Michael Zarrow, Janet Lavinio, and Richard Barnes, oral history on Grosvenor Atterbury, March 15, 2004, transcript from audiotape, Southampton Historical Museum.

Municipal Archives, New York, NY.

Olmsted Associates Records, Manuscripts Division, Library of Congress, Washington DC.

Reminiscences of Lawrence Veiller, 1949, in the Columbia University Oral History Research Office Collection.

Rockefeller Family Archive, Rockefeller Archive Center, Sleepy Hollow, NY.

Russell Sage Foundation Archives, Rockefeller Archive Center, Sleepy Hollow, NY.

Southampton Historical Museum, Southampton, NY.

University Archives and Columbiana Library, Columbia University.

William Adams Delano Papers, Manuscripts and Archives, Yale University.

ARTICLES AND LECTURES
BY GROSVENOR ATTERBURY

"Forest Hills Gardens: a Study and Demonstration in Town Planning and Home Building Undertaken by the Russell Sage Foundation at Forest Hills, Long Island." *Survey* 25 (January 9, 1911): 563–70.

"Model Towns in America." *Scribner's Magazine* 52 (July 1912): 20–35.

"Forest Hills Gardens: an Example of Collective Planning, Development and Control." *Brickbuilder* 21 (December 1912): 317–20.

"Garden Cities," *Proceedings of the Second National Conference on Housing, Housing Problems in America*. December 4–6, 1912.

"Hospitals and Esthetics: The Architectural Problem, with Particular Reference to Esthetics and the Art of Architecture." *American Medical Association Journal* 65 (September 25, 1915): 1080–85.

"What Can Be Done to Bring Art Closer to the People and Increase Their Love for It?" Lecture given at the Republican Club of the City of New York, Saturday Discussions Committee, March 4, 1916.

"How to Get Low Cost Houses: The Real Housing Problem and the Art of Construction." *The American Architect* 110 (November 22, 1916): 317–21.

The Community and the Home. A Preface to the Discussion of City Planning and Housing, Army Educational Commission, March 31, 1919.

"Housing Costs Can Be Cut: New Production Principles May Effect Revolutionary Revisions in Building Costs." *Building Investment and Maintenance* 1 (May 1926): 23–25.

"Our Monster City and Its Life." *New York Times Magazine* (January 13, 1929): 1–2, 20.

"The House, the Owner and the Element of Design." *New York Herald* (March 10, 1929): 9, 12.

Notes on the Architectural and Other Esthetic Problems Involved in the Development of our Great National Parks Made During August and September 1929. United States Department of the Interior, National Park Service, Yellowstone National Park.

The Economic Production of Workingmen's Homes: An Outline of a Scientific Solution of the Housing Problem and its Relation to the Development of the City. January 1930.

"Bricks Without Brains: A Challenge to Science, and the Factory-Made House." *Architecture* 73 (April 1936): 193–96.

"The Cooling Fountains of Stone Ashley." *Bulletin of the Garden Club of America* 23 (September 1936): 40–48.

Atterbury, Corbett, and Holden, *Report on the Use of Prefabricated Fireproof Construction as Exemplified by the Atterbury Precast Sectional System as Proposed in Concrete for a Typical Six-Story Unit of the Amsterdam Houses*. New York: Housing Authority, May 1943.

The Scientific Approach to Economic Construction. Two addresses given on the Economic and Esthetic Aspects of "Prefabrication" during the First Exhibition of the "Prefabrication" held under the auspices of the Architectural League of New York, March 1944.

ACKNOWLEDGMENTS

Grosvenor Atterbury was one of the most inventive and prolific architects of the early twentieth century. We were well familiar with many of his buildings and projects before we began researching our book, and it was clear to us from the start that his body of work deserved a closer look. Early in our study, we realized that Atterbury was both an artist and a scientist in his approach to architecture and that this range of skills fostered a career of unparalleled variety. Sadly, Atterbury's architectural drawings—a prime source for research—were discarded at the end of his career. Nonetheless, his persistent and persuasive voice can be heard through his many articles and writings, and his legacy survives in his many buildings that endure today. Donald Dwyer's article on Atterbury in the Society for the Preservation of Long Island Antiquities's *Long Island Country Houses and Their Architects, 1860–1940* and Susan L. Klaus's *A Modern Arcadia: Frederick Law Olmsted Jr. and the Plan for Forest Hills Gardens* provided an excellent starting point for our research.

Among the many people and organizations who shared information and recollections, gave us access to Atterbury's buildings, and supported our research, we are grateful to: at the Rockefeller Archive Center, Nancy Adgent and Kenneth Rose; Shantia Anderheggen; at the Medical History Cushing/Whitney Medical Library Yale, Toby A. Appel; at the Long Island Institute, Victoria Aspinwall; Tyler Bagwell; at the East Hampton Historical Society, Richard Barons; at City Hall, Mary Beth Betts, Joan Bright, Keri Butler, and Matthew Kelly; Mosette Broderick; at the SVF Foundation, Peter M. Borden, Peter Davis, and Joanie Tripp; at the Museum of the City of New York, Melanie Bower and Chris Murtha; Roberta Burkhardt; at the Worcester Historical Museum, Robyn Christensen; at the Olmsted National Historic Site, Michele Clark; William Coleman; at Planting Fields, Marianne Della Croce; at the Southampton Historical Museum, Mary Cummings and Laurie Collins; at the House of the Redeemer, Judy Counts; at the LaGuardia & Wagner Archives, Douglas DiCarlo; David Dwyer; Donald Dwyer; at the Nassau County Department of Parks, Recreation & Museum, George W. Fisher; at the Century Association Archives Foundation, Russell Flinchum; at the Metropolitan Museum of Art, Alice Cooney Frelinghuysen and Morrison Heckscher; Forest Hills Gardens Corporation; John L. Fox; Juergen A. Friedrich; Sharon Frisbie; at Westbury Gardens, Richard Gachot; at the Unicoi County Public Library, Jane Garrett; Cynthia Gibson; at the New-York Historical Society, Eleanor Gillers, Susan Kriete, and Itty Matthews; Gregory Gilmartin; Christopher Gray; at Cornell University's Carl A. Koch Library, Ana Guimaraes and Laura Linke; at Hofstra University, Barbara Guzowski; at the American Institute of Architects Archives, Nancy Hadley; Dorrance Hamilton; Robert Hammer; at the Johns Hopkins Medical Institutions, Andrew J. Harrison; Harry W. Havemeyer; William Havemeyer; Huyler Held; at the Stone Barns Center for Food and Agriculture, Erica Helms; Susanna Hof; at the Kingsport Public Library, Brianna Johnson; at the Liederkranz Foundation, Cynthia Kessel; at the Cincinnati Historical Society Library, M'Lissa Kesterman; Star Lawrence; at the St. Paul's School, David Levesque; Katherine Longfield; at the Parrish Art Museum, Alicia G. Longwell, Chris McNamara, and Sam Bridger-Carroll; at Yale University Library's Manuscripts and Archives, William Massa and Cynthia Ostroff; at the Society for the Preservation of Long Island Antiquities, Robert MacKay and Judy Estes; at the Roslyn Landmark Society, Jefferson Mansell; at the Seatuck Environmental Association, Enrico Marclone; at the New York City Housing Authority, Howard Marder; John Maseman; Finlay Matheson; Aleks Matviak; at Acadia National Park, John McDade; at Columbia University's Avery Architectural and Fine Arts Library, Janet Parks and Inna Guzenfeld; Stowe Phelps; Asa Phillips; at the National Academy Museum, Paula Pineda; Day E. Ravenscroft; at Harvard Design School, Alix Reiskind; Katie Ridder; at Rosemont College, Deloris Richardi; at the Unitarian Church of Montclair, Irene Sanderson; Scott Schneider; Elizabeth Seeler; at the Maine Historic Preservation Commission, Earle G. Shettleworth Jr.; at the Methuen Historical Commission, Lynn Smiledge; at the Adirondack Museum, Angela Snye; at the Winterthur Library, Jeanne Solensky; Mark Stevens; at the Pittsburgh History and Landmarks Foundation, Albert M. Tannler; at the Trinity-Pawling School, Margaret Taylor; Peter Tcherepnine; W. Barry Thomson; at the East Hampton Library, Marci Vail; Samuel G. White; Douglas Williams; Linden Havemeyer Wise; Eric Woodward; and at the Bedford Historical Society, Emily Zucker.

Finally, a special thanks to Robert A. M. Stern, who continues to inspire and encourage us; Jonathan Wallen, whose photography brings the color and vividness of Atterbury's work alive; Martha Ann Underhill for her dedicated research assistance; Abigail Sturges for designing such a lovely book; and the team at W. W. Norton & Company and our editor, Nancy Green, who has made this book possible.

INDEX

Note: Illustrations are indicated by *italic type.*

Printed in Canada